Commercial Pilot Flight Maneuvers and Practical Test Prep is one of four related Gleim books that are cross-referenced and interdependent. Please obtain and use the following books as a package:

Commercial Pilot Flight Maneuvers and Practical Test Prep
Commercial Pilot FAA Written Exam
Commercial Pilot Syllabus
Aviation Weather and Weather Services
Pilot Handbook
FAR/AIM

All of the aviation books and software by Gleim are listed on the order form provided at the back of this book. Thank you for choosing Gleim.

Gleim Publications, Inc.
P.O. Box 12848, University Station
Gainesville, Florida 32604
(800) 87-GLEIM or (800) 874-5346
(352) 375-0772
FAX: (352) 375-6940
Internet: www.gleim.com
E-mail: admin@gleim.com

Orders must be prepaid. Prices are subject to change without notice. We ship latest editions. Shipping and handling charges are added to all orders. Library and company orders may be on account. Add applicable sales tax to shipments within Florida. All payments must be in U.S. funds and payable on a U.S. bank. Please write or call for prices and availability of all foreign country shipments. Books will usually be shipped the day after your order is received. Allow 10 days for delivery in the United States. Please contact us if you do not receive your shipment within 2 weeks.

Gleim Publications, Inc. guarantees the immediate refund of all resalable texts returned within 30 days. The guaranteed refund applies only to books purchased direct from Gleim Publications, Inc. Shipping and handling charges are nonrefundable.

This book contains a systematic discussion and explanation of the FAA's Commercial Pilot Practical Test Standards (Airplane, Single-Engine Land), which will assist you in (1) preparing for and (2) successfully completing your Commercial Pilot FAA Practical Test!

REVIEWERS AND CONTRIBUTORS

Karen A. Hom, B.A., University of Florida, is our book production coordinator. Ms. Hom coordinated the production of the manuscripts and provided assistance throughout the project.

Joshua B. Moore, CFII, MEI; B.A., University of Florida, is our aviation technical editor and a flight instructor with Gulf Atlantic Airways in Gainesville, FL. Mr. Moore added new material, incorporated numerous revisions, and provided technical assistance throughout the project.

John F. Rebstock, B.S.A., University of Florida, reviewed the final manuscript.

Jan M. Strickland is our book production assistant. Ms. Strickland reviewed the manuscript and prepared the page layout.

Ian T. Twombly, CFI; B.S., University of Florida, is an aviation technical research assistant and a flight instructor with Kitty Hawke Aviation in Archer, FL.

The many FAA employees who helped, in person or by telephone, primarily in Gainesville, FL; Orlando, FL; Oklahoma City, OK; and Washington, DC.

A PERSONAL THANKS

This manual would not have been possible without the extraordinary efforts and dedication of Terry Hall and Teresa Soard, who typed the entire manuscript and all revisions, and prepared the camera-ready pages.

The authors also appreciate the production and editorial assistance of Jim Broughton, Aminta Bumrungsup, Michelle Buscemi, Devin Dupree, Rich Fought, Rachel Goodwin, Vanessa Haufler, Nico Medina, Pranav Patel, Shivani Patel, Blenda Perez, Shane Rapp, and Dean Swinford.

Finally, I appreciate the encouragement, support, and tolerance of my family throughout this project.

Groundwood Paper and Highlighters -- This book is printed on high quality groundwood paper. It is lightweight and easy-to-recycle. We recommend that you purchase a highlighter specifically designed to be non-bleed-through (e.g., Avery *Glidestick*™) at your local office supply store.

GLEIM FLIGHT TRAINING SERIES →

COMMERCIAL PILOT

FLIGHT MANEUVERS AND PRACTICAL TEST PREP
FOURTH EDITION

by Irvin N. Gleim, Ph.D., CFII

ABOUT THE AUTHOR

Irvin N. Gleim earned his private pilot certificate in 1965 from the Institute of Aviation at the University of Illinois, where he subsequently received his Ph.D. He is a commercial pilot, flight instructor (instrument), and FAA Aviation Safety Counselor. He is a member of the Aircraft Owners and Pilots Association, American Bonanza Society, Civil Air Patrol, Experimental Aircraft Association, and Seaplane Pilots Association. He is author of flight maneuvers and practical test prep books for the private, instrument, commercial, and flight instructor certificates/ratings, and study guides for the private/recreational, instrument, commercial, flight/ground instructor, fundamentals of instructing, airline transport pilot, and flight engineer FAA knowledge tests. Three additional pilot training books are *Pilot Handbook*, *Aviation Weather and Weather Services*, and *FAR/AIM*.

Dr. Gleim has also written articles for professional accounting and business law journals and is the author of widely used review manuals for the CIA exam (Certified Internal Auditor), the CMA exam (Certified Management Accountant), the CPA exam (Certified Public Accountant), and the EA exam (IRS Enrolled Agent). He is Professor Emeritus, Fisher School of Accounting at the University of Florida, and is a CFM, CIA, CMA, and CPA.

Gleim Publications, Inc.

P.O. Box 12848 • University Station
Gainesville, Florida 32604

(352) 375-0772
(800) 87-GLEIM or (800) 874-5346
FAX: (352) 375-6940

Internet: www.gleim.com
E-mail: admin@gleim.com

ISSN: 1085-2913
ISBN 1-58194-252-4
First Printing: July 2002

This is the first printing of the fourth edition of
Commercial Pilot Flight Maneuvers and Practical Test Prep.
Please e-mail update@gleim.com with CPFM 4-1 in the subject or text. You will receive our current update as a reply.

EXAMPLE:

To: update@gleim.com
From: your e-mail address
Subject: CPFM 4-1

CAUTION: This book is an academic presentation for training purposes only. Under **NO** circumstances can it be used as a substitute for your *Pilot's Operating Handbook* or FAA-approved *Airplane Flight Manual*. **You must fly and operate your airplane in accordance with your *Pilot's Operating Handbook* or FAA-approved *Airplane Flight Manual*.**

HELP !!

Please send any corrections and suggestions for subsequent editions to me, Irvin N. Gleim, Gleim Publications, Inc. • P.O. Box 12848 • University Station • Gainesville, Florida • 32604. The last page in this book has been reserved for you to make your comments and suggestions. It should be torn out and mailed to me.

Also, please bring this book to the attention of flight instructors, fixed-base operators, and others interested in flying. Wide distribution of these books and increased interest in flying depend on your assistance and good word. Thank you.

NOTE: UPDATES

If necessary, we will develop an UPDATE for *Commercial Pilot Flight Maneuvers and Practical Test Prep*. Send e-mail to update@gleim.com as described at the top right of this page, and visit our Internet site for the latest updates and information on all of our products. To continue providing our customers with first-rate service, we request that questions about our books and software be sent to us via mail, e-mail, or fax. The appropriate staff member will give each question thorough consideration and a prompt response. Questions concerning orders, prices, shipments, or payments will be handled via telephone by our competent and courteous customer service staff.

TABLE OF CONTENTS

FOURTH EDITION (07/02) CHANGES

1. This book has been revised to reflect the FAA's new Commercial Pilot Practical Test Standards, effective August 1, 2002:

Tasks Added	Tasks Deleted
Airworthiness Requirements	Physiological Aspects of Night Flying
Power-Off 180° Accuracy Approach & Landing	Lighting and Equipment for Night Flying
Steep Spirals	Emergency Descent
	A Post-Flight Procedure Task by combining two tasks into one task

PREFACE

This book will facilitate your commercial pilot flight training and prepare you to pass your COMMERCIAL PILOT FAA PRACTICAL TEST. In addition, this book will assist you and your flight instructor in planning and organizing your flight training.

The commercial pilot practical test is a rigorous test of both concept knowledge and motor skills. This book explains all of the knowledge that your instructor and FAA examiner will expect you to demonstrate and discuss with him/her. Previously, commercial pilot candidates had only the FAA PTS "reprints" to study. Now you have PTSs followed by a thorough explanation of each task and a step-by-step description of each flight maneuver. Thus, through careful organization and presentation, we will decrease your preparation time, effort, and frustration, **and** increase your knowledge and under-standing.

To save you time, money, and frustration, we have listed some of the common errors made by pilots in executing each flight maneuver or operation. You will be aware of *what not to do*. We all learn by our mistakes, but our *common error* list provides you with an opportunity to learn from the mistakes of others.

Most books create additional work for the user. In contrast, *Commercial Pilot Flight Maneuvers and Practical Test Prep* facilitates your effort; i.e., it is easy to use. The outline format, numerous illustrations and diagrams, type styles, indentions, and line spacing are designed to improve readability. Concepts are often presented as phrases rather than complete sentences.

Relatedly, our outline format frequently has an "a" without a "b" or a "1" without a "2." While this violates some journalistic *rules of style*, it is consistent with your cognitive processes. This book was designed, written, and formatted to facilitate your learning and understanding. Another similar counterproductive "rule" is *not to write in your books*. I urge you to mark up this book to facilitate your learning and understanding.

I am confident this book will facilitate speedy completion of your flight training and practical test. I also wish you the very best in subsequent flying, and in obtaining additional ratings and certificates. If you have *not* passed your FAA commercial pilot knowledge test and do *not* have *Commercial Pilot FAA Written Exam* (another book with a red cover) and *FAA Test Prep* software, please order today. Almost everything you need to pass the FAA's knowledge and practical tests for the commercial pilot certificate is available from Gleim in our new Commercial Pilot Kit. If your FBO, flight school, or aviation bookstore is out of stock, call (800) 87-GLEIM, or (800) 874-5346.

I encourage your suggestions, comments, and corrections for future printings and editions. The last page of this book has been designed to help you note corrections and suggestions throughout your preparation process. Please use it, tear it out, and mail it to me. Thank you.

Enjoy Flying -- Safely!

Irvin N. Gleim

July 2002

PART I
GENERAL INFORMATION

Part I (Chapters 1 through 3) of this book provides general information to assist you in obtaining your commercial pilot certificate:

Part II consists of Chapters I through XI, which provide an extensive explanation of each of the 43 tasks required of those taking the commercial pilot FAA practical test in a single-engine land airplane. Part II is followed by Appendix A, FAA Commercial Pilot Practical Test Standards Reprinted (FAA-S-8081-12A with Change 3) Single Engine Land Only, which is a reprint of all 43 tasks in one location.

Commercial Pilot Flight Maneuvers and Practical Test Prep is one book in a series of six books for obtaining your commercial pilot certificate. The six books are

1. *Commercial Pilot Flight Maneuvers and Practical Test Prep*
2. *Commercial Pilot Syllabus*
3. *Commercial Pilot FAA Written Exam*
4. *Aviation Weather and Weather Services*
5. *Pilot Handbook*
6. *FAR/AIM*

Gleim's Commercial Pilot Kit contains all of the above books except *Pilot Handbook* and *FAR/AIM* (which were included in Gleim's Private Pilot Kit), and *Aviation Weather and Weather Services* (which was included in Gleim's Instrument Pilot Kit). These books are available at your local FBO, flight school, bookstore, etc., or call 800-87-GLEIM (see order form at back of book).

Commercial Pilot Syllabus is a step-by-step syllabus of ground and flight training lesson plans for your commercial pilot training.

Commercial Pilot FAA Written Exam contains all of the FAA's commercial pilot knowledge airplane-related questions and organizes them into logical topics called modules. The book consists of 84 modules, which are grouped into 11 chapters. Each chapter begins with a brief, user-friendly outline of what you need to know, and answer explanations are provided next to each question. This book will transfer knowledge to you and give you the confidence to do well on the FAA commercial pilot knowledge test.

Aviation Weather and Weather Services combines all of the information from the FAA's *Aviation Weather* (AC 00-6A), Aviation Weather Services (AC 00-45E), and numerous other FAA publications into one easy-to-understand book. It will help you study all aspects of aviation weather and provide you with a single reference book.

Pilot Handbook is a complete text and reference for all pilots. Aerodynamics, airplane systems and instruments, and airspace are among the topics explained.

Gleim's *FAR/AIM* is an easy-to-read reference book containing all of the Federal Aviation Regulations (FARs) applicable to general aviation flying, plus the full text of the FAA's *Aeronautical Information Manual* (*AIM*).

RECAP OF REQUIREMENTS TO OBTAIN A COMMERCIAL PILOT CERTIFICATE

1. Be at least 18 years of age.

2. Be able to read, write, and converse fluently in English.

3. Hold a current FAA medical certificate.

4. Receive and log ground training from an authorized instructor or complete a home-study course, such as studying this book, *Commercial Pilot FAA Written Exam* (and the related Gleim *FAA Test Prep* software), and *Pilot Handbook*. Subjects include

   a. FAR
   b. NTSB Part 830
   c. Aerodynamics
   d. Aviation weather
   e. Operation of aircraft
   f. Weight and balance
   g. Performance charts
   h. Effects of exceeding limitations
   i. VFR charts
   j. Navigation facilities
   k. Aeronautical Decision Making (ADM)
   l. Aircraft systems
   m. Maneuvers, procedures, and emergency operations in the airplane
   n. Night and high-altitude operations
   o. National airspace system

5. Pass the FAA commercial pilot knowledge test with a score of 70% or better.

6. Accumulate flight experience (FAR 61.129). You must log at least 250 hr. of flight time as a pilot that consists of at least

   a. 100 hr. in powered aircraft, of which 50 hr. must be in airplanes

   b. 100 hr. as pilot in command flight time, which includes at least

      1) 50 hr. in airplanes
      2) 50 hr. in cross-country flight of which at least 10 hr. must be in airplanes

   c. 20 hr. of training in the areas of operation listed in item 8. on page 3, including at least

      1) 10 hr. of instrument training of which at least 5 hr. must be in a single-engine airplane

      2) 10 hr. of training in an airplane that has a retractable landing gear, flaps, and controllable pitch propeller, or is turbine-powered

      3) One cross-country flight of at least 2 hr. in a single-engine airplane in day-VFR conditions, consisting of a total straight-line distance of more than 100 NM from the original point of departure

      4) One cross-country flight of at least 2 hr. in a single-engine airplane in night-VFR conditions, consisting of a straight-line distance of more than 100 NM from the original point of departure

      5) 3 hr. in a single-engine airplane in preparation for the practical test within the 60 days preceding the test

d. 10 hr. of solo flight (meaning no one else is in the airplane) in a single-engine airplane training in the areas of operation listed in item 8. below, which includes at least

    1) One cross-country flight of not less than 300 NM total distance, with landings at a minimum of three points, one of which is a straight-line distance of at least 250 NM from the original departure point

        a) In Hawaii, the longest segment need have only a straight-line distance of at least 150 NM.

    2) 5 hr. in night-VFR conditions with 10 takeoffs and 10 landings (with each landing involving a flight in the traffic pattern) at an airport with an operating control tower

e. The 250 hr. of flight time as a pilot may include 50 hr. in a flight simulator or flight training device that is representative of a single-engine airplane.

7. Hold an instrument rating or your commercial certificate will be issued with a limitation against carrying passengers for hire on flights beyond 50 NM or at night.

8. Receive flight instruction and demonstrate skill. Obtain a logbook sign-off by your CFI on the following areas of operation:

    a. *Preflight preparation*
    b. *Preflight procedures*
    c. *Airport and seaplane base operations*
    d. *Takeoffs, landings, and go-arounds*
    e. *Performance maneuvers*
    f. *Ground reference maneuvers*
    g. *Navigation*
    h. *Slow flight and stalls*
    i. *Emergency operations*
    j. *High-altitude operations*
    k. *Postflight procedures*

9. Successfully complete a practical test, which will be given as a final exam by an FAA inspector or designated pilot examiner. The practical test will be conducted as specified in Part II of this book.

4

Gleim's *FAA Test Prep for Windows*™ contains many of the same features found in earlier versions. However, we have simplified the study process by incorporating the outlines and figures from our books into the new software. Everything you need to study for any of the FAA knowledge tests will be contained in one unique, easy-to-use program. Below are some of the enhancements you will find with our new study software.

Gleim's *FAA Test Prep for Windows*™
32-Bit, CD-ROM Version

NEW for Students:

⇨ A complete on-screen library of FAA figures

⇨ The familiar Gleim outlines and questions contained in one convenient program

⇨ Customizable test sessions that emulate the testing vendors (AvTest, CATS, LaserGrade)

⇨ Improved performance analysis charts and graphs to track your study progress

NEW for Instructors:

⇨ More ways to create and customize tests

⇨ Print options that allow you to design and create quizzes for your students

⇨ One comprehensive program to meet all of your students' needs

Visit our Web site at <u>www.gleim.com</u>
for more information!

CHAPTER ONE
THE COMMERCIAL CERTIFICATE

1.1 WHY GET YOUR COMMERCIAL CERTIFICATE?

Attaining a commercial pilot certificate is not only a fun pursuit but also a worthwhile accomplishment. It provides the satisfaction of knowing that you have gone a step beyond the average pilot and have demonstrated the skill and determination to achieve a higher and safer set of standards. For those not planning a career as a professional pilot, the effort and expense can be justified several ways, including by

1. **Increased skill:** The training and maneuvers accomplished are more advanced and have tighter tolerances than those for the private certificate. Only the airline transport pilot (ATP) certificate is more demanding. The private pilot certificate required you to learn how to fly. To become a commercial pilot, you must learn to fly with the precision of a professional.

2. **Increased safety:** The more precise and thorough your piloting skill and knowledge are, the safer you will be. Safety should be the foremost concern of all pilots. By flying to higher standards (closer tolerances), you will increase the safety of every flight.

3. **Lowered insurance premiums:** A major factor in the cost of aviation insurance is the skill level of the pilot. Insurance companies do not send someone to fly with each client/customer. The level of pilot proficiency is assumed on the basis of the number of hours flown and the certificates and ratings held. By gaining your commercial pilot certificate, you are elevating yourself into a safer category, which may lower the cost of your insurance.

4. **Challenge:** Many pilots are lured to aviation for the challenge of doing something special. For those who have been private pilots for a while, the challenge may now be dwindling, and flying may be becoming mundane. Pursuit of the commercial certificate will hopefully revitalize that interest.

For those considering a career as a pilot, the commercial certificate is required and the above justifications support the decision to become a professional. A professional pilot career, whether in flight instruction, charter, corporate, or airline, is appealing to many beginning pilots. For some, the love of flying is strong enough for them to make a career of aviation.

1.2 WHAT IS A COMMERCIAL PILOT CERTIFICATE?

A. A commercial pilot certificate is identical to your private pilot certificate except that it allows you to fly an airplane and carry passengers and/or property for compensation or hire. The certificate is sent to you by the FAA upon satisfactory completion of your training program, a knowledge test, and a practical test. A sample commercial pilot certificate is reproduced below.

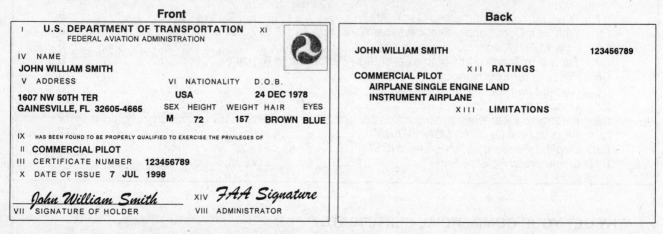

B. The requirements to obtain a commercial pilot certificate are thoroughly explained in the Introduction, The FAA Pilot Knowledge Test, of the *Commercial Pilot FAA Written Exam* book.

1.3 HOW TO GET STARTED

A. **Talk to several people who have recently attained their commercial certificate.** Visit several flight training schools and ask for the names of several people who have just completed their pilot training. One person can usually refer you to another. How did they do it?

1. Flight training: Airplane? CFI? Period of time? Cost? Structure of the program?
2. Ask for their advice. How would they do it differently? What do they suggest to you?
3. What difficulties did they encounter?

B. **Talk to several CFIs.** Tell them you are considering becoming a commercial pilot. Evaluate each as a prospective instructor.

1. What does each CFI recommend?

2. What are the projected costs?

3. What is the rental cost for their training aircraft, solo and dual?

4. Ask for the names and phone numbers of several persons who recently obtained commercial pilot certificates under his/her direction.

5. Does the flight instructor's schedule and the schedule of available aircraft fit your schedule?

6. Where will the instructor recommend that you take your practical test? What is its estimated cost?

7. Is a structured training syllabus used so that you will know exactly what to expect?

C. Once you have made a preliminary choice of flight instructor and/or FBO, **sit down with your CFI and plan a schedule of flight instruction.**

    1. When and how often you will fly

    2. When you will take the FAA commercial pilot knowledge test

    3. When you should plan to take your practical test

    4. When and how payments will be made for your instruction

    5. Review, revise, and update the total cost to obtain your commercial pilot certificate (see below).

D. **Prepare a tentative written time budget and a written expenditure budget.**

Hours Solo: ____ hours × $_____	$_____
Hours Dual: ____ hours × $_____	$_____
FAA commercial pilot knowledge test	$_____
Practical test (examiner)	$_____
Practical test (airplane)	$_____
Medical exam (at least a third-class medical certificate)	$_____
This book*	$ 16.95
Gleim's Commercial Pilot Syllabus*	$ 14.95
Gleim's *Commercial Pilot FAA Written Exam**	$ 14.95
Gleim's *FAA Test Prep* Software (CD for Windows 95, 98, or NT 4.0 or higher)*	$ 59.95
Gleim's *Pilot Handbook*	$ 13.95
Gleim's *FAR/AIM*	$ 15.95
Gleim's *Aviation Weather and Weather Services*	$ 22.95
Other materials:	
One or more sectional chart(s)	$_____
Airport/Facility Directory	$_____
Information manual for your training airplane(s)	$_____
Gleim's flight computer and navigation plotter	$ 15.90
TOTAL	$_____
*Included in Gleim's Commercial Pilot Kit	

E. **Consider purchasing an airplane** (yourself, or through joint ownership) **or joining a flying club.** Frequently, shared expenses through joint ownership can significantly reduce the cost of flying.

    1. Inquire about local flying clubs.

    2. Call a member and learn about the club's services, costs, etc.

1.4 TRANSITION TRAINING TO COMPLEX AND HIGH-PERFORMANCE AIRPLANES

A. You should receive a thorough checkout when changing from one make or model airplane to another with which you are not familiar.

   1. Accident records indicate that some pilots take unnecessary risks when they attempt to fly a different type of airplane without familiarizing themselves with its peculiarities, limitations, and systems.

   2. The goal is to prevent an accident by ensuring that you have the proper training in the specific systems and operating characteristics of every airplane model you fly.

B. Commercial pilot training requires you to be familiar with, knowledgeable about, and comfortable with complex airplanes. Complex airplanes are defined in FAR 61.31(e) as those with retractable landing gear, flaps, and a controllable pitch propeller.

C. The objective of your complex airplane transition training is to obtain the skills, the proficiency, and the aeronautical knowledge required to operate that specific airplane safely.

   1. You should receive comprehensive ground and flight training in that airplane.

   2. If you are instrument rated, your transition training should include key instrument flight maneuvers so that you can practice them under the supervision of an instructor. These maneuvers should include

      a. Departure and arrival procedures
      b. Holding
      c. Approaches (including missed approaches)

D. The following is a list of steps to take when transitioning to a complex airplane. This procedure should be followed for every new airplane to be flown. Even ATPs should get checked out when flying a different airplane.

   1. **Thoroughly study the *Pilot's Operating Handbook* (or FAA-approved *Airplane Flight Manual*).**

      a. A thorough understanding of the fuel system, electrical and/or hydraulic system, landing gear system, empty and maximum allowable weights, loading schedule, and normal and emergency operating procedures, including all checklists, is essential.

      b. For introductory information on operating high-performance airplanes, see Appendix B, Complex and High-Performance Airplanes, beginning on page 299.

   2. **Learn the cockpit arrangement.**

      a. You should study the engine and flight controls, engine and flight instruments, fuel management controls, wing flaps and landing gear controls and indicators, and radio equipment until proficient enough to pass a blindfold cockpit check in the airplane in which qualification is sought.

      b. One method of gaining cockpit familiarity is by running through the normal operating and emergency checklists while the airplane is on the ground.

      c. Obtain a picture or schematic of the instrument panel. Take a blank sheet of paper and make your own sketch from the picture or schematic or from the actual instrument panel while you are sitting in the airplane.

         1) Label each instrument, switch, radio, etc.
         2) Note its purpose.

      d. The objective of this exercise is for you to feel entirely "at home" with the instrument panel, radios, and controls before you begin flying the airplane. This procedure definitely puts you ahead of the competition!

3. **Hire a flight instructor.**

    a. You should obtain the services of a flight instructor who is fully qualified in the airplane concerned. THIS IS VERY IMPORTANT.

    b. The flight instructor not only should be well qualified in the airplane to be used but also should be capable of effectively communicating the techniques essential for the safe operation of the airplane.

4. **Learn the flight and operating characteristics.**

    a. You should not limit familiarization flights to the practice of normal takeoffs and landings.

    b. It is extremely important to learn the V-speeds and become thoroughly familiar with the slow flight and stall characteristics, maximum performance techniques, all normal operating procedures, and all emergency procedures.

5. **Learn the gross weight and CG limitations.**

    a. You should include in the checkout at least a demonstration of takeoffs, landings, and flight maneuvers with the airplane fully loaded.

    b. Most four-place and larger airplanes handle quite differently when loaded to near-maximum gross weight, as compared to operation with only two occupants.

    c. You should compute weight and balance for various loading conditions.

E. Before you can act as pilot in command (PIC) in a complex airplane, you must have your logbook endorsed by a CFI. While this is a one-time endorsement for a complex airplane, you should get a complete checkout for each different make and model of airplane you fly.

    1. An example of an endorsement for a pilot to act as PIC in a complex airplane, FAR 61.31(e), appears below:

        I certify that (First name, MI, Last name) , (pilot certificate) (certificate number) has received the required training of Sec. 61.31(e) in a (make and model of complex airplane). I have determined that he/she is proficient in the operation and systems of a complex airplane.

        _____   _____   _____   _____
        Date   *Signature*   *CFI No.*   *Expiration Date*

F. A high-performance airplane is defined by FAR 61.31(f) as an airplane with an engine of more than 200 horsepower.

    1. For transition training into a high-performance airplane, follow the recommended steps listed in item D. beginning on page 8.

    2. Before you can act as PIC of a high-performance airplane, you must have a one-time logbook endorsement by a CFI. An example of an endorsement, FAR 61.31(f), appears below:

        I certify that (First name, MI, Last name) , (pilot certificate) (certificate number) has received the required training of Sec. 61.31(f) in a (make and model of high-performance airplane) . I have determined that he/she is proficient in the operation and systems of a high-performance airplane.

        _____   _____   _____   _____
        Date   *Signature*   *CFI No.*   *Expiration Date*

1.5 *PILOT'S OPERATING HANDBOOK (POH)*

A.   The FAA requires a *Pilot's Operating Handbook* (also called an FAA-approved *Airplane Flight Manual*) (FAR 23.1581). These usually are 6" x 8" ring notebooks, so pages can be updated, deleted, added, etc. They typically have nine sections:

```
1.  General . . . . . . . . . . . . . . . . . . . . . . . . . . . . . . . . . . . . . . . . . . . . . . . . . . Description of the airplane
2.  Limitations . . . . . . . . . . . . . . . . . . . . . . . . . . . . . . . . . . . . . . Description of operating limits
3.  Emergency Procedures . . . . . . . . . . . . . . . . . . . . . . . . . . . . . . What to do in each situation
4.  Normal Procedures . . . . . . . . . . . . . . . . . . . . . . . . . . . . . . . . . . . . . . . . . . . Checklists
5.  Performance  . . . . . . . . . . . . . . . . . . . . . . . . . Graphs and tables of airplane capabilities
6.  Weight and Balance . . . . . . . . . . . . . . . . . . . . . . . . . Equipment list, airplane empty weight
7.  Description of Operating Systems  . . . . . . . . . . . . . . . . . . . . . As discussed in this chapter
8.  Servicing and Maintenance . . . . . . . . . . . . . . . . . . . . . . . . . . . Explanation of what and when
9.  Supplements  . . . . . . . . . . . . . . . . . . . . . . . . Usually describes available optional equipment
```

B.   The *POH* is your primary source of information on the airplane's specific operating procedures and limitations.

   1.   Your *POH* is critical for emergency operations.

      a.   Your *POH* must be easily accessible to you during flight.

   2.   Also be aware that some *POHs* have two parts to each section:

      a.   Abbreviated procedures (which are checklists)
      b.   Amplified procedures (which consist of discussion of the checklists)

   3.   As a practical matter, after you study your *POH* and gain some experience in your airplane, you may wish to retype some of the standard checklists on heavy manila paper.

      a.   Having the checklists available is more convenient than finding checklists in your *POH* while engaged in other cockpit activities.

      b.   Also, electronic checklists are available which provide checklist items one at a time.

C.   Most late-model popular airplanes have *POHs* reprinted as perfect-bound books (called Information Manuals) available at FBOs and aviation bookstores. If possible, purchase a *POH* for your training airplane before you begin your flight lessons. Read it cover-to-cover and study (committing to memory) the normal operating checklists, standard airspeeds, and emergency procedures.

1.6 COCKPIT FAMILIARITY

A.   Just as you need to understand the operation of all systems and equipment prior to flying an airplane, you also must be conversant with the control panel layout, flight controls, and various equipment/systems controls.

B.   Your *POH* should have a control panel diagram similar to that of the Piper Arrow illustrated on page 11. Before beginning your flight lessons, make a photocopy of the control panel diagram in your airplane's *POH* and/or take several photographs of your control panel.

   1.   Study the diagram/photo. Go over each control, gauge, switch, etc. Know its exact function and/or its normal reading.

   2.   Next, take a blank sheet of paper and, without the aid of a diagram or photo, sketch your control panel and review normal control positions and normal gauge indications.

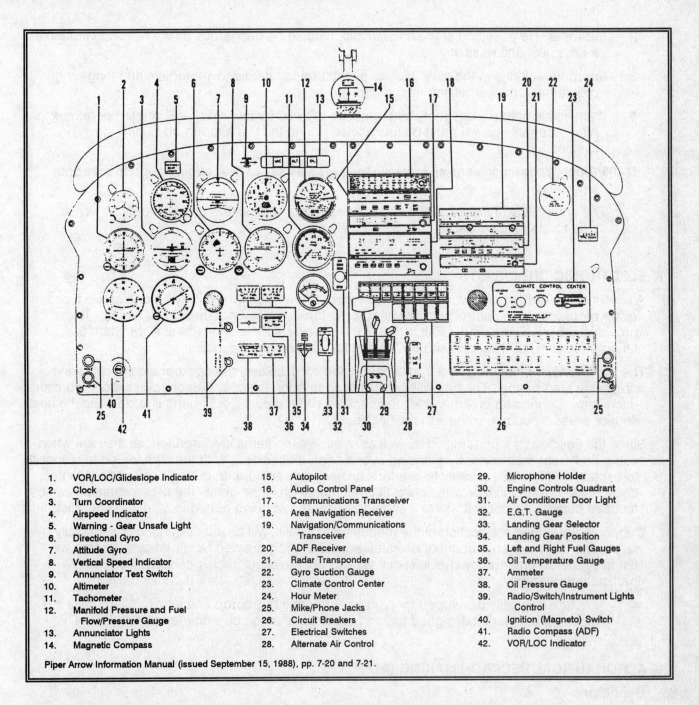

1.	VOR/LOC/Glideslope Indicator	15.	Autopilot
2.	Clock	16.	Audio Control Panel
3.	Turn Coordinator	17.	Communications Transceiver
4.	Airspeed Indicator	18.	Area Navigation Receiver
5.	Warning - Gear Unsafe Light	19.	Navigation/Communications Transceiver
6.	Directional Gyro	20.	ADF Receiver
7.	Attitude Gyro	21.	Radar Transponder
8.	Vertical Speed Indicator	22.	Gyro Suction Gauge
9.	Annunciator Test Switch	23.	Climate Control Center
10.	Altimeter	24.	Hour Meter
11.	Tachometer	25.	Mike/Phone Jacks
12.	Manifold Pressure and Fuel Flow/Pressure Gauge	26.	Circuit Breakers
13.	Annunciator Lights	27.	Electrical Switches
14.	Magnetic Compass	28.	Alternate Air Control

29.	Microphone Holder
30.	Engine Controls Quadrant
31.	Air Conditioner Door Light
32.	E.G.T. Gauge
33.	Landing Gear Selector
34.	Landing Gear Position
35.	Left and Right Fuel Gauges
36.	Oil Temperature Gauge
37.	Ammeter
38.	Oil Pressure Gauge
39.	Radio/Switch/Instrument Lights Control
40.	Ignition (Magneto) Switch
41.	Radio Compass (ADF)
42.	VOR/LOC Indicator

Piper Arrow Information Manual (issued September 15, 1988), pp. 7-20 and 7-21.

1.7 CHECKLISTS

A. Everyone operating any airplane safely has no alternative but to use the checklists pertinent to that particular airplane. They are found in the airplane's *POH*.

B. Complex airplanes characteristically have many more controls, switches, instruments, and indicators. Failure to position or check any of these controls, switches, instruments, and indicators may have much more serious results than would a similar error in the more basic single-engine airplane.

   1. Failure to turn off the heat or air conditioner (depending on the airplane) for takeoff and landing could result in inadequate power during an emergency situation such as a partial engine failure.

2.   Improper use or setting of the pressurization could be dangerous as well as uncomfortable for the pilot and passengers.

3.   Improper settings of the cowl flaps or air intakes could lead to immediate and long-range problems from overheating or cooling.

4.   If anti-ice is needed, adequate time must be allowed for it to reach desired temperatures. Also, adequate power must be maintained during the taxi and run-up to operate the system.

5.   Proper propeller settings and operations are essential for best engine performance and longevity.

6.   The complexity of autopilot and compass systems requires the proper inputs as well as time for them to stabilize.

1.8 ELECTRONIC CHECKLISTS

A.   A recent aid to reduce pilot workload is the electronic checklist, which may be one of two types, either mounted in the control panel or hand-held. The unit is about the size of a radio. It provides either an aural or a visual listing of the checklists for each stage of flight (start, taxi, takeoff, descent, landing, and shutdown) and for possible emergencies.

B.   The pilot, instead of reading off a traditional printed card, selects the appropriate checklist and presses a start button. The box will then proceed through the specified checklist, stopping after each item. Depending on the model, the pilot will either verbally command it to go on to the next item or press a button moving it to the next item.

C.   Since the checklist is standardized as well as complete, no items are forgotten, as they are when pilots do it from memory or by glancing over a printed checklist. With the pilot forced to respond to each item, (s)he is less likely to overlook an item, as can happen during busy periods in the cockpit. Also, with the electronic checklist mounted high in the panel, the pilot's attention can be focused outside the cockpit where it should be, instead of being buried in a printed checklist.

D.   Depending on the sophistication of the model, the checklist will be either generic or especially tailored to the make and model of aircraft flown. One programmed for a particular aircraft will usually have an emergency checklist that will call out the exact items needed to cope with a particular emergency.

1.   Although originally developed for high-performance turboprop and jet aircraft, models are reaching the market designed for, and in the price range of, single-engine airplanes.

1.9 AERONAUTICAL DECISION MAKING (ADM)

A.   **Definitions**

1.   **ADM** is a systematic approach to the mental process used by aircraft pilots to consistently determine the best course of action in response to a given set of circumstances.

2.   **Attitude** is a personal motivational predisposition to respond to persons, situations, or events in a given manner that can, nevertheless, be changed or modified through training.

a.   A sort of "mental shortcut" to decision making

3.   **Attitude management** is the ability to recognize hazardous attitudes in oneself and the willingness to modify them as necessary through the application of appropriate antidote thoughts.

4. **Cockpit resource management (CRM)**, in single-pilot or multiperson crew configurations, is the effective use of all personnel and material assets available to a pilot or a flight crew.

    a. CRM emphasizes good communication and other interpersonal relationship skills.

5. **Headwork** is required to accomplish a conscious, rational thought process when making decisions.

    a. Good decision making involves risk identification and assessment, information processing, and problem solving.

6. **Judgment** is the mental process of recognizing and analyzing all pertinent information in a particular situation, rationally evaluating alternative actions in response to it, and making a timely decision on which action to take.

7. **Personality** is the embodiment of personal traits and characteristics of an individual that are set at a very early age and are extremely resistant to change.

8. **Poor judgment (PJ) chain** is a series of mistakes that may lead to an accident or incident.

    a. Two basic principles generally associated with the creation of a PJ chain are

        1) One bad decision often leads to another.

        2) As a string of bad decisions grows, it reduces the number of subsequent alternatives for continued safe flight.

    b. ADM is intended to break the PJ chain before it can cause an accident or incident.

9. **Risk management** is the part of the decision-making process which relies on situational awareness, problem recognition, and good judgment to reduce risks associated with each flight.

10. **Risk elements** in ADM take into consideration the four fundamental risk elements:

    a. The pilot
    b. The aircraft
    c. The environment
    d. The type of operation that comprises any given aviation situation

11. **Situational awareness** is the accurate perception and understanding of all the factors and conditions within the four fundamental risk elements that affect safety before, during, and after the flight.

12. **Skills and procedures** are the procedural, psychomotor, and perceptual skills used to control a specific aircraft or its systems.

    a. They are the "stick and rudder" or airmanship abilities that are gained through conventional training, are perfected, and become almost automatic through experience.

13. **Stress management** is the personal analysis of the kinds of stress experienced while flying and the application of appropriate stress assessment tools and coping mechanisms.

B. **ADM Process**

1. ADM enhances the decision-making process to decrease the probability of pilot error. The figure below illustrates the ADM process and shows the interactions of the ADM steps and how these steps can produce a safe outcome.

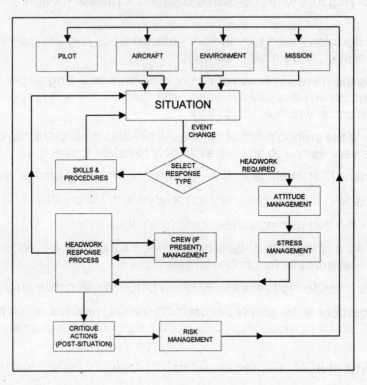

2. ADM provides a structured, systematic approach to analyzing changes that occur during a flight and the effect these changes might have on a flight's safe outcome.

    a. Starting with the recognition of change, and following with an assessment of alternatives, a decision to act or not to act is made, and the results are monitored.

3. ADM enhances the conventional decision-making process with an awareness of the importance of attitudes in decision making, a learned ability to search for and establish the relevance of all information, and the motivation to choose and execute the actions which assure safety in a time frame permitted by the situation.

4. The ADM process addresses all aspects of decision making in the cockpit and identifies the steps involved in good decision making. These steps are

    a. Identifying personal attitudes hazardous to safe flight
    b. Learning behavior modification
    c. Learning how to recognize and cope with stress
    d. Developing risk assessment skills
    e. Using all resources in a single-pilot or multiperson crew situation
    f. Evaluating the effectiveness of one's ADM skills

C. **Hazardous Attitudes**

  1. **Antiauthority (*Don't tell me!*).** This attitude is found in people who do not like anyone telling them what to do. In a sense, they are saying, "No one can tell me what to do." They may be resentful of having someone tell them what to do or may regard rules, regulations, and procedures as silly or unnecessary. Of course, it is always your prerogative to question authority if you feel it is in error.

  2. **Impulsivity (*Do something quickly!*)** is the attitude of people who frequently feel the need to do something-anything-immediately. They do not stop to think about what they are about to do, they do not determine the best alternative, and they do the first thing that comes to mind.

  3. **Invulnerability (*It won't happen to me.*).** Many people feel that accidents happen to others, but never to them. They know accidents can happen, and they know that anyone can be affected. However, they never really feel or believe that they will be personally involved. Pilots who think this way are more likely to take chances and increase risk.

  4. **Macho (*I can do it.*).** Pilots who are always trying to prove that they are better than anyone else are thinking *I can do it -- I'll show them*. Pilots with this type of attitude will try to prove themselves by taking risks in order to impress others. While this pattern is thought to be a male characteristic, women are equally susceptible.

  5. **Resignation (*What's the use?*).** Pilots who think *What's the use?* do not see themselves as being able to make a great deal of difference in what happens to them. The pilot is apt to think that things go well due to good luck. When things go badly, the pilot may feel that someone is out to get him/her or may attribute the situation to bad luck. The pilot will leave the action to others, for better or worse. Sometimes, such pilots will even go along with unreasonable requests just be to a "nice guy."

D. **Antidotes for Hazardous Attitudes**

  1. Hazardous attitudes which contribute to poor pilot judgment can be effectively counteracted by redirecting each hazardous attitude so that appropriate action can be taken.

     a. Recognition of hazardous thoughts is the first step in neutralizing them in the ADM process.

  2. After recognizing and labeling a thought as hazardous, the pilot should correct the hazardous thought by stating the corresponding antidote.

     a. Antidotes should be memorized for each of the hazardous attitudes so that they automatically come to mind when needed.

  3. The hazardous attitude antidotes, shown below, should be learned thoroughly and practiced.

Hazardous Attitude	Antidote
Antiauthority: *Don't tell me!*	Follow the rules. They are usually right.
Impulsivity: *Do something quickly!*	Not so fast. Think first.
Invulnerability: *It won't happen to me.*	It could happen to me.
Macho: *I can do it.*	Taking chances is foolish.
Resignation: *What's the use?*	I'm not helpless. I can make a difference.

1.10 COCKPIT RESOURCE MANAGEMENT (CRM)

A.   CRM is an extension of the ADM concepts previously discussed to the multiperson flight crew. The only difference is the additional focus on communication.

     1.   CRM means the effective use of all resources (people and materials) to achieve safe and efficient flight operations.

B.   One of the most important keys to good cockpit management, as in any management position, is communication among crew members.

     1.   Information must be requested, offered, and/or given freely in a timely way to permit the captain to make accurate, effective decisions.

     2.   Good cockpit management also requires an understanding of communication styles used by other members of the crew for interpretation and for determination of the proper emphasis for a response.

     3.   Finally, good cockpit management requires an understanding and acceptance of the unique role and leadership responsibility of each member of the crew.

C.   The most important aspect of CRM training is interpersonal communication. Management is conducted through communication.

     1.   Effective communication means making the other person understand what you are saying as well as understanding what the other person is saying because it can mean the safety of the flight.

     2.   It is the responsibility of all crew members to communicate effectively.

D.   Following are five elements of good communication that are independent of each other and cover the aspects of cockpit communication very well.

     1.   Inquiry

         a.   Inquiry or information seeking represents the beginning point to making effective decisions. Good decisions are based on good information.

            1)   In the cockpit, it consists of both visually scanning the cockpit for information and questioning other crewmembers or controllers for information.

            2)   Inquiry also means asking for clarification when the information is not clearly understood.

         b.   In the cockpit, crewmembers with fragile egos are often reluctant to ask for clarification because it may reflect badly on either their intellect or their hearing, both of which are important for maintaining not only flying status but also the respect of peers.

            1)   This feeling of insecurity, which is often fed by equally insecure peers and/or controllers who fire back a statement about how foolish you look to have to ask such a question, must be overcome if complete understanding is to be reached and safe decisions are to be made consistently.

     2.   Advocacy

         a.   Advocacy refers to the need to state what you know or believe in a forthright manner.

         b.   It means not only stating your position but also maintaining your position until completely convinced by the facts, not the authority of another, that it is wrong.

3.   Listening

    a.   Listening requires the listener to open up to the other person, inquire actively through questions and other forms of feedback, and respond appropriately (i.e., agreement, acknowledgment, disagreement), but always to accept that what is said may be true to the other person.

    b.   Passive listeners have the following traits:

       1)   Preplan: Passive listeners are intent on what they want to say, so they do not listen to what you are saying.

       2)   Debate: No matter what is said, some people want to take the other side.

       3)   Detour: These people resemble those who preplan, but they wait for a key word to take the discussion to another area of interest to them.

       4)   Tune out: Whatever you have to say, it is not important enough for their attention.

    c.   Active listeners will

       1)   Ask questions
       2)   Paraphrase: Did I hear you right?
       3)   Provide eye contact
       4)   Use body language

    d.   Active listening results in better communication, safety, efficiency, relationships, decision making, and harmony.

    e.   To summarize active listening, the following points are offered:

       1)   It is a basic human need to be heard and understood -- active listening serves that need.

       2)   Active listening is a skill that must be learned.

       3)   In an emergency, active listening is a critical skill.

       4)   In normal situations, active listening enhances communication, eliminates barriers, and lays the groundwork for good communication during emergencies.

4.   Conflict resolution

    a.   If you and your other crewmembers are each advocating your position properly, conflict is inevitable. Thus, an effective process is needed to resolve those conflicts.

    b.   Conflicts are not necessarily bad as long as they arise over issues within the cockpit.

       1)   They can become destructive when issues from outside the cockpit (i.e., personality factors, personal weaknesses, social status, etc.) are brought into the argument.

          a)   It can also be destructive when the argument is over who is right rather than what is right.

          b)   Such arguments can have a serious effect on the quality of the decisions made because thinking is focused on the wrong issues.

    c.   The proper way to resolve conflicts is to

        1)   Have a policy of crew coordination that is known and accepted by everyone.

        2)   Keep the discussion on the issues needing resolution within the cockpit.

        3)   Bring out all issues of disagreement.

        4)   Acknowledge and express all feelings that are deep enough to cloud your thinking.

    d.   Properly handled conflict resolution is the key to the highest level of problem solving known.

        1)   It leads to deeper thinking, creative new ideas, mutual respect, and higher self-esteem, which strengthens team effectiveness.

        2)   For these reasons, conflict should not be avoided when differences of opinion arise. Rather, it should be recognized as an opportunity to seek better solutions to problems that may not have been thought of previously.

5.   Critique

    a.   Even more difficult than conflict resolution is the ability to provide an effective critique of fellow crewmembers.

        1)   A critique is necessary because it teaches us how to improve.

    b.   To improve cockpit skills such as problem solving, monitoring traffic, communication, etc., we need feedback in the form of a critique from our fellow crewmembers.

1.11 COMMERCIAL RELATED FARs

A.   Study Chapter 4, Federal Aviation Regulations, in the *Commercial Pilot FAA Written Exam* book.

    1.   Remember to purchase Gleim's *FAR/AIM* as your official FAR and *AIM* reference. Its revised formatting and larger type make it easier to read, and it has better indices. In addition, an automatic e-mail update service is provided for *FAR/AIM*.

END OF CHAPTER

CHAPTER TWO
OPTIMIZING YOUR FLIGHT
AND GROUND TRAINING

The purpose of this chapter is to help you get the most out of your ground training and your flight training. They should support each other. Ground training should facilitate your flight training and vice versa. While your immediate objective is to pass your practical test, your long-range goal is to become a safe and proficient pilot and enjoy a successful aviation career. Thus, you have to work hard to be able to **do your best**. No one can ask for more!

2.1 PART 61 vs. PART 141 FLIGHT TRAINING PROGRAMS

A. The general requirement for attaining the commercial pilot certificate is a minimum of 250 hr. of flight experience. The program laid out in FAR Part 61 is available to anyone in conjunction with a flight program taught by any CFI.

B. An alternative is a FAR Part 141 training program, which is a program conducted by an FAA-approved flight school. Part 141 flight schools are more highly regulated and require physical facility inspection, approval of the ground and flight training syllabi, etc., by the FAA.

1. The Part 141 commercial pilot certification course (airplane) includes a minimum of 35 hr. of ground training and a minimum of 120 hr. of flight training, all of which must be conducted at a Part 141 school.

2.2 GROUND TRAINING

A. First and foremost: Ground training is extremely important to facilitate flight training. Each preflight and postflight discussion is as important as the actual flight training of each flight lesson!

1. Unfortunately, most students and some CFIs incorrectly overemphasize the in-airplane portion of a flight lesson.

a. The airplane, all of its operating systems, ATC, other traffic, etc., are major distractions from the actual flight maneuver and the aerodynamic theory/factors underlying the maneuver.

b. Recognizing the importance of ground training does not diminish the importance of dealing with operating systems, ATC, other traffic, etc.

2. Note that the effort and results are those of the student. Instructors are responsible for directing student effort so that optimal results are achieved.

3. Formal ground schools to support flight training generally do **not** exist except at aeronautical universities and some Part 141 programs. Most community colleges, adult education programs, and FBO ground schools are directed toward the FAA commercial pilot knowledge test.

B.   Again, **the effort and results are dependent on you.** Prepare for each flight lesson so you know exactly what is going to happen and why. The more you prepare, the better you will do, both in execution of maneuvers and acquisition of knowledge.

　　1.   At the end of each flight lesson, find out exactly what is planned for the next flight lesson.

　　2.   At home, begin by reviewing everything that occurred during the last flight lesson -- preflight briefing, flight, and postflight briefing. Make notes on follow-up questions and discussion to be pursued with your CFI at the beginning of the next preflight briefing.

　　3.   Study all new flight maneuvers scheduled for the next flight lesson, and review flight maneuvers that warrant additional practice (refer to the appropriate chapters in Part II of this book). Make notes on follow-up questions and discussion to be pursued with your CFI at the beginning of the next preflight briefing.

　　4.   Before each flight, sit down with your CFI for a preflight briefing. Begin with a review of the last flight lesson. Then focus on the current flight lesson. Go over each maneuver to be executed, including maneuvers to be reviewed from previous flight lessons.

　　5.   During each flight lesson, be diligent about safety (continuously check traffic and say so as you do it). During maneuvers, compare your actual experience with your expectations (based on your prior knowledge from completing your Flight Maneuver Analysis Sheet).

　　6.   Your postflight briefing should begin with a self-critique, followed by evaluation by your CFI. Ask questions until you are satisfied that you have expert knowledge. Finally, develop a clear understanding of the tasks and maneuvers to be covered in your next flight lesson.

2.3 FLIGHT TRAINING

A.   Once you are in the airplane, the FAA recommends that your CFI use the "telling and doing" technique:

　　1.   Instructor tells, instructor does.
　　2.   Student tells, instructor does.
　　3.   Student tells, student does.
　　4.   Student does, instructor evaluates.

B.   Each attribute of the maneuver should be discussed before, during, and after execution of the maneuver.

C.   Integrated flight training: The FAA strongly encourages flight by reference to instruments in conjunction with initial flight instruction, i.e., "from the first time each maneuver is introduced."

　　1.   The intent is to instruct students to perform flight maneuvers both by outside visual references and by reference to flight instruments.

　　2.   This approach was instituted by the FAA in reaction to accidents that occurred when pilots encountered instrument weather conditions.

D.   Additional student home study of flight maneuvers needs to be **integrated** with in-airplane training to make in-airplane training both more effective and more efficient.

　　1.   Effectiveness refers to learning as much as possible (i.e., getting pilot skills "down pat" so as to be a safe and proficient pilot).

　　2.   Efficiency refers to learning as much as possible in a reasonable amount of time.

2.4 FLIGHT MANEUVER ANALYSIS SHEET (FMAS)

A. We have developed a method of analyzing and studying flight maneuvers that incorporates 10 variables:

1. Maneuver
2. Objective
3. Flight path
4. Power setting(s)
5. Altitude(s)

6. Airspeed(s)
7. Control forces
8. Time(s)
9. Traffic considerations
10. Completion standards

B. A copy of an FMAS (front and back) appears on pages 22 and 23 for your convenience. When you reproduce the form for your own use, photocopy on the front and back of a single sheet of paper to make the form more convenient. The front contains space for analysis of the above variables. The back contains space for

1. Make- and model-specific information

   a. Weight
   b. Airspeeds
   c. Fuel
   d. Center of gravity
   e. Performance data

2. Flight instrument review of maneuver

   a. Attitude indicator . . . . AI
   b. Airspeed indicator . . . . ASI
   c. Turn coordinator . . . . TC
   d. Heading indicator . . . . HI
   e. Vertical speed indicator . . . . . . VSI
   f. Altimeter . . . . ALT

3. Common errors

C. You should prepare/study/review the FMAS for each maneuver you intend to perform before each flight lesson. Changes, amplifications, and other notes should be added subsequently. Blank sheets of paper should be attached (stapled) to the FMAS, including self-evaluations, "to do" items, questions for your CFI, etc., for your home study during your flight training program. FMASs are also very useful to prepare for the practical test.

1. A major benefit of the FMAS is preflight lesson preparation. It serves as a means to discuss maneuvers with your CFI before and after flight. It emphasizes preflight planning, make and model knowledge, and flight instruments.

2. Also, the FMAS helps you, in general, to focus on the operating characteristics of your airplane, including weight and balance. Weight and balance, which includes fuel, should be carefully reviewed prior to each flight.

GLEIM'S
FLIGHT MANEUVER ANALYSIS SHEET

CFI _____
Student _____
Date _____

1. **MANEUVER** _____

2. **OBJECTIVES/PURPOSE** _____
   _____

3. **FLIGHT PATH (visual maneuvers)**

4. **POWER SETTINGS**   5. **ALT**   6. **A/S**

MP	RPM	SEGMENT OF MANEUVER		
____	____	a. _____	____	____
____	____	b. _____	____	____
____	____	c. _____	____	____

Pencil in expected indication on each of 6 flight instruments on reverse side.

7. **CONTROL FORCES**
   a. _____
      _____
   b. _____
      _____
   c. _____
      _____

8. **TIME(S), TIMING** _____
   _____

9. **TRAFFIC CONSIDERATIONS**   **CLEARING TURNS REQUIRED** ____
   _____

10. **COMPLETION STANDARDS/ATC CONSIDERATIONS** _____
    _____
    _____

AIRPLANE MAKE/MODEL _____

WEIGHT

Gross _____

Empty _____

Pilot/Pasngrs _____

Baggage _____

Fuel (gal × 6) _____

AIRSPEEDS

V_{S0} _____

V_{S1} _____

V_X _____

V_Y _____

V_A _____

V_{NO} _____

V_{NE} _____

V_{FE} _____

V_{LO} _____

V_R _____

ASI   AI   ALT

TC   HI   VSI

CENTER OF GRAVITY

Fore Limit _____

Aft Limit _____

Current CG _____

FUEL

Capacity   L ____ gal   R ____ gal

Current Estimate   L ____ gal   R ____ gal

Endurance (Hr.) _____

Fuel Flow -- Cruise (GPH) _____

PRIMARY vs. SECONDARY INSTRUMENTS

(IFR maneuvers) -- instruments: AI, ASI, ALT, TC, HI, VSI, RPM and/or MP
(most relevant to instrument instruction)

	PITCH	BANK	POWER
ENTRY			
primary	_____	_____	_____
secondary	_____	_____	_____
ESTABLISHED			
primary	_____	_____	_____
secondary	_____	_____	_____

PERFORMANCE DATA

	Airspeed	Power* MP	RPM
Takeoff Rotation	_____	_____	_____
Climbout	_____	_____	_____
Cruise Climb	_____	_____	_____
Cruise Level	_____	_____	_____
Cruise Descent	_____	_____	_____
Approach**	_____	_____	_____
Approach to Land (Visual)	_____		_____
Landing Flare	_____		_____

If you do not have a constant-speed propeller, ignore manifold pressure (MP).
** *Approach speed is for holding and performing instrument approaches.*

COMMON ERRORS

_____

_____

_____

_____

2.5 GLEIM'S COMMERCIAL PILOT SYLLABUS

A.   This syllabus is designed for pilots with over 200 hr. and an instrument rating (see page 311). Gleim also has a commercial pilot syllabus for pilots who have just completed their instrument training.

B.   Our syllabus consists of a flight training syllabus and a ground training syllabus, and meets the requirements of Part 61. Ground training and flight training may be completed together as an integrated course of instruction, or each may be completed separately. If they are completed separately, the ground syllabus may be conducted as a home-study course or as a formal ground school.

  1.   This syllabus was constructed using the building-block progression of learning, in which the student is required to perform each simple task correctly before a more complex task is introduced. This method will promote the formation of correct habit patterns from the beginning.

C.   **Flight Training Syllabus**

  1.   The flight training syllabus contains 18 lessons. It is recommended that each lesson be completed in sequential order. However, the syllabus is flexible enough to meet individual student needs or the particular training environment.

  2.   A listing of the 18 lessons is presented in the table below.

Lesson	Topic
1.	Introduction to Complex Airplanes
2.	Slow Flight and Stalls
3.	Emergency Operations
4.	Complex Airplane Review
5.	Dual Cross-Country
6.	Dual Night Cross-Country
7.	Solo Cross-Country
8.	Chandelles, Lazy 8's, and Steep Turns
9.	Eights-on-Pylons and Steep Spirals
10.	Solo Practice
11.	Review of Slow Flight and Stalls
12.	Review of Emergency Operations
13.	Solo Practice
14.	Maneuvers Review
15.	Solo Practice
16.	Maneuvers Review
17.	Solo Practice
18.	Practice Practical Test

  3.   The syllabus is reprinted in Appendix C, which begins on page 311.

D.   **Ground Training**

  1.   The ground training syllabus contains 12 lessons.

    a.   The ground training can be conducted concurrently with the flight training.

    b.   Ground training may also be conducted as part of a formal ground school or as a home-study program.

  2.   Each ground lesson involves studying the appropriate chapter in Gleim's *Pilot Handbook*. After each chapter is completed, you need to answer the questions in the appropriate chapter in Gleim's *Commercial Pilot FAA Written Exam* book and review incorrect responses with your instructor.

END OF CHAPTER

CHAPTER THREE
YOUR FAA PRACTICAL (FLIGHT) TEST

After all the training, studying, and preparation, the final step to receive your commercial pilot certificate is the FAA practical test. It requires that you exhibit to your examiner your previously gained knowledge and that you demonstrate that you are a proficient and safe commercial pilot.

Your practical test will be similar to previous practical tests. It is merely repeating to an examiner flight maneuvers that are familiar and well practiced. Conscientious flight instructors do not send applicants to an examiner until the applicant can pass the practical test on an average day; i.e., an exceptional flight will not be needed. Theoretically, the only way to fail would be to commit an error beyond the scope of what your CFI expects.

Most applicants pass the commercial practical test on the first attempt. The vast majority of those having trouble will succeed on the second attempt. This high pass rate is due to the high quality of flight training and the fact that most examiners test on a human level, not a NASA shuttle pilot level. The FAA Commercial Pilot Practical Test Standards are reprinted in Chapters I through XI and again in their entirety in Appendix A. Study Chapters I through XI so you know exactly what will be expected of you. Your goal is to exceed each requirement. This will ensure that even a slight mistake will fall within the limits, especially if you recognize it and explain your error to your examiner.

As you proceed with your flight training, you and your instructor should plan ahead and schedule your practical test. Several weeks before your practical test is scheduled, contact one or two individuals who took the commercial pilot practical test with your examiner. Ask each person to explain the routine, length, emphasis, maneuvers, and any peculiarities (i.e., surprises). This is a very important step because, like all people, examiners are unique. One particular facet of the practical test may be tremendously important to one examiner, while another examiner may emphasize an entirely different area. By gaining this information beforehand, you can focus on the areas of apparent concern to the examiner. Also, knowing what to expect will relieve some of the apprehension and tension about your practical test.

When you schedule your practical test, ask your examiner for the cross-country flight you should plan for on the day of your test. The Commercial Pilot PTS Task I.C., Cross-Country Flight Planning, beginning on page 62, states that you are to present and explain a preplanned VFR cross-country flight, as previously assigned by your examiner. However, some examiners may want to wait until the day of your test to assign you a cross-country flight.

3.1 FAA PRACTICAL TEST STANDARDS

A.   The intent of the FAA is to structure and standardize practical tests by specifying required tasks and acceptable performance levels to FAA inspectors and FAA-designated pilot examiners. These tasks (procedures and maneuvers) listed in the PTS are mandatory on each practical test unless specified otherwise.

B.   The 43 tasks for the commercial pilot certificate (airplane, single-engine land) are listed in 11 areas of operation as organized by the FAA.

   1.   The 12 tasks that can be completed away from the airplane are indicated below as "oral" and are termed "knowledge only" tasks by the FAA.

   2.   The 31 tasks that are usually completed in the airplane are indicated "flight" and are termed "knowledge and skill" tasks by the FAA.

NOTE: In the PTS format, the FAA has done away with reference to "oral tests" and "flight tests." The current FAA position is that all tasks require oral examining about applicant knowledge. Nonetheless, we feel it is useful to separate "knowledge only" tasks from "knowledge and skill" tasks.

C.   This book is based on the FAA's *Commercial Pilot Practical Test Standards* (FAA-S-8081-12B), dated August 2002. E-mail update@gleim.com with CPFM 4-1 in the subject line to determine if new PTSs have been released or if there are any updates to this book. See page iv.

3.2 FORMAT OF PTS TASKS

A.   Each of the FAA's 43 commercial pilot tasks listed on the opposite page is presented in a shaded box in Chapters I through XI, similar to Task I.A. reproduced below.

I.A. TASK: CERTIFICATES AND DOCUMENTS

   REFERENCES: 14 CFR Parts 43, 61, 91; FAA-H-8083-3, AC 61-23/FAA-H-8083-25; Pilot's Operating Handbook, FAA-Approved Airplane Flight Manual.

Objective. To determine that the applicant exhibits knowledge of the elements related to certificates and documents by:

1.   Explaining --

   a.   Commercial pilot certificate privileges, limitations, and recent flight experience requirements.

   b.   Medical certificate, class and duration.

   c.   Pilot logbook or flight records.

2.   Locating and explaining --

   a.   Airworthiness and registration certificates.

   b.   Operating limitations, placards, instrument markings, and Pilot's Operating Handbook/Airplane Flight Manual.

   c.   Weight and balance data and equipment list.

---

1.   The task number is followed by the title.

2.   The reference list identifies the FAA publication(s) that describe(s) the task.

   a.   Our discussion of each task is based on the FAA reference list. We will provide references to *Pilot Handbook* for additional reading on specific topics.

   b.   A listing of the FAA references used in the PTS begins on page 40.

3.   Next, the task has "**Objective**. To determine that the applicant . . . ," followed by a number of "Exhibits knowledge . . ." of aviation concepts and "Demonstrates . . ." various maneuvers.

B.   Each task in this book is followed by the following general format:

A.   General information

   1.   The FAA's objective and/or rationale for this task

   2.   Additional reading: Reference to Gleim's *Pilot Handbook* chapters and/or modules that provide additional discussion of the task, as appropriate

   3.   Any general discussion relevant to the task

B.   Comprehensive discussion of each concept or item listed in the FAA's task

C.   Common errors for each of the flight maneuvers, i.e., tasks appearing in Chapters II through IX and XI, relative to knowledge and skill tasks. Chapters I and X contain "knowledge only" tasks.

3.3 AIRPLANE AND EQUIPMENT REQUIREMENTS

A.   You are required to provide an appropriate and airworthy airplane for the practical test. Your airplane must have fully functioning dual controls and be equipped for, and its operating limitations must not prohibit, any task required on the practical test.

B.   The takeoff and landing maneuvers, and appropriate emergency procedures, must be accomplished in a complex airplane. A complex airplane is defined as an airplane that has retractable landing gear, flaps, and a controllable pitch propeller.

C.   You may provide a complex airplane for the entire test or elect to provide another airplane for those tasks that do not require a complex airplane. Your CFI can discuss the pros and cons of using two airplanes for training and the practical test. Regardless of the airplane(s) used, you are required to meet the commercial pilot knowledge and skill standards throughout the entire test.

3.4 WHAT TO TAKE TO YOUR PRACTICAL TEST

A.   You should ensure that you are completely prepared to begin your practical test before you meet your examiner. If you are unprepared, the test will become time-consuming and awkward for you and the examiner as you search for items that should have ben located beforehand.

B.   The following checklist from the FAA's Private Pilot Practical Test Standards should be reviewed with your instructor both 1 week and 1 day before your scheduled practical test:

   1.   Acceptable Airplane with Dual Controls

      a.   Aircraft Documents

         1)   Before your practical test, we suggest that you gather the following documents in one place so that you do not waste time looking for them once the test has started.

            a)   Airworthiness Certificate
            b)   Registration Certificate
            c)   Operating Limitations

               i)   Review the information in your *Pilot's Operating Handbook* or (FAA-Approved *Airplane Flight Manual)*

                  •   Before the practical test, perform a weight and balance computation based upon the anticipated conditions on the day of your flight;

                  •   Determine the takeoff and landing distances for that day's flight; and

                  •   List your airplane's V-speeds on an index card for quick reference.

b. Aircraft Maintenance Records

1) Logbook Record of Airworthiness Inspections and AD Compliance

a) Paperclip or otherwise indicate the location of the following items in your aircraft's airframe, powerplant, and propeller (if applicable) logbooks and other records.

i) Most recent Annual Inspection (must be within the preceding 12 calendar months)

ii) Most-recent 100-hr. Inspection (must be within the preceding 100 hours of flight time if the airplane is operated for compensation or hire)

iii) ELT Battery Due Date (must be after the date of the practical test)

iv) Most-recent Transponder Test and Inspection (must be within the preceding 24 calendar months)

v) Most-recent Altimeter and Static System Test and Inspection (must be within the preceding 24 calendar months)

vi) Most-recent VOR Receiver Check (must be within the preceding 30 days)

vii) Records of compliance with each one-time and recurring Airworthiness Directives (ADs) (records of compliance with recurring ADs must be within the appropriate interval)

2. Personal Equipment

a. View-Limiting Device (on FAA list, but not required by PTSs)
b. Current Aeronautical Charts, including appropriate Airport Diagrams
c. Computer and Plotter
d. Flight Plan Form
e. Flight Logs
f. Current *AIM, Airport/Facility Directory,* and Appropriate Publications (e.g., FARs)
g. A calculator to perform any weight and balance or performance computations

3. Personal Records

a. Before your practical test, we suggest that you gather the following items in a folder or other container.

1) Identification — photo/signature ID
2) Pilot Certificate (i.e., student or recreational)
3) Current Medical Certificate
4) Completed Application for an Airman Certificate and/or Rating (FAA Form 8710-1)
5) Airman Computer Test Report (pilot knowledge test grade report)
6) Logbook with Instructor's Endorsement for your Private Pilot Practical Test

a) Paperclip or otherwise mark the page with your practical test endorsement.

b) Total the last page's times in pencil so your application can be compared at a glance.

7) Notice of Disapproval (only if you previously failed your practical test)
8) Approved School Graduation Certificate (if applicable)
9) Examiner's Fee

3.5 PRACTICAL TEST APPLICATION FORM

C.   Prior to your practical test, your instructor will assist you in completing FAA Form 8710-1 (which appears on pages 32 and 33), and will sign the top of the back side of the form.

    1.   An explanation on how to complete the form is attached to the original, and we have reproduced it on page 31.

        a.   The form is not largely self-explanatory.
        b.   For example, the FAA wants dates shown as 12-13-97, **not** 12/13/97.

    2.   Do not go to your practical test without FAA Form 8710-1 properly filled out; remind your CFI about it as you schedule your practical test.

D.   If you are enrolled in a Part 141 flight school, the Air Agency Recommendation block of information on the back side may be completed by the chief instructor of your Part 141 flight school. (S)he, rather than a designated examiner or an FAA inspector, will administer the practical test if examining authority has been granted to your flight school.

E.   Your examiner or Part 141 flight school chief instructor will forward this and other required forms (listed on the bottom of the back side) to the nearest FSDO for review and approval.

    1.   Then they will be sent to Oklahoma City. From there, your new commercial pilot certificate will be issued and mailed to you.

    2.   However, you will be issued a temporary certificate when you successfully complete the practical test (see Module 3.9, Your Temporary Pilot Certificate, beginning on page 36).

AIRMAN CERTIFICATE AND/OR RATING APPLICATION
INSTRUCTIONS FOR COMPLETING FAA FORM 8710-1

I. APPLICATION INFORMATION. *Check appropriate blocks(s).*

Block A. Name. Enter legal name. Use no more than one middle name for record purposes. Do not change the name on subsequent applications unless it is done in accordance with 14 CFR Section 61.25. If you do not have a middle name, enter "NMN". If you have a middle initial only, indicate "Initial only." If you are a Jr., or a II, or III, so indicate. If you have an FAA certificate, the name on the application should be the same as the name on the certificate unless you have had it changed in accordance with 14 CFR Section 61.25.

Block B. Social Security Number. Optional: See supplemental Information Privacy Act. Do not leave blank: Use only **US Social Security Number.** Enter either "SSN" or the words "Do not Use" or "None." SSN's are not shown on certificates.

Block C. Date of Birth. Check for accuracy. Enter eight digits; Use numeric characters, i.e., 07-09-1925 instead of July 9, 1925. Check to see that DOB is the same as it is on the medical certificate.

Block D. Place of Birth. If you were born in the USA, enter the city and state where you were born. If the city is unknown, enter the county and state. If you were born outside the USA, enter the name of the city and country where you were born.

Block E. Permanent Mailing Address. Enter residence number and street, P.O. Box or rural route number in the top part of the block above the line. The City, State, and ZIP code go in the bottom part of the block below the line. Check for accuracy. Make sure the numbers are not transposed. FAA policy requires that you use your permanent mailing address. **Justification must be provided on a separate sheet of paper signed and submitted with the application when a PO Box or rural route number is used in place of your permanent physical address. A map or directions must be provided if a physical address is unavailable.**

Block F. Citizenship. Check USA if applicable. If not, enter the country where you are a citizen.

Block G. Do you read, speak, write and understand the English language? Check yes or no.

Block H. Height. Enter your height in inches. Example: 5'8" would be entered as 68 in. No fractions, use whole inches only.

Block I. Weight. Enter your weight in pounds. No fractions, use whole pounds only.

Block J. Hair. Spell out the color of your hair. If bald, enter "Bald." Color should be listed as black, red, brown, blond, or gray. If you wear a wig or toupee, enter the color of your hair under the wig or toupee.

Block K. Eyes. Spell out the color of your eyes. The color should be listed as blue, brown, black, hazel, green, or gray.

Block L. Sex. Check male or female.

Block M. Do You Now Hold or Have You Ever Held An FAA Pilot Certificate? Check yes or no. (NOTE: A student pilot certificate is a "Pilot Certificate.")

Block N. Grade of Pilot Certificate. Enter the grade of pilot certificate (i.e., Student, Recreational, Private, Commercial, or ATP). Do NOT enter flight instructor certificate information.

Block O. Certificate Number. Enter the number as it appears on your pilot certificate.

Block P. Date Issued. Enter the date your pilot certificate was issued.

Block Q. Do You Now Hold A Medical Certificate? Check yes or no. If yes, complete Blocks R, S, and T.

Block R. Class of Certificate. Enter the class as shown on the medical certificate, i.e., 1st, 2nd, or 3rd class.

Block S. Date Issued. Enter the date your medical certificate was issued.

Block T. Name of Examiner. Enter the name as shown on medical certificate.

Block U. Narcotics, Drugs. Check appropriate block. Only check "Yes" if you have actually been convicted. If you have been charged with a violation which has not been adjudicated, check ."No".

Block V. Date of Final Conviction. If block "U" was checked "Yes" give the date of final conviction.

II. CERTIFICATE OR RATING APPLIED FOR ON BASIS OF:
Block A. Completion of Required Test.
1. AIRCRAFT TO BE USED. (If flight test required) – Enter the make and model of each aircraft used. If simulator or FTD, indicate.
2. TOTAL TIME IN THIS AIRCRAFT (Hrs.) – (a) Enter the total Flight Time in each make and model. (b) Pilot-In-Command Flight Time - In each make and model.

Block B. Military Competence Obtained In. Enter your branch of service, date rated as a military pilot, your rank, or grade and service number. In block 4a or 4b, enter the make and model of each military aircraft used to qualify (as appropriate).

Block C. Graduate of Approved Course.
1. NAME AND LOCATION OF TRAINING AGENCY/CENTER. As shown on the graduation certificate. Be sure the location is entered.
2. AGENCY SCHOOL/CENTER CERTIFICATION NUMBER. As shown on the graduation certificate. Indicate if 142 training center.
3. CURRICULUM FROM WHICH GRADUATED. As shown on the graduation certificate.
4. DATE. Date of graduation from indicated course. Approved course graduate must also complete Block "A" COMPLETION OF REQUIRED TEST.

Block D. Holder of Foreign License Issued By.
1. COUNTRY. Country which issued the license.
2. GRADE OF LICENSE. Grade of license issued, i.e., private, commercial, etc.
3. NUMBER. Number which appears on the license.
4. RATINGS. All ratings that appear on the license.

Block E. Completion of Air Carrier's Approved Training Program.
1. Name of Air Carrier.
2. Date program was completed.
3. Identify the Training Curriculum.

III. RECORD OF PILOT TIME. The minimum pilot experience required by the appropriate regulation must be entered. It is recommended, however, that ALL pilot time be entered. If decimal points are used, be sure they are legible. Night flying must be entered when required. You should fill in the blocks that apply and ignore the blocks that do not. Second In Command "SIC" time used may be entered in the appropriate blocks. Flight Simulator, Flight Training Device and PCATD time may be entered in the boxes provided. Total, Instruction received, and Instrument Time should be entered in the top, middle, or bottom of the boxes provided as appropriate.

IV. HAVE YOU FAILED A TEST FOR THIS CERTIFICATE OR RATING? Check appropriate block.

V. APPLICANT'S CERTIFICATION.
  A. SIGNATURE. The way you normally sign your name.
  B. DATE. The date you sign the application.

TYPE OR PRINT ALL ENTRIES IN INK

Form Approved OMB No: 2120-0021

DEPARTMENT OF TRANSPORTATION
FEDERAL AVIATION ADMINISTRATION

Airman Certificate and/or Rating Application

I Application Information

- ☐ Student
- ☐ Recreational
- ☐ Private
- ☐ Commercial
- ☐ Airline Transport
- ☐ Instrument
- ☐ Additional Rating
- ☐ Airplane Single-Engine
- ☐ Airplane Multiengine
- ☐ Rotorcraft
- ☐ Balloon
- ☐ Airship
- ☐ Glider
- ☐ Powered-Lift
- ☐ Flight Instructor ____ Initial ____ Renewal ____ Reinstatement
- ☐ Additional Instructor Rating
- ☐ Ground Instructor
- ☐ Medical Flight Test
- ☐ Reexamination
- ☐ Reissuance of _____ certificate
- ☐ Other _____

A. Name (Last, First, Middle)	B. SSN (US Only)	C. Date of Birth Month Day Year	D. Place of Birth

E. Address	F. Citizenship ☐ USA ☐ Other _____ Specify	G. Do you read, speak, write, & understand the English language? ☐ Yes ☐ No

City, State, Zip Code	H. Height	I. Weight	J. Hair	K. Eyes	L. Sex ☐ Male ☐ Female

M. Do you now hold, or have you ever held an FAA Pilot Certificate? ☐ Yes ☐ No	N. Grade Pilot Certificate	O. Certificate Number	P. Date Issued

Q. Do you hold a Medical Certificate? ☐ Yes ☐ No	R. Class of Certificate	S. Date Issued	T. Name of Examiner

U. Have you ever been convicted for violation of any Federal or State statutes relating to narcotic drugs, marijuana, or depressant or stimulant drugs or substances? ☐ Yes ☐ No	V. Date of Final Conviction

II. Certificate or Rating Applied For on Basis of:

☐ A. Completion of Required Test	1. Aircraft to be used (if flight test required)	2a. Total time in this aircraft / SIM / FTD hours	2b. Pilot in command hours

☐ B. Military Competence Obtained In	1. Service	2. Date Rated	3. Rank or Grade and Service Number
	4a. Flown 10 hours PIC in last 12 months in the following Military Aircraft.	4b. US Military PIC & Instrument check in last 12 months (List Aircraft)	

☐ C. Graduate of Approved Course	1. Name and Location of Training Agency or Training Center	1a. Certification Number
	2. Curriculum From Which Graduated	3. Date

☐ D. Holder of Foreign License Issued By	1. Country	2. Grade of License	3. Number
	4. Ratings		

☐ E. Completion of Air Carrier's Approved Training Program	1. Name of Air Carrier	2. Date	3. Which Curriculum ☐ Initial ☐ Upgrade ☐ Transition

III RECORD OF PILOT TIME (Do not write in the shaded areas.)

	Total	Instruction Received	Solo	Pilot in Command (PIC)	Cross Country Instruction Received	Cross Country Solo	Cross Country PIC	Instrument	Night Instruction Received	Night Take-off/ Landings	Night PIC	Night Take-Off/ Landing PIC	Number of Flights	Number of Aero-Tows	Number of Ground Launches	Number of Powered Launches
Airplanes				PIC / SIC			PIC / SIC				PIC / SIC	PIC / SIC				
Rotor-craft				PIC / SIC			PIC / SIC				PIC / SIC	PIC / SIC				
Powered Lift				PIC / SIC			PIC / SIC				PIC / SIC	PIC / SIC				
Gliders																
Lighter Than Air																
Simulator																
Training Device																
PCATD																

IV. Have you failed a test for this certificate or rating? ☐ Yes ☐ No

V. Applicants's Certification -- I certify that all statements and answers provided by me on this application form are complete and true to the best of my knowledge and I agree that they are to be considered as part of the basis for issuance of any FAA certificate to me. I have also read and understand the Privacy Act statement that accompanies this form.

Signature of Applicant	Date

FAA Form 8710-1 (4-00) Supersedes Previous Edition

NSN: 0052-00-682-5007

Instructor's Recommendation

I have personally instructed the applicant and consider this person ready to take the test.

Date	Instructor's Signature (Print Name & Sign)	Certificate No:	Certificate Expires

Air Agency's Recommendation

The applicant has successfully completed our _____ course, and is recommended for certification or rating without further _____ test.

Date	Agency Name and Number	Officials Signature
		Title

Designated Examiner or Airman Certification Representative Report

- ☐ Student Pilot Certificate Issued (Copy attached)
- ☐ I have personally reviewed this applicant's pilot logbook and/or training record, and certify that the individual meets the pertinent requirements of 14 CFR Part 61 for the certificate or rating sought.
- ☐ I have personally reviewed this applicant's graduation certificate, and found it to be appropriate and in order, and have returned the certificate.
- ☐ I have personally tested and/or verified this applicant in accordance with pertinent procedures and standards with the result indicated below.
    - ☐ Approved -- Temporary Certificate Issued (Original Attached)
    - ☐ Disapproved -- Disapproval Notice Issued (Original Attached)

Location of Test (Facility, City, State)	Duration of Test		
	Ground	Simulator/FTD	Flight

Certificate or Rating for Which Tested	Type(s) of Aircraft Used	Registration No.(s)

Date	Examiner's Signature (Print Name & Sign)	Certificate No.	Designation No.	Designation Expires

Evaluator's Record (Use For ATP Certificate and/or Type Ratings)

	Inspector	Examiner	Signature and Certificate Number	Date
Oral	☐	☐		
Approved Simulator/Training Device Check	☐	☐		
Aircraft Flight Check	☐	☐		
Advanced Qualification Program	☐	☐		

Aviation Safety Inspector or Technician Report

I have personally tested this applicant in accordance with or have otherwise verified that this applicant complies with pertinent procedures, standards, policies, and or necessary requirements with the result indicated below.

- ☐ Approved -- Temporary Certificate Issued (Original Attached)
- ☐ Disapproved -- Disapproval Notice Issued (Original Attached)

Location of Test (Facility, City, State)	Duration of Test		
	Ground	Simulator/FTD	Flight

Certificate or Rating for Which Tested	Type(s) of Aircraft Used	Registration No.(s)

- ☐ Student Pilot Certificate Issued
- ☐ Examiner's Recommendation
    - ☐ Accepted ☐ Rejected
- ☐ Reissue or Exchange of Pilot Certificate
- ☐ Special Medical test conducted -- report forwarded to Aeromedical Certification Branch, AAM-330
- ☐ Certificate or Rating Based on
    - ☐ Military Competence
    - ☐ Foreign License
    - ☐ Approved Course Graduate
    - ☐ Other Approved FAA Qualification Criteria
- ☐ Flight Instructor ☐ Ground Instructor
- ☐ Renewal
- ☐ Reinstatement
- Instructor Renewal Based on
    - ☐ Activity ☐ Training Course
    - ☐ Test ☐ Duties and Responsibilities

Training Course (FIRC) Name	Graduation Certificate No.	Date

Date	Inspector's Signature (Print Name & Sign)	Certificate No.	FAA District Office

Attachments:
- ☐ Student Pilot Certificate (Copy)
- ☐ Knowledge Test Report
- ☐ Temporary Airman Certificate
- ☐ Notice of Disapproval
- ☐ Superseded Airman Certificate

☐ Airman's Identification (ID)

Form of ID _____

Number _____

Expiration Date _____

Telephone Number _____

ID:
Name: _____
Date of Birth: _____
Certificate Number: _____
E-Mail Address _____

FAA Form 8710-1 (4-00) Supersedes Previous Edition   NSN: 0052-00-682-5007

3.6 AUTHORIZATION TO TAKE THE PRACTICAL TEST

A. Before applicants for the commercial pilot certificate take the practical test, FAR 61.127 requires them to have logged ground and flight training from an authorized flight instructor in the following areas of operations:

1. Preflight preparation
2. Preflight procedures
3. Airport and seaplane base operations
4. Takeoffs, landings, and go-arounds
5. Performance maneuvers
6. Ground reference maneuvers
7. Navigation
8. Slow flight and stalls
9. Emergency operations
10. High-altitude operations
11. Postflight procedures

B. Your logbook must contain the following endorsement from your CFI certifying

1. That (s)he has found that you are prepared for the practical test

2. That (s)he has given you at least 3 hr. of flight training in a single-engine airplane in preparation for the practical test within the preceding 60 days and

3. That (s)he has found that you have demonstrated knowledge of the subject areas in which you were shown to be deficient in your knowledge test report.

I certify that (First name, MI, Last name) has received the required training of Secs. 61.127 and 61.129. I have determined he/she is prepared for the commercial pilot (airplane, single-engine land) practical test. He/She has demonstrated satisfactory knowledge of the subject areas found deficient on his/her knowledge test.

_____ _____ _____ _____
Date   *Signature*   *CFI No.*   *Expiration Date*

3.7 ORAL PORTION OF THE PRACTICAL TEST

C.   Your practical test will probably begin in your examiner's office.

    1.   You should have with you

        a.   This book

        b.   Your *Pilot's Operating Handbook (POH)* for your airplane (including weight and balance data)

        c.   Your copy of Gleim's *FAR/AIM*

        d.   All of the items listed on pages 28 and 29 (This is the FAA's list and they omitted the FARs.)

        e.   A positive attitude

    2.   Your examiner will probably begin by reviewing your paperwork (FAA Form 8710-1, Airman Knowledge Computer Test Report, logbook signoff, etc.) and receiving payment for his/her services.

    3.   Typically, your examiner will begin with questions about your preplanned VFR cross-country flight with discussion of weather, charts, FARs, etc. When you schedule your practical test, your examiner will probably assign a cross-country flight for you to plan and bring to your practical test.

    4.   As your examiner asks you questions, follow the guidelines listed below:

        a.   Attempt to position yourself in a discussion mode with him/her rather than being interrogated by the examiner.

        b.   Be respectful but do not be intimidated. Both you and your examiner are professionals.

        c.   Draw on your knowledge from this book and other books, your CFI, and your prior experience.

        d.   Ask for amplification of any points you feel uncertain about.

        e.   If you do not know an answer, try to explain how you would research the answer.

    5.   Be confident that you will do well. You are a good pilot. You have thoroughly prepared for this discussion by studying the subsequent pages and have worked diligently with your CFI.

D.   After you discuss various aspects of the 12 "knowledge only" tasks, you will move out to your airplane to begin the flight portion of your practical test, which consists of 31 "knowledge and skill" tasks.

    1.   If possible and appropriate in the circumstances, thoroughly preflight your airplane just before you go to your examiner's office.

    2.   As you and your examiner approach your airplane, explain that you have already preflighted the airplane (explain any possible problems and how you resolved them).

    3.   Volunteer to answer any questions.

    4.   Make sure you walk around the airplane to observe any possible damage by ramp vehicles or other aircraft while you were in your examiner's office.

    5.   As you enter the airplane, make sure that your cockpit is organized and you feel in control of your charts, clock, navigation logs, etc.

3.8 FLIGHT PORTION OF THE PRACTICAL TEST

A. As you begin the flight portion of your practical test, your examiner will have you depart on the VFR cross-country flight you previously planned.

    1. You will taxi out, depart, and proceed on course to your destination.

    2. Your departure procedures usually permit demonstration/testing of many of the tasks in Areas of Operation III, IV, and VII. After you complete these tasks, your examiner will probably have you discontinue your cross-country flight so you can demonstrate additional flight maneuvers.

B. Note that you are required to perform all 43 tasks during your practical test.

C. Remember that at all times you are the pilot in command of this flight. Take polite, but firm, charge of your airplane and instill in your examiner confidence in you as a safe and competent pilot.

D. To evaluate your ability to utilize proper control technique while dividing attention both inside and/or outside the cockpit, your examiner will cause a realistic distraction during the flight portion of your practical test to evaluate your ability to divide attention while maintaining safe flight.

3.9 YOUR TEMPORARY PILOT CERTIFICATE

A. When you successfully complete your practical test, your examiner will prepare a temporary pilot certificate similar to the one illustrated below.

    1. The temporary certificate is valid for 120 days.

B. Your permanent certificate will be sent to you directly from the FAA Aeronautical Center in Oklahoma City in about 60 to 90 days.

    1. If you do not receive your permanent certificate within 120 days, your examiner can arrange an extension of your temporary certificate.

3.10 FAILURE ON THE PRACTICAL TEST

A. About 90% of applicants pass their commercial pilot practical test the first time, and virtually all who experienced difficulty on their first attempt pass the second time.

B. If you have a severe problem with a maneuver or have so much trouble that the examiner has to take control of the airplane to avoid a dangerous situation, your examiner will fail you. If so, the test will be terminated at that point.

   1. When on the ground, your examiner will complete the Notice of Disapproval of Application, FAA Form 8060-5, which appears below, and will indicate the areas necessary for re-examination.

   2. Your examiner will give you credit for those tasks which you have successfully completed.

C. You should do the following:

   1. Indicate your intent to work with your instructor on your deficiencies.

   2. Inquire about rescheduling the next practical test.

      a. Many examiners have a reduced fee for a retake (FAA inspectors do not charge for their services).

   3. Inquire about having your flight instructor discuss your proficiencies and deficiencies with the examiner.

```
                    UNITED STATES OF AMERICA                           NOTE
   DEPARTMENT OF TRANSPORTATION-FEDERAL AVIATION ADMINISTRATION
                                                               PRESENT THIS FORM
      NOTICE OF DISAPPROVAL OF APPLICATION                     UPON APPLICATION
                                                               FOR REEXAMINTION

   NAME AND ADDRESS OF APPLICANT                               CERTIFICATE OR RATING
                                                               SOUGHT



   On the date shown, you failed the examination indicated below:
      ☐ FLIGHT            ☐ ORAL                   ☐ PRACTICAL
   AIRCRAFT USED (Make and Model)         FLT. TIME RECORDED IN LOGBOOK
                                      PILOT-IN-COMM.   INSTRUMENT    DUAL
                                      OR SOLO

   UPON REAPPLICATION YOU WILL BE REEXAMINED ON THE FOLLOWING:

   I have personally tested this applicant and deem his performance unsatisfactory for the issuance of the
   certificate or rating sought.
   DATE OF EXAMINATION   SIGNATURE OF EXAMINER OR INSPECTOR   DESIGNATION OR
                                                              OFFICE NO.

   FAA Form 8060—5 (5-80)
```

END OF CHAPTER

This is the end of Part I. Part II consists of Chapters I through XI. Each chapter covers one Area of Operation in the Commercial Pilot Practical Test Standards.

PART II
FAA PRACTICAL TEST STANDARDS
AND FLIGHT MANEUVERS:
DISCUSSED AND EXPLAINED

Part II of this book (Chapters I through XI) provides an in-depth discussion of the Commercial Pilot Practical Test Standards (PTS). Each of the 11 areas of operation with its related task(s) is presented in a separate chapter.

	Number of Tasks	Number of Pages
I. Preflight Preparation	8	47*
II. Preflight Procedures	5	23
III. Airport Operations	3	20
IV. Takeoffs, Landings, and Go-Arounds	8	63*
V. Performance Maneuvers	4	22
VI. Ground Reference Maneuver	1	6
VII. Navigation	4	12
VIII. Slow Flight and Stalls	4	18
IX. Emergency Operations	3	13
X. High-Altitude Operations	2	10
XI. Postflight Procedures	1	5
	43	239

* Larger chapters because they have more tasks.

Each task, reproduced verbatim from the PTS, appears in a shaded box within each chapter. General discussion is presented under "A. General Information." This is followed by "B. Task Objectives," which is a detailed discussion of each element of the FAA's task. Additionally, each "knowledge and skill" task (e.g., flight maneuver) common errors are listed and briefly discussed under "C. Common Errors . . . ."

Each objective of a task lists, in sequence, the important elements that must be satisfactorily performed. The objective includes

1. Specific abilities that are needed
2. The conditions under which the task is to be performed
3. The acceptable standards of performance

Be confident. You have prepared diligently and are better prepared and more skilled than the average commercial pilot applicant. Satisfactory performance to meet the requirements for certification is based on your ability to safely

1. Perform the tasks specified in the areas of operation for the certificate or rating sought within the approved standards

2. Demonstrate mastery of your airplane with the successful outcome of each task performed never seriously in doubt

3. Demonstrate satisfactory proficiency and competency within the approved standards

4. Demonstrate sound judgment

Each task has an FAA reference list which identifies the publication(s) that describe(s) the task. Our discussion is based on the current issue of these references. The following FAA references are used in the Commercial Pilot PTS.

14 CFR part 43	Maintenance, Preventive Maintenance, Rebuilding, and Alteration
14 CFR part 61	Certification: Pilots, Flight Instructors, and Ground Instructors
14 CFR part 91	General Operating and Flight Rules
AC 00-6	Aviation Weather
AC 00-45	Aviation Weather Services
AC 61-23/ FAA-H-8083-25	Pilot's Handbook of Aeronautical Knowledge
AC 61-65	Certification: Pilots and Flight Instructors
AC 61-67	Stall and Spin Awareness Training
AC 61-84	Role of Preflight Preparation
AC 90-48	Pilot's Role in Collision Avoidance
AC 90-66	Recommended Standard Traffic Patterns and Practices for Aeronautical Operations At Airports Without Operating Control Towers.
AC 120-51	Crew Resource Management Training
FAA-H-8083-1	Aircraft Weight and Balance Handbook
FAA-H-8083-3	Airplane Flying Handbook
FAA-H-8083-15	Instrument Flying Handbook
AIM	Aeronautical Information Manual
AFD	Airport Facility Directory
NOTAMs	Notices to Airmen
Other	Pilot Operating Handbook
	FAA-Approved Flight Manual
	Navigation Charts

In each task, as appropriate, we will provide you with the chapter and/or module from Gleim's *Pilot Handbook* for additional discussion of an element (or concept) of the task, along with the approximate number of pages of discussion. You should refer to *Pilot Handbook* when you desire a more detailed discussion than that provided in the task.

CHAPTER I
PREFLIGHT PREPARATION

This chapter explains the eight tasks (A-G, and J) of Preflight Preparation. These tasks are "knowledge only." Your examiner is required to test you on all eight of these tasks.

CERTIFICATES AND DOCUMENTS

I.A. TASK: CERTIFICATES AND DOCUMENTS

REFERENCES: 14 CFR Parts 43, 61, 91; FAA-H-8083-3; AC 61-23/FAA-H-8083-25; Pilot's Operating Handbook, FAA-Approved Airplane Flight Manual.

Objective. To determine that the applicant exhibits knowledge of the elements related to certificates and documents by:

1. Explaining --

a. Commercial pilot certificate privileges, limitations, and recent flight experience requirements.

b. Medical certificate class and duration.

c. Pilot logbook or flight records.

2. Locating and explaining --

a. Airworthiness and registration certificates.

b. Operating limitations, placards, instrument markings, and Pilot's Operating Handbook/Airplane Flight Manual.

c. Weight and balance data and equipment list.

A.   General Information

   1.   The objective of this task is to determine your knowledge of various pilot and airplane certificates and documents.

   2.   Additional reading: See Chapter 4, Federal Aviation Regulations, in *Pilot Handbook* for the following:

   a.   FAR 61.56, Flight Review, for information on the requirements of a biennial flight review (BFR)

B.   Task Objectives

   1.   You must be able to exhibit your knowledge of the following certificates and documents by explaining them to your examiner.

   a.   Commercial pilot certificate privileges, limitations, and recent flight experience requirements.

   1)   FAR 61.133, Commercial Pilot Privileges and Limitations, states that you can act as PIC of an airplane carrying passengers or property for compensation or hire, provided you are qualified under the FARs that apply to the type of flying you are conducting.

   a)   Most operations performed for compensation or hire are done with a Part 121, 125, or 135 certificate holder.

2) FAR 119.1, Applicability, specifically lists those operations that you can perform for compensation or hire without flying for a Part 121, 125, or 135 operation. These operations are

   a) Student instruction

   b) Nonstop sightseeing flights that are conducted in an airplane having a passenger seating configuration of 30 or fewer, excluding each crewmember seat, and a payload capacity of 7,500 lb. or less; that begin and end at the same airport; and that are conducted within a 25-SM radius of that airport

   c) Ferry or training flights

   d) Aerial work operations, including

      i) Crop dusting, seeding, spraying, and bird chasing
      ii) Banner towing
      iii) Aerial photography or survey
      iv) Fire fighting
      v) Powerline or pipeline patrol

   e) Nonstop flights conducted within a 25-SM radius of the airport of takeoff carrying persons for the purpose of intentional parachute jumps

   f) Emergency mail service conducted under appropriate regulations

   g) Operations conducted under FAR 91.321, Carriage of Candidates in Federal Elections

3) If you do not have an instrument rating, your certificate will be endorsed with a limitation prohibiting the carriage of passengers for hire in an airplane on cross-country flights of more than 50 NM, or at night.

4) General experience. To act as PIC of an aircraft carrying passengers, you must have completed three takeoffs and landings within the preceding 90 days as sole manipulator of the flight controls in an aircraft of the same category and class and, if a type rating is required, of the same type of aircraft. If made in a tailwheel aircraft, the landings must be to a full stop. (Category means airplane, rotorcraft, glider, or lighter than air. Class means single-engine land, multiengine land, single-engine sea, or multiengine sea.)

5) Night experience. Night officially begins (for logging night experience under FAR 61.57) 1 hr. after sunset and ends 1 hr. before sunrise. To act as PIC of an aircraft carrying passengers at night, you must have made, within the preceding 90 days, three takeoffs and landings to a full stop during night flight in an aircraft of the same category, class, and type (if a type rating is required)

6) You may not act as PIC unless you have completed a flight review (commonly referred to as a biennial flight review or BFR) within the preceding 24 months.

b. **Medical certificate class and duration**

   1) To exercise the privileges of your commercial pilot certificate, you must hold a first- or second-class medical certificate.

   2) A first- or second-class medical certificate will expire at the end of the last day of the 12th month (1 yr.) after the date of examination for operations requiring a commercial pilot certificate.

   3) A first- or second-class medical certificate will expire at the end of the last day of the 24th month (for a pilot aged 40 or older on the date of examination) or 36th month (for a pilot under the age of 40 on the date of examination) after the date of examination for operations requiring a recreational or private pilot certificate (i.e., the medical certificate effectively becomes a third-class certificate).

c.   Pilot logbook or flight record. FAR 61.51 requires you to log aeronautical training and experience to meet the requirements for obtaining a certificate or rating, or for meeting recent flight experience requirements.

   1)   A pilot logbook or flight record should be used to indicate the

   a)   Date
   b)   Length of flight
   c)   Place, or points of departure and arrival
   d)   Type and identification of aircraft used
   e)   Type of experience or training (e.g., solo/PIC, flight instruction from a CFI)
   f)   Conditions of flight (e.g., day or night VFR)

   2)   While you are required to carry your medical and pilot certificates, you are not required to have your logbooks with you at all times.

2.   You must be able to demonstrate your knowledge of the following certificates and documents by locating and explaining each of them to your examiner:

a.   Airworthiness and registration certificates. Your airplane must have both an airworthiness certificate and a certificate of aircraft registration.

   1)   An airworthiness certificate is issued to an aircraft by the FAA at the time of manufacture. It remains valid as long as all maintenance, airworthiness directives, and equipment FARs are complied with.

   2)   A registration certificate is issued to the current owner of an aircraft as registered with the FAA.

UNITED STATES OF AMERICA
DEPARTMENT OF TRANSPORTATION – FEDERAL AVIATION ADMINISTRATION
CERTIFICATE OF AIRCRAFT REGISTRATION

NATIONALITY AND REGISTRATION MARKS N 66421

AIRCRAFT SERIAL NO. D-10267

This certificate must be in the aircraft when operated.

MANUFACTURER AND MANUFACTURER'S DESIGNATION OF AIRCRAFT
BEECH   V35B

O T   D E C U S S I   TO
GLEIM IRVIN N
UNIVERSITY STATION PO BOX 12848
GAINESVILLE FL   32604

INDIVIDUAL

This certificate is issued for registration purposes only and is not a certificate of title. The Federal Aviation Administration does not determine rights of ownership as between private persons.

DATE OF ISSUE
JUNE 04, 1980

It is certified that the above described aircraft has been entered on the register of the Federal Aviation Administration, United States of America, in accordance with the Convention on International Civil Aviation dated December 7, 1944, and with the Federal Aviation Act of 1958, and regulations issued thereunder.

Langhorne Bond
Administrator

AC Form 8050-3 (5-77)

---

department of transportation federal aviation administration
STANDARD AIRWORTHINESS CERTIFICATE
united states of america

1. NATIONALITY AND REGISTRATION MARKS	2. MANUFACTURER AND MODEL	3. AIRCRAFT SERIAL NUMBER	4. CATEGORY
N66421	BEECH AIRCRAFT CORP. -V35B	D-10267	UTILITY

5. AUTHORITY AND BASIS FOR ISSUANCE
This airworthiness certificate is issued pursuant to the Federal Aviation Act of 1958 and certifies that, as of the date of issuance, the aircraft to which issued has been inspected and found to conform to the type certificate therefor, to be in condition for safe operation, and has been shown to meet the requirements of the applicable comprehensive and detailed airworthiness code as provided by Annex 8 to the Convention on International Civil Aviation, except as noted herein.
Exceptions:

NONE

6. TERMS AND CONDITIONS
Unless sooner surrendered, suspended, revoked, or a termination date is otherwise established by the Administrator, this airworthiness certificate is effective as long as the maintenance, preventative maintenance, and alterations are performed in accordance with Parts 21, 43, and 91 of the Federal Aviation Regulations, as appropriate, and the aircraft is registered in the United States.

DATE OF ISSUANCE	FAA REPRESENTATIVE	DESIGNATION NUMBER
June 22, 1979	*D. M. Porteous* D. M. Porteous	DOA, PC#8

Any alteration, reproduction, or misuse of this certificate may be punishable by a fine not exceeding $1,000, or imprisonment not exceeding 3 years, or both. THIS CERTIFICATE MUST BE DISPLAYED IN THE AIRCRAFT IN ACCORDANCE WITH APPLICABLE FEDERAL AVIATION REGULATIONS.

FAA Form 8100-2 (7-67) FORMERLY FAA FORM 1362   ☆ U.S. Government Printing Office — 1976-675-526

b.   Operating limitations, placards, instrument markings, and *Pilot's Operating Handbook/Airplane Flight Manual*.

1)   You may not operate an airplane unless the operating limitations (i.e., airspeed, powerplant, weight, CG, load factor, etc.) are in the airplane and are accessible to you during flight.

2)   These operating limitations will be found in the *POH*, placards, and/or instrument markings.

    a)   See Section 2, Limitations, of your *POH*.

        i)   The operating limitations of any optional equipment installed in your airplane (e.g., an autopilot) will be found in Section 9, Supplements, of the *POH*.

    b)   The *POH* is also referred to as the FAA-approved *Airplane Flight Manual*.

        i)   Airplanes manufactured prior to March 1, 1979 do not have the formal *POHs*.

c.   Weight and balance data and equipment list.

1)   Weight and balance data are very important and are presented and explained in the *POH* or included with that type of information. It is important that you understand the weight and balance calculations for the airplane in which you will be training and that you work through several examples to verify that you will be in the proper weight and balance, given one or two persons aboard the airplane and various fuel loads.

    a)   Obtain a weight and balance form for your airplane from your *POH* or CFI.

2)   The equipment list is in Section 6, Weight and Balance/Equipment List, of the airplane's *POH*. It shows the weight and moment of each accessory added to the basic airframe. After each modification or equipment addition, the repair facility will recompute the airplane's empty weight and center of gravity. These figures are used in your weight and balance computations.

END OF TASK

AIRWORTHINESS REQUIREMENTS

I.B. TASK: AIRWORTHINESS REQUIREMENTS

      REFERENCES: 14 CFR part 91; AC 61-23/FAA-H-8083-25.

Objective. To determine that the applicant exhibits knowledge of the elements related to airworthiness requirements by:

1. Explaining --

    a. Required instruments and equipment for day/night VFR.

    b. Procedures and limitations for determining airworthiness of the airplane with inoperative instruments and equipment with and without an MEL.

    c. Requirements and procedures for obtaining a special flight permit.

2. Locating and explaining --

    a. Airworthiness directives.
    b. Compliance records.
    c. Maintenance/inspection requirements.
    d. Appropriate record keeping.

A. General Information

    1. The objective of this task is to determine your knowledge of aircraft airworthiness requirements.

    2. Additional Reading: See Chapter 4, Federal Aviation Regulations, in *Pilot Handbook*, for the following:

        a. FAR 91.213, Inoperative Instruments and Equipment, for a detailed discussion of operating an airplane with or without an approved minimum equipment list (MEL).

B. Task Objectives

    1. **You must be able to exhibit your knowledge of the following items related to required instruments and equipment by explaining them to your examiner.**

        a. **Required instruments and equipment for day/night VFR**

           1) You may not operate a powered civil aircraft with a standard category U.S. airworthiness certificate without the specified operable instruments and equipment.

           2) Required equipment: VFR - day

               a) Airspeed indicator

               b) Altimeter

               c) Magnetic direction indicator (compass)

               d) Tachometer for each engine

               e) Oil pressure gauge for each engine using a pressure system

               f) Temperature gauge for each liquid-cooled engine

               g) Oil temperature gauge for each air-cooled engine

               h) Manifold pressure gauge for each altitude engine

               i) Fuel gauge indicating the quantity of fuel in each tank

               j) Landing gear position indicator, if the aircraft has a retractable landing gear

k)   For small airplanes certificated after March 11, 1996, an approved anticollision light system

l)   Approved flotation gear for each occupant and one pyrotechnic signaling device if the aircraft is operated for hire over water beyond power-off gliding distance from shore

m)   Approved safety belt with approved metal-to-metal latching device for each occupant who is 2 yr. of age or older

n)   For small civil airplanes manufactured after July 18, 1978, an approved shoulder harness for each front seat

o)   An emergency locator transmitter (ELT), if required by FAR 91.207

p)   For normal, utility, and acrobatic category airplanes with a seating configuration, excluding pilot seats, of nine or less, manufactured after December 12, 1986, a shoulder harness for each seat in the airplane

3)   Required equipment: VFR - night

a)   All equipment listed in 2) on the previous page

b)   Approved position (navigation) lights

c)   Approved aviation red or white anticollision light system on all U.S.-registered civil aircraft

d)   If the aircraft is operated for hire, one electric landing light

e)   An adequate source of electricity for all electrical and radio equipment

f)   A set of spare fuses or three spare fuses for each kind required which are accessible to the pilot in flight

b.   **Procedures and limitations for determining the airworthiness of an airplane having inoperative instruments and equipment, both with and without an MEL.**

1)   Except as provided in FAR 91.213, you may not take off in an airplane with any inoperative instruments or equipment installed, i.e., in an airplane that is not airworthy.

2)   FAR 91.213 describes the acceptable methods for the operation of an airplane with certain inoperative instruments and equipment that are not essential for safe flight. These acceptable methods of operation are

a)   Operation with an approved minimum equipment list (MEL)

i)   An MEL is a specific inoperative equipment document for a particular make and model aircraft by serial and registration number.

ii)   An MEL is designed to provide owners/operators with the authority to operate an aircraft with certain items or components inoperative, provided the FAA finds an acceptable level of safety maintained by

• Appropriate operations limitations

• A transfer of the function to another operating component

• Reference to other instruments or components providing the required information

    b) Operation without an MEL (probably the way your airplane is operated)

        i) You may take off in an aircraft with inoperative instruments and equipment without an approved MEL provided the inoperative instruments and equipment are not

- Part of the VFR-day type certification instruments and equipment under which the aircraft was type certificated

- Indicated as required on the aircraft's equipment list or on the Kinds of Operations Equipment List for the kind of flight operation being conducted

- Required by any FAR

- Required by an airworthiness directive

        ii) The inoperative instruments or equipment must be

- Removed from the airplane with the cockpit control placarded and the maintenance properly recorded, or

- Deactivated and placarded "inoperative."

        iii) A determination must be made by a certificated and appropriately rated pilot or an appropriately certificated mechanic that the inoperative instrument or equipment does not constitute a hazard to the aircraft.

        iv) By following these procedures, the aircraft is considered to be in a properly altered condition acceptable to the FAA.

c. **Requirements and procedures for obtaining a special flight permit**

    1) When a special flight permit is required

        a) A special flight permit may be issued to an airplane with inoperable instruments or equipment under FAR Part 21, Certification Procedures for Products and Parts

            i) This can be done despite any provisions listed in FAR 91.213

        b) Special flight permits may be issued for an airplane that does not currently meet applicable airworthiness requirements but is capable of safe flight in order for the pilot to fly the airplane to a base where repairs, alterations, or maintenance can be performed or to a point of storage (FAR 21.197).

    2) Procedures for obtaining a special flight permit

        a) To obtain a special flight permit, you must submit a written request to the nearest FSDO indicating

            i) The purpose of the flight

            ii) The proposed itinerary

            iii) The crew required to operate the airplane (e.g., pilot, co-pilot)

            iv) The ways, if any, the airplane does not comply with the applicable airworthiness requirements

            v) Any restriction that you consider is necessary for safe operation of your airplane

            vi) Any other information considered necessary by the FAA for the purpose of prescribing operating limitations

2.   **You must be able to exhibit your knowledge of the following items related to your aircraft's inspection and maintenance requirements by locating and explaining them to your examiner.**

   a.   **Airworthiness directives**

   1)   Airworthiness directives (ADs) are issued by the FAA to require correction of unsafe conditions found in an airplane, an airplane engine, a propeller, or an appliance when such conditions exist and are likely to exist or develop in other products of the same design.

   a)   ADs may be divided into two categories:

   i)   Those of an emergency nature requiring immediate compliance

   ii)   Those of a less urgent nature requiring compliance within a relatively longer period of time

   b)   ADs are regulatory (i.e., issued under FAR Part 39, Airworthiness Directives) and must be complied with unless a specific exemption is granted.

   b.   **Compliance records**

   1)   FAR 91.417, Maintenance Records, requires that a record be maintained that shows the current status of applicable ADs, including the method of compliance, the AD number, the revision date, and the signature and certificate number of the repair station or mechanic who performed the work.

   a)   If the AD involves recurring action (e.g., an inspection every 50 hr.), a record must be kept of the time and date when the next action is required.

   c.   **Maintenance/inspection requirements**

   1)   The maintenance requirements on aircraft that are used in commercial operations (i.e., flight training, charter, etc.) are more stringent than on non-commercial Part 91, which requires a maintenance inspection only on an annual basis.

   a)   All aircraft must undergo an annual inspection by a certificated airframe and powerplant (A&P) mechanic who also possesses an Inspection Authorization (IA).

   b)   Aircraft used to carry people for hire or to provide flight instruction for hire must undergo an annual or 100-hr. inspection within the preceding 100 hr. of flight time. The 100-hr. interval may be exceeded by no more than 10 hr. to facilitate transport of the aircraft to a maintenance location where the inspection can be performed.

   i)   However, if the 100-hr. inspection is overflown, the next inspection will be due after 100 hr. of flight time **less** the amount overflown.

   ii)   EXAMPLE: If the check is performed at the 105-hr. point, the next 100-hr. check is due at the end of 95 hr., not 100 hr.; thus, it would be due at the 200-hr. point.

   c)   Based on the specific make and model aircraft, further checks beyond the 100-hr. check may be necessary to comply with the FARs. This additional maintenance may be required at the 50-, 150-, or 250-hr. point.

d) You may not use an ATC transponder unless it has been tested and inspected within the preceding 24 calendar months.

e) The emergency locator transmitter (ELT) battery must be replaced after half its useful life has expired (as established by the transmitter manufacturer), or after 1 hr. of cumulative use.

i) The ELT must be inspected every 12 calendar months for
- Proper installation
- Battery corrosion
- Operation of the controls and crash sensor
- Sufficient signal radiated from its antenna

d. **Appropriate record keeping**

1) Examine the engine logbooks and the airframe logbook of your training airplane (presumably the one you will use for your practical test), and ask your instructor for assistance as appropriate. Locate and paperclip the most recent signoff for

a) Annual inspection

b) 100-hr. inspection

c) Transponder and static system inspection

d) ELT inspection and battery expiration (The expiration date is on the outside of the ELT and in the airframe logbook.)

2) The owner or operator is primarily responsible for maintaining an airplane in an airworthy condition and for ensuring compliance with all pertinent ADs.

a) The term operator includes the PIC. Thus, as PIC, you are responsible for ensuring that the airplane is maintained in an airworthy condition (e.g., 100-hr. and/or annual inspections) and that there is compliance with all ADs.

e. Supplemental Type Certificates (STCs). FAA method of allowing modifications to aircraft without recertifying the aircraft, e.g., a new and improved landing gear. The FAA requires engineering data and static and flight testing information. When issued, an STC may be used by the aircraft owner to maintain FAA airworthiness authorization and to justify the aircraft modification.

f. An easy way to remember the required documents is by using the memory aid
ARROW
A irworthiness certificate
R egistration
R adio station license
O perating limitations
W eight and balance

NOTE: A radio station license is required only if the airplane is flown outside of U.S. airspace (i.e., to another country). Additionally, on these flights you are required to have a restricted radiotelephone operator permit. These are requirements of the Federal Communications Commission (FCC), not FAA requirements.

END OF TASK

WEATHER INFORMATION

I.C. TASK: WEATHER INFORMATION

REFERENCES: 14CFR Part 91; AC 00-6, AC 00-45, AC 61-23/FAA-H-8083-25, AC 61-84; AIM.

Objective. To determine that the applicant:

1. Exhibits knowledge of the elements related to weather information by analyzing weather reports, charts, and forecasts from various sources with emphasis on --

    a. METAR, TAF, and FA
    b. Surface analysis chart
    c. Radar summary chart
    d. Winds and temperature aloft chart
    e. Significant weather prognostic charts
    f. Convective outlook chart
    g. AWOS, ASOS, and ATIS reports

2. Makes a competent "go/no-go" decision based on available weather information.

A. General Information

    1. The objective of this task is to determine your knowledge of analyzing aviation weather information and making a competent "go/no-go" decision based on that information.

    2. Gleim's *Aviation Weather and Weather Services* is a 442-page book in outline format that combines the FAA's *Aviation Weather* (AC 00-6A) and *Aviation Weather Services* (AC 00-45E) and numerous FAA publications into one easy-to-understand book. It will help you to learn all aspects of aviation weather, weather reports, and weather forecasts. It is a single, easy-to-use reference that is more up-to-date than the FAA's weather books. The table of contents is on the next page.

        a. "Aviation Weather" and "Aviation Weather Services" are Chapters 7 and 8 in *Pilot Handbook*, which are summaries of both topics.

    3. Flight Service Stations (FSSs) are the primary source for obtaining preflight briefings and in-flight weather information.

        a. Prior to your flight, and before you meet with your examiner, you should visit or call the nearest FSS for a complete briefing.

        b. There are four basic types of preflight briefings to meet your needs:

            1) Standard briefing

                a) A standard briefing should be requested anytime you are planning a flight and have not received a previous briefing.

            2) Abbreviated briefing

                a) Request an abbreviated briefing when you need information to supplement mass disseminated data (e.g., TIBS) or to update a previous briefing, or when you need only one or two specific items.

            3) Outlook briefing

                a) Request an outlook briefing whenever your proposed time of departure is 6 hr. or more from the time of the briefing.

            4) In-flight briefing

                a) In situations in which you need to obtain a preflight briefing or an update by radio, you should contact the nearest FSS to obtain this information.

                b) After communications have been established, advise the FSS of the type of briefing you require.

                c) You may be advised to shift to the Flight Watch frequency (122.0) when conditions indicate that it would be advantageous.

GLEIM'S
AVIATION WEATHER AND WEATHER SERVICES

Table of Contents

Call (800) 87-GLEIM to order.

B.   Task Objectives

     1.   **Exhibit your knowledge of the elements related to weather information by analyzing weather reports, charts, and forecasts from various sources with emphasis on the following items:**

         a.   **METAR, TAF, and FA.**

            1)   **Aviation routine weather report (METAR):**

                a)   A METAR is a statement of a weather observer's interpretation of the weather conditions at a given site and time.

                     i)   The weather observation can be made by a trained human observer or by a machine (e.g., an AWOS or ASOS station).

                b)   **Elements:** A METAR report contains the following sequence of elements in the order listed:

                     i)   Type of report

                     ii)   ICAO station identifier

                     iii)   Date and time of report

                     iv)   Modifier (as required)

> NOTE: The elements in the body of a METAR report are separated by a space, except temperature and dew point, which are separated with a solidus, /. When an element does not occur or cannot be observed, that element is omitted from that particular report.

                     v)   Wind

                     vi)   Visibility

                     vii)   Runway visual range (RVR)

                     viii)   Weather

                     ix)   Sky condition

                     x)   Temperature/dew point

                     xi)   Altimeter

                     xii)   Remarks (RMK)

                c)   **Example of a METAR Report**

```
METAR  KGNV  201953Z  24015KT  3/4SM  R28/2400FT  +TSRA
BKN008  OVC015CB  26/25  A2985  RMK  TSB32RAB32
```

To aid in the discussion, we have divided the report into the 12 elements:

METAR	KGNV	201953Z	___	24015KT	3/4SM	R28/2400FT	+TSRA
i)	ii)	iii)	iv)	v)	vi)	vii)	viii)

BKN008 OVC015CB	26/25	A2985	RMK TSB32RAB32
ix)	x)	xi)	xii)

- i)   Aviation routine weather report

- ii)   Gainesville, FL

- iii)   Observation taken on the 20th day at 1953 UTC (or Zulu)

- iv)   Modifier omitted; i.e., not required for this report

- v)   Wind 240° true at 15 kt.

- vi)   Visibility 3/4 statute miles

- vii)   Runway 28, runway visual range 2,400 ft.

- viii)   Thunderstorm with heavy rain

- ix)   Ceiling 800 ft. broken, 1,500 ft. overcast, cumulonimbus clouds

- x)   Temperature 26°C, dew point 25°C

- xi)   Altimeter 29.85

- xii)   Remarks: Thunderstorm began at 32 min. past the hour; rain began at 32 min. past the hour.

- d)   Additional reading: For a more-detailed discussion of METARs, refer to the following sections of *Aviation Weather and Weather Services* and *Pilot Handbook*:

    - i)   Part III, Chapter 2, Aviation Routine Weather Report (METAR), in *Aviation Weather and Weather Services*, or

    - ii)   Chapter 8, Aviation Weather Services, Module 8.2, Aviation Routine Weather Report (METAR), in *Pilot Handbook*.

2)   **Terminal Aerodrome Forecast (TAF):**

- a)   The TAF is a concise statement of the expected meteorological conditions at an airport during a specific period (usually 24 hr.).

    - i)   The TAF covers a geographic area within a 5-SM radius of the airport's center.

- b)   **Elements**. TAFs contain the following sequence of elements in the order listed:

    - i)   Type of report
    - ii)   ICAO station identifier
    - iii)   Date and time of origin
    - iv)   Valid period date and time
    - v)   Forecast of meteorological conditions
    - vi)   Wind
    - vii)   Visibility
    - viii)   Weather
    - ix)   Sky condition
    - x)   Wind shear (optional)

c)   **Example of a TAF**

```
TAF
KOKC 051130Z 051212 14008KT 5SM BR BKN030 WS018/32030KT
TEMPO 1316 1 1/2SM BR
FM1600 16010KT P6SM SKC
BECMG 2224 20013G20KT 4SM SHRA OVC020 PROB40 0006 2SM TSRA OVC008CB=
```

To aid in the discussion, we have divided the TAF above into the following 13 elements

TAF	KOKC	051130Z	051212	14008KT	5SM	BR	BKN030	WS018/32030KT
i)	ii)	iii)	iv)	v)	vi)	vii)	viii)	ix)

TEMPO 1316 1 1/2SM BR   FM1600 16010KT P6SM SKC
           x)   xi)

BECMG 2224 20013G20KT 4SM SHRA OVC020   PROB40 0006 2SM TSRA OVC008CB=
                  xii)   xiii)

i)   Routine terminal aerodrome forecast

ii)   Oklahoma City, OK

iii) Forecast prepared on the 5th day at 1130 UTC (or Z)

iv)   Forecast valid from the 5th day at 1200 UTC until 1200 UTC on the 6th

v)   Wind 140° true at 8 kt.

vi)   Visibility 5 statute miles

vii) Visibility obscured by mist

viii) Ceiling 3,000 ft. broken

ix)   Low-level wind shear at 1,800 ft., wind 320° true at 30 kt.

x)   Temporary (spoken as occasional) visibility 1½ SM in mist between
      1300 UTC and 1600 UTC

xi)   From (or after) 1600 UTC, wind 160° true at 10 kt., visibility more
      than 6 SM, sky clear

xii) Becoming (gradual change) wind 200° true at 13 kt. gusts to 20 kt.,
      visibility 4 SM in moderate rain showers, ceiling 2,000 ft. overcast
      between 2200 UTC and 2400 UTC

xiii) Probability (40% chance) between 0000 UTC and 0600 UTC of
      visibility 2 SM, thunderstorm, moderate rain, ceiling 800 ft.
      overcast, cumulonimbus clouds. The equal sign (=) indicates the
      end of the TAF.

d)   Additional reading: For a more-detailed discussion of TAFs, refer to the
      following sections of *Aviation Weather and Weather Services* and *Pilot
      Handbook*:

      i)   Part III, Chapter 7, Terminal Aerodrome Forecast (TAF), in *Aviation
            Weather and Weather Services*, or

      ii)   Chapter 8, Aviation Weather Services, Module 8.4, Terminal
            Aerodrome Forecast (TAF), in *Pilot Handbook*.

3)   **Aviation Area Forecast (FA):**

a)   An aviation area forecast (FA) is a forecast of VFR weather, clouds, and general weather conditions over an area the size of several states. It is used to determine forecast en route weather and to interpolate conditions at airports that do not have TAFs issued.

i)   FAs are issued three times a day by the Aviation Weather Center (AWC) in Kansas City, MO, for each of the six areas in the contiguous 48 states.

ii) The FA is comprised of four sections:

- Communication and product header section
- A precautionary statement section
- SYNOPSIS section
- VFR CLOUDS/WX section

b)   **Example.** A portion of an FA is presented below.

```
MIAC FA 221745
SYNOPSIS AND VFR CLDS/WX
SYNOPSIS VALID UNTIL 231200
CLDS/WX VALID UNTIL 230600...OTLK VALID 230600-231200
NC SC GA FL AND CSTL WTRS
.
SEE AIRMET SIERRA FOR IFR CONDS AND MTN OBSCN.
TS IMPLY SEV OR GTR TURB SEV ICE LLWS AND IFR CONDS.
NON MSL HGTS DENOTED BY AGL OR CIG.
.
SYNOPSIS...SLO MOVG CDFNT XTRM NRN FL FCST BECM NRLY STNR BY 06Z.
HI PRES FCST BLD SEWD FROM GREAT LAKE RGN THRU 12Z WITH RIDGE
AXIS SWD OVR CNTRL CAROLINAS BY 12Z. ..SMITH..
.
FL
PNHDL...SCT-BKN030 SCT-BKN100. TOPS FL250. SCT TSRA. CB TOPS ABV 450. 02Z
SCT030 SCT100..BKN CI. ISOL -TSRA. CB TOPS FL350. OTLK...MVFR BR.
NRN PEN...SCT-BKN030 BKN100. SCT TSRA. CB TOPS ABV FL450. 02Z SCT030
BKN100. TOPS FL250. ISOL -TSRA. CB TOPS FL350. OTLK...MVFR BR.
CNTRL/SRN PEN/KEYS...SCT035 SCT100. WDLY SCT TSRA. CB TOPS FL450. 02Z
SCT030 SCT120. OTLK...VFR.
.
CSTL WTRS
NS SC WTRS...SCT040. OTLK...VFR.
GA-NRN FL ATLC WTRS...SCT-BKN040 BKN100. SCT TSRA. CB TOPS FL400. OTLK...VFR.
NRN FL GULF WTRS...SCT030 SCT100. SCT TSRA. CB TOPS FL350. OTLK...VFR.
CNTRL/SRN FL WTRS...SCT030 SCT100. WDLY SCT TSRA. CB TOPS FL400. OTLK...VFR.
....
```

c)   Additional reading: For a more-detailed discussion of FAs, refer to the following sections of *Aviation Weather and Weather Services* and *Pilot Handbook*:

i)   Part III, Chapter 8, Aviation Area Forecast (FA), in *Aviation Weather and Weather Services*, or

ii) Chapter 8, Aviation Weather Services, Module 8.5, Aviation Area Forecast (FA), in *Pilot Handbook*.

b. Surface analysis chart.

1) The surface analysis chart is a computer-generated chart that depicts the observed weather conditions that existed at the valid time shown on the chart.

   a) The surface analysis chart displays the following weather information for specific locations in the form of multiple "station circles" (i.e., a group of symbols representing the observed weather at a specific location):

   i)   Surface wind direction and speed
   ii)   Surface temperature and dew point
   iii) Total sky cover
   iv)   Obstructions to vision
   v)   Precipitation type
   vi)   Predominant type of low, middle, and high clouds
   vii) Sea level pressure
   viii) Pressure change during the past 3 hours
   ix)   Precipitation recorded during the past 6 hours

   b) The chart also displays the following large-scale weather phenomena:

   i)   Position and type of fronts
   ii)   Position of highs and lows
   iii) Position of ridges and troughs
   iv)   Isobars (lines of constant pressure)

2) Additional reading: For a more-detailed discussion of surface analysis charts, refer to Part III, Chapter 16, Surface Analysis Chart, in *Aviation Weather and Weather Services.*

c. Radar summary chart.

1) A radar summary chart graphically displays a collection of automated radar weather reports (SDs).

   a) The chart displays the type of precipitation echoes, their intensity, configuration, coverage, echo tops and bases, and movement.

   i)   Severe weather watches are plotted if they are in effect when the chart is valid.

2) Radar primarily detects particles of precipitation size within a cloud or falling from a cloud.

   a) The type of precipitation can be determined by the radar operator from the scope presentation in combination with other sources.

3) The intensity is obtained from the Doppler radar and is indicated on the chart by **contours**. The six intensity levels are paired and combined into three contours.

   a) The contours are coded as follows:

   i)   The outermost contour indicates precipitation of light or moderate intensity.

   ii)   The second contour indicates precipitation of heavy or very heavy intensity.

   iii) The innermost contour indicates precipitation of intense or extreme intensity.

   b) Note that all three contours will not always be present; e.g., if all precipitation in a given area is of light to moderate intensity, only one contour will be shown.

4) Additional reading: For a more-detailed discussion of radar summary charts, refer to the following sections of *Aviation Weather and Weather Services* and *Pilot Handbook*:

    a) Part III, Chapter 18, Radar Summary Chart, in *Aviation Weather and Weather Services*, or

    b) Chapter 8, Aviation Weather Services, Module 8.9, Radar Summary Chart, in *Pilot Handbook*.

d. Winds and temperature aloft chart.

1) There are two types of computer-generated winds and temperatures aloft charts:

    a) Forecast winds and temperatures aloft charts are prepared for eight levels ranging from 6,000 ft. MSL to 39,000 ft. MSL on eight separate panels.

        i) Each station that prepares a winds and temperatures aloft forecast is represented on the panel by a station circle.

           • This station circle indicates wind speed and direction in the form of an arrow that is aligned with the wind direction. Barbs and pennants on the upwind end of the arrow indicate speed.

           • Temperature is shown in degrees Celsius above and to the right of the station circle.

           • A calm or light and variable wind is shown by "99" entered to the lower left of the station circle.

        ii) There is also a textual version of the forecast winds and temperatures aloft chart called a winds and temperatures aloft forecast (FD).

    b) Observed winds and temperatures aloft charts are prepared for four levels ranging from approximately 2,000 ft. AGL to 34,000 ft. MSL

        i) Information collected at each reporting station is shown by a station circle using symbols that are similar to the forecast winds and temperatures aloft chart.

2) Additional reading: For a more-detailed discussion of winds and temperatures aloft charts, refer to Part III, Chapter 21, Winds and Temperatures Aloft Charts, in *Aviation Weather and Weather Services*.

e. Significant weather prognostic charts.

1) Significant weather prognostic charts (called progs for brevity) are four-panel charts.

    a) Both low- and high-level significant weather prognostic charts are available to pilots, but our discussion will focus on the low-level charts because these are most likely to be used by pilots of piston-engine airplanes.

    b) For information about high-level significant weather prognostic charts, refer to *Aviation Weather and Weather Services*.

2) Low-level significant weather prognostic charts have the following general characteristics:

   a) They are composed of 4 panels

      i) The two lower panels are 12- and 24-hr. surface progs.

      ii) The two upper panels are 12- and 24-hr. progs of significant weather from the surface to 400 mb/hPa (24,000 ft. MSL).

   b) The charts show conditions as they are forecast to be at the valid time of the chart.

   c) They are issued four times daily with the 12- and 24-hr. forecasts based on the 0000Z, 0600Z, 1200Z, and 1800Z synoptic data.

3) The two lower panels are called surface progs and use standard symbols for fronts, significant troughs, and pressure centers.

   a) High and low pressure centers are depicted.

   b) Isobars depicting forecast pressure patterns are included on some 24-hr. surface progs.

   c) The surface prog also outlines areas of forecast precipitation and/or thunderstorms.

   d) Symbols are used to indicate precipitation type and character.

      i) If precipitation affects half or more of an area, that area is shaded.

        • The absence of shading denotes more sparse precipitation, specifically coverage of less than half of the area.

4) The upper panels depict IFR, MVFR, turbulence, and freezing levels.

   a) Smooth lines enclose areas of forecast IFR weather, and scalloped lines enclose areas of marginal weather (MVFR). VFR areas are not outlined.

   b) Forecast areas of non-convective turbulence of moderate or greater intensity are enclosed by long, dashed lines.

      i) Since thunderstorms always imply moderate or greater turbulence, areas of thunderstorm-related turbulence will not be outlined.

      ii) A symbol entered within a general area of forecast turbulence denotes intensity.

      iii) Numbers below and above a short line show expected bases and tops of the turbulent layer in hundreds of feet MSL.

   c) Freezing level height contours for the **highest** freezing level are drawn at 4,000-ft. intervals.

      i) Contours are labeled in hundreds of feet MSL.

      ii) The zig-zag line shows where the freezing level is forecast to be at the surface and is labeled "SFC."

   d) The low-level significant weather prog does not specifically outline areas of icing. However, icing is implied in clouds and precipitation above the freezing level. Interpolate for freezing levels between the given contours.

5)   Additional reading: For a more-detailed discussion of significant weather prognostic charts, refer to the following sections of *Aviation Weather and Weather Services* and *Pilot Handbook*:

   a)   Part III, Chapter 22, U.S. Low-Level Significant Weather Prog, and Chapter 23, U.S. High-Level Significant Weather Prog, in *Aviation Weather and Weather Services*, or

   b)   Chapter 8, Aviation Weather Services, Module 8.10, Low-Level Significant Weather Prog, in *Pilot Handbook*.

f.   Convective outlook chart.

1)   The convective outlook chart is a 48-hr. outlook for thunderstorm activity presented in two panels.

2)   The left-hand panel covers the first 24-hr. period beginning at 1200Z and depicts areas of possible general and severe thunderstorm activity in the continental U.S.

   a)   A line with an arrowhead delineates an area of probable thunderstorm activity located to the right of the line when facing in the direction of the arrow.

   b)   If severe thunderstorm activity is expected in an area, that area is labeled with a risk category.

      i)   **SLGT** means that there is a slight risk of severe thunderstorms and that they are expected to cover 2% to 5% of the depicted area.

      ii)   **MDT** means that there is a moderate risk of severe thunderstorms and that they are expected to cover 6% to 10% of the depicted area.

      iii)   **HIGH** means that there is a high risk of severe thunderstorms and that they are expected to cover more than 10% of the depicted area.

      iv)   **SEE TEXT** means that a **SLGT** risk was considered for the area, but at the time of the forecast, it was not warranted.

         •   You should refer to a textual convective outlook (AC) for more information if there is a **SEE TEXT** notation.

   c)   If general (i.e., non-severe) thunderstorm activity is expected in an area, that area is not labeled with a risk category.

3)   The right-hand panel covers the following day beginning at 1200Z and is similar to the left-hand panel, except that it is issued less frequently.

4)   Additional reading: For a more-detailed discussion of convective outlook charts, refer to Part III, Chapter 24, Convective Outlook Chart, in *Aviation Weather and Weather Services*.

g.   AWOS, ASOS, and ATIS reports.

1)   Definitions:

   a)   **AWOS**–Automated Weather Observing System: This is an older automated reporting system that may provide only basic observed weather information for an airport (e.g., an altimeter setting), or it may be capable of generating a complete automated METAR. AWOS capabilities vary from location to location.

   b)   **ASOS**–Automated Surface Observing System: This automated weather reporting system is more advanced than AWOS and is gradually replacing the older system. All ASOS stations are capable of providing at least the following information:

      i)   Altimeter setting
      ii)   Wind speed and direction
      iii)   Temperature and dewpoint
      iv)   Density altitude
      v)   Visibility
      vi)   Cloud cover and ceiling height
      vii) Precipitation
      viii) Remarks

   c)   **ATIS**–Automatic Terminal Information Service: ATIS is a continuous broadcast of recorded information in selected terminal areas. In addition to providing current observed weather information, ATIS broadcasts also reduce controller workload by including recorded airport information such as runways/approaches in use or local NOTAMs.

2)   You should listen to the appropriate AWOS, ASOS, or ATIS broadcast prior to entering the pattern at any airport at which you intend to make a landing, if one is available.

   a)   This will help you to anticipate the weather conditions you can expect, as well as which runway is in use.

   b)   In addition, when flying cross-country under VFR, you can periodically update your altimeter setting using broadcasts from airports along your route.

3)   Be aware that the information contained in AWOS, ASOS, and especially ATIS reports may be up to 1 hour old, so conditions at the airport may differ from those reported.

4)   Additional reading: For a more-detailed discussion of AWOS and ASOS, refer to Part III, Chapter 2, Aviation Routine Weather Report (METAR), in *Aviation Weather and Weather Services*.

2.   Make a competent "go/no-go" decision based on the available weather information.

   a.   In a well-equipped airplane with a proficient pilot flying, any ceiling and visibility within legal weather minimums should be flyable. In a poorly equipped airplane or with a new or rusty pilot, flying in low IFR (LIFR -- ceiling less than 500 ft. and/or visibility less than 1 SM) should be avoided. This is not to say that you must be an ATP to fly LIFR, but if your last actual approach was 4 months ago and only to 1,500 ft., it is not a good idea to tackle LIFR.

b. Another factor to consider in your go/no-go decision is the weather. MVFR or IFR in smooth air caused by a stalled front is considerably different from heavy turbulence ahead of a strong front or in a squall line. The following forecast conditions may lead to a no-go decision:

1) Thunderstorms

2) Embedded thunderstorms

3) Lines of thunderstorms

4) Fast-moving fronts or squall lines

5) Flights that require you to cross strong or fast-moving fronts

6) Extensive IFR that would require long periods of instrument flying (less of a problem with an autopilot)

7) Reported turbulence that is moderate or greater (Remember, moderate turbulence in a Boeing 727 is usually severe in a Piper Arrow.)

8) Icing

9) Fog (Unlike when in a ceiling, you usually cannot break out and land with ground fog. This is especially important if sufficient fuel may be a concern.)

10) Wind shear

c. These factors must be considered in relation to the equipment to be flown. Thunderstorms are less of a problem in a radar-equipped airplane. The only way to fly safely is to be able to weigh each factor against the other. This is done only by using common sense and gaining experience.

d. Flying is a continuing process of decision making throughout the whole flight. You must gain experience, but you must also temper the pursuit of experience so you do not get in beyond your capabilities or the capabilities of your airplane.

e. A final factor to consider in the go/no-go decision is your physical and mental condition. Are you sick, tired, upset, depressed, etc.? These factors greatly affect your ability to handle normal and abnormal problems.

END OF TASK

CROSS-COUNTRY FLIGHT PLANNING

I.D. TASK: CROSS-COUNTRY FLIGHT PLANNING

> REFERENCES: 14 CFR Part 91; AC 61-23/FAA-H-8083-25, AC 61-84; Navigation Charts; Airport/Facility Directory; AIM.

Objective. To determine that the applicant:

1. Exhibits knowledge of the elements related to cross-country flight planning by presenting and explaining a pre-planned VFR cross-country flight, as previously assigned by the examiner. On the day of the practical test, the final flight plan shall be to the first fuel stop, based on maximum allowable passengers, baggage, and/or cargo loads using real time weather.

2. Uses appropriate and current aeronautical charts.

3. Properly identifies airspace, obstructions, and terrain features.

4. Selects easily identifiable en route checkpoints.

5. Selects most favorable altitudes, considering weather conditions and equipment capabilities.

6. Computes headings, flight time, and fuel requirements.

7. Selects appropriate navigation system/facilities and communication frequencies.

8. Applies pertinent information from NOTAMs, the Airport/Facility Directory, and other flight publications.

9. Completes a navigation log and simulates filing a VFR flight plan.

A. General Information

1.   The objective of this task is for you to demonstrate your ability to plan a cross-country flight properly.

2.   Additional reading: See *Pilot Handbook* for the following:

   a.   Chapter 9, Navigation: Charts, Publications, Flight Computers, for a 44-page discussion of interpreting sectional charts, using flight publications, and using a manual flight computer

   b.   Chapter 11, Cross-Country Flight Planning, for steps to perform in planning a cross-country flight and examples of a standard navigation log, an abbreviated navigation log, and an FAA flight plan form

B. Task Objectives

1.   **Exhibit your knowledge of the elements related to cross-country flight planning by presenting and explaining a preplanned VFR cross-country flight, as previously assigned by the examiner. On the day of the test, the final flight plan shall be to the first fuel stop. Computations shall be based on maximum allowable passengers, baggage, and/or cargo loads and real-time weather.**

   a.   Before meeting with your examiner, you should complete your flight planning for your cross-country flight using the current weather.

      1)   This recommendation assumes that you have asked for, and your examiner has given you, a cross-country flight to plan before your practical test.

2.   **Use appropriate and current aeronautical charts.**

   a.   You must bring current VFR navigational charts (e.g., a sectional chart) to your practical test.

   b.   Obsolete charts must be discarded and replaced by new editions. Updating charts is important because revisions in aeronautical information occur constantly.

      1)   These revisions may include changes in radio frequencies, new obstructions, temporary or permanent closing of certain runways and airports, and other temporary or permanent hazards to flight.

      2)   On average, each new sectional chart incorporates over 275 changes from the previous chart.

c. The National Aeronautical Charting Office (NACO), which is part of the FAA (formerly a part of NOS), publishes and sells aeronautical charts of the United States and foreign areas. The type of charts most commonly used by pilots flying VFR include the following:

   1) Sectional charts are normally used for VFR navigation, and we will refer to this chart in this task. The scale on sectional charts is 1:500,000 (1 in. = 6.86 NM).

   2) VFR terminal area charts depict the airspace designated as Class B airspace. The information found on these charts is similar to that found on sectional charts. They exist for large metropolitan areas such as Atlanta and New York. The scale on terminal charts is 1:250,000 (1 in. = 3.43 NM).

   3) Both the sectional and VFR terminal area charts are revised semiannually.

3. **Properly identify airspace, obstructions, and terrain features.**

   a. You should be able to identify airspace, obstructions, and terrain features on your sectional chart.

      1) The topographical information featured on sectional charts consists of elevation levels and a great number of checkpoints.

         a) Checkpoints include populated places (i.e., cities, towns), drainage patterns (i.e., lakes, rivers), roads, railroads, and other distinctive landmarks.

      2) The aeronautical information on sectional charts includes visual and radio aids to navigation, airports, controlled airspace, special-use airspace, obstructions, and related data.

   b. Within each quadrangle bounded by lines of longitude and latitude on the sectional chart are large, bold numbers that represent the maximum elevation figure (MEF).

      1) The MEF shown is given in thousands and hundreds of feet MSL.

         a) EXAMPLE: 1^9 means 1,900 ft. MSL.

      2) The MEF is based on information available concerning the highest known feature in each quadrangle, including terrain and obstructions (trees, towers, antennas, etc.).

      3) Since the sectional chart is published once every 6 months, you must also check the Aeronautical Chart Bulletin in the *Airport/Facility Directory (A/FD)* for major changes to the sectional chart (e.g., new obstructions).

4. **Select easily identifiable en route checkpoints.**

   a. There is no set rule for selecting a landmark as a checkpoint. Every locality has its own peculiarities. The general rule to follow is never to place complete reliance on any single landmark.

      1) Use a combination of two or more, if available.

   b. Select prominent landmarks as checkpoints.

5. **Select the most favorable altitudes considering weather conditions and equipment capabilities.**

    a.   Your selection of the most favorable altitude is based on a number of factors, which include

          1)   Winds aloft
          2)   Basic VFR weather minimums
          3)   Obstacle and/or terrain clearance
          4)   Navigation systems to be used
          5)   VFR cruising altitudes, if applicable
          6)   Airplane performance
          7)   Special-use airspace

6. **Compute headings, flight time, and fuel requirements.**

    a.   Use your flight computer to determine headings, flight time, and fuel requirements.

7. **Select appropriate navigation systems/facilities and communication frequencies.**

    a.   From studying your course on your sectional chart, you can determine which radio navigation systems/facilities (e.g., VOR, NDB, LORAN, GPS) you may use for navigation.

    b.   You should use the *A/FD* to determine the appropriate communication frequencies (e.g., ground, tower, radar facilities, etc.).

8. **Apply pertinent information from NOTAMs, the *Airport/Facility Directory* and other flight publications.**

    a.   Notices to Airmen (NOTAMs) offer time-critical aeronautical information that is of a temporary nature not sufficiently known in advance to permit publication on aeronautical charts or on other operational publications.

    b.   The *A/FD* is a civil flight information publication published and distributed every 8 weeks by the NACO.

          1)   It is a directory of all airports, seaplane bases, and heliports open to the public; communications data; navigational facilities; and certain special notices and procedures.

    c.   The *AIM* provides you with a vast amount of basic flight information and ATC procedures in the United States.

          1)   This information is vital to you as a pilot so that you may understand the structure and operation of the ATC system and your part in it.

9. **Complete a navigation log and simulate filing a VFR flight plan.**

    a.   Always use a navigation log to assist you in planning and conducting a cross-country flight.

    b.   The final step in your cross-country flight planning is to complete and file a VFR flight plan.

          1)   VFR flight plans are not mandatory, but they are highly recommended as a safety precaution. In the event you do not reach your destination as planned, the FAA will institute a search for you. This process begins 30 min. after you were scheduled to reach your destination.

          2)   This element requires that you simulate filing a VFR flight plan. Complete a VFR flight plan form, and explain to your examiner how you would file the flight plan.

END OF TASK

NATIONAL AIRSPACE SYSTEM

I.E. TASK: NATIONAL AIRSPACE SYSTEM

    REFERENCES: 14 CFR Parts 71, 91; Navigation Charts; AIM.

Objective. To determine that the applicant exhibits knowledge of the elements related to the National Airspace System by explaining:

1. Basic VFR Weather Minimums -- for all classes of airspace.

2. Airspace classes -- their operating rules, pilot certification and airplane equipment requirements for the following:

    a. Class A
    b. Class B
    c. Class C
    d. Class D
    e. Class E
    f. Class G

3. Special use airspace and other airspace areas.

A.   General Information

1.   The objective of this task is to determine your knowledge of the National Airspace System (NAS).

2.   The diagram below should be used with the airspace classification explanations of requirements and services available on the following pages.

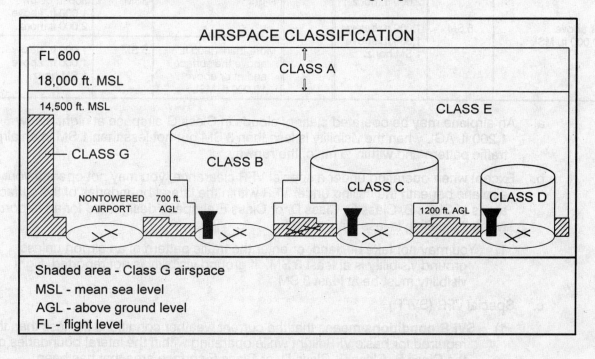

AIRSPACE CLASSIFICATION

Shaded area - Class G airspace
MSL - mean sea level
AGL - above ground level
FL - flight level

B.   Task Objectives

1.   **Explain basic VFR weather minimums for all classes of airspace.**

Cloud Clearance and Visibility Required for VFR

Airspace	Flight Visibility	Distance from Clouds		Airspace	Flight Visibility	Distance from Clouds
Class A	Not applicable	Not applicable		**Class G:** 1,200 ft. or less above the surface (regardless of MSL altitude)		
Class B	3 SM	Clear of clouds		Day	1 SM	Clear of clouds
Class C	3 SM	500 ft. below 1,000 ft. above 2,000 ft. horiz.		Night, except as provided in a. below	3 SM	500 ft. below 1,000 ft. above 2,000 ft. horiz.
Class D	3 SM	500 ft. below 1,000 ft. above 2,000 ft. horiz.		More than 1,200 ft. above the surface but less than 10,000 ft. MSL		
Class E: Less than 10,000 ft. MSL	3 SM	500 ft. below 1,000 ft. above 2,000 ft. horiz.		Day	1 SM	500 ft. below 1,000 ft. above 2,000 ft. horiz.
				Night	3SM	500 ft. below 1,000 ft. above 2,000 ft. horiz.
At or above 10,000 ft. MSL	5 SM	1,000 ft. below 1,000 ft. above 1 SM horiz.		More than 1,200 ft. above the surface and at or above 10,000 ft. MSL	5 SM	1,000 ft. below 1,000 ft. above 1 SM horiz.

a.   An airplane may be operated clear of clouds in Class G airspace at night below 1,200 ft. AGL when the visibility is less than 3 SM but not less than 1 SM in an airport traffic pattern and within ½ mi. of the runway.

b.   Except when operating under a special VFR clearance, you may not operate your airplane beneath the ceiling under VFR within the lateral boundaries of the surface areas of Class B, Class C, Class D, or Class E airspace designated for an airport when the ceiling is less than 1,000 ft.

   1)   You may not take off, land, or enter the traffic pattern of an airport unless ground visibility is at least 3 SM. If ground visibility is not reported, flight visibility must be at least 3 SM.

c.   Special VFR (SVFR)

   1)   **SVFR conditions** means that the current weather conditions are less than that required for basic VFR flight while operating within the lateral boundaries of the Class B, Class C, Class D, or Class E surface area that has been designated for an airport and in which some aircraft are permitted to operate under VFR.

   2)   SVFR operations may only be conducted

      a)   With an ATC clearance (You must request the clearance.)
      b)   Clear of clouds
      c)   With flight visibility of at least 1 SM

3) To take off or land under a SVFR clearance, you must have ground visibility of at least 1 SM.

    a) If ground visibility is not reported, then flight visibility must be at least 1 SM.

4) To request a SVFR clearance at night, you must have an instrument rating.

2. **Explain airspace classes -- their operating rules, pilot certification and airplane equipment requirements.**

  a. **Class A** airspace is generally the airspace from 18,000 ft. MSL up to and including flight level (FL) 600, including the airspace overlying the waters within 12 NM of the coast of the 48 contiguous states and Alaska.

    1) Operating rules and pilot/equipment requirements

      a) An IFR clearance to enter and operate within Class A airspace is mandatory. Thus, you must be instrument-rated to act as PIC of an airplane in Class A airspace.

      b) Two-way radio communication, appropriate navigational capability, and a Mode C transponder are required.

  b. **Class B** airspace is generally the airspace from the surface to 10,000 ft. MSL surrounding the nation's busiest airports in terms of IFR operations or passenger enplanements (e.g., Atlanta, Chicago).

    1) The configuration of each Class B airspace area is individually tailored and consists of a surface area and two or more layers.

    2) Operating rules and pilot/equipment requirements for VFR operations

      a) An ATC clearance is required prior to operating within Class B airspace.

      b) Two-way radio communication capability is required.

      c) Mode C transponder is required within, and above the lateral limits of, Class B airspace and within 30 NM of the primary airport regardless of altitude.

      d) The PIC must be at least a private pilot, or a student or recreational pilot who is under the supervision of a CFI.

  c. **Class C** airspace surrounds those airports that have an operational control tower, are serviced by a radar approach control, and have a certain number of IFR operations or passenger enplanements.

    1) Class C airspace normally consists of

      a) A 5-NM radius surface area (formerly called the inner circle) that extends from the surface to 4,000 ft. above the airport elevation

      b) A 10-NM radius shelf area (formerly called the outer circle) that extends from 1,200 ft. to 4,000 ft. above the airport elevation

    2) Operating rules and pilot/equipment requirements

      a) Two-way radio communications must be established and maintained with ATC before entering and while operating in Class C airspace.

      b) Mode C transponder is required within and above the lateral limits of Class C airspace.

      c) No specific pilot certification is required.

d. **Class D** airspace surrounds those airports that have both an operating control tower and weather services available, and are not associated with Class B or C airspace.

   1) Class D airspace normally extends from the surface up to and including 2,500 ft. AGL.

   2) Operating rules and pilot/equipment requirements

      a) Two-way communications must be established and maintained with ATC prior to entering and while operating in Class D airspace.

      b) No specific pilot certification is required.

e. **Class E** airspace is any controlled airspace that is not Class A, B, C, or D airspace.

   1) Except for 18,000 ft. MSL (the floor of Class A airspace), Class E airspace has no defined vertical limit, but rather it extends upward from either the surface or a designated altitude to the overlying or adjacent controlled airspace.

   2) There are no specific pilot certification or equipment requirements to operate in Class E airspace.

f. **Class G** airspace is that airspace that has not been designated as Class A, Class B, Class C, Class D, or Class E airspace (i.e., it is uncontrolled airspace).

   1) No specific pilot certification or airplane equipment is required in Class G airspace.

NOTE: While generally no equipment is required to operate VFR in Class E or Class G airspace, there are some airports with operational control towers within the surface area of Class E or Class G airspace. In these circumstances, you must establish and maintain two-way radio communication with the control tower if you plan to operate to, from, or through an area within 4 NM from the airport, from the surface up to an including 2,500 ft. AGL.

3. **Explain special-use airspace and other airspace areas.**

   a. Special-use airspace (SUA)

      1) **Prohibited areas** -- airspace within which flight is prohibited. Such areas are established for security or other reasons of national welfare.

      2) **Restricted areas** -- airspace within which flight, while not wholly prohibited, is subject to restrictions. Restricted areas denote the existence of unusual, often invisible hazards to aircraft such as artillery firing, aerial gunnery, or guided missiles.

      3) **Warning areas** -- airspace of defined dimensions, extending from 3 NM outward from the coast of the U.S., that contains activity that may be hazardous to nonparticipating aircraft. The purpose of a warning area is to warn nonparticipating pilots of the potential danger (such as those in restricted areas).

         a) A warning area may be located over domestic or international waters or both.

      4) **Military operations areas (MOA)** -- airspace established to separate certain military training activities from IFR traffic

         a) VFR aircraft should operate with caution while in an active MOA.

5) **Alert areas** -- areas depicted on aeronautical charts to inform nonparticipating pilots that the areas may contain a high volume of pilot training or an unusual type of aerial activity

6) **Controlled firing areas** -- areas containing activities that, if not conducted in a controlled environment, could be hazardous to nonparticipating aircraft

   a) The activities are suspended immediately when spotter aircraft, radar, or ground lookout positions indicate an aircraft might be approaching the area.

b. Other airspace areas

1) **National security areas (NSA)** -- airspace of defined vertical and lateral dimensions established at locations where there is a requirement for increased security and safety of ground facilities. Pilots are requested to voluntarily avoid flying through the depicted NSA.

   a) A NOTAM will be issued to prohibit flight in NSAs when it is necessary to provide a greater level of security and safety.

2) **Airport advisory areas** encompass the areas within 10 SM of airports that have no operating control towers but where FSSs are located. At such locations, the FSS provides advisory service to arriving and departing aircraft. Participation in the Local Airport Advisory (LAA) program is recommended but not required.

3) **Military training routes (MTRs)** are developed for use by the military for the purpose of conducting low-altitude (below 10,000 ft. MSL), high-speed training (more than 250 kt.).

4) Temporary flight restrictions (FAR 91.137) may be put into effect in the vicinity of any incident or event which by its nature may generate such a high degree of public interest that hazardous congestion of air traffic is likely.

5) Flight limitations in the proximity of space flight operations (FAR 91.143) are designated in a NOTAM.

6) Flight restrictions in the proximity of Presidential and other parties (FAR 91.141) are put into effect by a regulatory NOTAM to establish flight restrictions.

7) Tabulations of parachute jump areas in the U.S. are contained in the *A/FD*.

8) **VFR flyway** is a general flight path not defined as a specific course but used by pilots planning flights into, out of, through, or near complex terminal airspace to avoid Class B airspace.

   a) VFR flyways are depicted on the reverse side of some of the VFR terminal area charts.

   b) An ATC clearance is not required to fly these routes since they are not in Class B airspace.

9) **VFR corridor** is airspace through Class B airspace, with defined vertical and lateral boundaries, in which aircraft may operate without an ATC clearance or communication with ATC. A VFR corridor is, in effect, a hole through the Class B airspace.

10) **Class B airspace VFR transition route** is a specific flight course depicted on a VFR terminal area chart for transiting a specific Class B airspace.

    a)   These routes include specific ATC-assigned altitudes, and you must obtain an ATC clearance prior to entering the Class B airspace.

    b)   On initial contact, you should inform ATC of your position, altitude, route name desired, and direction of flight.

        i)   After a clearance is received, you must fly the route as depicted, and most importantly, follow ATC instructions.

11) **Terminal area VFR route** is a specific flight course for optional use by pilots to avoid Class B, Class C, and Class D airspace areas while operating in complex terminal airspace (e.g., Los Angeles).

    a)   An ATC clearance is not required to fly these routes.

12) **Terminal Radar Service Area (TRSA)**

    a)   TRSAs are not controlled airspace from a regulatory standpoint (i.e., they do not fit into any of the airspace classes) because TRSAs were never subject to the rulemaking process.

        i)   Thus, TRSAs are not contained in FAR Part 71 nor are there any TRSA operating rules in FAR Part 91.

        ii)   TRSAs are areas where participating pilots can receive additional radar services, known as TRSA Service.

    b)   The primary airport(s) within the TRSA are in Class D airspace.

        i)   The remaining portion of the TRSA normally overlies Class E airspace beginning at 700 or 1,200 ft. AGL.

    c)   Pilots operating under VFR are encouraged to participate in the TRSA service. However, participation is voluntary.

    d)   TRSAs are depicted on sectional charts with a solid black line and with altitudes for each segment expressed in hundreds of feet MSL.

        i)   The Class D portion is depicted with a blue segmented line.

END OF TASK

PERFORMANCE AND LIMITATIONS

I.F. TASK: PERFORMANCE AND LIMITATIONS

REFERENCES: AC 61-23/FAA-H-8083-25; FAA-H-8083-1; AC 61-84; Pilot's Operating Handbook, FAA-Approved Airplane Flight Manual.

Objective. To determine that the applicant:

1. Exhibits knowledge of the elements related to performance and limitations by explaining the use of charts, tables, and data to determine performance and the adverse effects of exceeding limitations.

2. Computes weight and balance. Determines if the computed weight and center of gravity is within the airplane's operating limitations and if the weight and center of gravity will remain within limits during all phases of flight.

3. Demonstrates use of the appropriate performance charts, tables, and data.

4. Describes the effects of various atmospheric conditions on the airplane's performance.

A. General Information

   1. The objective of this task is for you to demonstrate your knowledge of determining your airplane's performance and limitations.

   2. Additional reading: See Chapter 5, Airplane Performance and Weight and Balance, in *Pilot Handbook* for a 17-page discussion on airplane performance and a 12-page discussion on weight and balance.

   3. This task is make- and model-specific, and applies to the most complex airplane used on your practical test. This task covers Sections 2, 5, and 6 of your *POH*.

      a. Section 2: Limitations
      b. Section 5: Performance
      c. Section 6: Weight and Balance/Equipment List

B. Task Objectives

   1. **Exhibit your knowledge of the elements related to performance and limitations by explaining the use of charts, tables, and data to determine performance and the adverse effects of exceeding limitations.**

      a. Airplane performance can be defined as the ability to operate or function, i.e., the ability of an airplane to accomplish certain things that make it useful for certain purposes.

         1) The various items of airplane performance result from the combination of airplane and powerplant characteristics.

            a) The aerodynamic characteristics of the airplane generally define the power and thrust requirements at various conditions of flight.

            b) Powerplant characteristics generally define the power and thrust available at various conditions of flight.

            c) The matching of these characteristics is done by the manufacturer.

b.   Operating limitations are found in Section 2, Limitations, of your airplane's *POH*. These limits establish the boundaries (i.e., flight envelope) in which the airplane must be operated.

    1)   You should be able to explain the adverse effects of exceeding your airplane's limitations. These may include

        a)   Attempting a takeoff or landing without a long enough runway

        b)   Not having enough fuel to make your airport of intended landing, while cruising at a high power setting

        c)   Exceeding your airplane's structural limits by being over gross weight and/or outside center of gravity limits

c.   Performance charts, tables, and/or data are found in Section 5, Performance, of your airplane's *POH*.

    1)   You must be able to explain the use of each chart, table, and/or set of data.

2.   Compute weight and balance. Determine if the weight and center of gravity is within the airplane's operating limitations and if the weight and center of gravity will remain within the limits during all phases of flight.

a.   You will need to use Section 6, Weight and Balance/Equipment List, in your airplane's *POH* to accomplish this element. You should calculate the weight and balance for takeoff, cruise, and landing.

    1)   The subject of weight and balance is concerned with not only the weight of the airplane but also the location of its center of gravity (CG). You should not attempt a flight until you are satisfied with the weight and balance condition.

3.   Demonstrate use of the appropriate performance charts, tables, and data.

a.   Appropriate performance charts, tables, and data are found in Section 5, Performance of your airplane's *POH*.

    1)   Such charts provide take off and landing distance information, climb performance information, and cruise performance information.

    2)   You must be able to explain the use of each chart, table, and/or set of data.

b.   As a commercial pilot, you must display sound judgment when determining whether the required performance is within your airplane's and your own capabilities and operating limitations.

    1)   Remember the performance charts in your *POH* do not make allowance for pilot proficiency or mechanical deterioration of the aircraft.

    2)   You can determine your airplane's performance in all phases of flight if you follow and use the performance charts in your *POH*.

4.   Describe the effects of various atmospheric conditions on the airplane's performance.

a.   **Calibrated airspeed (CAS)** is indicated airspeed (IAS) corrected for installation and instrument errors.

    1)   Although manufacturers attempt to keep airspeed errors to a minimum, it is not possible to eliminate them along the entire airspeed operating range.

        a)   Installation (position) error is caused by the static port(s) sensing erroneous static pressure. The slipstream flow causes disturbances at the static port(s) preventing true static pressure measurement.

        b)   Also, at varying angles of attack, the pitot tube does not always point directly into the relative wind, which causes erroneous total (or impact) pressure measurement.

2)   At certain airspeeds and with certain flap settings, the installation and instrument error may be several knots. This error is generally greatest at low airspeeds.

3)   In the cruising and higher airspeed ranges, IAS and CAS are approximately the same.

4)   The airspeed indicator is calibrated to display an airspeed representative of a given dynamic pressure, only at sea-level values; thus the airspeed indicator does not reflect changes in density altitude.

   a)   Remember that dynamic pressure is a variable in the lift equation.

   b)   Since the airspeed indicator measures dynamic pressure, you use the same indicated airspeeds regardless of density altitude.

5)   The effect of this can be observed, for example, when an airplane, taking off at high density altitudes, takes longer to develop the dynamic pressure required to produce enough lift for takeoff. This will lead to a longer takeoff distance.

b.   **True airspeed (TAS)** is CAS corrected for density altitude. TAS is the true speed of an airplane through the air.

1)   Because air density decreases with an increase in altitude, the airplane must be flown faster at higher altitudes (i.e., higher density altitude) to cause the same dynamic pressure to be measured in the ASI.

   a)   Therefore, for a given TAS, IAS decreases as altitude increases.
   b)   For a given IAS, TAS increases with an altitude increase.

c.   **Pressure altitude** is the altitude indicated on the altimeter when the altimeter is set to 29.92.

1)   In the International Standard Atmosphere (ISA), the standard datum plane is a theoretical plane where air pressure (corrected to 15°C) is equal to 29.92 in. of mercury.

   a)   As atmospheric pressure changes, the standard datum plane may be below, at, or above sea level.

      i)   High barometric pressure decreases pressure altitude; low barometric pressure increases pressure altitude.

2)   Pressure altitude is important as a basis for determining airplane performance.

d.   **Density altitude** is pressure altitude corrected for nonstandard temperature.

1)   Air density is perhaps the single most important factor affecting airplane performance. The general rule is that, as air density decreases, so does airplane performance.

   a)   Temperature, altitude, barometric pressure, and humidity all affect air density. The density of the air DECREASES

      i)   As air temperature INCREASES
      ii)   As altitude INCREASES
      iii) As barometric pressure DECREASES
      iv)   As humidity INCREASES

   b)   The engine produces power in proportion to the weight or density of the air.

      i)   As air density decreases, the power output of the engine decreases.

         •   This is true of all engines not equipped with a supercharger or turbocharger.

    c)   The propeller produces thrust in proportion to the mass of air being accelerated through the rotating blades.

        i)   As air density decreases, propeller efficiency decreases.

    d)   The wings produce lift as a result of the air passing over and under them.

        i)   As air density decreases, the lift efficiency of the wing decreases.

2)   At power settings of less than 75%, or at density altitudes above 5,000 ft., it is essential that normally aspirated engines be leaned for maximum power on takeoff, unless equipped with an automatic altitude mixture control.

    a)   The excessively rich mixture adds another detriment to overall performance.

    b)   Turbocharged engines need not be leaned for takeoff in high density altitude conditions because they are capable of producing manifold pressure equal to or higher than sea-level pressure.

    c)   At airports of higher elevations, such as those in the western U.S., high temperatures sometimes have such an effect on density altitude that safe operations may be impossible.

        i)   Even at lower elevations with excessively high temperature or humidity, airplane performance can become marginal, and it may be necessary to reduce the airplane's weight for safe operations.

END OF TASK

OPERATION OF SYSTEMS

I.G. TASK: OPERATION OF SYSTEMS

> REFERENCES: AC 61-23/FAA-H-8083-25; Pilot's Operating Handbook, FAA-Approved Airplane Flight Manual.

Objective.   To determine that the applicant exhibits knowledge of the elements related to the operation of systems on the airplane provided for the practical test by explaining at least five (5) of the following systems:

1. Primary flight controls and trim.

2. Flaps, leading edge devices, and spoilers.

3. Powerplant and propeller.

4. Landing gear.

5. Fuel, oil, and hydraulic.

6. Electrical.

7. Avionics.

8. Pitot-static, vacuum/pressure, and associated flight instruments.

9. Environmental.

10. Deicing and anti-icing.

A. General Information

    1. The objective of this task is for you to demonstrate your knowledge of your airplane's systems and their operation.

       a. This task is make- and model-specific and applies to the most complex airplane used on your practical test.

       b. Your examiner is required to have you explain only five of the 10 systems, as a minimum.

    2. Additional reading: See *Pilot Handbook* for the following:

       a. Chapter 1, Airplanes and Aerodynamics, Module 1.4, Flight Controls and Control Surfaces, for a five-page discussion on the primary flight controls, trim devices, flaps, leading edge devices, and spoilers

       b. Chapter 2, Airplane Instruments, Engines, and Systems, for a 50-page discussion of the operation of the various airplane instruments, engines, and systems

    3. To prepare for this task, systematically study, not just read, Sections 1, 7, 8, and 9 of your *POH*:

       a. Section 1. General.
       b. Section 7. Airplane and Systems Descriptions.
       c. Section 8. Airplane Handling, Service and Maintenance.
       d. Section 9. Supplement (Optional Systems Description and Operating Procedures).

    4. Finally, make a list of the make and model of all avionics equipment in your training airplane. Know the purpose, operation, and capability of each unit. You should be constantly discussing your airplane's systems with your CFI.

B. Task Objectives

    1. Explain primary flight controls and trim.

       a. The airplane's attitude is controlled by the deflection of the primary flight controls.

         1) The primary flight controls are the rudder, elevator (or stabilizer on some airplanes), and ailerons.

       b. Trim devices are commonly used to relieve you of the need of maintaining continuous pressure on the primary flight controls.

         1) The most common trim devices used on general aviation airplanes are trim tabs and anti-servo tabs.

2. **Explain flaps, leading edge devices, and spoilers.**

   a. Wing flaps are used on most airplanes. Flaps increase both lift and drag and have three important functions:

      1) First, they permit a slower landing speed, which decreases the required landing distance.

      2) Second, they permit a comparatively steep angle of descent without an increase in speed. This makes it possible to clear obstacles safely when making a landing approach to a short runway.

      3) Third, they may also be used to shorten the takeoff distance and provide a steeper climb path.

   b. Leading edge devices are used on many larger airplanes. These devices (slots and slats) are designed to allow smooth airflow over the wing at higher angles of attack and delay the airflow separation.

   c. Spoilers are used on some airplanes to disrupt the smooth flow of air over the wing. Using spoilers is a means of increasing the rate of descent without increasing the airplane's speed.

3. **Explain the powerplant and the propeller.**

   a. An airplane's engine is commonly referred to as the powerplant. Not only does the engine provide power to propel the airplane, but it powers the units that operate a majority of the airplane's systems.

      1) You should be able to explain your airplane's powerplant, including

         a) The operation of the engine
         b) Engine type and horsepower
         c) Ignition system
         d) Induction system
         e) Cooling system

   b. The airplane propeller consists of two or more blades and a central hub to which the blades are attached. Each blade of an airplane propeller is essentially a rotating wing which produces forces that create the thrust to pull, or push, the airplane through the air.

      1) Complex airplanes have a **controllable-pitch propeller**; i.e., the pitch of the propeller blades can be changed in flight by the pilot.

      2) See Appendix B, Complex and High-Performance Airplanes, for a discussion on constant-speed propellers beginning on page 305.

      3) The power needed to rotate the propeller blades is furnished by the engine. The engine rotates the airfoils of the blades through the air at high speeds, and the propeller transforms the rotary power of the engine into forward thrust.

4. **Explain the landing gear system.**

   a. The landing gear system supports the airplane during the takeoff run, landing, and taxiing, and when parked. The landing gear can be fixed or retractable and must be capable of steering, braking, and absorbing shock.

      1) Complex airplanes are equipped with retractable landing gear.

b. Gear systems can be operated in a number of different ways. Some are electric, some are hydraulic, and some are hybrids called electro-hydraulic.

1) The electric system uses a reversible electric motor to power the system. Through a gear assembly, the electric motor turns a bellcrank, operating the push-pull cables and tubes that extend and retract the landing gear.

2) The hydraulic system uses an engine-driven hydraulic pump to force fluid under pressure through a series of valves, pipes, and actuators. The hydraulic pressure drives the gear up or down.

3) The electro-hydraulic system uses a reversible electric motor to drive the hydraulic pump. The gear selector switch is an electric switch which activates the electric motor and controls the direction of the hydraulic fluid to move the gear up or down.

5. **Explain fuel, oil, and hydraulic systems**.

a. The fuel system stores fuel and transfers it to the airplane engine.

b. The oil system provides a means of storing and circulating oil throughout the internal components of a reciprocating engine.

1) Each engine is equipped with an oil pressure gauge and an oil temperature gauge to be monitored to determine that the oil system is functioning properly.

c. Most airplanes have an independent hydraulic brake system powered by master cylinders in each main landing gear wheel, similar to those in your car.

1) An airplane with retractable landing gear normally uses hydraulic fluid in the operation of the landing gear.

d. You should be able to explain the fuel, oil and hydraulic systems for your airplane, including

1) Approved fuel grade(s) and quantity (usable and nonusable)
2) Oil grade and quantity (minimum and maximum operating levels)
3) Hydraulic systems (i.e., brakes, landing gear, etc.)

6. **Explain the electrical system.**

a. Electrical energy is required to operate the starter, navigation and communication radios, lights, and other airplane equipment.

b. You should be able to explain the electrical system for your airplane, including

1) Battery location, voltage, and capacity (i.e., amperage)
2) Electrical system and alternator (or generator) voltage and capacity

a) Advantages and disadvantages of an alternator and a generator

3) Circuit breakers and fuses -- location and purpose
4) Ammeter indications

7. **Explain the avionics systems.**

a. Avionics systems are all of your airplane's aviation electronic equipment.

1) Be able to explain how all your communication and navigation systems operate.

2) Make a list of the make, model, and type of radio and related equipment in your airplane. As appropriate, consult and study their instruction manuals.

8. **Explain the pitot-static system, the vacuum/pressure system, and associated flight instruments.**

    a. The pitot-static system provides the source for the operation of the

        1) Altimeter
        2) Vertical speed indicator
        3) Airspeed indicator

    b. The vacuum/pressure system provides the source for the operation of the following gyroscopic flight instruments:

        1) Heading indicator
        2) Attitude indicator

    c. While not normally part of the vacuum/pressure system, the turn coordinator is a gyroscopic flight instrument but is normally powered by the electrical system.

9. **Explain the environmental system.**

    a. Heating in most training airplanes is accomplished by an air intake in the nose of the airplane.

        1) The air is directed into a shroud, where it is heated by the engine.
        2) The heated air is then delivered through vents into the cabin or used for the defroster.

    b. Cooling and ventilation are controlled by outlets.

        1) Some airplanes are equipped with an air conditioner for cooling.
        2) Outside air used for cooling and ventilation is normally supplied through air inlets that are located in the wings or elsewhere on the airplane.
        3) Learn how your airplane's system works by reading your airplane's *POH*.

    c. Heat and defrost controls are located on the instrument panel or within easy reach.

        1) Most aircraft are equipped with outlets that can be controlled by each occupant of the airplane.
        2) Your airplane's *POH* will explain the operation of the controls.

10. **Explain deicing and anti-icing systems.**

    a. An induction system ice-protection system is the basic, and probably the only, ice-protection system in your airplane.

        1) Carburetor heat warms the air before it enters the carburetor.

            a) It is used to remove and/or prevent ice formation.
            b) Carburetor ice can occur at temperatures much warmer than freezing due to fuel vaporization and a drop in pressure through the carburetor venturi.

        2) Fuel-injected airplanes will have an alternate air source that functions automatically or manually.

            a) If the air intake or filter becomes clogged with ice, a spring-loaded door will open automatically to allow the induction system to operate from the alternate air source.
            b) You can also manually open the door if it does not operate automatically.

b. Fuel system icing results from the presence of water in the fuel system. This may cause freezing of screen, strainers, and filters. When fuel enters the carburetor, the additional cooling may freeze the water.

   1) Normally, proper use of carburetor heat can warm the air sufficiently in the carburetor to prevent ice formation.

   2) Some airplanes are approved to use anti-icing fuel additives.

      a) Remember that an anti-icing additive is not a substitute for carburetor heat.

c. Pitot heat is an electrical system and may put a severe drain on the electrical system on some airplanes.

   1) Pitot heat is used to prevent ice from blocking the ram air hole of the pitot tube.

      a) Pitot heat should be used prior to encountering visible moisture.

   2) Monitor your ammeter for the effect pitot heat has on your airplane's electrical system.

d. Be emphatic with your examiner that icing conditions are to be avoided both in flight planning and in the air!

   1) Most training airplanes have placards that prohibit flight into known icing conditions.

e. Check your airplane's *POH* for the appropriate system, if any, installed in the airplane.

END OF TASK

AEROMEDICAL FACTORS

I.J. TASK: AEROMEDICAL FACTORS

REFERENCES: AC 61-23/FAA-H-8083-25; AIM.

Objective.   To determine that the applicant exhibits knowledge of the elements related to aeromedical factors by explaining:

1. The symptoms, causes, effects, and corrective actions of at least four (4) of the following --

    a. Hypoxia.
    b. Hyperventilation.
    c. Middle ear and sinus problems.
    d. Spatial disorientation.
    e. Motion sickness.
    f. Carbon monoxide poisoning.
    g. Stress and fatigue.
    h. Dehydration

2. The effects of alcohol, drugs, and over-the-counter medications.

3. The effects of excess nitrogen during scuba dives upon a pilot and/or passenger in flight.

A.   General Information

    1.   The objective of this task is to determine your knowledge of aeromedical factors as they relate to safety of flight.

    2.   Pilot personal checklist

        a.   Aircraft accident statistics show that pilots should conduct preflight checklists on themselves as well as their aircraft. Pilot impairment contributes to many more accidents than do failures of aircraft systems.

        b.   I'M SAFE -- I am NOT impaired by

            I llness
            M edication

            S tress
            A lcohol
            F atigue
            E motion

B.   Task Objectives

    1.   Exhibit your knowledge of the elements related to aeromedical factors, including the symptoms, causes, effects, and corrective actions of at least four of the following.

        a.   Hypoxia is a state of oxygen deficiency in the body sufficient to impair functions of the brain and other organs.

            1)   Significant effects of altitude hypoxia usually do not occur in the normal, healthy pilot below 12,000 ft. MSL.

                a)   A deterioration in night vision occurs as low as 5,000 ft. MSL.

            2)   From 12,000 to 15,000 ft. MSL (without supplemental oxygen), judgment, memory, alertness, coordination, and ability to make calculations are impaired. Headache, drowsiness, dizziness, and either a sense of well-being (euphoria) or belligerence occur.

            3)   At altitudes above 15,000 ft. MSL, the periphery of the visual field turns gray. Only central vision remains (tunnel vision). A blue color (cyanosis) develops in the fingernails and lips.

            4)   Corrective action if hypoxia is suspected or recognized includes

                a)   Use of supplemental oxygen
                b)   An emergency descent to a lower altitude

b. **Hyperventilation**, which is an abnormal increase in the volume of air breathed in and out of the lungs, can occur subconsciously when you encounter a stressful situation.

   1) This abnormal breathing flushes from your lungs and blood much of the carbon dioxide your system needs to maintain the proper degree of blood acidity.

      a) The resulting chemical imbalance in the body produces dizziness, tingling of the fingers and toes, hot and cold sensations, drowsiness, nausea, and suffocation. Often you may react to these symptoms with even greater hyperventilation.

   2) It is important to realize that early symptoms of hyperventilation and hypoxia are similar. Also, hyperventilation and hypoxia can occur at the same time.

   3) The symptoms of hyperventilation subside within a few minutes after the rate and depth of breathing are consciously brought back under control.

      a) This can be hastened by controlled breathing in and out of a paper bag held over the nose and mouth. Also, talking, singing, or counting aloud often helps.

c. **Middle ear and sinus problems**

   1) As the cabin pressure decreases during ascent, the expanding air in the middle ear pushes the eustachian tube open and escapes down it to the nasal passages, thus equalizing ear pressure with the cabin pressure.

      a) Either an upper respiratory infection (e.g., a cold or a sore throat) or nasal allergies can produce enough congestion around the eustachian tube to make equalization difficult if not impossible.

      b) The difference in pressure between the middle ear and the airplane's cabin can build to a level that will hold the eustachian tube closed. This problem, commonly referred to as "ear block," produces severe ear pain and loss of hearing that can last from several hours to several days.

         i) Rupture of the ear drum can occur in flight or after landing.
         ii) Fluid can accumulate in the middle ear and become infected.

   2) During ascent and descent, air pressure in the sinuses equalizes with aircraft cabin pressure through small openings that connect the sinuses to the nasal passages.

      a) Either an upper respiratory infection (e.g., a cold or sinusitis) or nasal allergies can produce enough congestion around one or more of these small openings to slow equalization.

      b) As the difference in pressure between the sinus and the cabin mounts, the opening may become plugged, resulting in "sinus block." A sinus block, experienced most frequently during descent, can occur in the frontal sinuses, located above each eyebrow, or in the maxillary sinuses, located in each upper cheek.

         i) It usually produces excruciating pain over the sinus area.
         ii) A maxillary sinus block can also make the upper teeth ache.
         iii) Bloody mucus may discharge from the nasal passages.

   3) Middle ear and sinus problems are prevented by not flying with an upper respiratory infection or a nasal allergic condition.

      a) Adequate protection is not provided by decongestant spray or drops to reduce congestion around the eustachian tubes or the sinus openings.

      b) Oral decongestants have side effects that can significantly impair pilot performance.

d. Spatial disorientation

1) Spatial disorientation is a state of temporary spatial confusion resulting from misleading information sent to the brain by various sensory organs. To a pilot this means simply the inability to tell "which way is up."

2) Sight, the semicircular canals of the inner ear, and pressure-sensitive nerve endings (located mainly in your muscles and tendons) are used to maintain spatial orientation.

    a) However, during periods of limited visibility, conflicting information among these senses makes you susceptible to spatial disorientation.

3) Your brain relies primarily on sight when there is conflicting information.

    a) When outside references are limited due to limited visibility and/or darkness, you must rely on your flight instruments for information.

4) Spatial disorientation can be corrected by relying on and believing your airplane's instruments or by focusing on reliable, fixed points on the ground.

e. Motion sickness

1) Motion sickness is caused by continued stimulation of the tiny portion of the inner ear which controls your sense of balance. The symptoms are progressive.

    a) First, the desire for food is lost.
    b) Then saliva collects in the mouth and you begin to perspire freely.
    c) Eventually, you become nauseated and disoriented.
    d) The head aches and there may be a tendency to vomit.

2) If suffering from airsickness, you should

    a) Open the air vents.
    b) Loosen clothing.
    c) Use supplemental oxygen, if available.
    d) Keep the eyes on a point outside the airplane.
    e) Avoid unnecessary head movements.
    f) Cancel the flight and land as soon as possible.

f. Carbon monoxide poisoning

1) Carbon monoxide is a colorless, odorless, and tasteless gas contained in exhaust fumes and tobacco smoke.

    a) When inhaled even in minute quantities over a period of time, it can significantly reduce the ability of the blood to carry oxygen.

    b) Consequently, effects of hypoxia occur.

2) Most heaters in light aircraft work by air flowing over the exhaust manifold.

    a) Using these heaters when exhaust fumes are escaping through manifold cracks and seals is responsible every year for both nonfatal and fatal aircraft accidents from carbon monoxide poisoning.

    b) If you detect the odor of exhaust or experience symptoms of headache, drowsiness, or dizziness while using the heater, you should suspect carbon monoxide poisoning and immediately shut off the heater and open the air vents.

        i) If symptoms are severe, or continue after landing, medical treatment should be sought.

g. Stress and fatigue

1) Stress from the pressures of everyday living can impair pilot performance, often in very subtle ways.

    a) Difficulties can occupy thought processes so as to decrease alertness.

    b) Distraction can so interfere with judgment that unwarranted risks are taken.

    c) When you are under more stress than usual, you should consider delaying flight until your difficulties have been resolved.

2) Acute fatigue is the everyday tiredness felt after long periods of physical or mental strain.

    a) Coordination and alertness can be reduced.

    b) Acute fatigue is prevented by adequate rest and sleep, as well as regular exercise and proper nutrition.

3) Chronic fatigue occurs when there is not enough time for full recovery between episodes of acute fatigue.

    a) Performance continues to fall off, and judgment becomes impaired.
    b) Recovery from chronic fatigue requires a prolonged period of rest.

h. Dehydration is the lack of adequate body fluids for the body to carry on normal functions at an optimal level.

1) Dehydration occurs by either inadequate intake of fluids or loss of fluids through perspiration, vomiting, diarrhea, and excessive urination.

    a) Vomiting, diarrhea, and excessive urination are separate health problems that usually preclude piloting activities.

    b) As the atmosphere becomes thinner, it also contains less moisture and more body fluids are lost.

2) Losses of only a few percent of body fluids can adversely affect both mental and physical processes.

3) On all extended flights, carry water or other suitable liquids to consume as appropriate, i.e., to satisfy thirst.

    a) Do NOT over-consume so as to require otherwise unnecessary landings to urinate.

4) Advise passengers regarding the need to consume appropriate amounts of liquids.

2. Exhibit your knowledge of the effects of alcohol, drugs, and over-the-counter medications.

a. There is only one safe rule to follow with respect to combining flying and drinking -- **DON'T**.

1) As little as 1 oz. of liquor, 1 bottle of beer, or 4 oz. of wine can impair flying skills.

    a) Even after your body has completely destroyed a moderate amount of alcohol, you can still be impaired for many hours by hangover.

    b) Alcohol also renders you much more susceptible to disorientation and hypoxia.

2)   The FARs prohibit pilots from performing cockpit duties within 8 hr. after drinking any alcoholic beverage or while under the influence of alcohol.

    a)   An excellent rule is to allow at least 12 to 24 hr. "from bottle to throttle," depending on how much you drank.

b.   Pilot performance can be seriously impaired by both prescribed and over-the-counter (OTC) medications.

1)   Many medications have primary or side effects that may impair judgment, memory, alertness, coordination, vision, and the ability to make calculations.

2)   Any medication that depresses the nervous system (i.e., sedative, tranquilizer, antihistamine) can make you more susceptible to hypoxia.

3)   The safest rule is not to fly while taking any medication, unless approved by the FAA.

4)   The table below lists the common over-the-counter medications and outlines some of their possible side effects that could affect your flying abilities. As with all drugs, side effects may vary with the individual and with changes in altitude and other flight conditions.

MOST COMMONLY EXPERIENCED SIDE EFFECTS AND INTERACTIONS OF OTC MEDICATIONS

	MEDICATIONS	SIDE EFFECTS	INTERACTIONS
PAIN RELIEF/FEVER	**ASPIRIN** Alka-Seltzer Bayer Aspirin Bufferin	Ringing in ears, nausea, stomach ulceration, hyperventilation	Increase effect of blood thinners
	ACETAMINOPHEN Tylenol	Liver toxicity (in large doses)	
	IBUPROFEN Advil Motrin Nuprin	Upset stomach, dizziness, rash, itching	Increase effect of blood thinners
COLDS/FLU	**ANTIHISTAMINES** Actifed Dristan Benadryl Drixoral Cheracol-Plus Nyquil Chlortrimeton Sinarest Contac Sinutab Dimetapp	Sedation, dizziness, rash, impairment of coordination, upset stomach, thickening of bronchial secretions, blurring of vision	Increase sedative effects of other medications
	DECONGESTANTS Afrin Nasal Spray Sine-Aid Sudafed	Excessive stimulation, dizziness, difficulty with urination, palpitations	Aggravate high blood pressure, heart disease, and prostate problems
	COUGH SUPPRESSANTS Benylin Robitussin CF/DM Vicks Formula 44	Drowsiness, blurred vision, difficulty with urination, upset stomach	Increase sedative effects of other medications
BOWEL PREPARATIONS	**LAXATIVES** Correctol Ex-Lax	Unexpected bowel activity at altitude, rectal itching	
	ANTI-DIARRHEALS Imodium A-D Pepto-Bismol	Drowsiness, depression, blurred vision (See Aspirin)	
APPETITE SUPPRESSANTS	Acutrim Dexatrim	Excessive stimulation, dizziness, palpitations, headaches	Increase stimulatory effects of decongestants, interfere with high blood pressure medications
SLEEPING AIDS	Nytol Sominex	(Contain antihistamine) Prolonged drowsiness, blurred vision	Cause excessive drowsiness when used with alcohol
STIMULANTS	**CAFFEINE** Coffee, tea, cola, chocolate	Excessive stimulation, tremors, palpitations, headache	Interfere with high blood pressure medications

3. **Exhibit your knowledge of the effects of excess nitrogen absorbed during scuba dives upon a pilot and/or passenger in flight.**

   a. If you or one of your passengers intends to fly after scuba diving, you should allow the body sufficient time to rid itself of excess nitrogen absorbed during diving.

      1) If this is not done, decompression sickness due to evolved gas (i.e., the nitrogen changes from a liquid to a gas and forms bubbles in the bloodstream) can occur at low altitudes and create a serious in-flight emergency.

   b. The recommended waiting time before a flight to flight altitudes of up to 8,000 ft. is at least 12 hr. after a dive that has not required controlled ascent (nondecompression diving).

      1) You should allow at least 24 hr. after diving that has required controlled ascent (decompression diving).

      2) The waiting time before a flight to flight altitudes above 8,000 ft. should be at least 24 hr. after any scuba diving.

   c. The recommended altitudes are actual flight altitudes above mean sea level (MSL), not pressurized cabin altitudes. These recommendations take into consideration the risk of decompression of aircraft during flight.

END OF TASK - - END OF CHAPTER

CHAPTER II
PREFLIGHT PROCEDURES

This chapter explains the five tasks (A-D, and F) of Preflight Procedures. These tasks include both knowledge and skill. Your examiner is required to test you on all five tasks.

PREFLIGHT INSPECTION

II.A. TASK: PREFLIGHT INSPECTION

    REFERENCES: FAA-H-8083-3; Pilot's Operating Handbook, FAA-Approved Airplane Flight Manual.

Objective. To determine that the applicant:

1. Exhibits knowledge of the elements related to preflight inspection. This shall include which items must be inspected, the reasons for checking each item, and how to detect possible defects.

2. Inspects the airplane with reference to an appropriate checklist.

3. Verifies that the airplane is in condition for safe flight.

A. General Information

   1. The objective of this task is for you to demonstrate the proper preflight inspection procedures.

   2. You, as pilot in command, are responsible for determining whether your airplane is airworthy and safe to fly. FAR 91.7 states, "The pilot in command is responsible for determining whether that aircraft is in condition for safe flight."

B. Task Objectives

   1. Exhibit your knowledge of the elements related to a preflight inspection including which items must be inspected, the reasons for checking each item, and how to detect possible defects.

     a. The objective of the preflight inspection is to ensure that your airplane has no obvious problems prior to taking off. The preflight is carried out in a systematic walk around the airplane and begins in the cockpit.

       1) Make sure all necessary documents, maps, safety equipment, etc., are aboard.

       2) Check to ensure all inspections are current (i.e., 100-hr., annual, transponder).

       3) Make sure your airplane has the required equipment for the flight you are about to take, e.g., a Mode C transponder for an operation in Class B or Class C airspace.

b. Next, inspect items outside of the cockpit to determine that the airplane is in condition for safe flight.

    1) Fuel quantity and grade

        a) You should check the level of fuel in the tanks to verify roughly fuel gauge indications.

        b) Refer to your *POH* for the manufacturer's recommendation regarding the minimum grade. Dyes are added by the refinery to help you identify the various grades of aviation fuel.

            i)   80 is red.
            ii)   100LL is blue.
            iii) 100 is green.
            iv)   Jet fuel is clear.

        c) Every aircraft engine has been designed to use a specific grade of aviation fuel for satisfactory performance.

            i)   When you are faced with a shortage of the correct grade of fuel, always use the alternate fuel grade specified by the manufacturer or the next higher grade.

        d) DO NOT USE AUTOMOTIVE FUEL unless an FAA supplemental type certificate (STC) has been obtained for your airplane that approves auto gas use.

    2) Fuel contamination safeguards

        a) Always assume that the fuel in your airplane is contaminated. A transparent container should be used to collect a generous fuel sample from each sump drainage valve at the lowest point of each tank and from other parts of the fuel system.

        b) Water, the most common fuel contaminant, is usually caused by condensation inside the tank.

            i)   Since water is heavier than fuel, it will be located at the lowest levels in the fuel system.

            ii)   If water is found in the first sample, drain further samples until no water appears.

            iii) Do not hold your fuel sample cup up to the sky to check for water contamination. If the sample is 100% water (no fuel at all), it may appear to be 100% fuel when seen against the blue sky.

            iv)   Over time the dye used to color the fuel will stain your fuel sample cup. If the sample is 100% water, it may appear as 100% fuel.

        c) Also check for other contaminants, e.g., dirt, sand, rust.

            i)   Keep draining until no trace of the contaminant appears.

            ii) A preventive measure is to avoid refueling from cans and drums, which may introduce fuel contaminants such as dirt or other impurities.

        d) Wait at least 15 min. after your airplane has been refueled before you take a fuel sample.

            i)   Waiting will allow time for any contaminants to settle to the bottom of the tank.

3) Fuel venting

    a) Fuel tank vents allow air to replace the fuel consumed during flight, so the air pressure inside the tank remains the same as outside the tank. It is very important that you visually inspect these vents to ensure that they are not blocked.

        i) Any degree of blockage (partial or complete) can cause a vacuum to form in the fuel tank and may prevent the flow of fuel to the engine.

    b) Rather than a vent tube, some systems have a small vent hole in the fuel cap.

        i) Some of these vents face forward on the fuel cap, and, if replaced backwards with the tube facing rearward, fuel-flow difficulty or in-flight siphoning may occur.

    c) Fuel tanks also have an overflow vent that prevents the rupture of the tank due to fuel expansion, especially on hot days.

        i) This vent may be combined with the fuel tank vent or separate from it.

    d) Study your *POH* to learn the system on your airplane.

4) Oil quantity, grade, and type

    a) Usually the oil is stored in a sump at the bottom of the engine crankcase. An opening to the oil sump is provided through which oil can be added, and a dipstick is provided to measure the oil level.

        i) Your *POH* will specify the quantity of oil needed for safe operation.

        ii) Always make certain that the oil filler cap and the oil dipstick are secure after adding and/or checking the oil level. If these are not properly secured, oil loss may occur.

    b) Use only the type and grade of oil recommended by the engine manufacturer, or its equivalent. Never use any oil additive that has not been recommended by the engine manufacturer or authorized by the FAA.

        i) The type and grade of oil to use can be found in your *POH*, or on placards on or near the oil filler cap.

    c) The wrong type of oil or an insufficient oil supply may interfere with any or all of the basic oil functions and can cause serious engine damage and/or an engine failure during flight.

5) Fuel, oil, and hydraulic leaks

    a) Check to see that there are no oil puddles or other leakages under your airplane, inside the engine cowling, or on the wheel struts.

    b) Ask someone more experienced and/or knowledgeable to look at any leakage. Know the cause and make the necessary repairs before flying.

6) Flight controls

   a) Visually inspect the flight control surfaces (ailerons, elevators, rudder) to ensure that they move smoothly and freely for their entire movement span.

      i) They also must be securely attached, with no missing, loose, or broken nuts, bolts, or rivets.

   b) Inspect any mass balance weights on control surfaces (designed to keep the control surface's center of gravity forward of the hinge so as to preclude possible shudder).

   c) Check to see that the control yoke moves in the proper direction as the control surfaces move.

   d) Place the flaps in the full down position to examine the attaching bolts and the entire flap surface.

      i) Ensure that the flaps operate correctly with the flap control and that they lock into position.

7) Structural damage

   a) Check for dents, cracks, or tears (cloth cover) on all surfaces of the airplane. These can disrupt the smooth airflow and change your airplane's performance.

      i) Surface deformities can lead to structural weakness and/or failures due to the stress that is put on the airplane during flight.

         • These deformities result from bent or broken underlying structure.

      ii) One method of checking the wings on a cloth-covered airplane is to grasp the wing spars at the wingtip and gently push down and pull up.

         • Any damage may be evident by sound and/or wrinkling of the skin.

   b) Inspect the propeller for nicks and/or cracks. A small nick that is not properly repaired can become a stress point where a crack could develop and cause the blade to break.

   c) If you have any doubts, get assistance from a qualified mechanic.

8) Exhaust system

   a) Check the exhaust system for visible damage and/or holes, which could lead to carbon monoxide poisoning.

9) Tiedown, control lock, and wheel chock removal

10) Ice and frost removal

   a) Frost, ice, frozen rain, or snow may accumulate on parked airplanes. All of these must be removed before takeoff.

      i) Ice is removed by parking the airplane in a hangar or spraying deicing compounds on the airplane.

      ii) Frost must be removed from all airfoils before flight. Even small amounts can disrupt the airflow, increase stall speed, and reduce lift.

11) Security of baggage, cargo, and equipment

   a) Secure all baggage, cargo, and equipment during the preflight inspection. Make sure everything is in its place and secure.

      i) You do not want items flying around the cockpit if you encounter turbulence.

      ii) Cargo and baggage should be secured to prevent movement that could damage the airplane and/or cause a shift in the airplane's CG.

      iii) An item of cargo is not more secure because it is heavy; it is more dangerous because it moves with greater force.

2. Inspect your airplane with reference to an appropriate checklist.

a. Each airplane has a specific list of preflight procedures recommended by the airplane manufacturer, which are found in Section 4, Normal Procedures, of your *POH*.

   1) The written checklist is a systematic set of procedures.
   2) Always have your checklist in hand and follow it item by item.

b. Your CFI will instruct you in a systematic method of performing a preflight inspection. This inspection will most likely be more detailed than the checklist in your *POH*.

   1) Always have your checklist in hand to be used as a reference to ensure that all items have been checked. If you become distracted during the preflight inspection, you should use the checklist to determine the last item to be checked.

3. Verify that your airplane is in condition for safe flight.

a. During your preflight inspection of your airplane, you must note any discrepancies and make sound judgments on the airworthiness of your airplane.

   1) As pilot in command, you are responsible for determining that the airplane is airworthy.

   2) If you have any doubt, you should ask someone with more experience and/or knowledge.

   3) Do not attempt a flight unless you are completely satisfied that the airplane is safe and airworthy.

b. After you have completed the preflight inspection, take a step back and look at your entire airplane.

   1) During your inspection, you were looking at individual items for airworthiness. Now you should look at the airplane as a whole and ask, "Is this airplane safe to fly?"

C.   Common Errors during the Preflight Inspection

    1.   Failure to use, or the improper use of, the checklist.

        a.   Checklists are guides for use in ensuring that all necessary items are checked in a logical sequence.

        b.   You must not get the idea that the list is merely a crutch for poor memory.

    2.   Hazards which may result from allowing distractions to interrupt a preflight inspection.

        a.   Distractions could lead to missing items on the checklist or not recognizing a discrepancy.

            1)   You must keep your thoughts on the preflight inspection.

        b.   If you are distracted, either start at the beginning of the preflight inspection or repeat the preceding two or three items.

    3.   Inability to recognize discrepancies.

        a.   You must understand what you are looking at during the preflight inspection.

        b.   Look for smaller items such as missing screws, drips of oil, etc.

    4.   Failure to assure servicing with the proper fuel and oil.

        a.   It is easy to determine whether the correct grade of fuel has been used. Even if you are present during fueling, you should be in the habit of draining a sample of fuel from the airplane to check for the proper grade and for any contamination.

        b.   Oil is not color-coded for identification. You will need to check the proper grade before you or any line personnel add oil to the airplane.

END OF TASK

COCKPIT MANAGEMENT

II.B. TASK: COCKPIT MANAGEMENT

   REFERENCE: FAA-H-8083-3; Pilot's Operating Handbook, FAA-Approved Airplane Flight Manual.

Objective. To determine that the applicant:

1. Exhibits knowledge of the elements related to cockpit management procedures.

2. Ensures all loose items in the cockpit and cabin are secured.

3. Organizes material and equipment in an efficient manner so they are readily available.

4. Briefs occupants on the use of safety belts, shoulder harnesses, doors, and emergency procedures.

A. General Information

   1. The objective of this task is for you to explain and demonstrate efficient procedures for good cockpit management and related safety factors.

     a. This objective includes both maintaining an organized cockpit and understanding the aeronautical decision-making process.

   2. Additional reading: Chapter 6, Aeromedical Factors and Aeronautical Decision Making, of *Pilot Handbook*, see Modules 6.10 through 6.14 for a 12-page discussion of the aeronautical decision-making process and related topics.

B. Task Objectives

   1. Exhibit your knowledge of the elements related to cockpit management procedures.

     a. Cockpit management is more than just maintaining an organized and neat cockpit. Cockpit management is a process that combines you, your airplane, and the environment for safer and more efficient operations.

     b. Some of the elements of cockpit management include

       1) Communication -- the exchange of information with ATC, FSS personnel, maintenance personnel, and other pilots

         a) To be effective, you must develop good speaking and listening skills.

       2) Decision making and problem solving -- the manner in which you respond to problems that you encounter from preflight preparation to your postflight procedures

       3) Situational awareness -- your knowledge of how you, your airplane, and the environment are interacting. This is a continuous process throughout your flight.

         a) As you increase your situational awareness, you will become a safer pilot by being able to identify clues that signify a loss of situational awareness prior to an impending accident or incident.

       4) Standardization -- your use of standardized checklists and procedures

         a) Checklist discipline will help you because you will develop a habit of reading a checklist item and then performing the task.

         b) Procedural learning is learning a standardized procedure pattern while using the checklist as a backup, as you may do in the first few steps of an emergency.

5) Leader/follower. Below are the desirable characteristics of both:

   a) A leader will manage those resources that contribute to a safe flight, e.g. ensuring the proper quantity, grade, and type of fuel.

   b) A good follower will ask for help at the first indication of trouble.

6) Psychological factors -- your attitude, personality, and motivation in the decision-making process

   a) Hazardous attitudes include antiauthoritarian, impulsive, invulnerable, macho, and resigned.

   b) Personality is the way you cope with problems.

   c) Your motivation to achieve a goal can be internal (you are attracted to the goal) or external (an outside force is driving you to perform).

7) Planning ahead -- anticipation of and preparation for future situations

   a) Always think and stay ahead of what needs to be done at any specific time.

   b) Always picture your location and your heading with respect to nearby navigational aids (NAVAIDs), airports, and other geographical fixes.

   c) Confirm your present position and anticipate future positions with as many NAVAIDs as possible; i.e., use them all.

8) Stress management -- the manner in which you manage the stress in your life, which will follow you into the cockpit. Stress is your reaction to a perceived (real or imaginary) threat to your body's equilibrium.

   a) Learn to reduce the stress in your life or to cope with it better.

9) Checklist use

   a) You should use the appropriate checklist for a specific phase of your flight while on the ground or in the air (e.g., before starting engine, during climb, before landing, etc.).

   b) We emphasize the appropriate use of checklists throughout this book.

      i) A checklist provides a listing of "actions" and or "confirmations." For example, you either "turn on the fuel pump" or confirm that the fuel pump is on.

      ii) If the desired condition is not available, you have to decide whether to accept the situation or take action. For example, if your engine oil temperature is indicating a higher-than-normal temperature while en route, you may continue your flight or attempt to divert for a landing, depending upon the level of overheating and relative changes in the temperature.

      iii) Each item on the checklist requires evaluation and possible action:

         • Is the situation safe?

         • If not, what action is required?

         • Is the overall airplane/environment safe when you take all factors into account?

        iv) There are different types of checklists:

- "Read and do," e.g., before-takeoff checklist
- "Do and read," e.g., in reacting to emergencies. Do everything that comes to mind and then confirm or research in your *POH*.

        v) In other words, checklists are not an end in and of themselves. Checklists are a means of flying safely. Generally, they are to be used as specified in the *POH* and to accomplish safe flight.

    c) ALL CHECKLISTS should be read aloud at all times.

        i) Call out each item on the checklist as you undertake the action or make the necessary observation.

    d) When using a prescribed checklist, you must consider proper scanning vigilance and division of attention at all times.

2. Ensure that all loose items in the cockpit and cabin are secured.

    a. Loose objects in the cockpit or cabin are hazards. They may

        1) Distract you from flying the airplane at a critical moment by getting in the way,

        2) Become lodged under a rudder pedal or otherwise prevent you from achieving full control travel, or

        3) Become projectiles in the event of a turbulence encounter or a forced landing.

    b. Any objects that you will need during the flight (e.g., charts, pencils, timer, etc.) should be securely stowed in an accessible location, such as in a seat-back pocket.

        1) All other objects should be placed in the baggage area or another out-of-the-way location.

    c. Seatbelts in all unoccupied seats should be securely fastened in order to avoid entanglement during an evacuation, or possible obstruction of the flight controls.

        1) Securing unused seatbelts is particularly critical in older-style tandem-seat trainers, where an unfastened seatbelt could become wrapped around the control stick and lead to loss of control.

    d. Advise passengers that they should not scatter personal items around the cabin during flight.

        1) While it is acceptable to read a book, listen to a portable CD/cassette player, etc. during the flight, passengers should stow objects that are not in use.

        2) Advise your passengers to put away any personal objects during taxi, takeoff, approach, and landing, and during any encounters with turbulence.

3. Organize material and equipment in an efficient manner so they are readily available.

    a. On every flight, you should be in the habit of organizing and neatly arranging your materials and equipment in an efficient manner that makes them readily available.

    b. Be in the habit of "good housekeeping."

        1) A disorganized cockpit will complicate even the simplest of flights.

    c. Organization will contribute to safe and efficient flying.

4. **Brief your passengers on the use of safety belts, shoulder harnesses, doors, and emergency procedures.**

   a. You are required to brief each passenger on how to fasten and unfasten the safety belt and, if installed, the shoulder harness (FAR 91.107).

      1) You cannot taxi, takeoff, or land before notifying each passenger to fasten his/her safety belt and, if installed, shoulder harness and ensuring that (s)he has done so.

   b. At this time, you need to brief the occupants on the airplane's emergency procedures that are relevant to them.

      1) Inform them of what they should do before and after an off-airport landing.

      2) You can determine if an occupant is competent to assist you in reading an emergency checklist. Assistance would allow you to perform the tasks as they are read item by item.

      3) Ensure that each passenger can open all exit doors and unfasten their safety belts.

   c. Remember, you must brief your examiner on these items as you would any passenger.

C. Common Errors in Cockpit Management

   1. **Failure to place and secure essential materials and equipment for easy access during flight.**

      a. Do not use the top of the instrument panel as a storage area.
      b. Maintain an organized cockpit and stress the safety factors of being organized.

   2. **Failure to brief passengers.**

      a. Always brief your passengers on the use of their safety belts and shoulder harnesses.
      b. Also brief your passengers on emergency procedures.

   3. **Failure to use the appropriate checklist.**

      a. Always use the appropriate checklist for a specific phase of your flight while on the ground or in the air.

END OF TASK

ENGINE STARTING

II.C. TASK: ENGINE STARTING

REFERENCES: FAA-H-8083-3, AC 61-23/FAA-H-8083-25, AC 91-13, AC 91-55; Pilot's Operating Handbook, FAA-Approved Airplane Flight Manual.

Objective. To determine that the applicant:

1. Exhibits knowledge of the elements related to recommended engine starting procedures. This shall include the use of an external power source, hand propping safety, and starting under various atmospheric conditions.

2. Positions the airplane properly considering structures, surface conditions, other aircraft, and the safety of nearby persons and property.

3. Utilizes the appropriate checklist for starting procedure.

A. General Information

    1. The objective of this task is for you to explain and demonstrate correct engine starting procedures.

    2. In Chapter 2, Airplane Instruments, Engines, and Systems, of *Pilot Handbook*, see Module 2.14, Ignition System, for a one-page discussion on hand-propping procedures.

B. Task Objectives

    1. Exhibit your knowledge of the elements related to recommended engine starting procedures, including the use of an external power source, hand propping safety, and starting under various atmospheric conditions.

        a. The correct engine starting procedure for your airplane is explained in your *POH*.

        b. Some airplanes are equipped with an external power receptacle.

            1) This receptacle allows you to connect an external power (battery) to your airplane's electrical system without accessing the battery in the airplane.

            2) You can also use an external battery and connect it to the airplane's battery to provide power to the starter.

            3) Read your *POH* for the correct procedures.

        c. While most airplanes are now equipped with electric starters, it is still helpful to be familiar with the procedures used to start the engine by hand (called "hand propping").

            1) Hand propping should always be done with 2 people, both of whom are thoroughly familiar with the airplane's controls and hand propping techniques.

                a) The person pulling the propeller blades directs all activity and is in charge of the procedure, while the other person must be seated in the airplane with the brakes set.

                b) Hand propping should never be attempted alone.

            2) The ground surface near the propeller should be stable and free of debris.

                a) If the person pulling the propeller blades is unable to get a firm footing, (s)he may slip into the path of the blades after the engine has started.

                b) If a firm footing is not available where the airplane is located, move elsewhere.

3) Both participants should discuss the procedure beforehand and agree on voice commands and the associated actions.

   a) To begin the procedure, the fuel system and engine controls should be positioned for a normal start.

   b) With the magnetos OFF, the person pulling the propeller blades should rotate the propeller until the descending blade is in a position slightly above horizontal.

      i) The person pulling the propeller blades should stand facing the descending blade squarely at slightly less than one arm's length from the blade.

         • Standing too far away would require leaning toward the propeller and would increase the chances of falling forward into the rotating blades after the engine has started.

         • Standing too close increases the chances of being struck by the propeller when the engine has started.

4) The procedure and commands for hand propping are:

   a) **Person pulling the propeller blades**: Says, "GAS ON, SWITCH (i.e., magnetos) OFF, BRAKES SET."

   b) **Person in the pilot seat:** Makes certain that the fuel is on, the mixture is rich, the magentos are off, the throttle is set for engine start, and the brakes are set, and says, "GAS ON, SWITCH OFF, CLOSED THROTTLE, BRAKES SET."

   c) **Person pulling the propeller blades:** Pulls the propeller through several times to prime the engine and says, "BRAKES AND CONTACT (i.e., magnetos on)."

   d) **Person in the pilot seat:** Verifies that the brakes are set, turns the magnetos on, and says "BRAKES AND CONTACT."

   e) **Person pulling the propeller blades:** Swings the blade down rapidly by pushing with the palms of both hands while simultaneously stepping backward away from the propeller.

      i) Do not grip the propeller blade tightly with your fingers or you may be pulled into the blades when the engine starts or injured if the propeller turns backward due to a misfire.

   f) Note that the words "CONTACT" and "SWITCH OFF" sound significantly different from one another and are used to avoid confusion on a noisy ramp.

5) If you are pulling the person pulling the propeller blades, remember that the propeller is essentially invisible once the engine has started. Do not step into the propeller arc as you remove the chocks or walk toward the door.

6) Refer to your airplane's *POH* for specific instructions regarding hand propping procedures.

d.   You must be able to explain engine starting procedures under various atmospheric conditions (i.e., cold or hot weather).

   1)   During cold weather, the oil in your airplane's engine becomes congealed (or thick). There are several methods to assist in starting a cold engine. Check your *POH* for the recommended procedure.

      a)   One method is that the propeller should be pulled through (turned) several times to loosen the oil.

         i)   This saves battery energy, which is already low due to the low temperature.

         ii)   When performing this procedure, ensure that the ignition/magneto switch is off, throttle is closed, mixture is lean/idle cut-off position, nobody is standing in or near the propeller arc, the parking brake is on, and the airplane is chocked and/or tied down.

         iii)   A loose or broken groundwire on either magneto could cause the engine to fire or backfire.

      b)   Cold weather starting can be made easier by preheating the engine.

         i)   Many FBOs in cold weather locations offer this service.

         ii)   Small, portable heaters are available which can blow hot air into the engine to warm it.

         iii)   Preheating the engine is generally required when outside air temperatures are below -18°C (0°F) and is recommended by most engine manufacturers when the temperature is below 7°C (20°F).

      c)   To start a cold engine, prime it with fuel first.

         i)   In carburetor engines, the primer is a small manual or electric pump which draws fuel from the tanks and vaporizes it directly into one or two of the cylinders through small fuel lines.

            •   Continuous priming may be required to keep the engine running until sufficient engine heat is generated to vaporize the fuel.

      d)   After a cold engine has been started, it should be idled at low RPMs for 2 to 5 min. to allow the oil to warm and begin circulating throughout the system.

   2)   During hot weather and/or with a hot engine, the cylinders tend to become overloaded with fuel. This could lead to a flooded engine situation.

      a)   Follow the appropriate checklist for either a HOT or FLOODED engine in your *POH*.

         i)   Flooded engine normally requires you to have the mixture in the lean position and the throttle full open.

            •   This helps clear the cylinders of the excess fuel and allows the engine to start.

         ii)   As the engine starts, ensure that you close the throttle and move the mixture to rich.

e.   Be sure to use the recommended starting procedures.

1)   Use the recommended starting procedures described in Section 4, Normal Procedures, of your airplane's *POH*.

a)   The following are some safety guidelines that may not be in your *POH*.

2)   Set the brakes.

a)   Some airplanes have a parking brake which should be set in the manner prescribed in your *POH*.

b)   In an airplane without a parking brake, you must ensure that your airplane's brakes are set, normally by applying appropriate pressure on the toe (or pedal) brakes.

c)   Before starting the engine, remember to position your airplane to avoid creating a hazard.

i)   If for some reason the brakes are not set properly and your airplane moves forward when the engine is started, you must have an area in which you can stop your airplane by engine shutdown.

3)   Determine that the area around your airplane is clear by observing the area and shouting, "Clear prop!" out your open window, before cranking the engine.

a)   Allow a few seconds for a response if someone is nearby or under the airplane.

4)   Adjust the engine controls.

a)   While activating the starter and during ground operations while the engine is running, you should keep one hand on the throttle at all times.

i)   Keeping a hand on the throttle allows you to advance the throttle if the engine falters during starting or to prevent excessive RPM just after starting.

5)   Prevent airplane movement after engine start.

a)   You must prevent your airplane from moving after you start the engine. This is done with your brakes.

b)   You must look outside your airplane to ensure that you are not moving. Be aware of what is happening around you.

6)   Avoid excessive engine RPM and temperatures.

a)   You must monitor your engine instruments during your ground operations.

i)   Your *POH* will have the recommended RPM and temperature ranges for the warm-up and other ground operations.

b)   Follow the checklist in your *POH* if the engine temperature begins to rise above the normal operating range.

7)   Check the engine instruments after engine start.

a)   As soon as the engine is started and operating, you should check the oil pressure gauge. If it does not rise to the normal operating range in about 30 sec. in summer or 60 sec. in winter, the engine may not be receiving proper lubrication and should be shut down immediately.

b)   Check all other engine instruments to ensure that they are also operating within the normal limits as prescribed in your *POH*.

    f.   Using incorrect starting procedures could be very hazardous. It could also lead to overpriming or priming your engine when it is not necessary.

        1)   Operating your starter motor for long periods of time may cause it to overheat and/or completely drain your battery.

        2)   Follow the recommendations and procedures that are in your *POH*.

2.   Position your airplane properly, considering structures, surface conditions, other aircraft, and the safety of nearby persons and property.

    a.   Always start the engine with enough room in front of the airplane so you can turn off the engine if the brakes fail.

    b.   Also, do not start the engine with the tail of the airplane pointed toward an open hangar door, parked cars, or a group of bystanders (i.e., think about direction of prop blast).

        1)   It is a violation of FAR 91.13 to operate your airplane on any part of the surface of an airport in a careless or reckless manner that endangers the life or property of another.

        2)   Be cautious of loose debris, e.g., rocks or dirt, that can become projectiles when you start the engine.

3.   Utilize the appropriate checklist for the starting procedure.

    a.   It is vital that you make a habit of appropriate use of a checklist for every operation in flying.

        1)   Using a checklist ensures that every item is completed and checked.

    b.   You must use the checklist in your *POH* for the before-starting and the starting procedures.

C.   Common Errors during Engine Start

1.   Failure to use, or the improper use of, the checklist.

    a.   You must be in the habit of properly using the correct checklist for engine starting.
    b.   Using a checklist ensures that every item is completed and checked in a logical order.

2.   Excessively high RPM after starting.

    a.   You should constantly monitor the engine instruments while the engine is operating.

3.   Improper preheat of the engine during severe cold weather conditions.

    a.   Severe cold weather will cause a change in the viscosity of engine oils, batteries may lose a high percentage of their effectiveness, and instruments may stick.

    b.   During preheating operations, do not leave the airplane unattended, and keep a fire extinguisher nearby.

    c.   There is a tendency to overprime, which washes down cylinder walls and may result in scoring of the walls.

    d.   Icing on the spark plug electrodes can short them out. The only remedy is heat.

4.   Failure to ensure proper clearance of the propeller.

    a.   During the preflight inspection, the propeller path should be checked for debris or obstructions, especially on the ground.

    b.   Before starting, ensure that no person or object will be struck by the propeller.

END OF TASK

TAXIING

II.D. TASK: TAXIING

       REFERENCES: FAA-H-8083-3; Pilot's Operating Handbook, FAA-Approved Airplane Flight Manual.

Objective. To determine that the applicant:

1. Exhibits knowledge of the elements related to safe taxi procedures.

2. Performs a brake check immediately after the airplane begins moving.

3. Positions flight controls properly for the existing wind conditions.

4. Controls direction and speed without excessive use of brakes.

5. Complies with airport/taxiway markings, signals, and ATC clearances and instructions.

6. Taxies so as to avoid other aircraft and hazards.

A. General Information

   1.   The objective of this task is to determine your knowledge of safe taxiing procedures.

B. Task Objectives

   1.   Exhibit your knowledge of the elements related to safe taxi procedures.

      a.   Taxiing is the controlled movement of the airplane under its own power while on the ground.

      b.   The brakes are used primarily to stop the airplane at a desired point, to slow the airplane, or to aid in making a sharp controlled turn.

          1)   Whenever used, they must be applied smoothly, evenly, and cautiously.

      c.   More engine power may be required to start moving the airplane forward, or to start or stop a turn, than is required to keep it moving in any given direction. Thus, you may find it necessary to use a large amount of power.

          1)   When used, the throttle should immediately be retarded once the airplane begins moving to prevent accelerating too rapidly.

      d.   Usually when an airplane is operated on a soft or muddy field, the taxi speed or power must be maintained slightly above that required under normal field operations; otherwise, the airplane may come to a stop.

          1)   Full power may be required to get the airplane moving, causing mud or stones to be picked up by the propeller and resulting in damage.

          2)   The use of additional power during taxiing will result in more slipstream acting on the rudder, thus providing better control.

      e.   Taxiing nosewheel airplanes

          1)   Taxiing an airplane equipped with a nosewheel is relatively simple. Nosewheel airplanes generally have better ground handling characteristics (relative to tailwheel airplanes). The nosewheel is usually connected to the rudder pedals by a mechanical linkage.

          2)   When starting to taxi, the airplane should always be allowed to roll forward slowly so the nosewheel turns straight ahead in order to avoid turning into an adjacent airplane or a nearby obstruction.

      3)   All turns conducted with a nosewheel airplane are started using the rudder pedals.

          a)   Power may be applied after entering the turn to counteract the increase in friction during the turn.

          b)   If it is necessary to tighten the turn after full rudder pedal deflection has been reached, the inside brake may be used as needed to aid in turning the airplane.

      4)   When stopping the airplane, you should always stop with the nosewheel straight in order to relieve any strain on the nose gear and to make it easier to start moving again.

          a)   This advice is particularly applicable when you are positioning yourself for the before-takeoff checklist during which you run up (operate at relatively high RPM) the airplane's engine.

2.   Perform a brake check immediately after your airplane begins moving.

    a.   To perform a brake check on your airplane, you need to begin moving your airplane forward by gradually adding power (moving the throttle forward slowly) to increase the engine RPM.

      1)   Reduce the power to idle as soon as your airplane begins rolling, and gently apply the brakes to stop the forward motion of your airplane.

    b.   If there is any question about the operation of the brakes, shut down the engine immediately and have them checked.

3.   Position the flight controls properly for the existing wind conditions.

    a.   The wind is a very important consideration when operating your airplane on the ground. The objective is to keep your airplane firmly on the ground, i.e., not to let the wind blow the airplane around.

      1)   If a wind from the side gets under the wing, it can lift the wing up and even blow the airplane over sideways. A wind from the rear can get under the tail of the airplane and blow the airplane over to the front.

      2)   Caution is recommended. Avoid sudden bursts of power and sudden braking.

    b.   When taxiing in windy conditions, you must position the control surfaces as shown in the following diagram:

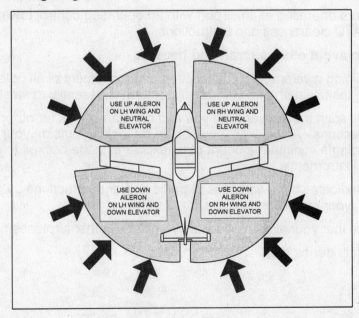

1) When the wind is from any forward direction, the aileron control should be turned or pushed fully toward the wind while keeping the elevator control neutral.

   a) The aileron on the side from which the wind is coming will be up, and the wind flowing over the wing will hold the wing down (rather than lifting the wing, which would permit the wind to get under the wing and possibly blow the airplane over on its back).

   b) The elevators should be in a neutral position, i.e., the control yoke held neither forward nor back, to permit the nosewheel to carry its normal weight and be used for directional control.

2) When the wind is from any rearward direction, the aileron control should be turned or pushed fully away from the wind while the elevator control should be full forward.

   a) The aileron on the side from which the wind is coming will be down, which will help keep the wind from getting under the wing and lifting it.

   b) The elevators should be down, i.e., the control yoke pushed full forward, to deter the wind from getting under the tail, raising the tail, and possibly blowing the airplane over (tail over front).

4. **Control direction and speed without excessive use of brakes.**

   a. There is no set rule for a safe taxiing speed. What is safe under some conditions may be hazardous under others.

      1) The primary requirement is safe, positive control -- the ability to stop or turn where and when desired.

      2) Normally, the speed should be at the rate at which movement of the airplane is dependent on the throttle, that is, slow enough so that when the throttle is closed the airplane can be stopped promptly.

   b. Turning very sharply or attempting to turn at too great a speed must be avoided as both tend to exert excessive pressure on the landing gear, and such turns are difficult to control once started.

5. **Comply with airport/taxiway markings, signals, ATC clearances, and instructions.**

   a. You must comply with airport/taxiway markings and signals.

   b. If you are operating at an airport with an operating control tower, you must comply with ATC clearances and instructions.

6. **Taxi so as to avoid other aircraft and hazards.**

   a. Maintaining awareness of the location and movement of all other aircraft and vehicles along the taxi path and in the traffic pattern is essential to safety.

   b. Visually scan the area around you and constantly look for other traffic and/or obstructions. At this time, you should be looking outside your airplane while spending a minimum amount of time looking in the cockpit to check your engine and flight instruments.

      1) Indicate your awareness of traffic and/or obstructions by pointing them out to your examiner.

   c. Be sure that your airplane's wings will clear all other airplanes or obstructions.

      1) If in doubt, stop.

    d.   Avoid prop washing people, aircraft, or vehicles while taxiing.

        1)   FAR 91.13 prohibits you from operating your airplane in a careless or reckless manner that endangers the life or property of another.

        2)   Be polite when operating around people and/or property.

    e.   Monitor the appropriate radio frequency for traffic and possible conflicts.

    f.   You must apply right-of-way rules and maintain adequate spacing behind other aircraft.

        1)   Generally, the right-of-way rules apply as they do while in the air; i.e., approaching head-on, alter course to the right; yield to an airplane on the right.

            a)   Ground control (at an airport with an operating control tower) may instruct one aircraft to stop or yield to another.

            b)   If in doubt, always yield to other aircraft. Be safe.

        2)   Avoid being too close to another airplane's prop or jet wash, which could cause you to lose control of your airplane. Maintain a safe separation.

C. Common Errors during Taxiing

  1. Improper use of brakes.

    a.   The most common error is the tendency to ride the brakes while taxiing.

        1)   Correct this by using the throttle to slow the airplane down, and use the brakes to completely stop the airplane.

  2. Improper positioning of flight controls for various wind conditions.

    a.   Always know the direction of the wind in relation to the airplane. Use all available means to determine direction, such as wind sock and/or ground control.

    b.   Picture the wind relative to your airplane at any given time by means of the heading indicator.

        1)   EXAMPLE: If the airplane is heading 090° and the wind is from 240°, you can use the heading indicator to determine that the wind is a right-quartering tailwind.

  3. Hazards of taxiing too fast.

    a.   This error occurs when you use the throttle improperly and sometimes when you feel rushed to get to the run-up area.

    b.   Taxi slowly in the ramp area and at a speed at which you can stop or turn where and when you desire.

        1)   Normally the speed should be such that, when the throttle is closed, the airplane can be stopped promptly.

  4. Failure to comply with markings, signals, or clearances.

    a.   Before starting to taxi at an airport with an operating control tower, ask yourself if the taxi instructions make sense and if you understand the clearance.

        1)   Contact ground control for clarification.

    b.   While taxiing, identify markings and signals to your examiner.

END OF TASK

BEFORE-TAKEOFF CHECK

II.F. TASK: BEFORE TAKEOFF CHECK

REFERENCES: FAA-H-8083-3; Pilot's Operating Handbook, FAA-Approved Airplane Flight Manual.

Objective. To determine that the applicant:

1. Exhibits knowledge of the elements related to the before takeoff check. This shall include the reasons for checking each item and how to detect malfunctions.
2. Positions the airplane properly considering other aircraft, wind and surface conditions.
3. Divides attention inside and outside of the cockpit.
4. Ensures the engine temperatures and pressure are suitable for run-up and takeoff.
5. Accomplishes the before takeoff checklist and ensures the airplane is in safe operating condition.
6. Reviews takeoff performance airspeeds, takeoff distances, departure and emergency procedures.
7. Avoids runway incursion and/or ensures no conflict with traffic prior to taxiing into takeoff position.

A. General Information

  1. The objective of this task is to determine your ability to perform the before-takeoff check.

B. Task Objectives

  1. **Exhibit your knowledge of the elements related to the before-takeoff check, including the reasons for checking each item and how to detect malfunctions.**

     a. The before-takeoff check is the systematic procedure for making a last-minute check of the engine, controls, systems, instruments, and radio prior to flight.

        1) Normally, it is performed after taxiing to a position near the takeoff end of the runway.

        2) Taxiing to that position usually allows sufficient time for the engine to warm up to at least minimum operating temperatures and ensures adequate lubrication of the internal moving parts of the engine before operating the engine at high power settings.

     b. Your *POH* will explain the proper operating limitations while you are performing your before-takeoff check.

        1) Any deviation from these normal operating limits means that there is a possible malfunction, and you should return to the ramp to determine the cause.

  2. **Position your airplane properly considering other aircraft and wind and surface conditions.**

     a. As you taxi to the active runway, turn your airplane somewhat diagonally to the taxiway or run-up area so you will not prop blast any aircraft behind you.

     b. The FAA recommends that you position your airplane into the wind, as nearly as possible, to obtain more accurate operating indications and to minimize engine overheating when the engine is run up.

     c. You should position your airplane on a firm surface (smooth turf or paved surface) that is free of debris.

        1) Otherwise, the propeller will pick up pebbles, dirt, mud, sand, or other loose particles and hurl them backward, not only damaging the tail of the airplane, but often inflicting damage to the propeller itself.

      d.   Straighten your nosewheel before stopping, as your magneto check requires an engine run-up which puts considerable stress on your nosewheel (which is better absorbed with the nosewheel straight).

3.   Divide your attention inside and outside of the cockpit, especially during the engine run-up.

      a.   If the parking brake slips, or if the application of the toe brakes is inadequate for the amount of power applied, the airplane could move forward unnoticed if your attention is fixed inside the airplane.

4.   Ensure that your airplane's engine temperatures and pressure are suitable for run-up and takeoff.

      a.   Most of the engine warm-up will have been conducted during taxi.

      b.   Any additional warm-up should be restricted to the before-takeoff check.

           1)   The takeoff can be made when the throttle can be advanced to full power without the engine faltering.

5.   Accomplish the before-takeoff checklist and confirm that your airplane is in safe operating condition.

      a.   You, as the pilot in command, are responsible for determining whether your airplane is in condition for safe flight (FAR 91.7). Remember that everything on your checklist is very important to ensure that your airplane is safe for flight.

      b.   Stop at each discrepancy and note its effect(s). How is any problem covered by another instrument, piece of equipment, pilot workload, etc.? Relate problems to FARs.

      c.   Exercise sound judgment in determining that your airplane is safe for flight.

           1)   If you have any doubts, explain them to your examiner and return to the ramp for further investigation.

6.   Review takeoff performance airspeeds, takeoff distances, and departure and emergency procedures.

      a.   Review the V_R, V_X, V_Y, and other takeoff performance airspeeds for your airplane.

           1)   As you reach these airspeeds, plan to call them out loud.

      b.   From your preflight planning, you have already determined the expected takeoff distance for the conditions. Review this performance data.

      c.   You should review your departure procedure before you depart the run-up area.

           1)   Know your initial direction of flight after takeoff.

           2)   At an airport with an operatng control tower, ATC will issue you a clearance on how to depart the traffic pattern.

           3)   At an airport without an operating control tower, you should depart the traffic pattern by continuing straight out or exiting with a 45° left turn (right turn if the runway has a right-hand traffic pattern) beyond the departure end of the runway, after reaching traffic pattern altitude.

d.   Takeoff emergency procedures are set forth in Section 3, Emergency Procedures, of your *POH*. Prepare ahead for all contingencies. Be prepared at all times to execute an emergency landing if you lose an engine. Remember, **maintain airspeed** so you control your situation rather than enter a stall/spin.

   1)   The most common emergency on takeoff is the loss of engine power during the takeoff roll or during the takeoff climb.

   a)   If engine power is lost during the takeoff roll, pull the throttle to idle, apply the brakes, and slow the airplane to a stop.

   b)   If you are just lifting off the runway and you lose your engine power, try to land the airplane on the remaining runway. Leave it in the flare attitude which it is already in. It will settle back down to the ground; i.e., land it like a normal landing.

   i)   It is very important not to lower the nose because you do not want to come down on the nosewheel.

   c)   If engine power is lost anytime during the climbout, a general rule is that, if the airplane is above 500 to 1,000 ft. AGL, you may have enough altitude to turn back and land on the runway from which you have just taken off. This decision must be based on distance from airport, wind condition, obstacles, etc.

   i)   Watch your airspeed! Avoiding a stall is the most important consideration. Remember that the control yoke should be forward (nose down) for more airspeed.

   d)   If the airplane is below 500 ft. AGL, do not try to turn back. If you turn back, you will probably either stall or hit the ground before you get back to the runway.

   i)   The best thing to do is to land the airplane straight ahead. Land in a clear area, if possible.

   ii)   If you have no option but to go into trees, slow the airplane to just above the stall speed (as close to the treetops as possible) to strike the trees with the slowest forward speed possible.

7.   **Avoid runway incursion and/or ensure that there is no conflict with traffic prior to taxiing into the takeoff position.**

   a.   Prior to taxiing onto the runway, you must make certain that the takeoff area and path are clear of other aircraft, vehicles, persons, livestock, wildlife (including birds), etc.

   1)   In addition, you must be certain that you have received an appropriate ATC clearance before crossing the hold short lines at an airport with an operating control tower.

   b.   At an airport with an operating control tower, ensuring that the takeoff area is clear is primarily a function of ATC, but you must also check for conflicts with other aircraft or other hazards.

   c.   At an airport without an operating control tower, you should announce your intentions on the appropriate common traffic advisory frequency (CTAF), and if possible, make a 360° turn on the taxiway in the direction of the runway traffic pattern to look for other aircraft.

8.   **Complete the appropriate checklist.**

   a.   Follow the prescribed (ground check and/or before-takeoff) checklists in your *POH*.

   1)   You must follow the checklist item by item.

C. Common Errors during the Before-Takeoff Check

1. **Failure to use, or the improper use of, the checklist.**

    a. You must be in the habit of properly using the appropriate checklist.
    b. Using a checklist ensures that every item is completed and checked in a logical order.

2. **Improper positioning of the airplane.**

    a. Position your airplane so you will not prop blast any airplanes behind you.

    b. The FAA recommends that the airplane be positioned into the wind as nearly as possible.

    c. The airplane should be on a surface that is firm and free of debris.

3. **Acceptance of marginal engine performance.**

    a. You may feel that you have to complete this flight at this time and thus must accept marginal engine performance.

        1) Marginal engine performance is not acceptable and may lead to a hazardous condition.

4. **Improper check of flight controls.**

    a. The flight controls should be visually checked for proper positioning and movement.
    b. The control yoke should move freely in the full range of positions.
    c. Call aloud the proper position and visually check it.

5. **Hazards of failure to review takeoff and emergency procedures.**

    a. Before taxiing onto the runway, review the critical airspeeds used for takeoff, the takeoff distance required, and takeoff emergency procedures.

    b. You will then be thinking about this review during the takeoff roll. It helps prepare you for any type of emergency that may occur.

6. **Failure to check for hazards and other traffic.**

    a. You, the pilot in command, are responsible for collision avoidance.

        1) ATC is not responsible but works with pilots to maintain separation.

    b. Other airplanes are not the only hazards for which you must look. Vehicles, persons, and livestock could be in a hazardous position during the takeoff.

END OF TASK -- END OF CHAPTER

CHAPTER III
AIRPORT OPERATIONS

This chapter explains the three tasks (A-C) of Airport Operations. These tasks include both knowledge and skill. Your examiner is required to test you on all three tasks.

RADIO COMMUNICATIONS AND ATC LIGHT SIGNALS

III.A. TASK: RADIO COMMUNICATIONS AND ATC LIGHT SIGNALS

REFERENCES: 14 CFR Part 91; AC 61-23/FAA-H-8083-25; AIM.

Objective. To determine that the applicant:

1. Exhibits knowledge of the elements related to radio communications and ATC light signals.

2. Selects appropriate frequencies.

3. Transmits using recommended phraseology.

4. Acknowledges radio communications and complies with instructions.

A. General Information

1. The objective of this task is for you to demonstrate your knowledge of radio communication procedures and radio communication failure procedures including ATC light signals.

2. Additional reading: See Chapter 3, Airports, Air Traffic Control, and Airspace, in *Pilot Handbook,* for a nine-page discussion on radio phraseology and communications at airports with, and without, operating control towers.

B. Task Objectives

1. **Exhibit your knowledge of the elements related to radio communications and ATC light signals.**

   a. During your flight training, your CFI will work with you to improve your communication procedures at airports with, and without, operating control towers, including what to do if you experience a radio failure.

   b. This task allows your examiner to evaluate your radio communication skills that you have been developing since you were a student pilot.

c. Remember that ATC light signals have the meaning shown in the following table:

Light Signal	On the Ground	In the Air
Steady Green	Cleared for takeoff	Cleared to land
Flashing Green	Cleared to taxi	Return for landing *(to be followed by steady green at proper time)*
Steady Red	Stop	Give way to other aircraft and continue circling
Flashing Red	Taxi clear of landing area (runway) in use	Airport unsafe -- Do not land
Flashing White	Return to starting point on airport	Not applicable
Alternating Red and Green	General warning signal -- Exercise extreme caution	General warning signal -- Exercise extreme caution

2. Select the appropriate frequencies.

a. You should make your radio technique as professional as possible. Selecting the appropriate frequency is obviously essential.

b. Your preflight planning should include looking up the frequencies of all facilities that you might use and/or need during your flight.

1) This information can be obtained from a current *A/FD*, sectional charts, etc.

2) Write this information on your navigation log, or organize it so you can locate it easily in the cockpit.

c. You may still have to look up frequencies while you are flying.

d. Always plan ahead as to frequencies needed.

1) Listen to hand-offs by your controller to airplanes ahead of you.
2) Look up frequencies before you need them.

3. Transmit using the recommended phraseology.

a. Radio communication is a very important task of flying, especially when you are working with ATC. The single most important concept in radio communication is understanding.

1) Using standard phraseology enhances safety and is a mark of professionalism in a pilot.

a) Jargon, chatter, and "CB" slang have no place in aviation radio communications.

b. In virtually all situations, radio broadcasts can be thought of as

1) Whom you are calling
2) Who you are
3) Where you are
4) What you want to do

4. **Acknowledge radio communications and comply with instructions.**

   a. Make sure your radios, speakers, and/or headset are in good working order so you can plainly hear radio communications. Acknowledge all ATC clearances by repeating key points; e.g., "Taxi to (or across) Runway 10," "Position and hold," "Clear for takeoff Runway 24," or "Left downwind 6," followed by your call sign.

      1) Always repeat altitudes and headings.

      2) Do not hesitate with "Say again" if your clearance was blocked or you did not hear or understand it.

      3) As appropriate, ask for amplification or clarification; e.g., ask for **progressives** if you need taxi instructions.

   b. FAR 91.123 states that once you, as pilot in command, obtain a clearance from ATC you may not deviate from that clearance, except in an emergency.

      1) You have the responsibility for the safe operation of your airplane.

      2) If you cannot accept a clearance from ATC (e.g., flying into clouds), inform ATC of the reason you cannot accept and obtain a new clearance.

   c. FAR 91.3 states that you, the pilot in command, are directly responsible for, and the final authority as to, the operation of your airplane.

      1) As a safe and competent pilot, you should obtain clarification on any clearance that you do not understand or that you feel would put you in a bad situation.

C. Common Errors with Radio Communications and ATC Light Signals

   1. **Use of improper frequencies.**

      a. This error is caused by inadequate planning, misreading the frequency on the chart or navigation log, or mistuning the frequency on the radio.

      b. Double-check and read aloud the frequency numbers that are to be set in the radio.

         1) Monitor the frequency before transmitting. Often you can confirm the correct frequency by listening to other transmissions.

   2. **Improper procedure and phraseology when using radio voice communications.**

      a. Think about what you are going to say before you transmit.

      b. Be sensitive to the controller's workload and tailor your broadcasts to match. Often pilots are taught correct phraseology only and never taught how to abbreviate transmissions on busy ATC frequencies.

   3. **Failure to acknowledge, or properly comply with, ATC clearances and other instructions.**

      a. This error normally occurs because you did not hear or understand the message.

      b. Developing your ability to properly divide your attention will help you not to miss ATC messages.

      c. Ask ATC to repeat its message or ask for clarification. Do not assume what ATC meant or instructed.

   4. **Failure to understand, or properly comply with, ATC light signals.**

      a. Periodically review the different light gun signals and their meanings.

      b. If you operate where you can ask ground control to direct some practice light signals toward you, the practice will help you learn the signals.

      c. Reviewing and practicing will help you understand and comply with ATC light signals.

END OF TASK

TRAFFIC PATTERNS

III.B. TASK: TRAFFIC PATTERNS

REFERENCES: FAA-H-8083-3, AC 61-23/FAA-H-8083-25, AC 90-66; AIM.

Objective. To determine that the applicant:

1. Exhibits knowledge of the elements related to traffic patterns. This shall include procedures at airports with and without operating control towers, prevention of runway incursions, collision avoidance, wake turbulence avoidance, and wind shear.

2. Complies with proper traffic pattern procedures.

3. Maintains proper spacing from other aircraft.

4. Corrects for wind-drift to maintain proper ground track.

5. Maintains orientation with runway/landing area in use.

6. Maintains traffic pattern altitude ±100 ft. (30 meters), and appropriate airspeed ±10 kt.

A. General Information

    1.   The objective of this task is for you to demonstrate your knowledge and skill in traffic pattern operations.

    2.   Additional reading: See Chapter 3, Airports, Air Traffic Control, and Airspace, in *Pilot Handbook* for the following:

        a.   A seven-page discussion on wake turbulence
        b.   A two-page discussion on collision avoidance

    3.   Safety first! Commit to it and practice it. Always look for traffic and talk about it (even when you are solo). Ask your examiner to watch for traffic.

B. Task Objectives

    1.   Exhibit your knowledge of the elements related to traffic patterns, including procedures at airports with and without operating control towers, prevention of runway incursions, collision avoidance, wake turbulence avoidance, and wind shear.

        a.   Runway incursion is a concern at airports with parallel or intersecting runways in use.

            1)   Runway incursion avoidance is accomplished by flying the correct traffic pattern for the runway you are to use.

            2)   Confirm runway number with heading indicator during all traffic pattern legs.

        b.   Scanning the sky for other aircraft is a key factor in collision avoidance. You and your copilot (or right-seat passenger), if there is one, should scan continuously to cover all areas of the sky visible from the cockpit.

            1)   Effective scanning is accomplished with a series of short, regularly spaced eye movements that bring successive areas of the sky into the central visual field.

                a)   Each eye movement should not exceed 10°.
                b)   Each area should be observed for at least 1 sec. to enable detection.

            2)   Visual tasks inside the cabin should represent no more than 1/4 to 1/3 of the scan time outside or no more than 4 to 5 sec. on the instrument panel for every 16 sec. outside.

                a)   You must realize that your eyes may require several seconds to refocus when switching your view from items in the cockpit to distant objects.

3) Effective scanning also helps avoid "empty-field myopia."

    a) When flying above the clouds or in a haze layer that provides nothing specific to focus on outside the aircraft, the eyes tend to relax and seek a comfortable focal distance which may range from 10 to 30 ft.

    b) For you, this means looking without seeing, which is dangerous.

c. Judgment aspects of collision avoidance.

1) Determining relative altitude -- Use the horizon as a reference point. If you see another aircraft above the horizon, it is probably on a higher flight path. If it appears to be below the horizon, it is probably flying at a lower altitude.

2) Taking appropriate action -- You must be familiar with the rules of right-of-way so that, if an aircraft is on an obvious collision course, you can take the appropriate evasive action.

3) Considering multiple threats -- The decision to climb, descend, or turn is a matter of personal judgment, but you should anticipate that the other pilot may also be making a quick maneuver. Watch the other aircraft during the maneuver, but begin your scanning again immediately. There may be even more aircraft in the area!

4) Improving windshield conditions -- Dirty or bug-smeared windshields can greatly reduce your ability to see other aircraft. Keep a clean windshield.

5) Considering visibility conditions -- Smoke, haze, dust, rain, and flying toward the sun can also greatly reduce the ability to detect other aircraft.

6) Being aware of visual obstructions in the cockpit

    a) You may need to move your head to see around blind spots caused by fixed aircraft structures, such as door posts, wings, etc. It may even be necessary occasionally to maneuver your airplane (e.g., lift a wing) to facilitate seeing.

    b) Check that curtains and other cockpit objects (e.g., maps that glare on the windshield) are removed and stowed during flight.

7) Using lights

    a) Day or night, exterior lights can greatly increase the visibility of any aircraft.

    b) Keep interior lights low at night so that you can see out in the dark.

d. The following wake turbulence avoidance procedures are recommended:

1) Landing behind a larger aircraft which is landing on the same runway -- Stay at or above the larger aircraft's final approach flight path. Note the aircraft's touchdown point and land beyond it.

2) Landing behind a larger aircraft which is landing on a parallel runway closer than 2,500 ft. to your runway -- Consider possible vortex drift to your runway. Stay at or above the larger aircraft's final approach path and note its touchdown point.

3) Landing behind a larger aircraft which is landing on a crossing runway -- Cross above the larger aircraft's flight path.

4) Landing behind a larger aircraft departing on the same runway -- Note the larger aircraft's rotation point. Land well prior to the rotation point.

5) Landing behind a larger aircraft departing on a crossing runway -- Note the larger aircraft's rotation point.

   a) If it rotates past the intersection, continue your approach and land prior to the intersection.

   b) If the larger aircraft rotates prior to the intersection, avoid flight below the larger aircraft's flight path.

      i) Abandon the approach unless your landing is assured well before reaching the intersection.

6) Departing behind a larger aircraft taking off -- Note the larger aircraft's rotation point. You should rotate prior to the larger aircraft's rotation point. Continue to climb above and stay upwind of the larger aircraft's climb path until turning clear of its wake.

   a) Avoid subsequent headings that will cross below and behind a larger aircraft.

   b) Be alert for any critical takeoff situation that could lead to a vortex encounter.

7) Intersection takeoffs on the same runway -- Be alert to adjacent larger aircraft operations, particularly upwind of your runway. If intersection takeoff clearance is received, avoid a subsequent heading which will cross below a larger aircraft's path.

8) Departing or landing after a larger aircraft has executed a low approach, a missed approach, or a touch-and-go landing -- Because vortices settle and move laterally near the ground, the vortex hazard may exist along the runway and in your flight path.

   a) Ensure that an interval of at least 2 min. has elapsed before your takeoff or landing.

e. Wind shear is the abrupt change in wind direction and/or wind speed. During an approach, it can cause severe turbulence and a possible decrease in your airspeed (when a headwind changes to a tailwind), causing your airplane to stall (and possibly crash).

   1) The best method of dealing with wind shear is avoidance. You should never conduct traffic pattern operations in close proximity to an active thunderstorm. Thunderstorms provide visible signs of possible wind-shear activity.

   2) Many large airports now have some type of wind-shear alert/detection system. By measuring differences in wind speed and/or direction at various points on the airport, or by use of Doppler radar, the controller will be able to warn arriving and departing aircraft of the possibility of wind shear.

      a) An example of a low-level wind-shear alert:

         "Delta One Twenty Four - center field wind two seven zero at one zero - south boundary wind one four zero at three zero."

      b) Elsewhere, pilot reports from airplanes preceding you on the approach can be very informational.

   3) If you are conducting an approach with possible wind shear or a thunderstorm nearby, you should consider

      a) Using more power during the approach

      b) Flying the approach at a faster airspeed (general rule: adding ½ the gust factor to your airspeed)

c)   Staying as high as feasible on the approach until it is necessary to descend for a safe landing

d)   Initiating a go-around at the first sign of a change in airspeed or an unexpected pitch change. The most important factor is to go to full power and get the airplane climbing.

i)   Many accidents caused by wind shear are due to a severe down-draft (or a rapid change from headwind to tailwind), punching the aircraft into the ground. In extreme cases, even the power of an airliner is unable to counteract the descent.

2. Comply with proper traffic pattern procedures.

a.   Established airport traffic patterns assure that air traffic flows into and out of an airport in an orderly manner. You should use the basic rectangular airport traffic pattern at the recommended altitude unless modified by air traffic control (ATC) or by approved visual markings at the airport.

1)   The basic traffic pattern altitude is usually 1,000 ft. above the elevation of the airport, unless otherwise specified in the *Airport/Facility Directory*. Using a common altitude is the key to minimizing collision risk.

2)   At all airports, the direction of traffic flow is to the left, unless right turns are indicated by

a)   Visual markings (i.e., traffic pattern indicators) at an airport without an operating control tower

b)   Control tower instructions

b.   The basic traffic pattern

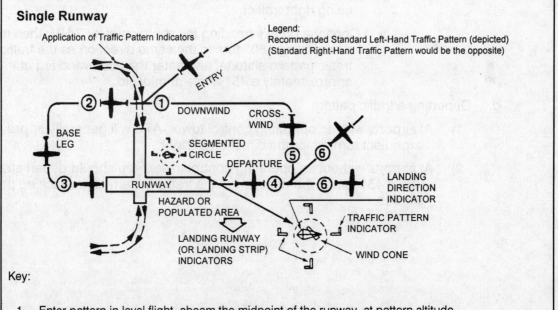

Single Runway

Application of Traffic Pattern Indicators

Legend:
Recommended Standard Left-Hand Traffic Pattern (depicted)
(Standard Right-Hand Traffic Pattern would be the opposite)

Key:

1.   Enter pattern in level flight, abeam the midpoint of the runway, at pattern altitude.
2.   Maintain pattern altitude until abeam approach end of the landing runway on the downwind leg.
3.   Complete turn to final at least ¼ mi. from the runway.
4.   Continue straight ahead until beyond departure end of runway.
5.   If remaining in the traffic pattern, commence turn to crosswind leg beyond the departure end of the runway, within 300 ft. of pattern altitude.
6.   If departing the traffic pattern, continue straight out, or exit with a 45° left turn (right turn for right traffic pattern) beyond the departure end of the runway, after reaching pattern altitude.

c.   Entering a traffic pattern

1)   At an airport with an operating control tower, the controller will direct when and where you should enter the traffic pattern.

2)   To enter the traffic pattern at an airport without an operating control tower, inbound pilots are expected to observe other aircraft already in the pattern and to conform to the traffic pattern in use.

a)   If no other aircraft are in the pattern, traffic and wind indicators on the ground must be checked to determine which runway and traffic pattern direction should be used.

i)   Overfly the airport at least 500 to 1,000 ft. above the traffic pattern altitude.

ii)   After the proper traffic pattern direction has been determined, you should proceed to a point well clear of the pattern before descending to the pattern altitude.

b)   When approaching an airport for landing, you should enter the traffic pattern at a 45° angle to the downwind leg at the midpoint of the runway.

i)   You should always be at the proper traffic pattern altitude before entering the pattern.

c)   One method to enter the traffic pattern at an airport without an operating control tower is to fly in the landing direction parallel to, and slightly to one side of, the runway.

i)   Once you are about 15 sec. past the departure end of the runway, turn 45° in the same direction as the traffic pattern direction (i.e., turn left if the runway is using left traffic; turn right if the runway is using right traffic).

ii)   Continue on this heading for approximately 2 NM; then make a descending 180° turn in the same direction as the traffic pattern, to traffic pattern altitude, and enter the downwind leg at approximately a 45° angle at midfield.

d.   Departing a traffic pattern

1)   At airports with an operating control tower, ATC will generally approve the most expedient turnout for the direction of flight.

2)   At airports without an operating control tower, you should depart straight out or with a 45° turn in the direction of the traffic pattern after reaching pattern altitude.

3. **Maintain proper spacing from other aircraft.**

    a.   As you fly in the traffic pattern, you must observe other traffic and maintain separation, especially when smaller airplanes may have relatively slower approach speeds than your airplane.

        1)   Faster aircraft typically fly a wider pattern than slower aircraft.

    b.   At an airport with an operating control tower, the controller may instruct you to adjust your traffic pattern to provide separation.

    c.   Remember, whether you are at an airport with or without an operating control tower, you are responsible for seeing and avoiding other aircraft.

4. **Correct for wind drift to maintain the proper ground track.**

    a.   This is a procedure that you have been developing since you flew your first rectangular course.

        1)   Ensure that you fly a good rectangular pattern.

    b.   It is important for you to know the wind direction when landing or taking off at an airport.

        1)   At an airport with an operating control tower, ATC provides this information.

            a)   At an airport with a Flight Service Station (FSS) and without an operating control tower, the FSS can provide you with the wind information.

        2)   At an airport without an operating control tower, you may be able to receive wind information from an FBO at the airport.

        3)   You may also be able to obtain wind information from automated weather stations located at some airports.

    c.   Virtually all airports have a wind indicator of one of the following types:

        1)   Wind socks (or cones) are fabric "socks" through which wind blows.

            a)   The large end of the wind sock points into the wind; thus the wind blows through the sock from the large end to the small end.

        2)   Wind (landing) tees have the stem (bottom) of the "T" pointing in the direction the wind is GOING (indicating that landings should be in the opposite direction). Think of the wind tee as a small airplane (with the wings represented by the crossbar or top of the "T") landing into the wind.

            a)   The landing tee indicates the direction of the wind but not the wind velocity.

        3)   Tetrahedrons point to the direction from which the wind is COMING (indicating that landings should be in that direction).

            a)   A tetrahedron will indicate the direction of the wind but not the wind velocity.

    d.   The segmented circle system, if installed, provides traffic pattern information at airports without operating control towers. It consists of the following:

        1)   The **segmented circle** is located in a position affording maximum visibility to pilots in the air and on the ground. A wind and/or landing direction indicator is usually in the center.

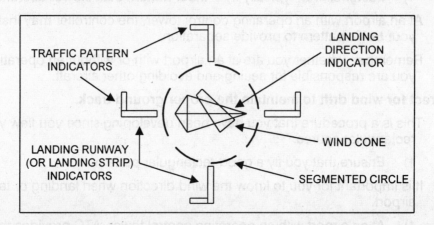

        2)   **Landing runway (strip) indicators** are installed in pairs as shown in the segmented circle above and are used to show the alignment of runways.

        3)   **Traffic pattern indicators** are arranged in pairs with the landing runway indicators and are used to indicate the direction of turns when there is a variation from the normal left traffic pattern.

           a)   If the airport has no segmented circle, traffic pattern indicators may be installed on or near the runway ends.

5.   Maintain orientation with the runway/landing area in use.

    a.   While conducting airport traffic pattern operations, you must remain oriented with the runway in use.

    b.   Know which runway is in use, and plan to enter properly and remain in the correct traffic pattern.

    c.   When approaching an airport, you should visualize your position from the airport and the relative direction of the runway. Use the airplane's heading indicator to assist you.

6.   *Maintain the traffic pattern altitude, ±100 ft., and the appropriate airspeed, ±10 kt.*

    a.   You must maintain the traffic pattern altitude until you are abeam the touchdown point on the downwind leg.

    b.   Maintain the proper airspeed for the portion of the traffic pattern prescribed in your *POH*.

        1)   If ATC requests that you maintain a specified airspeed, and if you determine it is safe for your operation, then maintain that airspeed.

C.   Common Errors during Traffic Patterns

    1.   Failure to comply with traffic pattern instructions, procedures, and rules.

        a.   Your noncompliance with ATC instructions may be caused by not understanding or hearing radio communications.

            1)   You must learn to divide your attention while in the traffic pattern among flying, collision avoidance, checklists, and radio communications.

    2.   Improper correction for wind drift.

        a.   Remember that a traffic pattern is no more than a rectangular course and should be performed in the same manner.

    3.   Inadequate spacing from other traffic.

        a.   This error occurs when you turn onto a traffic pattern leg too soon or you are flying an airplane that is faster than the one you are following.

            1)   Fly a slightly larger pattern when slower aircraft are present.

    4.   Poor altitude or airspeed control.

        a.   Know the airspeeds at various points in the traffic pattern.
        b.   Check the airplane and engine instruments.

END OF TASK

AIRPORT, RUNWAY, AND TAXIWAY SIGNS, MARKINGS, AND LIGHTING

III.C. TASK: AIRPORT, RUNWAY, AND TAXIWAY SIGNS, MARKINGS, AND LIGHTING

      REFERENCES: AC 61-23/FAA-H-8083-25; AIM.

Objective. To determine that the applicant:

1. Exhibits knowledge of the elements related to airport, runway, and taxiway operations with emphasis on runway incursion avoidance.	2. Properly identifies and interprets airport, runway, and taxiway signs, markings, and lighting.

A. General Information

    1. The objective of this task is for you to demonstrate your knowledge of airport and runway markings and lighting.

    2. Additional reading: See Chapter 3, Airports, Air Traffic Control, and Airspace, in *Pilot Handbook* for a sixteen-page discussion of airport taxiway markings, signs, and lights.

B. Task Objectives

    1. Exhibit your knowledge of the elements related to airport, runway, and taxiway operations, with emphasis on runway incursion avoidance.

        a. Surface operations are a critical phase of any flight. Do not allow yourself to become complacent during taxi operations just because the airplane is "safely on the ground."

            1) Give your examiner confidence in your abilities by exercising due caution during taxi operations.

                a) Do not taxi too fast for the conditions (i.e., a speed that might be appropriate for a wide, straight taxiway would be too fast for a crowded ramp).

                b) Make all turns at a reasonable speed.

                    i) Apply braking while moving straight ahead in order to reach the desired speed before entering the turn.

                c) Take precautions to avoid experiencing a runway incursion.

        b. The FAA defines a **runway incursion** as any occurrence at an airport involving an aircraft, vehicle, person, or object on the ground that creates a collision hazard or results in a loss of separation with an aircraft taking off, intending to take off, landing, or intending to land. Some examples of runway incursions are:

            1) At an airport without an operating control tower, a departing aircraft may taxi into position for takeoff without first checking for landing traffic. If an aircraft is on short final when this happens, a go-around will be necessary, or a collision could result.

            2) While taxiing at an airport with a complex taxiway layout, a pilot may become confused as to his/her location and inadvertently cross or turn onto a runway that is being used by another aircraft. Depending on the timing of the incursion, the other aircraft may have to abort a takeoff or perform a go-around. Unfortunately, a collision may result.

3) At an airport with an operating control tower, a pilot may misunderstand a clearance (or fail to obtain the correct clearance due to inattention) and cross a runway of which (s)he was instructed to hold short. The pilot could also turn onto the wrong runway when cleared for takeoff. Any aircraft using these runways may have to abort a takeoff or perform a go-around. Again, a collision may be unavoidable.

c. Runway incursions that are most likely to cause accidents are common at high-volume airports with complex taxiway layouts and multiple parallel or intersecting runways.

　　1) The vast majority are caused by general aviation pilots who are confused/disoriented, do not understand a controller's instructions, or are not paying attention to their surroundings.

　　2) The likelihood of an accident increases when the visibility is low.

d. The following practices will help you to avoid a runway incursion incident:

　　1) Read back all runway crossing and/or hold short instructions.

　　2) Review airport layouts as part of preflight planning, before descending to land, and while taxiing as needed.

　　3) Know airport signage.

　　4) Review Notices to Airmen (NOTAMs) for information on runway/taxiway closures and construction areas.

　　5) Do not hesitate to request progressive taxi instructions from ATC when you are unsure of the taxi route.

　　6) Check for traffic before crossing any runway or entering a taxiway.

　　7) Turn on your aircraft's lights and rotating beacon or strobe lights while taxiing.

　　8) When landing, clear the active runway as quickly as possible; then wait for taxi instructions before further movement.

　　9) Study and use proper radio phraseology as described in the *Aeronautical Information Manual*, Chapter 4, or Gleim's **Pilot Handbook,** Chapter 3, in order to respond to and understand ground control instructions.

　　10) Write down complex taxi instructions at unfamiliar airports.

2. **Properly identify and interpret airport, runway, and taxiway signs, markings, and lighting.**

a. You need to be able to identify and interpret the various runway and taxiway markings and airport lighting since you may be flying in and out of various airports.

b. Airport pavement markings and signs provide information that is useful to you during takeoff, landing, and taxiing.

　　1) Markings for runways are white.

　　2) Markings for taxiways, closed areas, hazardous areas, and holding positions (even if they are on a runway) are yellow.

c. Runway markings

　　1) **Designation marking**. Runway numbers and letters are determined from the approach direction. The runway number is the whole number nearest one-tenth the magnetic direction of the runway. Letters differentiate between left (L), right (R), or center (C) parallel runways, if applicable.

　　　　a) For two parallel runways -- "L," "R"

　　　　b) For three parallel runways -- "L," "C," "R"

2) **Centerline marking**. The runway centerline identifies the center of the runway and provides alignment guidance during takeoff and landing. The runway centerline is a dashed line.

3) **Threshold markings**. The runway threshold markings help you to identify the beginning of the runway that is available for landing. Threshold markings come in two configurations:

   a) Eight longitudinal stripes (four on each side of the centerline)
   b) The number of stripes designated according to the width of the runway

4) **Aiming point marker**. The aiming point marker serves as a visual aiming point during landing. The aiming point markings are two broad white stripes located on each side of the runway centerline approximately 1,000 ft. from the landing threshold.

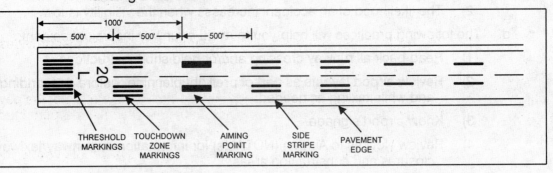

5) **Touchdown zone marker**. The touchdown zone markings identify the touchdown zone for landing operations and are coded to provide distance information in 500-ft. increments.

   a) These markings consist of groups of one, two, and three rectangular bars arranged on each side of the centerline, as shown above.

6) **Side stripe marking**. Runway side stripes are continuous white stripes located on each side of the runway to provide a visual contrast between the runway and the abutting terrain or shoulders.

7) **Runway shoulder markings** are yellow and may be used to supplement runway side stripes to identify the runway shoulder area that is not intended for use by aircraft.

8) A **runway threshold bar** is used to mark the beginning of the runway that is available for landing when the threshold has been relocated or displaced.

   a) A **relocated threshold** is a threshold that is temporarily relocated (due to construction, maintenance, etc.) toward the departure end of the runway.

   b) A **displaced threshold** is a threshold that is not at the beginning of the paved runway.

       i)   The paved area before the displaced runway threshold (marked by arrows) is available for taxiing, the takeoff of aircraft, and a landing rollout from the opposite direction, but not for landing in the direction of the runway in question.

9) **Chevrons** are used to show pavement areas (e.g., blast pads, stopways, etc.) aligned with the runway that are unusable for landing, takeoff, and taxiing. Chevrons are yellow.

10) A **demarcation bar** separates a runway that has a displaced threshold from a taxiway or an area marked by chevrons that precedes the runway. The demarcation bar is colored yellow since it is not on the runway.

11) **Closed or temporarily closed runway**

   a) A permanently closed runway has all runway lighting disconnected, all runway markings obliterated, and yellow crosses placed at each end of the runway and at 1,000-ft. intervals.

   b) A temporarily closed runway is marked by yellow crosses placed only at each end of the runway.

   i) A visual indication may not be present depending on the reason for the closure, the duration of the closure, airport configuration, and the existence (and operating hours) of a control tower.

d. Taxiway markings

   1) The **taxiway centerline** is a single continuous yellow line that provides a visual cue to permit taxiing along a designated path.

   2) **Taxiway edge markings** are primarily used to define the edge of the taxiway when the taxiway edge does not correspond with the edge of the pavement. There are two types depending on whether your airplane is permitted to cross the taxiway edge.

   a) A continuous marking consists of a continuous double yellow line that should not be crossed.

   b) A dashed marking consists of a broken double yellow line and indicates the edge of the taxiway where the adjoining pavement is also intended for use by aircraft, i.e., a parking ramp.

   3) **Taxiway shoulder markings** indicate that the paved shoulders along the taxiway are unusable. Taxiway shoulder markings are yellow.

   4) **Surface painted taxiway direction signs** have a yellow background with a black inscription and are provided when it is not possible to provide taxiway direction signs at intersections or when it is necessary to supplement such signs.

   a) These markings are located adjacent to the centerline with markings indicating turns to the left on the left side of the centerline and markings indicating turns to the right on the right side of the centerline.

   5) **Surface painted location signs** have a black background with a yellow inscription. When necessary, these markings are used to supplement location signs located alongside the taxiway and to confirm your taxiway designation.

   a) These markings are located on the right side of the centerline.

   6) **Geographic position markings** are located at points along low visibility taxi routes and are used to identify the location of taxiing aircraft during low visibility operations (i.e., when the runway visual range is below 1,200 ft.).

   a) The geographic position marker is positioned to the left of the taxiway centerline in the direction of taxiing and has a pink background with a black number or a number and letter.

   7) Closed or temporarily closed taxiway

   a) A permanently closed taxiway has all lighting disconnected and yellow crosses placed at each entrance of the taxiway and possibly at 1,000-ft. intervals.

   b) A temporarily closed taxiway is usually treated as a hazardous area that no part of the airplane may enter and is blocked with barricades.

e.   Holding position markings

1)   **Runway holding position markings** indicate where an aircraft is supposed to stop. They consist of four yellow lines, two solid and two dashed, extending across the width of the taxiway or runway. The solid lines are always on the side where the aircraft is to hold. Runway holding position markings are encountered at three locations.

a)   On taxiways, these markings identify the location where you are to stop when you do not have clearance to proceed onto the runway at an airport with an operating control tower or when you do not have adequate separation from other aircraft at an airport without an operating control tower.

i)   When exiting the runway, you are not clear of the runway until all parts of your airplane have crossed the holding position marking.

b)   On a runway, these markings are installed only if the runway is used by ATC for "land, hold short" operations or taxiing.

i)   A sign with a white inscription on a red background is installed adjacent to these holding position markings.

c)   Runway holding position markings are used at some airports when it is necessary to hold an aircraft on a taxiway located in the approach or departure area of a runway so that the aircraft does not interfere with the operation on the runway.

2)   **Holding position markings for ILS critical areas** consist of two yellow solid lines connected by pairs of solid lines extended across the width of the taxiway as shown in the figure below.

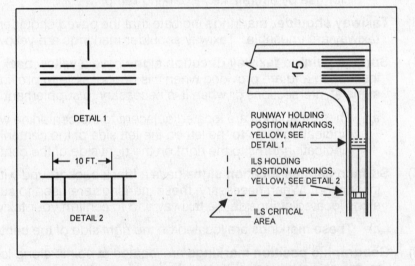

3)   **Holding position markings for taxiway/taxiway intersections** consist of one dashed line extending across the width of the taxiway.

4)   **Surface painted holding position signs** have a red background with the intersecting runway's designation in white.

a)   These markings may be used to supplement the runway holding position sign located alongside the taxiway.

b)   These markings are located on the left side of the centerline and prior to the holding position marking.

f.　Other markings

1)　**Vehicle roadway markings** are used to define a pathway for vehicle operations or crossing areas that are also intended for aircraft.

　　a)　Vehicle roadway markings consist of a white solid line to delineate each edge of the roadway and a dashed line to separate lanes within the edges of the roadway.

　　　　i)　An alternative to solid edge lines is the use of zipper markings (staggered lines).

2)　The **VOR receiver checkpoint marking** allows you to locate the position on the airport to perform a ground check of the VOR (VHF omnidirectional range) navigation instrument in your airplane, if equipped.

　　a)　The VOR receiver checkpoint marking consists of a painted circle with an arrow in the middle; the arrow is aligned in the direction of the checkpoint direction to the VOR.

3)　**Non-movement area boundary markings** delineate the movement area, i.e., the area under air traffic control. These markings are yellow and are located on the boundary between the movement and non-movement areas.

　　a)　The non-movement area boundary markings consist of two yellow lines, one solid and one dashed.

　　　　i)　The solid line is located on the non-movement area side, while the dashed line is located on the movement area side.

g.　Airport signs are used on runways and taxiways to provide information. Six types of signs are installed on airports.

1)　**Mandatory instruction signs** have white characters on a red background and are used to denote entrances to runways or critical areas and areas that airplanes are prohibited from entering.

　　a)　A **runway holding position sign** is located at the holding position on taxiways that intersect a runway or on runways that intersect other runways.

　　b)　**Runway approach area holding position sign.** At some airports, it is necessary to hold an aircraft on a taxiway located in the approach or departure area for a runway so that the aircraft does not interfere with operations on that runway.

　　c)　**ILS critical area holding position sign.** At some airports, when the instrument landing system (ILS) is being used, it is necessary to hold an aircraft on a taxiway at a location other than the marked runway holding position.

　　　　i)　In these situations, the holding position sign for these operations will have the inscription "ILS" and be located adjacent to an ILS holding position marking.

　　d)　A **no entry sign** prohibits an aircraft from entering an area.

2) **Location signs** are used to identify either a taxiway or a runway on which the aircraft is located. Other location signs provide visual clues to pilots to assist them in determining when they have exited an area.

   a) A **taxiway location sign** has yellow characters on a black background and a yellow border.

      i) These signs are installed along taxiways either by themselves or in conjunction with direction signs or runway holding position signs.

   b) A **runway location sign** is similar to the taxiway location sign except it will indicate on which runway the aircraft is located.

   c) A **runway boundary sign** has a yellow background with a black inscription and a graphic depicting the pavement holding position marking.

      i) This sign, which faces the runway and is visible to the pilot exiting the runway, is located adjacent to the holding position marking on the pavement.

   d) An **ILS critical area boundary sign** has a graphic depicting the ILS pavement holding position marking.

3) **Direction signs** have black characters on a yellow background. The inscription identifies the designation(s) of the intersecting taxiway(s) leading out of the intersection that a pilot would normally be expected to turn onto or hold short of. Each designation is accompanied by an arrow indicating the direction of the turn.

4) **Destination signs** also have black characters on a yellow background indicating a destination on the airport. These signs always have an arrow showing the direction of the taxiing route to that destination.

5) **Information signs** have black characters on a yellow background. They are used to provide the pilot with information on such things as areas that cannot be seen from the control tower, applicable radio frequencies, and noise abatement procedures.

6) **Runway distance remaining signs** are located along one or both side(s) of the runway. These signs have white numbers on a black background.

   a) The number on the sign indicates the distance (in thousands of feet) of runway remaining.

h. **Approach light systems (ALS)**

1) ALS provide the basic means to transition from instrument flight to visual flight for landing.

   a) Thus, ALS will be used only with precision and nonprecision instrument runways.

i.   Runway lights

    1)   **Runway edge lights** are used to outline the edges of the runway during periods of darkness or restricted visibility conditions.

        a)   Runway edge lights marking the ends of the runway (sometimes called runway end lights) show

            i)   Green to aircraft on approach, i.e., indicate the landing threshold

            ii)   Red to aircraft taking off or on the landing rollout, i.e., indicate the end of the runway

    2)   **In-runway lighting** is installed on some precision approach runways to facilitate landing under adverse visibility conditions.

        a)   **Touchdown zone lighting (TDZL)** is a row of flush white lights on either side of the centerline in the runway touchdown zone.

        b)   **Runway centerline lighting (RCLS)** consists of semi-flush centerline lights spaced at 50-ft. intervals beginning 75 ft. from the landing threshold and extending to within 75 ft. of the opposite end.

        c)   **Land and hold short lights** are a row of five semi-flush flashing white lights installed at the hold short point, perpendicular to the centerline of the runway on which they are installed.

            i)   When land and hold short operations are conducted continuously, the land and hold short lights will normally be "on" during that period. Thus, departing pilots and pilots who are cleared to land using the full length of the runway should ignore the lights.

        d)   **Taxiway lead-off lights** are semi-flush lights defining the curved path of travel from the runway centerline to a point on the taxiway.

j.   Taxiway lights

    1)   **Taxiway edge lights** are blue and outline the edges of taxiways during periods of darkness or restricted visibility conditions.

    2)   **Taxiway centerline lights** are used on some airports to mark the taxiway centerline during low visibility conditions. These lights are green.

    3)   **Clearance bar lights** consist of three in-pavement steady-burning yellow lights located at holding positions on taxiways to help you identify the holding position in low visibility conditions.

    4)   **Runway guard lights** are installed at taxiway/runway intersections and are primarily used to help you identify taxiway/runway intersections during low visibility conditions.

    5)   **Stop bar lights**, when installed, are used to confirm the ATC clearance to enter or cross the active runway in low visibility conditions.

k. **Runway end identifier lights (REIL)**

    1) The REIL system consists of a pair of synchronized flashing lights located laterally on each side of the runway threshold.

l. **Airport rotating beacons**

    1) The primary purpose of these beacons is to identify the location of airports at night.

    2) White and green alternating flashes indicate a lighted land airport for civil use.

m. Visual glideslope indicators

    1) The **visual approach slope indicator (VASI)** is a system of lights arranged to provide visual descent guidance during an approach.

        a) VASI may consist of 2, 4, 6, 12, or 16 light units arranged in bars that are referred to as near, middle, and far bars.

    2) The **precision approach path indicator (PAPI)** uses lights similar to the VASI but in a single row of either two or four lights.

    3) The **tri-color approach slope indicator** normally consists of a single light unit, projecting a three-color visual approach path into the final approach area of the runway.

    4) **Pulsating visual approach slope indicators** normally consist of a single light unit projecting a two-color (red and white) visual approach path.

    5) **Alignment of elements system** is a visual glideslope indicator, but it does not use lights as in the other systems.

        a) It is a low-cost system consisting of painted plywood panels, normally black and white or fluorescent orange.

            i) Some may be lighted for night operations.

END OF TASK -- END OF CHAPTER

CHAPTER IV
TAKEOFFS, LANDINGS, AND GO-AROUNDS

This chapter explains the eight tasks (A-F, K, L) of Takeoffs, Landings, and Go-Arounds. These tasks include elements of both knowledge and skill. Your examiner is required to test you on all eight tasks. You are required to perform these tasks in a complex airplane.

This chapter explains and describes the factors involved and the technique required for safely taking your airplane off the ground and departing the takeoff area under normal conditions, as well as in various situations in which maximum performance of your airplane is essential. Although the takeoff and climb maneuver is one continuous process, it can be divided into three phases.

1.   The **takeoff roll** is that portion of the maneuver during which your airplane is accelerated to an airspeed that provides sufficient lift for it to become airborne.

2.   The **liftoff**, or rotation, is the act of becoming airborne as a result of the wings lifting the airplane off the ground or your rotating the nose up, increasing the angle of attack to start a climb.

3.   The **initial climb** begins when your airplane leaves the ground and a pitch attitude is established to climb away from the takeoff area. Normally, it is considered complete when your airplane has reached a safe maneuvering altitude or an en route climb has been established.

This chapter also discusses the factors that affect your airplane during the landing approach under normal and critical circumstances, and the technique for positively controlling these factors. The approach and landing can be divided into five phases.

1.   The **base leg** is that portion of the traffic pattern during which you must accurately judge the distance in which your airplane must descend to the landing point.

2.   The **final approach** is the last part of the traffic pattern during which your airplane is aligned with the landing runway and a straight-line descent is made to the point of touchdown. The descent rate and descent angle are governed by your airplane's height and distance from the intended touchdown point and by the airplane's groundspeed.

3.   The **roundout**, or **flare**, is that part of the final approach during which your airplane makes a transition from the approach attitude to the touchdown or landing attitude.

4.   The **touchdown** is the actual contact or touching of the main wheels of your airplane on the landing surface, as the weight of the airplane is being transferred from the wings to the wheels.

5.   The **after-landing roll**, or **rollout**, is the forward roll of your airplane on the landing surface after touchdown while the airplane's momentum decelerates to a normal taxi speed or a stop.

NORMAL AND CROSSWIND TAKEOFF AND CLIMB

IV.A. TASK: NORMAL AND CROSSWIND TAKEOFF AND CLIMB

REFERENCES: FAA-H-8083-3; Pilot's Operating Handbook, FAA-Approved Airplane Flight Manual.

NOTE: If a crosswind condition does not exist, the applicant's knowledge of crosswind elements shall be evaluated through oral testing.

Objective. To determine that the applicant:

1. Exhibits knowledge of the elements related to normal and crosswind takeoff, climb operations and rejected takeoff procedures.

2. Positions the flight controls for the existing wind conditions.

3. Clears the area, taxies onto the takeoff surface, and aligns the airplane on the runway center/takeoff path.

4. Advances the throttle smoothly to takeoff power.

5. Lifts off at the recommended airspeed, and accelerates to V_Y.

6. Establishes a pitch attitude that will maintain V_Y, ±5 knots.

7. Retracts the landing gear, if appropriate, and flaps after a positive rate of climb is established.

8. Maintains takeoff power and V_Y, ±5 knots to a safe maneuvering altitude.

9. Maintains directional control, proper wind-drift correction throughout the takeoff and climb.

10. Complies with noise abatement procedures.

11. Completes appropriate checklist.

A. General Information

   1. The objective of this task is for you to demonstrate your ability to perform a normal and a crosswind takeoff and climb.

      a. If a crosswind condition does not exist, your knowledge of crosswind procedures will be orally tested.

B. Task Objectives

   1. **Exhibit your knowledge of the elements related to normal and crosswind takeoff and climb operations and rejected takeoff procedures.**

      a. A normal takeoff and climb is one in which your airplane is headed directly into the wind or the wind is very light, and the takeoff surface is firm, with no obstructions along the takeoff path, and is of sufficient length to permit your airplane to accelerate gradually to normal climbing speed.

         1) A crosswind takeoff and climb is one in which your airplane is NOT headed directly into the wind.

      b. Section 4, Normal Procedures, in your *POH* will provide you with the proper airspeeds, e.g., V_R, V_Y, and also the proper configuration.

         1) Best rate of climb (V_Y) is the speed which will produce the greatest gain in altitude for a given unit of time. V_Y gradually decreases as the density altitude increases.

      c. A rejected takeoff procedure is performed any time you are not satisfied with the development of the takeoff roll.

         1) Some situations that might call for a rejected takeoff procedure would be:

            a) Partial or total loss of engine power.

            b) Unexpectedly poor acceleration due to an engine malfunction, as of takeoff surface, low tire pressure, etc.

            c) Rapidly approaching the end of the runway before flying speed has been attained (e.g., during a misjudged touch and go landing).

2) A general rejected takeoff procedure is as follows:

    a) Close the throttle.
    b) Apply braking as needed, but do not skid the tires.
    c) Maintain directional control using the rudder pedals.

3) Refer to your airplane's *POH* for additional information about rejected takeoff procedures.

2. Position the flight controls for the existing wind conditions.

a. Always reverify wind direction as you taxi onto the runway by observing the windsock or other wind direction indicator, which may include grass or bushes.

b. For a crosswind takeoff, the ailerons should be FULLY deflected at the start of the takeoff roll.

    1) The aileron should be up on the upwind side of the airplane (i.e., the aileron control turned toward the wind).

    2) This position will impose a downward force on the upwind wing to counteract the lifting force of the crosswind and prevent that wing from rising.

c. Normally, wing flaps are in the retracted position for normal and crosswind takeoffs and climbs.

d. Follow the procedures prescribed in your *POH* for normal and crosswind takeoffs.

3. Clear the area, taxi onto the takeoff surface, and align your airplane on the runway centerline.

a. Before taxiing onto the runway, make certain that you have sufficient time to execute the takeoff before any aircraft in the traffic pattern turn onto the final approach.

    1) Check that the runway is clear of other aircraft, vehicles, persons, or other hazards.

    2) This check should be done at airports both with and without operating control towers.

b. Before beginning your takeoff roll, study the runway and related ground reference points, such as nearby buildings, trees, runway lights (at night), etc.

    1) You will gain a frame of reference for directional control during takeoff.
    2) You will feel more confident that you have everything under control.

c. After you taxi onto the runway, align your airplane with the runway centerline with the nosewheel straight.

4. Advance the throttle smoothly to takeoff power.

a. Recheck that the propeller control and mixture are set in accordance with your *POH*.

b. Power should be added smoothly to allow for a controllable transition to flying airspeed.

    1) Applying power too quickly can cause engine surging, backfiring, and a possible overboost situation (turbocharged engines). These conditions cause unnecessary engine wear as well as possible failure.

    2) Applying power too slowly wastes runway length.

c. Use the power setting that is recommended in your *POH*.

    d.   Manifold pressure (MP), RPM, and fuel flow instruments must be monitored during the entire maneuver.

        1)   Listen for any indication of power loss or engine roughness.

        2)   Monitoring the instruments enables you to notice immediately any malfunctions or indication of insufficient power or other potential problems. Do not commit to liftoff unless all engine indications are normal.

5.   *Lift off at the recommended airspeed and accelerate to V_Y.*

    a.   As your airplane accelerates, check your airspeed indicator to ensure that the needle is moving and operating properly.

        1)   Call out your airspeed as you accelerate to V_R, e.g., "40, 60, 80."

        2)   Your airplane's V_R _____.

    b.   If your *POH* does not recommend a V_R, use the following procedure from the FAA's *Airplane Flying Handbook* (FAA-H-8083-3).

        1)   When all the flight controls become effective during the takeoff roll, back elevator pressure should be gradually applied to raise the nosewheel slightly off the runway, thus establishing the liftoff attitude.

           a)   This is referred to as rotating.

        2)   At this point, the position of the nose in relation to the horizon should be noted, then elevator pressure applied as necessary to hold this attitude.

    c.   Forcing your airplane into the air by applying excessive back pressure only results in an excessively high pitch attitude and may delay the takeoff.

        1)   Excessive and rapid changes in pitch attitude result in proportionate changes in the effects of torque, thus making the airplane more difficult to control.

        2)   If you force your airplane to leave the ground before adequate speed is attained, the wing's angle of attack may be excessive, causing the airplane to settle back onto the runway or to stall.

        3)   Also, jerking the airplane off the ground reduces passenger comfort.

    d.   If not enough back pressure is held to maintain the correct takeoff attitude or the nose is allowed to lower excessively, the airplane may settle back to the runway. This occurs because the angle of attack is decreased and lift is diminished to the point where it will not support the airplane.

    e.   Some complex and many high-performance airplanes require conscious rearward elevator pressure at V_R to establish the liftoff.

        1)   Without this conscious control pressure, the airplane may start to wheelbarrow (i.e., the main wheels break ground before the nose wheel).

        2)   Note that, in general, high-performance airplanes have heavier control pressures and require more deliberate application of control movements.

    f.   During takeoffs in a strong, gusty wind, increase V_R to provide an additional margin of safety in the event of sudden changes in wind direction immediately after liftoff.

    g.   The best takeoff attitude requires only minimal pitch adjustments just after liftoff to establish the best-rate-of-climb airspeed, V_Y. The airplane should be allowed to fly off the ground in its normal takeoff (i.e., best-rate-of-climb) attitude, if possible.

    h.   Maintain V_Y during your climb. Some complex and high-performance airplanes may have two V_Y speeds, depending on the gear position. Check your *POH* for the proper airspeed(s).

        1)   Your airplane's V_Y (gear down) _____

                    V_Y (gear up) _____

6. **Establish a pitch attitude that will maintain V$_Y$ ±5 kt.**

    a. Experiment with your airplane in order to determine the approximate pitch attitude for V$_Y$ with takeoff power at various weights and in different configurations.

        1) You should be particularly interested in determining V$_Y$ pitch attitude for your airplane as it will be loaded during the practical test.

        V$_Y$ pitch attitude for practical test conditions _____

    b. When you reach V$_R$, rotate directly to the pitch attitude that will establish V$_Y$.

        1) If you hold this attitude, you should be able to maintain V$_Y$ ±5 kt. with no difficulty.

7. **Retract the landing gear, if appropriate, and flaps after a positive rate of climb is established.**

    a. Landing gear retraction is normally started when you can no longer land on the remaining runway and a positive rate of climb* is established on the VSI.

    b. Before retracting the landing gear, apply the brakes momentarily to stop the rotation of the wheels to avoid excessive vibration on the gear mechanism.

        1) Centrifugal force caused by the rapidly rotating wheels expands the diameter of the tires, and if mud or other debris has accumulated in the wheel wells, the rotating wheels may rub as they enter.

    c. Make necessary pitch adjustment to maintain V$_Y$, ±5 kt.

    d. Flaps should be retracted once you are above the height of any nearby obstacles.

    e. Follow the gear and flap retraction procedure in your *POH*.

*The FAA definition of a positive rate of climb is a steady clockwise rotation of the altimeter needle at a rate that you can interpret with experience, and a stable rate of climb, appropriate to the airplane, shown on the vertical speed indicator.

8. **Maintain takeoff power and V$_Y$, ±5 kt. to a safe maneuvering altitude.**

    a. After establishing V$_Y$ and completing gear and flap retraction, maintain takeoff power to a safe maneuvering altitude, normally 500 to 1,000 ft. AGL.

        1) Then the power (MP, RPM, and mixture) should be set to the climb power setting recommended in your *POH*.

            a) Adjust pitch as necessary to maintain airspeed.

    b. Maintain V$_Y$, ±5 kt. until reaching traffic pattern altitude (normally 1,000 ft. AGL); then transition to the recommended cruise climb airspeed.

        1) Cruise climb offers the advantages of higher airspeed for increased engine cooling, higher groundspeed, better visibility ahead of the airplane, and greater passenger comfort.

    c. Follow the procedures in your *POH*.

9. **Maintain directional control and proper wind-drift correction throughout the takeoff and climb.**

    a. Maintain directional control on runway centerline.

        1) Rudder pressure must be promptly and smoothly applied to counteract yawing forces (from wind and/or torque) so that your airplane will continue straight down the center of the runway.

        2) During a crosswind takeoff roll, you will normally apply downwind rudder pressure since on the ground your airplane may tend to weathervane into the wind.

3)   When takeoff power is applied, torque, which yaws the airplane to the left, may be sufficient to counteract the weathervaning tendency caused by a right crosswind.

    a)   On the other hand, it may also aggravate the tendency to swerve left with a left crosswind.

b.   Adjust aileron deflection during acceleration.

1)   During crosswind takeoffs, the aileron deflection into the wind should be decreased as appropriate airspeed increases.

    a)   As the forward speed of your airplane increases and the crosswind becomes more of a relative headwind, the holding of full aileron into the wind should be reduced.

2)   You will feel increasing pressure on the controls as the ailerons become more effective.

    a)   Your objective is to release enough pressure to keep the wings level.

    b)   The crosswind component does not completely vanish, so some aileron pressure will need to be maintained to prevent the upwind wing from rising.

        i)   The pressure will hold that wing down so that your airplane will, immediately after liftoff, be slipping into the wind enough to counteract drift.

c.   In a crosswind takeoff as the nosewheel rises off the runway, holding the aileron control into the wind should result in the downwind wing rising and the downwind main wheel lifting off the runway first, with the remainder of the takeoff roll being made on the other main wheel (i.e., on the side from which the wind is coming).

1)   This is preferable to side skipping (which would occur if you did not turn the control yoke into the wind and use opposite rudder).

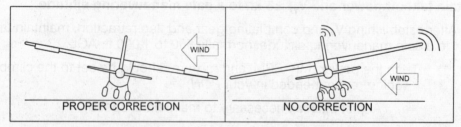

2)   If a significant crosswind exists, the main wheels should be held on the ground slightly longer than in a normal takeoff so that a smooth but very definite liftoff can be made.

    a)   Accomplish this by applying slightly less back pressure on the control yoke as you near V_R.

    b)   This procedure will allow the airplane to leave the ground under more positive control so that it will definitely remain airborne while the proper amount of drift correction is established.

    c)   More importantly, it will avoid imposing excessive side loads on the landing gear and prevent possible damage that would result from the airplane settling back to the runway while drifting (due to the crosswind).

3) As both main wheels leave the runway and ground friction no longer resists drifting, the airplane will be slowly carried sideways with the wind unless you maintain adequate drift correction.

d. In the initial crosswind climb, the airplane will be slipping (upwind wing down to prevent drift and opposite rudder to align your flight path with the runway) into the wind sufficiently to counteract the drifting effect of the wind and to increase stability during the transition to flight.

1) After your airplane is safely off the runway and a positive rate of climb has been established, the airplane should be headed toward the wind to establish just enough crab to counteract the wind, and then the wings should be rolled level. The climb while in this crab should be continued so as to follow a ground track aligned with the runway centerline.

2) Center the ball in the inclinometer with proper rudder pressure throughout the climb.

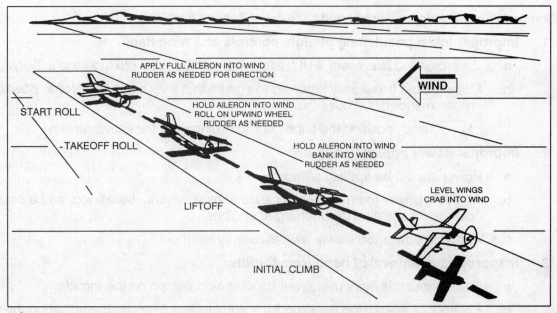

e. Maintain a straight track over the extended runway centerline until a turn is required.

1) In a crosswind condition, after you leave the initial side slip for liftoff and enter the crab for climbout, the crab should be maintained as needed to continue along the extended runway centerline until a turn on course or the crosswind leg is initiated.

2) It is important to remain aligned with the runway to avoid the hazards of drifting into obstacles or the path of another aircraft, which may be taking off from a parallel runway.

10. Comply with noise abatement procedures.

a. You must comply with any established noise abatement procedure.

1) A noise abatement policy is developed by the airport authority or city and is a local ordinance. Thus, you can be cited by the city for violation of the policy.

b. The *A/FD* will indicate that an airport has a noise abatement procedure in effect under "airport remarks."

1) Other pilot guides may contain more detailed information on an airport's noise abatement procedures.

    c.   A key to complying with noise abatement is to put as much distance as possible between you and the ground, as quickly as possible.

    1)   Use the longest runway available.
    2)   Rotate at V_R and climb out at V_X or V_Y, as recommended in your *POH*.
    3)   Reduce power to climb power, and transition to a cruise climb as appropriate.

        a)   The reduction to climb power will reduce the noise of your engine, and the transition to cruise climb airspeed will reduce the time you are over the noise monitors and noise-sensitive areas.

    d.   If you are flying from an unfamiliar airport that has a noise abatement policy, you should contact the airport's noise abatement office for details.

11. Complete the appropriate checklist.

    a.   Use and complete your takeoff and climb checklist from Section 4, Normal Procedures, of your *POH*.

C. Common Errors during a Normal and Crosswind Takeoff and Climb

1.   Improper initial positioning of flight controls and wing flaps.

    a.   If a crosswind is present, FULL aileron should be held into the wind initially.

    b.   Flaps should be visually checked to ensure that they are in the proper position recommended by your *POH*.

    1)   If used, position the flaps prior to taxiing onto the active runway.

2.   Improper power application.

    a.   Power should be applied smoothly.

    b.   Applying power too quickly can cause engine surging, backfiring, and a possible overboost situation (turbocharged engines).

    c.   Applying power too slowly wastes runway length.

3.   Inappropriate removal of hand from throttle.

    a.   Throughout this maneuver, your hand should remain on the throttle.

    b.   Exceptions are raising the wing flaps and landing gear, and/or adjusting the trim during the climb. After completing these, your hand should return to the throttle.

4.   Poor directional control.

    a.   Directional control is made with smooth, prompt, positive rudder corrections.

    1)   The effects of torque at the initial power application tend to pull the nose to the left.

    b.   The rudder will become more effective as airspeed increases.

    c.   A tendency to overcorrect will find you meandering back and forth across the centerline.

5.   Improper use of ailerons.

    a.   As the forward speed of the airplane increases and the ailerons become more effective, the holding of full aileron should be reduced.

    b.   Some aileron pressure must be maintained to keep the upwind wing from rising.

    c.   If the upwind wing rises, a "skipping" action may develop.

    1)   This side skipping imposes severe side stresses on the landing gear and could result in structural failure.

6. **Neglecting to monitor all engine and flight instruments.**

    a. Develop a quick scan of the engine gauges to detect any abnormality.

        1) Perform the scan several times during your ground roll and then several times during climbout.

            a) Engine temperatures: EGT, cylinder head, and oil
            b) MP, RPM, fuel pressure
            c) Oil pressure

        2) Call out full power when you attain it on the takeoff roll, e.g., "Three red lines."

            a) EXAMPLE: Three red lines mean that MP, RPM, and fuel flow are at the maximum red-line limit.

    b. Call out your airspeed as you accelerate.

7. **Improper pitch attitude during liftoff.**

    a. Applying excessive back pressure will result only in an excessively high pitch attitude and delay the takeoff.

    b. If not enough elevator pressure is held to maintain the correct attitude, your airplane may settle back onto the runway, and this will delay the climb to safe altitude.

    c. An improper trim setting will make it harder for you to maintain the proper takeoff attitude by causing an increase in control pressure that you must hold.

8. **Failure to establish and maintain proper climb configuration and airspeed.**

    a. Use your *POH* checklists to determine the proper climb configuration and airspeed.

    b. Maintain airspeed by making small pitch changes by outside visual references; then cross-check with the airspeed indicator.

9. **Raising the landing gear before a positive rate of climb is established.**

    a. Airplanes, especially in windy conditions, can become airborne in ground effect before sufficient airspeed is attained to sustain flight.

        1) If the landing gear is immediately raised on liftoff, the airplane may settle back down and strike the runway.

    b. Also, if an engine problem develops immediately after liftoff, the airplane should be landed immediately.

        1) If you have to wait for the landing gear to extend, there may be insufficient time and/or runway available.

10. **Drift during climb.**

    a. You must use all available outside references, including looking behind, to maintain a ground track of the runway centerline extension.

    b. This will assist you in avoiding hazardous obstacles or prevent drifting into the path of another airplane, which may be taking off from a parallel runway.

    c. Cross-check with the airplane's heading indicator, using enough right rudder to maintain heading with the wings level.

END OF TASK

NORMAL AND CROSSWIND APPROACH AND LANDING

IV.B. TASK: NORMAL AND CROSSWIND APPROACH AND LANDING

REFERENCES: FAA-H-8083-3; Pilot's Operating Handbook, FAA-Approved Airplane Flight Manual.

NOTE: If a crosswind condition does not exist, the applicant's knowledge of the crosswind elements shall be evaluated through oral testing.

Objective. To determine that the applicant:

1. Exhibits knowledge of the elements related to normal and crosswind approach and landing.

2. Considers the wind conditions, landing surface, obstructions, and selects a suitable touchdown point.

3. Establishes the recommended approach and landing configuration and airspeed and adjusts pitch attitude and power as required.

4. Maintains a stabilized approach and recommended airspeed, or in its absence, not more than 1.3 V_{SO}, ±5 kt. with wind gust factor applied.

5. Makes smooth, timely, and correct control application during the roundout and touchdown.

6. Touches down smoothly at approximate stalling speed.

7. Touches down at or within 200 ft. (60 meters) beyond a specified point, with no drift, and with the airplane's longitudinal axis aligned with and over the runway center/landing path.

8. Maintains crosswind correction and directional control throughout the approach and landing sequence.

9. Completes the appropriate checklist.

A. General Information

1. The objective of this task is for you to demonstrate your ability to perform normal and crosswind approaches and landings.

a. If a crosswind condition does not exist, your knowledge of crosswind procedures will be orally tested.

B. Task Objectives

1. **Exhibit your knowledge of the elements related to a normal and crosswind approach and landing.**

a. A normal approach and landing is one in which engine power is available, the wind is light or the final approach is made directly into the wind, the final approach path has no obstacles, and the landing surface is firm and of ample length to bring your airplane to a stop gradually.

1) A crosswind approach and landing involves the same basic principles as a normal approach and landing except the wind is blowing across rather than parallel to the final approach path.

a) Virtually every landing will require at least some slight crosswind correction.

b. The presence of strong, gusting winds or turbulent air may require you to increase your airspeed on final approach. Increased airspeed provides for more positive control of your airplane.

1) The gust factor, the difference between the steady-state wind and the maximum gust, should be factored into your final approach airspeed in some form.

a) It should also be added to your various approach segment airspeeds for downwind, base, and final.

2)   One recommended technique is to use the normal approach speed plus one-half the gust factor.

    a)   EXAMPLE: If the normal approach speed is 70 kt. and the wind gusts increase 20 kt., an airspeed of 80 kt. is appropriate.

    b)   Some pilots add all of the steady wind and one-half the gust, or all of the gust and no steady wind.

3)   Remember, your airspeed and whatever gust factor you select to add to your final approach speed should be flown only after all maneuvering has been completed and your airplane has been lined up on the final approach.

4)   When using a higher-than-normal approach speed, it may be expedient to use less than full flaps on landing.

5)   Follow the recommended procedures in your *POH*.

c.   An airplane may have a maximum crosswind component limitation, which is a limitation in Section 2, Limitations, of the airplane's *POH*.

    1)   Other airplanes may have a maximum demonstrated crosswind component, which is not an official *POH* limitation.

2.   Consider the wind conditions, landing surface, and obstructions, and select a suitable touchdown point.

a.   You should consider the wind conditions and obstacles when planning your approach.

    1)   A strong headwind on final will cause you to position the base leg closer to the approach end of the runway than you would if the wind were light.

    2)   Obstacles along the final approach path will cause you to plan to be at a higher altitude on final than you would if there were no obstacles.

b.   After considering the conditions, you should select a touchdown point that is beyond the runway's landing threshold but well within the first one-third portion of the runway.

    1)   After selecting your touchdown point, you should identify it to your examiner.

c.   Once you have selected your touchdown point, you need to select your aim point. The aim point will be the point at the end of your selected glide path, not your touchdown point. Thus, your aim point will be short of your touchdown point.

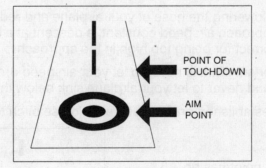

3.   Establish the recommended approach and landing configuration and airspeed, and adjust pitch attitude and power as required.

    a.   Properly configuring your airplane throughout the various approach segments will assist you in flying a stabilized approach.

        1)   On the downwind leg, you should complete the before-landing checklist in your *POH*, which includes gear extension.

            a)   When abeam of your intended landing point, reduce the power and hold altitude constant. As the airspeed slows below the maximum flap extended speed (V_{FE}), you should partially lower the flaps and begin your descent.

                i)   In your airplane, V_{FE} _____.

        2)   On the base leg, the flaps may be extended further, but full flaps are not recommended.

        3)   Once aligned with the runway centerline on the final approach, you should make the final flap selection. This is normally full flaps.

            a)   In turbulent air or strong gusty winds, you may elect not to use full flaps. This will allow you to maintain control more easily at a higher approach speed.

                i)   With less than full flaps, your airplane will be in a higher nose-up attitude.

    b.   The approach and landing configuration means that the gear is down, wing flaps are extended, and you are maintaining a reduced power setting.

    c.   The objective of a good approach and landing is to descend at an angle and airspeed that will permit your airplane to reach the desired touchdown point at an airspeed that will result in a minimum of floating just before touchdown.

        1)   A fundamental key to flying a stabilized approach is the interrelationship of pitch and power.

            a)   This interrelationship means that any changes to one element in the approach equation (e.g., airspeed, attitude) must be compensated for by adjustments in the other.

        2)   Power should be adjusted as necessary to control the airspeed, and the pitch attitude adjusted SIMULTANEOUSLY to control the descent angle or to attain the desired altitudes along the approach path.

            a)   By lowering the nose of your airplane and reducing power to keep your approach airspeed constant, a descent at a higher rate can be made to correct for being too high in the approach.

        3)   The important point is never to let your airspeed drop below your approach speed and never to let your airplane sink below the selected glide path.

    d.   When you are established on final, you should use pitch to fly your airplane to the aim point.

        1)   If the aim point has no apparent movement in your windshield, then you are on a constant glide path to the aim point. No pitch correction is needed.

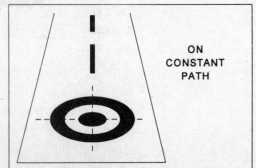

ON CONSTANT PATH

2)   If the aim point appears to move down your windshield or toward you, then you will overshoot the aim point and you need to pitch down.

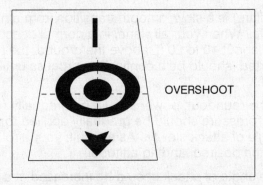

OVERSHOOT

a)   As you pitch down, reduce power to maintain approach speed.

3)   If the aim point appears to move up your windshield or away from you, then you will undershoot the aim point and you need to pitch up.

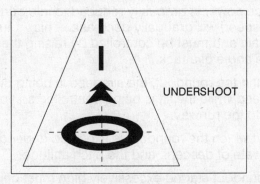

UNDERSHOOT

a)   As you pitch up, increase power to maintain approach speed.

4.   ***Maintain a stabilized approach and the recommended approach airspeed, or in its absence, not more than 1.3 V_{so}, ± 5 kt., with a wind gust factor applied.***

a.   Airspeed control is the most important factor in achieving landing precision. A well-executed landing begins in the traffic pattern with a stabilized approach.

1)   Once on final approach, slight adjustments in pitch and power may be necessary to maintain the descent attitude and the desired airspeed.

2)   Use the final approach speed in your *POH*. If one is not given, use 1.3 V_{so}.

a)   EXAMPLE: If V_{so} in your airplane is 60 kt., the airspeed on final approach should be 78 kt. (1.3 x 60).

b)   In your airplane, final approach speed (*POH*) _____, or 1.3 V_{so} _____.

c)   Make necessary adjustments to that speed if you are in turbulent air or strong, gusty winds.

d)   Inform your examiner of your final approach airspeed.

b.   The term **stabilized approach** means that your airplane is in a position in which minimum input of all controls will result in a safe landing.

1)   Excessive control input at any juncture could be an indication of improper planning.

c.   Remember to trim your airplane. A trimmed airplane makes it easier to fly a stabilized approach and maintain your approach speed within 5 kt.

5. **Make smooth, timely, and correct control application during the roundout and touchdown.**

   a. The roundout (flare) is a slow, smooth transition from a normal approach attitude to a landing attitude. When your airplane, in a normal descent, approaches what appears to be about 10 to 20 ft. above the ground, the roundout should be started and, once started, should be a continuous process until the airplane touches down on the ground.

      1) To start the roundout, power should be gradually reduced to idle, and back elevator pressure should be gradually applied to increase the pitch attitude and angle of attack slowly. As a result, your airplane's nose will rise gradually toward the desired landing attitude.

         a) The angle of attack should be increased at a rate that will allow your airplane to continue settling slowly as forward speed decreases.

      2) When the angle of attack is increased, the lift is momentarily increased, thereby decreasing the rate of descent.

         a) Since power is gradually reduced to idle during the roundout, the airspeed will gradually decrease. This, in turn, causes lift to decrease again and must be controlled by raising the nose and further increasing the angle of attack.

         b) During the roundout, the airspeed is being decreased to touchdown speed while the lift is being controlled so your airplane will settle gently onto the runway.

      3) The rate at which the roundout is executed depends on your height above the ground, rate of descent, and the pitch attitude.

         a) A roundout started excessively high must be executed more slowly than one from a lower height to allow your airplane to descend to the ground while the proper landing attitude is being established.

         b) The rate of rounding out must also be proportionate to the rate of closure with the ground. When your airplane appears to be descending slowly, the increase in pitch attitude must be made at a correspondingly slow rate.

      4) Once the actual process of rounding out is started, the elevator control should not be pushed forward. If too much back pressure has been exerted, this pressure should be either slightly relaxed or held constant, depending on the degree of error.

         a) In some cases, you may find it necessary to add power slightly to prevent an excessive rate of sink, or a stall, all of which would result in a hard, drop-in landing.

      5) You must be in the habit of keeping one hand on the throttle control throughout the approach and landing should a sudden and unexpected hazardous situation require an immediate application of power.

   b. The touchdown is the gentle settling of your airplane onto the runway. The touchdown should be made so that your airplane will touch down on the main gear at approximately stalling speed.

      1) As your airplane settles, the proper landing attitude must be attained by application of whatever back elevator pressure is necessary.

      2) It seems contradictory that the way to make a good landing is to try to hold your airplane's wheels a few inches off the ground as long as possible with the elevators.

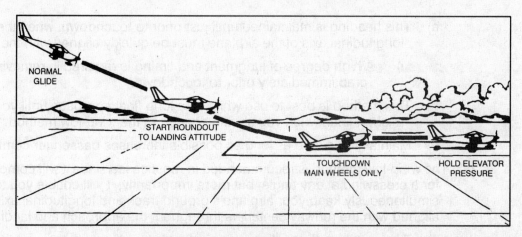

a) Normally, when the wheels are about 2 or 3 ft. off the ground, the airplane will still be settling too fast for a gentle touchdown. Thus, this descent must be retarded by further back pressure on the elevators.

b) Since your airplane is already close to its stalling speed and is settling, this added back pressure will only slow up the settling instead of stopping it. At the same time, it will result in your airplane's touching the ground in the proper nose-high landing attitude.

c. During a normal landing, your airplane should contact the ground in a tail-low attitude, with the main wheels touching down first so that little or no weight is on the nose wheel.

1) After the main wheels make initial contact with the ground, back pressure on the elevator control should be held to maintain a positive angle of attack for aerodynamic braking and to hold the nosewheel off the ground until the airplane decelerates.

2) As the airplane's momentum decreases, back pressure may be gradually relaxed to allow the nosewheel to settle gently onto the runway.

a) This will permit prompt steering with the nosewheel.

b) At the same time, it will cause a low angle of attack and negative lift on the wings to prevent floating or skipping and will allow the full weight of the airplane to rest on the wheels for better braking action.

6. ***Touch down smoothly at appropriate stalling speed.***

7. ***Touch down at or within 200 ft. beyond a specified point with no drift, and with your airplane's longitudinal axis aligned with and over the runway centerline.***

8. **Maintain crosswind correction and directional control throughout the approach and landing sequence.**

a. Immediately after the base-to-final approach turn is completed, the longitudinal axis of your airplane should be aligned with the centerline of the runway so that drift (if any) will be recognized immediately.

b. On a normal approach, with no wind drift, the longitudinal axis should be kept aligned with the runway centerline throughout the approach and landing.

1) Any corrections should be made with coordinated aileron and rudder pressure.

c. On a crosswind approach, there are two usual methods of maintaining the proper ground track on final approach. These are the crab method and the wing-low method.

1) The crab method is used first by establishing a heading (crab) toward the wind with the wings level so that your airplane's ground track remains aligned with the centerline of the runway.

     a)   This heading is maintained until just prior to touchdown, when the longitudinal axis of the airplane must be quickly aligned with the runway.

        i)   A high degree of judgment and timing is required in removing the crab immediately prior to touchdown.

     b)   This method is best to use while on a long final approach until you are on a short final, when you should change to the wing-low method.

     c)   Maintaining a crab as long as possible increases passenger comfort.

2)   The wing-low method is recommended in most cases since it will compensate for a crosswind at any angle, but more importantly, it will enable you to simultaneously keep your airplane's ground track and longitudinal axis aligned with the runway centerline throughout the approach and landing.

     a)   To use this method, align your airplane's heading with the centerline of the runway, note the rate and direction of drift, and then promptly apply drift correction by lowering the upwind wing.

        i)   The amount the wing must be lowered depends on the rate of drift.

     b)   When you lower the wing, the airplane will tend to turn in that direction. Thus, it is necessary to apply sufficient opposite rudder pressure simultaneously to prevent the turn and keep the airplane's longitudinal axis aligned with the runway.

        i)   Drift is controlled with aileron, and the heading with rudder.

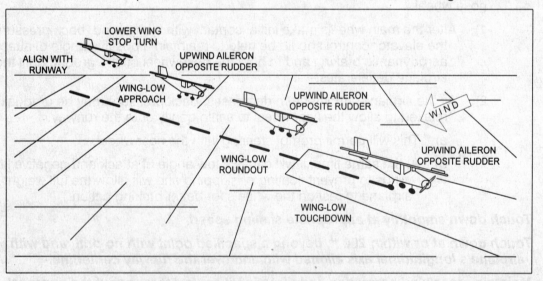

     c)   Your airplane will now be slipping into the wind just enough that both the resultant flight path and the ground track are aligned with the runway.

     d)   In a very strong crosswind, the required bank may be so steep that full opposite rudder will not prevent a turn. The wind is too strong to land safely on that particular runway with those wind conditions.

        i)   Since the airplane's capabilities would be exceeded, it is imperative that the landing be made on a more favorable runway either at that airport or at an alternate airport.

d.   The roundout during a crosswind landing can be made as in a normal landing, but the application of a crosswind correction must be continued as necessary to prevent drifting.

   1)   Since the airspeed decreases as the roundout progresses, the flight controls gradually become less effective. Thus, the crosswind correction being held would become inadequate.

      a)   It is therefore necessary to increase the deflection of the rudder and ailerons gradually to maintain the proper amount of drift correction.

   2)   Do not level the wings. Keep the upwind wing down throughout the crosswind roundout. If the wings are leveled, your airplane will begin drifting, and the touchdown will occur while drifting, which imposes severe side stresses (loads) on the landing gear.

e.   During a crosswind touchdown, you must make prompt adjustments to the crosswind correction to assure that your airplane does not drift as it touches down.

   1)   The crosswind correction should be maintained throughout the roundout, and the touchdown made on the upwind main wheel.

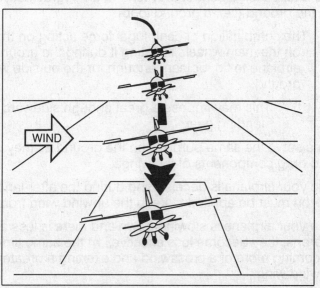

      a)   As the forward momentum decreases after initial contact, the weight of the airplane will cause the downwind main wheel to settle gradually onto the runway.

   2)   In those airplanes having nosewheel steering interconnected with the rudder, the nosewheel may not be aligned with the runway as the wheels touch down because opposite rudder is being held in the crosswind correction.

      a)   This is the case in airplanes which have no centering cam built into the nose gear strut to keep the nosewheel straight until the strut is compressed.

      b)   To prevent swerving in the direction that the nosewheel is offset, the corrective rudder pressure must be promptly relaxed just as the nosewheel touches down.

f.   Maintain directional control during the after-landing rollout on the runway.

   1)   The landing process must never be considered complete until your airplane decelerates to normal taxi speed during the landing roll or has been brought to a complete stop when clear of the runway.

      a)   Accidents have occurred as the result of pilots abandoning their vigilance and positive control after getting the airplane on the ground.

2)   You must be alert for directional control problems immediately upon and after touchdown due to the ground friction on the wheels. The friction creates a pivot point on which a moment arm can act.

   a)   Nosewheel-type airplanes make the task of directional control easier because the CG, being **ahead** of the main landing wheels, presents a moment arm that tends to straighten the airplane's path during the touchdown and the after-landing roll.

      i)   This should not lull you into a false sense of security.

3)   Another directional control problem in crosswind landings is due to the weathervaning tendency of your airplane. Characteristically, an airplane has a greater profile or side area behind the main landing gear than forward of it.

   a)   With the main landing wheels acting as a pivot point and the greater surface area exposed to a crosswind behind the pivot point, the airplane may tend to turn or weathervane into the wind.

4)   Loss of directional control may lead to an aggravated, uncontrolled, tight turn on the ground (i.e., a ground loop).

   a)   The combination of centrifugal force acting on the CG and ground friction on the main wheels resisting it during the ground loop may cause the airplane to tip, or lean, enough for the outside wingtip to contact the ground.

      i)   This may impose a great enough sideward force to collapse the landing gear.

g.   The ailerons serve the same purpose on the ground as they do in the air; they change the lift and drag components of the wings.

1)   While your airplane is decelerating during the after-landing roll, more and more aileron must be applied to keep the upwind wing from rising.

2)   Since your airplane is slowing down and there is less airflow around the ailerons, they become less effective. At the same time, the relative wind is becoming more of a crosswind and exerting a greater lifting force on the upwind wing.

   a)   Consequently, when the airplane is coming to a full stop, the aileron control must be held FULLY toward the wind.

h.   If available remaining runway permits, the speed of the airplane should be allowed to dissipate in a normal manner by the friction and drag of the wheels on the ground.

1)   Brakes may be used if needed to slow the airplane. Braking is normally done near the end of the after-landing roll to ensure that the airplane is moving slowly enough to exit the runway in a controlled manner.

9.   **Complete the appropriate checklist.**

a.   Prior to or as you enter the airport traffic pattern (usually on the downwind leg), you should complete a before-landing checklist to be sure that you and your airplane are ready to land. This should be a "do and review" (i.e., memorized) type of checklist and is found in your *POH*.

1)   Many pilots use **GUMPS**:

   G as
   U ndercarriage
   M ixture
   P rop and/or power
   S afety belts and shoulder harnesses

C.   Common Errors during a Normal and Crosswind Approach and Landing

    1.   Improper use of landing performance data and limitations.

        a.   Use your *POH* to determine the appropriate airspeeds for a normal and crosswind approach and landing.

        b.   In gusty and/or strong crosswinds, use the crosswind component chart to determine that you are not exceeding your airplane's crosswind limitations.

        c.   Use your *POH* to determine data and limitations, and do not attempt to do better than the data.

    2.   Failure to establish approach and landing configuration at the appropriate time or in proper sequence.

        a.   Use the before-landing checklist in your *POH* to ensure that you follow the proper sequence in establishing the correct approach and landing configuration for your airplane.

        b.   You should initially start the checklist at midpoint on the downwind leg with the power reduction beginning once you are abeam of your intended point of landing.

            1)   By the time you turn on final and align your airplane with the runway centerline, you should be in the final landing configuration. Confirm this by completing your checklist once again.

    3.   Failure to establish and maintain a stabilized approach.

        a.   Once you are on final and aligned with the runway centerline, you should make small adjustments to pitch and power to establish the correct descent angle (i.e., glide path) and airspeed.

            1)   Remember, you must make simultaneous adjustments to both pitch and power.

            2)   Large adjustments will result in a roller coaster ride.

        b.   Lock in your airspeed and glide path as soon as possible.

            1)   Never let your airspeed go below your approach speed.

            2)   Never let your airplane sink below your selected glide path or the glide path of a visual approach slope indicator (i.e., VASI or PAPI).

    4.   Inappropriate removal of hand from throttle.

        a.   One hand should remain on the control yoke at all times.

        b.   The other hand should remain on the throttle unless operating the microphone or making an adjustment, such as trim or flaps.

            1)   Once you are on short final, your hand should remain on the throttle, even if ATC gives you instruction (e.g., cleared to land).

                a)   Your first priority is to fly your airplane and avoid doing tasks that may distract you from maintaining control.

                b)   Fly first; talk later.

        c.   You must be in the habit of keeping one hand on the throttle in case a sudden and unexpected hazardous situation should require an immediate application of power.

5.   **Improper technique during roundout and touchdown.**

a.   High roundout

1)   This error occurs when you make the roundout too rapidly and your airplane is flying level too high above the runway.

a)   If you continue the roundout, you will increase the wings' angle of attack to the critical angle while reducing the airspeed. Thus, you will stall your airplane and drop hard onto the runway.

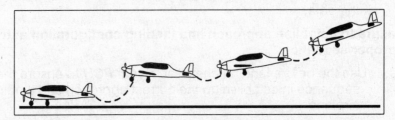

2)   To correct this problem, the pitch attitude should be held constant until the airplane decelerates enough to start descending again. Then the roundout can be continued to establish the proper landing attitude.

a)   Use this technique only when you have an adequate amount of airspeed. It may be necessary to add a slight amount of power to prevent the airspeed from decreasing excessively and to avoid losing lift too rapidly.

3)   Although back pressure on the elevator control may be relaxed slightly, the nose should not be lowered any perceptible amount to make the airplane descend when relatively close to the runway.

a)   The momentary decrease in lift that would result from lowering the nose (i.e., decreasing angle of attack) may be so great that a nosewheel-type airplane might contact the ground with the nosewheel, which could then collapse.

b)   Execute a go-around (see Task IV.L., Go-Around/Rejected Landing, on page 189) anytime it appears that the nose should be lowered significantly.

b.   Late or rapid roundout

1)   Starting the roundout too late or pulling the elevator control back too rapidly to prevent your airplane from touching down prematurely can impose a heavy load factor on the wing and cause an accelerated stall.

a)   This is a dangerous situation because it may cause your airplane to land extremely hard on the main landing wheels and then bounce back into the air.

i)   As your airplane contacts the ground, the tail will be forced down very rapidly by the back pressure on the elevator and the inertia acting downward on the tail.

2)   Recovery requires prompt and positive application of power prior to occurrence of the stall.

a)   The recovery may be followed by a normal landing, if sufficient runway is available; otherwise, execute an immediate go-around.

c.   Floating during roundout

1)   This error is caused by using excessive speed on the final approach. Before touchdown can be made, your airplane may be well past the desired landing point, and the available runway may be insufficient.

2)   If you dive your airplane excessively on final approach to land at the proper point, there will be an appreciable increase in airspeed. Consequently, the proper touchdown attitude cannot be established without producing an excessive angle of attack and lift. This will cause your airplane to gain altitude.

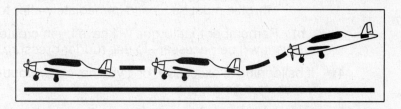

3)   Failure to anticipate ground effect may also result in floating.

4)   The recovery will depend on the amount of floating, the effect of a crosswind (if any), and the amount of runway remaining.

   a)   You must smoothly and gradually adjust the pitch attitude as your airplane decelerates to touchdown speed and starts to settle so that the proper landing attitude is attained at the moment of touchdown.

      i)   The slightest error in judgment will result in either ballooning or bouncing.

   b)   If, during your practical test or practice for your practical test, your landing cannot be completed within 200 ft. of a prespecified point, you should immediately execute a go-around.

d.   Ballooning during roundout

1)   If you misjudge the rate of sink during a landing and think your airplane is descending faster than it should, you may tend to increase the pitch attitude and angle of attack too rapidly.

   a)   This not only stops the descent, but actually starts your airplane climbing (i.e., ballooning).

   b)   Ballooning can be dangerous because the height above the ground is increasing and your airplane may be rapidly approaching a stalled condition.

2)   When ballooning is slight, a constant landing attitude may be held and the airplane allowed to settle onto the runway.

   a)   You must be extremely cautious of ballooning when there is a crosswind present because the crosswind correction may be inadvertently released or it may become inadequate.

   b)   Due to the lower airspeed after ballooning, the crosswind affects your airplane more. Consequently, the wing will have to be lowered even further to compensate for the increased drift.

      i)   You must ensure that the upwind wing is down and that directional control is maintained with opposite rudder.

3) Depending on the severity of ballooning, the use of power may be helpful in cushioning the landing.

   a) By adding power, thrust can be increased to keep the airspeed from decelerating too rapidly and the wings from suddenly losing lift, but the throttle must be closed immediately after touchdown.

   b) Remember that torque will have been created as power was applied; thus it will be necessary to use rudder pressure to counteract this effect.

4) If ballooning is excessive, or if you have any doubts, you should immediately execute a go-around.

e. Bouncing during touchdown

1) When your airplane contacts the ground with a sharp impact as the result of an improper attitude or an excessive rate of sink, it tends to bounce back into the air.

   a) Though your airplane's tires and shock struts provide some springing action, the airplane does not bounce as does a rubber ball.

   b) Your airplane rebounds into the air because the wing's angle of attack was abruptly increased, producing a sudden addition of lift.

      i) The change in angle of attack is the result of inertia instantly forcing the airplane's tail downward when the main wheels contact the ground sharply.

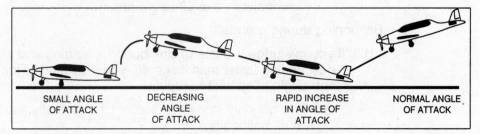

SMALL ANGLE OF ATTACK   DECREASING ANGLE OF ATTACK   RAPID INCREASE IN ANGLE OF ATTACK   NORMAL ANGLE OF ATTACK

   c) The severity of the bounce depends on the airspeed at the moment of contact and the degree to which the angle of attack, or pitch attitude, was increased.

2) The corrective action for a bounce is the same as for ballooning and similarly depends on its severity.

   a) When a bounce is very slight and there is not an extreme change in your airplane's pitch attitude, a follow-up landing may be executed by applying sufficient power to cushion the subsequent touchdown and smoothly adjusting the pitch to the proper touchdown attitude.

3) Extreme caution and alertness must be exercised, especially when there is a crosswind. The crosswind correction will normally be released by inexperienced pilots when the airplane bounces.

   a) When one main wheel of the airplane strikes the runway, the other wheel will touch down immediately afterwards, and the wings will become level.

   b) Then, with no crosswind correction as the airplane bounces, the wind will cause the airplane to roll with the wind, thus exposing even more surface to the crosswind and drifting the airplane more rapidly.

   c) Remember, the upwind wing will have to be lowered even further to compensate for the increased drift due to the slower airspeed.

f. Hard landing

1) When your airplane contacts the ground during landings, its vertical speed is instantly reduced to zero. Unless provision is made to slow this vertical speed and cushion the impact of touchdown, the force of contact with the ground may be so great as to cause structural damage to the airplane.

2) The purpose of pneumatic tires, rubber or oleo shock absorbers, and other such devices is, in part, to cushion the impact and to increase the time in which the airplane's vertical descent is stopped.

   a) The importance of this cushion may be understood from the computation that a 6-in. free fall on landing is roughly equivalent to a 340-fpm descent.

   b) Within a fraction of a second, your airplane must be slowed from this rate of vertical descent to zero, without damage.

      i) During this time, the landing gear together with some aid from the lift of the wings must supply the necessary force to counteract the force of the airplane's inertia and weight.

3) The lift decreases rapidly as the airplane's forward speed is decreased, and the force on the landing gear increases as the shock struts and tires are compressed by the impact of touchdown.

   a) When the descent stops, the lift will practically be zero, leaving the landing gear alone to carry both the airplane's weight and inertial forces.

   b) The load imposed at the instant of touchdown may easily be three or four times the actual weight of the airplane depending on the severity of contact.

g. Touchdown in a drift or crab

1) If you have not taken adequate corrective action to avoid drift during a crosswind landing, the main wheels' tire treads offer resistance to the airplane's sideward movement in respect to the ground. Consequently, any sideward velocity of the airplane is abruptly decelerated, as shown in the figure below.

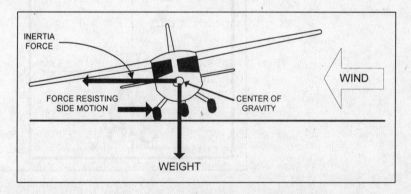

   a) This creates a moment around the main wheel when it contacts the ground, tending to overturn or tip the airplane.

   b) If the windward wingtip is raised by the action of this moment, all the weight and shock of landing will be borne by one main wheel. This may cause structural damage.

   c) Retractable gear is particularly susceptible to collapse from side loads.

2) It is vital to prevent drift and keep the longitudinal axis of the airplane aligned with the runway during the roundout and touchdown.

6. **Poor directional control after touchdown.**

a. Ground loop

1) A ground loop is an uncontrolled turn during ground operation that may occur while taxiing or taking off, but especially during the after-landing roll.

a) It is not always caused by drift or weathervaning, although these may cause the initial swerve. Other reasons may include careless use of rudder, an uneven ground surface, or a soft spot that retards one main wheel of the airplane.

2) If your airplane touches down while drifting or in a crab, you should apply aileron toward the high wing and stop the swerve with the rudder.

3) Brakes should be used to correct for turns or swerves only when the rudder is inadequate. You must exercise caution when applying corrective brake action because it is very easy to over-control and aggravate the situation.

a) If brakes are used, sufficient brake should be applied on the low-wing (outside of the turn) to stop the swerve.

b) When the wings are approximately level, the new direction must be maintained until the airplane has slowed to taxi speed or has stopped.

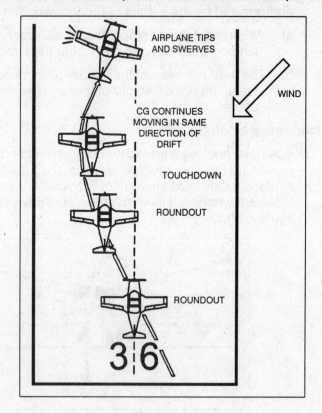

b. Wing rising after touchdown

   1) When landing in a crosswind, you may experience instances in which a wing will rise during the after-landing roll.

   2) Anytime an airplane is rolling on the ground in a crosswind condition, the upwind wing is receiving a greater force from the wind than is the downwind wing. This causes a lift differential.

      a) Also, the wind striking the fuselage on the upwind side may further raise the wing by tending to tip or roll the fuselage.

   3) The corrective action is for you immediately to apply more aileron pressure toward the high wing and maintain directional control.

      a) The sooner the aileron is applied, the more effective it will be.

      b) The farther a wing is allowed to rise before you take corrective action, the more airplane surface is exposed to the force of the crosswind. This reduces the effectiveness of the aileron.

7. **Improper use of brakes.**

   a. Use the minimum amount of braking required, and let your airplane slow by the friction and drag of the wheels on the ground, if runway length permits.

   b. Never attempt to apply brakes until your airplane is firmly on the runway under complete control.

   c. Use equal pressure on both brakes to help prevent swerving and/or loss of directional control.

END OF TASK

SOFT-FIELD TAKEOFF AND CLIMB

IV.C. TASK: SOFT-FIELD TAKEOFF AND CLIMB

REFERENCES: FAA-H-8083-3; Pilot's Operating Handbook, FAA-Approved Airplane Flight Manual.

Objective. To determine that the applicant:

1. Exhibits knowledge of the elements related to a soft-field takeoff and climb.

2. Positions the flight controls for existing conditions and to maximize lift as quickly as possible.

3. Clears the area; taxies onto takeoff surface at a speed consistent with safety without stopping while advancing the throttle smoothly to takeoff power.

4. Establishes and maintains a pitch attitude that will transfer the weight of the airplane from the wheels to the wings as rapidly as possible.

5. Lifts off at the lowest possible airspeed and remains in ground effect while accelerating to V_X or V_Y, as appropriate.

6. Establishes a pitch attitude for V_X or V_Y, as appropriate, and maintains selected airspeed ±5 knots, during the climb.

7. Retracts the landing gear, if appropriate, and flaps after clear of any obstacles, or as recommended by the manufacturer.

8. Maintains takeoff power and V_X or V_Y ±5 knots to a safe maneuvering altitude.

9. Maintains directional control and proper wind-drift correction throughout the takeoff and climb.

10. Completes appropriate checklist.

A. General Information

1. The objective of this task is for you to demonstrate your ability to perform a soft-field takeoff and climb.

2. Additional reading: See Chapter 1, Airplanes and Aerodynamics, of *Pilot Handbook*, see Module 1.7, Ground Effect, for a one-page discussion of the aerodynamic effects when flying just above the ground.

3. Before landing at a soft (unpaved) field, determine your capability to take off in your airplane from that field. Also, consider the possibility of damage and extra wear on your airplane. You may decide to wait until the takeoff surface conditions improve.

    a. Some complex and high-performance airplanes have poor soft-field handling characteristics. You must know and understand both your airplane's and your limitations.

        1) You may decide to land at the nearest suitable hard-surfaced airport.

    b. Many types of professional flying, such as agricultural spraying or providing medical services to remote areas, require takeoffs from soft fields.

    c. If the need arises to make a soft-field takeoff, follow the procedures provided by the manufacturer in your airplane's *POH*.

        1) Practice and perfect soft-field takeoffs.

4. If your airplane is parked on a soft surface, other airplanes or the wind may have blown unwanted debris onto your airplane. Such materials, when trapped in the control surfaces, may jam the controls or limit their travel, which can cause disaster.

    a. Soft fields are often remote fields. Birds and animals can seek refuge or build nests (even overnight) under the cowling, in landing gear wheel wells, and elsewhere.

    b. Also, be cautious of possible vandalism of your airplane at remote airfields.

5. Inspect your taxi route and your takeoff runway. Normally, you should walk the entire route carefully.

    a. Note wet or soft spots and mark them as necessary (use pieces of cloth or paper tied to objects, e.g., fence posts, or anchor them to the ground at the side of the takeoff surface with stakes, sticks, etc.).

    b. Determine and mark your takeoff abort point -- exactly where you will cut power if not airborne.

        1) 75% of V_R by the halfway point on the runway is a general rule.

6. If the airplane wheels have settled into the ground, move the airplane forward before getting into the cockpit.

    a. Use leverage of the wing by holding the wingtip and rocking the wingtip back and forth.

    b. Be careful not to stress the nose wheel with side loads (have someone lift the nose or push down on the tail).

    c. Use help as available.

B. Task Objectives

1. **Exhibit your knowledge of the elements related to a soft-field takeoff and climb.**

    a. The goals of this takeoff are

        1) To get the airplane airborne as soon as possible

        2) To transfer as much weight as possible to the wings to minimize wheel friction in the soft surface

            a) The combination of considerable back pressure on the control yoke and the manufacturer's recommended flap setting is the best means of achieving a soft-field takeoff.

            b) Weight is transferred to the wings and away from the wheels because of the high angle of attack produced by the back elevator pressure.

2. **Position the flight controls for the existing conditions and to maximize lift as quickly as possible.**

    a. Always verify the wind direction as you taxi onto the takeoff surface by observing the windsock or other wind direction indicator, which may include grass or bushes.

    b. For a crosswind takeoff, the ailerons should be FULLY deflected at the start of the takeoff roll.

    c. Use full or nearly full back pressure on the control yoke so as to maximize lift as quickly as possible during the takeoff roll.

        1) Back pressure helps remove some of the stress from the nosewheel and minimize rolling resistance during taxiing.

    d. If the use of flaps is recommended, the flaps must be extended prior to starting the takeoff roll.

        1) Always check your flap setting visually.

3. **Clear the area and taxi onto the takeoff surface at a speed consistent with safety without stopping, while advancing the throttle smoothly to takeoff power.**

   a. Before taxiing onto the takeoff surface, you must make certain that you have sufficient time to execute the takeoff before any aircraft in the traffic pattern turns onto the final approach.

      1) Check that the takeoff surface is clear of other aircraft, vehicles, persons, or other hazards.

      2) Recheck that the mixture is set in accordance with the *POH* and the propeller is at high RPM.

   b. Keep moving once your airplane is rolling. If your airplane becomes bogged down, the thrust available may be insufficient for the airplane to pull out of the mud and/or ruts, and the only choice would be to shut down and move the airplane by hand or with equipment.

      1) Grass, sand, mud, and snow require more power than is necessary to taxi on a hard surface.

         a) Be cautious of your propeller blast and its effect on others.

      2) Also, debris may be sucked up by the propeller, causing propeller damage and/or wear and damage to your paint job when the debris strikes the airplane.

      3) You should taxi your airplane onto the takeoff surface as fast as possible, consistent with safety.

         a) Line your airplane up as done on a hard-surfaced runway with a centerline.

   c. Keep your airplane moving with sufficient power while lining up for the takeoff roll.

      1) Power should be applied smoothly and as rapidly as possible to allow for a controllable transition to flying airspeed.

         a) Applying power too quickly can cause engine surging, backfiring, and a possible overboost situation (turbocharged engines). These conditions cause unnecessary engine wear as well as possible failure.

         b) Applying power too slowly wastes runway length.

   d. The engine instruments must be monitored during the entire maneuver.

      1) Monitoring enables you to notice immediately any malfunction or indication of insufficient power or other potential problems.

      2) Listen for any indication of power loss or engine roughness.

      3) Do not hesitate to abort the takeoff if there is any indication of trouble.

   e. Check your airspeed indicator for movement as you accelerate.

      1) If the airspeed indicator does not move, abort the takeoff.

4. **Establish and maintain a pitch attitude that will transfer the weight of the airplane from the wheels to the wings as rapidly as possible.**

   a. Enough back elevator pressure should be applied to establish a positive angle of attack.

      1) This reduces the weight supported by the nosewheel.

      2) The nose-high attitude will allow the weight to transfer from the wheels to the wings as lift is developed.

    b.   When the airplane is held at a nose-high attitude throughout the takeoff, the wings will, as speed increases and lift develops, progressively relieve the wheels of more and more of the airplane's weight, thus reducing the drag on the wheels caused by surface irregularities or adhesion.

        1)   As the airplane picks up speed, back pressure must be reduced somewhat to avoid an excessive angle of attack, while weight is transferred to the wings and liftoff into ground effect is accomplished as quickly as possible.

5.   **Lift off at the lowest possible airspeed and remain in ground effect while accelerating to V_X or V_Y, as appropriate.**

    a.   If the pitch attitude is accurately maintained during the takeoff roll, the airplane should become airborne at an airspeed slower than a safe climb speed because of the action of ground effect.

    b.   After your airplane becomes airborne, the nose must be lowered very gently with the wheels just clear of the surface to allow your airplane to accelerate in ground effect to V_X or V_Y.

        1)   Failure to level off will cause the airplane to climb out of ground effect at too slow a speed, and the increase in drag could reduce the lift sufficiently to cause the airplane to settle back onto the takeoff surface.

    c.   If there are no obstacles in your takeoff and climb path, then accelerate in ground effect to V_Y.

        1)   If obstacles are present, you should accelerate to V_X and climb at V_X until clear of the obstacle, then adjust pitch and climb at V_Y.

        2)   During your practical test, if you are using a runway which would allow a V_Y climb, your examiner may request that you simulate an obstacle at the departure end of the runway.

6.   *Establish a pitch attitude for V_X or V_Y, as appropriate, and maintain the selected airspeed, ±5 kt., during the climb.*

    a.   During the climb, maintain V_Y, ±5 kt., to the traffic pattern altitude, unless obstacles are a factor.

        1)   If obstacles are a factor, maintain V_X ± 5 kt. until you are clear of them.

    b.   After clearing the obstacles, transition to V_Y, ±5 kt.

7.   **Retract the landing gear, if appropriate, and flaps after clearing any obstacles or as recommended by the manufacturer.**

    a.   Before retracting the landing gear, apply the brakes momentarily to stop the rotation of the wheels to avoid excessive vibration on the gear mechanism.

        1)   Centrifugal force caused by the rapidly rotating wheels expands the diameter of the tires, and if mud or other debris has accumulated in the wheel wells, the rotating wheels may rub as they enter.

    b.   When to retract the landing gear varies among manufacturers. Thus, it is important that you know what procedure is prescribed by your airplane's *POH*.

        1)   Some manufacturers recommend gear retraction after a positive rate of climb has been established, while others recommend gear retraction only after the obstacles have been cleared.

        2)   Normally, the landing gear will be retracted before the flaps.

        3)   Make necessary pitch adjustments to maintain the appropriate airspeed.

   c.   Flaps are normally retracted when you have established V_Y and a positive rate of climb.

      1)   Raise the flaps in increments (if appropriate) to avoid sudden loss of lift and settling of the airplane.

      2)   Make needed pitch adjustments to maintain V_Y.

   d.   Follow the procedure in your airplane's *POH*.

8.   *Maintain takeoff power and V_X or V_Y, ± 5 kt., to a safe maneuvering altitude.*

   a.   After establishing V_X or V_Y, as appropriate, and completing gear and flap retraction, maintain takeoff power to a safe maneuvering altitude, normally 500 to 1,000 ft. AGL.

      1)   Then the power (MP, RPM, and mixture) should be set to the climb power setting recommended in your airplane's *POH*.

         a)   Adjust pitch as necessary to maintain airspeed.

   b.   Maintain V_X or V_Y, ± 5 kt., until reaching traffic pattern altitude; then transition to the recommended cruise climb airspeed.

   c.   Follow the procedures in your airplane's *POH*.

9.   Maintain directional control and proper wind-drift correction throughout the takeoff and climb.

   a.   Crosswind takeoff techniques are consistent with a soft-field takeoff and should be employed simultaneously, as needed.

      1)   A common error is to become preoccupied with the soft-field effort at the expense of neglecting crosswind correction. The results are directional control problems.

   b.   For additional information on a crosswind takeoff, see Task IV.A., Normal and Crosswind Takeoff and Climb, beginning on page 132.

10. Complete the appropriate checklist.

   a.   In Section 4, Normal Procedures, of your *POH*, find the soft-field takeoff checklist and study it and any amplified procedures.

   b.   Complete the checklist for climb to ensure that your airplane is in the proper configuration for the continued climb to cruising altitude.

   c.   Follow the checklist(s) in your *POH*.

C. Common Errors during a Soft-Field Takeoff and Climb

1.   Improper initial positioning of the flight controls or wing flaps.

   a.   The control yoke should be held in the full back position and turned into the crosswind (if appropriate).

   b.   If wing flaps are recommended by your *POH*, they should be lowered prior to your taxiing onto the takeoff surface.

2.   Allowing the airplane to stop on the takeoff surface prior to initiating takeoff.

   a.   Once stopped, your airplane may become bogged down and may not have the power to begin rolling again.

3. **Improper power application.**

   a. Power must be used throughout the entire ground operation in a positive and safe manner.

   b. Power must be applied smoothly and as quickly as the engine will accept (without faltering).

   c. Remember, the goal is to get your airplane airborne as quickly as possible.

4. **Inappropriate removal of hand from throttle.**

   a. Keep your hand on the throttle at all times except during

      1) Flap retraction
      2) Gear retraction
      3) Trim adjustment

5. **Poor directional control.**

   a. Maintain the center of the takeoff surface by use of the rudder.
   b. Divide your attention between the soft-field takeoff technique and directional control.

6. **Improper use of brakes.**

   a. Brakes should never be used on a soft field.
   b. Keep your feet off the brakes.

7. **Improper pitch attitude during liftoff.**

   a. During the takeoff roll, excessive back elevator may cause the angle of attack to exceed that required for a climb, which would generate more drag.

      1) Also, the tail of your airplane may drag on the ground.

   b. You must slowly lower the nose after liftoff to allow the airplane to accelerate in ground effect.

      1) If the nose is lowered too quickly, you will settle back onto the takeoff surface.

   c. Attempting to climb without the proper airspeed may cause you to settle back onto the takeoff surface due to the increase in drag.

8. **Settling back to takeoff surface after becoming airborne, resulting in**

   a. Reduction of takeoff performance
   b. A wheel digging in, causing an upset of the airplane
   c. Side loads on the landing gear if in a crosswind crab
   d. A gear-up landing or a prop strike if the landing gear is retracted early

9. **Failure to establish and maintain proper climb configuration and airspeed.**

   a. Follow the procedures in your *POH.*

   b. Fly your airplane by the numbers. Failure to do so means reduced performance, which may be devastating on a short soft-field takeoff, especially if there is an obstacle to be cleared.

10. **Drift during climbout.**

    a. Maintain the extended centerline of the takeoff surface during the climb to avoid other obstacles.

    b. Other pilots in the traffic pattern will be expecting you to maintain the centerline. If you drift, they may be forced to take measures to avoid a collision.

END OF TASK

SOFT-FIELD APPROACH AND LANDING

IV.D. TASK: SOFT-FIELD APPROACH AND LANDING

        REFERENCES: FAA-H-8083-3; Pilot's Operating Handbook, FAA-Approved Airplane Flight Manual.

Objective. To determine that the applicant:

1. Exhibits knowledge of the elements related to soft-field approach and landing.

2. Considers the wind conditions, landing surface, and obstructions, and selects the most suitable touchdown area.

3. Establishes the recommended approach and landing configuration and airspeed; adjusts pitch attitude and power as required.

4. Maintains a stabilized approach and recommended airspeed, or in its absence, not more than 1.3 V_{so}, ±5 kt. with wind gust factor applied.

5. Makes smooth, timely, and correct control application during the roundout and touchdown.

6. Touches down softly, with no drift, and with the airplane's longitudinal axis aligned with the runway/landing path.

7. Maintains crosswind correction and directional control throughout the approach and landing sequence.

8. Maintains proper position of the flight controls and sufficient speed to taxi on the soft surface.

9. Completes appropriate checklists.

A. General Information

   1. The objective of this task is for you to demonstrate your ability to perform a soft-field approach and landing.

B. Task Objectives

   1. Exhibit your knowledge of the elements related to a soft-field approach and landing.

      a. The approach for the soft-field landing is similar to the normal approach used for operating into long, firm landing areas.

        1) The major difference between the two is that, during the soft-field landing, the airplane is held 1 to 2 ft. off the surface as long as possible to dissipate the forward speed sufficiently to allow the wheels to touch down softly at minimum speed.

      b. Landing on fields that are rough or have soft surfaces (e.g., snow, mud, sand, or tall grass) requires special techniques.

        1) When landing on such surfaces, you must control your airplane in a manner such that the wings support the weight of the airplane as long as practicable.

          a) Supporting the airplane's weight with the wings minimizes drag and stress put on the landing gear from the rough or soft surfaces.

      c. Follow the procedures prescribed in your *POH*.

   2. Consider the wind conditions, landing surface, and obstructions, and select the most suitable touchdown area.

      a. You must know the wind conditions and the effect they will have upon your airplane's approach and landing performance. The effect of wind on the landing distance may be significant and deserves proper consideration.

        1) A headwind will decrease the landing distance, while a tailwind will greatly increase the landing distance.

        2) Wind conditions are important if the landing area is short and/or in a confined area.

b.   A soft field is any surface other than a paved one. You must take into account a hard-packed turf or a wet, high grass turf. Know the condition of the landing surface you will be operating into.

1)   If a surface is soft or wet, consider what effect that will have if you perform a crosswind landing, when one main wheel touches down before the other main wheel.

c.   During your approach, you must look for any hazards or obstructions and then evaluate how they may affect your approach and selection of a suitable touchdown point.

1)   Be aware of traffic, both in the air and on the ground.

2)   Look out for vehicles and/or people on or near the runway.

3)   Check the approach area for any natural or man-made obstacles (e.g., trees, towers, or construction equipment).

4)   Your angle of descent on final approach may need to be steepened if obstacles are present.

d.   After considering the wind conditions, landing surface, and obstructions, you should select the most suitable touchdown point.

1)   After you select your touchdown point, you should identify it to your examiner.

e.   Once you have selected your touchdown point, you need to select your aim point.

1)   See Task IV.B., Normal and Crosswind Approach and Landing, beginning on page 140, for a discussion on the use of the aim point.

3.   Establish the recommended approach and landing configuration and airspeed, and adjust pitch attitude and power as required.

a.   Establish your airplane in the proper soft-field configuration and at the proper airspeed as prescribed in your *POH*. The configuration is usually similar to that used for a normal approach.

1)   The use of flaps during soft-field landings will aid in touching down at minimum speed and is recommended whenever practicable.

a)   In low-wing airplanes, however, the flaps may suffer damage from mud, stones, or slush thrown up by the wheels. In such cases, it may be advisable to use partial or no flaps.

b.   See Task IV.B., Normal and Crosswind Approach and Landing, beginning on page 140, for the discussion of how to use pitch and power on the approach.

4.   *Maintain a stabilized approach and the recommended airspeed, or in its absence, not more than 1.3 V_{S0}, ±5 kt., with wind gust factor applied.*

a.   For information on gust factors and a stabilized approach, see Task IV.B., Normal and Crosswind Approach and Landing, beginning on page 140.

5.   Make smooth, timely, and correct control application during the roundout and touchdown.

a.   Use the same technique during the roundout and touchdown as discussed in Task IV.B., Normal and Crosswind Approach and Landing, beginning on page 140.

1)   The only exception is that you will use partial power during the roundout and touchdown.

b.   Do not misjudge the roundout too high, since this may cause you to stall above the surface and drop your airplane in too hard for a soft surface.

6. ***Touch down softly, with no drift, and with your airplane's longitudinal axis aligned with the runway/landing path.***

   a. Maintain slight power throughout the roundout (flare) to assist in producing as soft a touchdown (i.e., minimum descent rate) as possible.

      1) Attempt to hold your airplane about 1 to 2 ft. above the ground as long as possible to allow the touchdown to be made at the slowest possible airspeed with your airplane in a nose-high pitch attitude.

   b. After the main wheels touch the surface, you should hold sufficient back elevator pressure to keep the nosewheel off the ground until it can no longer aerodynamically be held off the surface.

      1) At this time, you should let the nosewheel come down to the ground on its own. Maintain full back elevator pressure at all times on a soft surface.

         a) Maintaining slight power during and immediately after touchdown usually will aid in easing the nosewheel down.

   c. Use the proper crosswind technique to ensure your airplane's longitudinal axis is aligned with the landing surface.

7. **Maintain crosswind correction and directional control throughout the approach and landing sequence.**

   a. If a crosswind is present, use the crosswind and directional control techniques described in Task IV.B., Normal and Crosswind Approaches and Landings, beginning on page 140.

8. **Maintain proper position of the flight controls and sufficient speed to taxi on the soft surface.**

   a. Maintain full back elevator pressure and the proper aileron deflection for a crosswind condition while on the ground.

   b. Brakes are not needed on a soft surface. Avoid using the brakes because their use may impose a heavy load on the nosegear due to premature or hard contact with the landing surface, causing the nosewheel to dig in.

      1) The soft or rough surface itself will normally provide sufficient friction to reduce your airplane's forward speed.

   c. You must maintain enough speed while taxiing to prevent becoming bogged down on the soft surface.

      1) You will often need to increase power after landing on a very soft surface to keep your airplane moving and prevent becoming stuck.

      2) Care must be taken not to taxi excessively fast because if you taxi onto a very soft area, your airplane may bog down and bend the landing gear and/or nose over.

      3) Keep your airplane moving at all times until you are at the point where you will be parking your airplane.

9. **Complete the appropriate checklist.**

   a. The before-landing checklist should be completed on the downwind leg of the traffic pattern.

      1) The last GUMPS check should be completed on final.

   b. On a soft field, the after-landing checklist should normally be accomplished only after you have parked your airplane.

      1) Some items can be done while taxiing (e.g., turning the carburetor heat OFF, if it was used).

      2) You should maintain control of the airplane and, on a soft field, only come to a complete stop at the point at which you are parking your airplane.

C. Common Errors during a Soft-Field Approach and Landing

   1. **Improper use of landing performance data and limitations.**

      a. Use your *POH* to determine the appropriate airspeeds and performance for a soft-field approach and landing.

      b. The most common error, as well as the easiest to avoid, is to attempt a landing that is beyond the capabilities of your airplane and/or your flying skills. Be sure that the surface of the field you plan to use is suitable for landing. Plan ahead!

   2. **Failure to establish approach and landing configuration at appropriate time or in proper sequence.**

      a. Use the before-landing checklist in your *POH* to ensure that you follow the proper sequence in establishing the correct approach and landing configuration for your airplane.

      b. You should initially start the checklist at midpoint on the downwind leg with the power reduction beginning once you are abeam your intended point of landing.

         1) By the time you turn on final and align your airplane with the landing surface, you should be in the proper configuration. Confirm this by completing your checklist once again.

   3. **Failure to establish and maintain a stabilized approach.**

      a. Once you are on final and aligned with the landing surface, you should make small adjustments to pitch and power to establish the correct descent angle (i.e., glide path) and airspeed.

         1) Remember, you must make simultaneous adjustments to both pitch and power.

   4. **Failure to consider the effect of wind and landing surface.**

      a. Proper planning will ensure knowledge of the landing surface condition, e.g., wet, dry, loose, hard packed.

      b. Understand how the wind affects the landing distance required on a soft field.

   5. **Improper technique in use of power, wing flaps, and trim.**

      a. Use power and pitch adjustments simultaneously to maintain the proper descent angle and airspeed.

      b. Wing flaps should be used in accordance with your *POH*.

      c. Trim to relieve control pressures to help in stabilizing the final approach.

      d. Remember to maintain power throughout the roundout, touchdown, and after-landing roll.

6. **Inappropriate removal of hand from throttle.**

   a. One hand should remain on the control yoke at all times.

   b. The other hand should remain on the throttle unless you are operating the microphone or making an adjustment, such as trim or flaps.

      1) Your first priority is to fly your airplane and avoid doing tasks which may distract you from maintaining control.

   c. You must be in the habit of keeping one hand on the throttle in case a sudden and unexpected hazardous situation should require an immediate application of power.

7. **Improper technique during roundout and touchdown.**

   a. Maintain a little power, and hold the airplane off the ground as long as possible.

   b. See Task IV.B., Normal and Crosswind Approach and Landing, beginning on page 140, for a detailed discussion of general landing errors.

   c. Remember, if you have any doubts about the suitability of the field, go around.

8. **Failure to hold back elevator pressure after touchdown.**

   a. Holding back elevator pressure will keep weight off the nosewheel, which otherwise could get bogged down causing the gear to bend and/or nose over the airplane.

9. **Closing the throttle too soon after touchdown.**

   a. On a soft field, you must keep your airplane moving at all times.

10. **Poor directional control after touchdown.**

   a. Use rudder to steer your airplane on the landing surface, and increase aileron deflection into the wind as airspeed decreases.

   b. See Common Errors of Task IV.B., Normal and Crosswind Approach and Landing, beginning on page 149, for a discussion on ground loops and other directional control problems after touchdown.

11. **Improper use of brakes.**

   a. Brakes are not needed on a soft field and should be avoided.

   b. On a very soft surface, you may even need full power to avoid stopping and/or becoming bogged down on the runway.

END OF TASK

SHORT-FIELD TAKEOFF AND MAXIMUM PERFORMANCE CLIMB

IV.E. TASK: SHORT-FIELD TAKEOFF AND MAXIMUM PERFORMANCE CLIMB

REFERENCES: FAA-H-8083-3; Pilot's Operating Handbook, FAA-Approved Airplane Flight Manual.

Objective. To determine that the applicant:

1. Exhibits knowledge of the elements related to a short-field takeoff and maximum performance climb.

2. Positions the flight controls for the existing wind conditions, sets flaps as recommended.

3. Clears the area; taxies into takeoff position utilizing maximum available takeoff area and aligns the airplane on the runway center/takeoff path.

4. Applies brakes (if appropriate) while advancing the throttle smoothly to takeoff power.

5. Lifts off at the recommended airspeed, and accelerates to recommended obstacle clearance airspeed, or V_X.

6. Establishes a pitch attitude that will maintain the recommended obstacle clearance airspeed, or V_X, +5/−0 kt. until the obstacle is cleared, or until the airplane is at least 50 ft. (20 meters) above the surface.

7. After clearing the obstacle, establishes the pitch attitude for V_Y, accelerates to V_Y, and maintains V_Y, ±5 kt. during the climb.

8. Retracts the landing gear, if appropriate, and flaps after clear of any obstacles, or as recommended by manufacturer.

9. Maintains takeoff power and V_Y, ±5 kt. to a safe maneuvering altitude.

10. Maintains directional control and proper wind-drift correction throughout the takeoff and climb.

11. Completes appropriate checklist.

A. General Information

1. The objective of this task is to determine your ability to perform a short-field takeoff and maximum performance climb.

B. Task Objectives

1. **Exhibit your knowledge of the elements related to a short-field takeoff and maximum performance climb.**

   a. When taking off from a field where the available runway is short and/or where obstacles must be cleared, you must operate your airplane to its maximum capability.

      1) Positive and accurate control of your airplane attitude and airspeed is required to obtain the shortest ground roll and the steepest angle of climb.

   b. Section 4, Normal Procedures, in your *POH* will provide you with the proper airspeeds, e.g., V_R, V_X, V_Y, and also the proper configurations.

      1) Best angle of climb, V_X, is the speed which will result in the greatest gain of altitude for a given distance over the ground. This speed increases slowly as higher density altitudes are encountered.

         a) In some airplanes, a deviation of more than +5/−0 kt. from V_X can result in a significant reduction in climb performance.

      2) Always climb above the altitude of obstacles (usually powerlines or treelines) or, if no obstacles are involved, until an altitude of at least 50 ft. AGL before accelerating to V_Y. This acceleration involves a reduction in pitch.

    c.   Check the takeoff distance graph or table in Section 5, Performance, of your *POH* before attempting a short-field takeoff, specifically taking into account the existing temperature, barometric pressure, field length, wind, type of runway surface, and airplane operating condition and weight.

        1)   The takeoff distance graph or table will also list associated conditions, such as

            a)   Power
            b)   Mixture
            c)   Flap setting

        2)   Since the performance charts assume good pilot technique, consider your short-field takeoff proficiency.

        3)   Recognize that, in some situations, you should decide NOT to attempt to take off because the margin of safety is too small. You may have to

            a)   Remove fuel, people, baggage.
            b)   Wait for different wind and/or temperature conditions.
            c)   Retain a more experienced pilot to make the flight.
            d)   Have the airplane moved to a safer takeoff location.

    d.   Attempting a tailwind takeoff will drastically increase your takeoff distance.

2.   Position the flight controls for the existing conditions and set flaps as recommended.

    a.   Always reverify wind direction as you taxi onto the runway by observing the windsock or other wind direction indicator, which may include grass or bushes.

    b.   For a crosswind takeoff, the ailerons should be FULLY deflected at the start of the takeoff roll.

    c.   If the use of flaps is recommended, they should be extended prior to starting the takeoff roll.

        1)   Always check your flap setting visually.

3.   Clear the area and taxi into takeoff position utilizing maximum available takeoff area, and align the airplane on the runway center/takeoff path.

    a.   Before taxiing onto the runway, you must make certain that you have sufficient time to execute the takeoff before any aircraft in the traffic pattern turn onto the final approach.

        1)   Check that the runway is clear of other aircraft, vehicles, persons, or other hazards.

        2)   This should be done at airports both with and without operating control towers.

    b.   You should taxi to the very beginning of the runway that is available for takeoff and come to a complete stop, thus making full use of the runway.

        1)   This may require a back taxi; announce your intentions on the CTAF or request permission from the tower.

        2)   Be sure to align your airplane on the runway centerline with the nosewheel straight before coming to a complete stop.

    c.   Before beginning your takeoff roll, study the runway and related ground reference points (e.g., building, trees, obstacles).

        1)   You will gain a frame of reference for directional control during takeoff.
        2)   You will feel more confident that you have everything under control.

4. **Apply brakes, if appropriate, while advancing the throttle smoothly to takeoff power.**

    a. Recheck that the mixture is set in accordance with your *POH* and the propeller is at high RPM.

    b. While holding the brakes, add takeoff power, and then release the brakes smoothly. Confirm that the engine is developing takeoff power under prevailing conditions before releasing the brakes.

        1) Applying power too quickly can cause engine surging, backfiring, and a possible overboost situation (turbocharged engines). These conditions cause unnecessary engine wear as well as possible failure.

        2) Follow the recommended procedures for the use of brakes and the takeoff technique in your airplane's *POH*.

    c. Engine instruments must be monitored during the entire maneuver.

        1) Monitoring enables you to notice immediately any malfunctions or indication of insufficient power or other potential problems.

        2) Listen for any indication of power loss or engine roughness.

        3) Do not hesitate to abort the takeoff if all engine indications are not normal.

    d. Check your airspeed indicator for movement as you accelerate.

        1) Call out your airspeed as you accelerate to V_R, e.g., "40, 60, 80."

5. **Lift off at the recommended airspeed and accelerate to the recommended obstacle clearance airspeed or V_X.**

    a. Lift-off speed varies with aircraft weight. The appropriate airspeed is found on the takeoff distance graph or table in Section 5, Performance, of your airplane's *POH*.

        1) Most *POHs* will provide you with a range of weights and an associated liftoff airspeed and a 50-ft. airspeed.

        2) Rotation (V_R) should be approximately 5 kt. (or 5 mph) before the published lift-off speed.

            a) EXAMPLE: Given a takeoff weight of 2,750 lb. the liftoff speed is 59 kt. Thus, use a rotation speed (V_R) of 54 kt. (59 − 5).

    b. At V_R, you should smoothly apply back elevator pressure to raise the nose of the airplane to the pitch attitude that will produce the best-angle-of-climb airspeed, V_X.

        1) After becoming airborne, accelerate to V_X or the manufacturer's recommended obstacle clearance airspeed by holding this attitude.

    c. DO NOT attempt to raise the nose until V_R because this will create unnecessary drag and will prolong the takeoff roll.

        1) Keep the elevator in a neutral position to maintain a low drag attitude until rotation.

    d. Your airplane's V_R _____ at _____ lb.

6. ***Establish a pitch attitude that will maintain the recommended obstacle clearance airspeed, or V$_X$, +5/−O kt., until the obstacle is cleared, or until your airplane is at least 50 ft. above the surface.***

   a. The "50-ft." airspeed provided in the takeoff distance graph or table is V$_X$.

      1) If you pass through 50 ft. AGL at a lower airspeed, the pitch attitude is too high.

      2) If you pass through 50 ft. AGL at a higher airspeed, the pitch attitude is too low.

      3) If you pass through 50 ft. AGL at the recommended airspeed, then the pitch attitude is correct, and you are operating your airplane at the manufacturer's optimum level.

   b. While you are practicing short-field takeoffs, you should learn the pitch attitude required to maintain the recommended V$_X$.

      1) Observe the position of the airplane's nose on the horizon.
      2) Note the position of the aircraft bar on the attitude indicator.

   c. You should rotate to this predetermined pitch angle as soon as you reach V$_R$. As you climb out at V$_X$, you should maintain visual references, but occasionally glance at the attitude indicator and airspeed indicator to check the pitch angle and airspeed.

   d. Maintain V$_X$, +5/−0 kt., until the obstacle is cleared or, if no obstacles are involved, until an altitude of at least 50 ft. AGL.

   e. Your airplane's V$_X$ _____ at _____ lb.

7. ***After clearing the obstacle, establish the pitch attitude for V$_Y$, accelerate to V$_Y$, and maintain V$_Y$, ±5 kt., during the climb.***

   a. In addition to determining the pitch attitude required to maintain V$_X$, you should also determine the attitude required to maintain V$_Y$ during your practice of short-field takeoffs.

      1) After clearing the obstacle, lower the nose to the appropriate V$_Y$ attitude and accelerate to V$_Y$.

      2) Maintain V$_Y$, ± 5 kt., during the climb.

8. **Retract the landing gear, if appropriate, and flaps after clear of any obstacles, or as recommended by the manufacturer.**

   a. Before retracting the landing gear, apply the brakes momentarily to stop the rotation of the wheels to avoid excessive vibration on the gear mechanism.

      1) Centrifugal force caused by the rapidly rotating wheels expands the diameter of the tires, and if mud or other debris has accumulated in the wheel wells, the rotating wheels may rub as they enter.

b.   When to retract the landing gear varies among manufacturers. Thus, it is important that you know what procedure is prescribed by your airplane's *POH*.

    1)   Some manufacturers recommend gear retraction after a positive rate of climb has been established, while others recommend gear retraction only after the obstacles have been cleared.

    2)   It is generally unwise for you to be looking in the cockpit to confirm that you have the landing gear control until obstacle clearance is assured.

    3)   In some airplanes, the drag of the extended landing gear at V_x has little or no effect on climb performance, especially when looking at the big picture, which includes pilot proficiency and technique, engine performance, etc.

    4)   Normally, the landing gear will be retracted before the flaps.

c.   Flaps are normally retracted when you are clear of any obstacle(s) and the best-rate-of-climb speed, V_Y, has been established.

    1)   Raise the flaps in increments (if appropriate) to avoid sudden loss of lift and settling of the airplane.

d.   Make needed pitch adjustments during gear and flap retraction to maintain V_Y.

9.   *Maintain takeoff power and V_Y, ± 5 kt., to a safe maneuvering altitude.*

a.   After establishing V_Y and completing gear and flap retraction, maintain takeoff power to a safe maneuvering altitude, normally 500 to 1,000 ft. AGL.

    1)   Then the power (MP, RPM, and mixture) should be set to the climb power setting recommended in your airplane's *POH*.

        a)   Adjust pitch as necessary to maintain airspeed.

b.   Maintain V_Y until reaching traffic pattern altitude (normally 1,000 ft. AGL); then transition to the recommended cruise climb airspeed.

c.   Follow the procedures in your airplane's *POH*.

10.   Maintain directional control and proper wind-drift correction throughout the takeoff and climb.

a.   Maintain directional control and wind-drift correction as discussed in Task IV.A., Normal and Crosswind Takeoff and Climb, beginning on page 132.

b.   Crosswind takeoff techniques are consistent with a short-field takeoff and should be employed simultaneously, as needed.

    1)   A common error is to become preoccupied with the short-field effort at the expense of neglecting crosswind correction. The results are directional control problems.

11.   Complete the appropriate checklist.

a.   Follow the short-field takeoff checklist in your *POH*.

b.   Complete the checklist for climb to ensure that your airplane is in the proper configuration for the continued climb to cruising altitude.

C.   Common Errors during a Short-Field Takeoff and Climb

    1.   Failure to use the maximum amount of runway available for the takeoff.

        a.   Instead of making a wide turn onto the runway, you should taxi to the beginning of the usable portion of the runway for takeoff. The usable portion includes any runway before a displaced threshold.

            1)   Paved areas that are marked with arrows pointing toward the beginning of the runway for landings may be used for takeoff. Chevron-marked areas are to be used only in an emergency.

    2.   Improper positioning of flight controls and wing flaps.

        a.   If a crosswind is present, FULL aileron should be held into the wind initially to prevent the crosswind from raising the upwind wing.

        b.   Flaps should be visually checked to ensure that they are in the proper position recommended by your *POH*.

            1)   The short-field takeoff performance chart in your *POH* will also list the flap setting used to attain the chart performance.

            2)   Position the flaps prior to taxiing onto the active runway.

    3.   Improper engine operation during short-field takeoff and climbout.

        a.   In an attempt to gain the most performance, some pilots use very rapid throttle movements, overboost the engine, and use improper power settings.

            1)   Operating the engine in this manner can degrade engine performance, cause long-term engine wear, and add to the risk of engine failure.

        b.   The performance for short-field takeoffs should be obtained by the flap settings, runway selection, rotation speed, climbout attitude, and climbout airspeed indicated in your *POH*, not by misusing the engine.

    4.   Inappropriate removal of hand from throttle.

        a.   Throughout this maneuver, your hand should remain on the throttle.

        b.   Exceptions are when you are raising the flaps, raising the landing gear, and/or adjusting the trim during the climb. After you complete these tasks, your hand should return to the throttle.

    5.   Poor directional control.

        a.   Maintain the runway centerline throughout the takeoff roll by use of the rudder.

        b.   Poor directional control can lead to a longer takeoff roll and control problems at liftoff.

        c.   Positive and accurate control of your airplane is required to obtain the shortest ground roll and the steepest angle of climb (V_x).

        d.   The higher pitch attitude required for V_x will result in increased torque effects; thus, more right rudder will be required than during a climb at V_y.

            1)   Slipping will degrade your airplane's climb performance.

    6.   Improper use of brakes.

        a.   You should not release the brakes until the engine is producing full power and you have checked that the engine instruments are operating normally.

            1)   Follow the procedures in your airplane's *POH*.

        b.   When the brakes are released, ensure that your feet move to the bottom of the rudder pedal and are not on the brakes so that no further braking can take place.

            1)   Any use of brakes will increase the takeoff distance.

7. **Improper pitch attitude during liftoff.**

   a. If not enough back pressure is held to maintain the correct takeoff attitude or the nose is allowed to lower excessively, the airplane may settle back to the runway. This occurs because the angle of attack is decreased and lift is diminished to the point where it will not support the airplane.

      1) Too much back pressure will result in too low of an airspeed, approaching a stall.

   b. The attitude to maintain V_x will be significantly higher than that to maintain V_y; thus, a pilot not completely comfortable with his/her airplane may find it difficult to pull the airplane into a high pitch angle.

   c. Have confidence in your airplane's abilities, and fly it by the numbers.

8. **Failure to establish and maintain proper climb configuration and airspeed.**

   a. Follow the recommended procedures in your *POH*.

   b. Maintain V_x because a deviation of more than +5/–0 kt. can result in a reduction of climb performance.

9. **Drift during climbout.**

   a. Maintain the extended runway centerline until a turn is required.

   b. Remember that an airport traffic pattern can be a very busy area, and collision avoidance and awareness are of extreme importance.

      1) Your fellow pilots will be expecting you to maintain the extended runway centerline during your initial climb.

END OF TASK

SHORT-FIELD APPROACH AND LANDING

IV.F. TASK: SHORT-FIELD APPROACH AND LANDING

  REFERENCES: FAA-H-8083-3; Pilot's Operating Handbook, FAA-Approved Airplane Flight Manual.

Objective. To determine that the applicant:

1. Exhibits knowledge of the elements related to a short-field approach and landing.

2. Considers the wind conditions, landing surface, and obstructions, and selects the most suitable touchdown point.

3. Establishes the recommended approach and landing configuration and airspeed; adjusts pitch attitude and power.

4. Maintains a stabilized approach and recommended approach airspeed, or in its absence, not more than 1.3 V_{S0}, ±5 kt., with wind gust factor applied.

5. Makes smooth, timely, and correct control application during the roundout and touchdown.

6. Touches down smoothly at minimum control airspeed.

7. Touches down at or within 100 ft. (30 meters) beyond a specified point, with no side drift, minimum float, and with the airplane's longitudinal axis aligned with and over the runway center/landing path.

8. Maintains crosswind correction and directional control throughout the approach and landing sequence.

9. Applies brakes, as necessary, to stop in the shortest distance consistent with safety.

10. Completes appropriate checklist.

A.   General Information

  1.   The objective of this task is for you to demonstrate your ability to perform a short-field approach and landing.

B.   Task Objectives

  1.   **Exhibit your knowledge of the elements related to a short-field approach and landing.**

    a.   This maximum performance operation requires the use of procedures and techniques for the approach and landing at fields that have a relatively short landing area and/or where an approach must be made over obstacles that limit the available landing area.

      1)   This is a critical maximum performance operation, as it requires you to fly your airplane at one of its critical performance capabilities while close to the ground in order to land safely in a confined area.

    b.   To land within a short field or a confined area, you must have precise, positive control of your airplane's rate of descent and airspeed to produce an approach that will clear any obstacles, result in little or no floating during the roundout, and permit your airplane to be stopped in the shortest possible distance.

    c.   You must know, understand, and respect both your own and your airplane's limitations.

      1)   Think ahead. Do not attempt to land on a short field from which a takeoff is beyond your capability or that of your airplane.

  2.   **Consider the wind conditions, landing surface, and obstructions, and select the most suitable touchdown point.**

    a.   The height of obstructions will dictate how steep the approach will have to be. Know the type and height of the obstructions.

    b.   The landing surface will affect your airplane's braking/stopping distance. A headwind may shorten the distance, while a tailwind will significantly lengthen the landing distance.

    c.   Locate and study the Landing Distance graph or table in Section 5, Performance, of your airplane's *POH*.

        1)   Most charts will provide an approach speed for a specified weight. Others will provide only the approach speed at the maximum landing weight.

            a)   These airspeeds are listed as "speed at 50 ft."

        2)   The Landing Distance chart will provide you with the total landing distance to clear a 50-ft. obstacle and the ground roll.

    d.   During your preflight preparation, you have a regulatory requirement (FAR 91.103) to ensure that you can land on the available runway under the known or expected conditions.

        1)   Remember to check that you can depart, since the required landing distance may be less than the required takeoff distance.

    e.   To avoid surprises, pump your brakes to ensure that you have brake pressure.

    f.   Select an aim point that allows you to clear any obstacles and to touch down with the greatest amount of remaining runway available.

        1)   Your descent angle may be steeper than the one used on a normal approach.

            a)   This steeper descent angle helps you pick a touchdown aim point closer to the base of any obstacle, which means a shorter landing distance.

        2)   Remember, your aim point will be the point at the end of your selected glide path, not your touchdown point. Thus, your aim point will be short of your actual touchdown point.

            a)   See Task IV.B., Normal and Crosswind Approach and Landing, beginning on page 140, for a discussion of the use of the aim point.

    g.   You should also select points along the approach path at which you will decide between continuing the approach or executing a go-around.

        1)   A go-around may be necessary if you are too low, too high, too slow, or too fast and/or if you are not stabilized on the final approach.

    h.   After you select your point, you should identify it to your examiner.

3.   Establish the recommended approach and landing configuration and airspeed, and adjust pitch attitude and power as required.

    a.   Follow the procedures in your airplane's *POH* to establish the proper short-field approach and landing configuration and airspeed.

    b.   After the landing gear and full flaps have been extended, you should simultaneously adjust the power and pitch attitude to establish and maintain the proper descent angle and airspeed.

        1)   Since short-field approaches are power-on approaches, the pitch attitude is adjusted as necessary to establish and maintain the desired rate or angle of descent, and power is adjusted to maintain the desired airspeed.

            a)   However, a coordinated combination of both pitch and power adjustments is required.

            b)   When the proper adjustments are made and the final approach is stabilized, very little change in your airplane's pitch attitude and power will be necessary to make corrections in the angle of descent and airspeed.

2)   If it appears that the obstacle clearance is excessive and touchdown will occur well beyond the desired spot, leaving insufficient room to stop, power may be reduced while lowering the pitch attitude to increase the rate of descent and while maintaining the proper airspeed.

3)   If it appears that the descent angle will not ensure safe clearance of obstacles, power should be increased while simultaneously raising the pitch attitude to decrease the rate of descent and while maintaining the proper airspeed.

4)   Care must be taken to avoid excessively slow airspeed.

  a)   If the speed is allowed to become too slow, an increase in pitch and application of full power may only result in a further rate of descent.

     i)   The rate of descent increases when the angle of attack is so great and creates so much drag that the maximum available power is insufficient to overcome it.

c.   The final approach is normally started from an altitude of at least 500 ft. higher than the touchdown area, when you are approximately 3/4 to 1 SM from the runway threshold.

1)   The steeper descent angle means more altitude for a longer period of time, which can be converted to airspeed, if needed, by lowering the nose. This is good for safety because it prevents an approach that is simultaneously too low and too slow.

4.   *Maintain a stabilized approach and the recommended airspeed or, in its absence, not more than 1.3 V_{SO}, ±5 kt., with wind gust factor applied.*

a.   A stabilized approach and controlled rate of descent can be accomplished only by making minor adjustments to pitch and power while on final approach.

1)   To do this, you must maintain your selected glide path and airspeed.

b.   Your approach speed will be determined by the "speed at 50 ft." in the Landing Distance graph or table in Section 5, Performance, in your airplane's *POH*.

1)   This approach airspeed is based on the landing weight of your airplane.

2)   The FAA recommends that no more than one-half the gust factor be applied to the approach airspeed, if required.

3)   Once you clear the obstacle, or 50 ft. AGL, you will begin to slowly reduce power in preparation for the landing.

c.   An excessive amount of airspeed may result in touchdown too far from the runway threshold or an after-landing roll that exceeds the available landing area.

5.   Make smooth, timely, and correct control application during the roundout and touchdown.

a.   Use the same technique during the roundout and touchdown as discussed in Task IV.B., Normal and Crosswind Approach and Landing, beginning on page 140.

6.   Touch down smoothly at minimum control airspeed.

a.   Your airplane's minimum control airspeed is just above stalling speed.

b.   At this speed, any further increase in angle of attack will result in a stall.

1)   Touching down at minimum controllable airspeed will result in minimal float during the roundout and flare and will allow for the lowest possible touchdown speed, thus reducing the ground roll.

2)   Take care to avoid a stall prior to touchdown, however.

  a)   Do not hesitate to add power or go around if an excessive sink rate develops.

7. ***Touch down at or within 100 ft. beyond a specified point, with no side drift, minimum float, and with your airplane's longitudinal axis aligned with and over the runway center/landing path.***

    a.   Since the final approach over obstacles is made at a steep approach angle and close to the stalling speed, the initiation of the roundout (flare) must be judged accurately to avoid flying into the ground, or stalling prematurely and sinking rapidly.

    1)   During the roundout, the power should be smoothly reduced so that at touchdown the airplane is at the power-off stall attitude with the throttle at idle (or closed).

    b.   You must touch down at or within 100 ft. beyond a specified point.

    1)   Touchdown should occur at the minimum controllable airspeed at a pitch attitude which will produce a power-off stall.

    2)   Upon touchdown, hold the nosewheel off the runway, as long as the elevators/stabilator remains effective, to provide aerodynamic braking.

    3)   A lack of floating during the roundout, with sufficient control to touch down properly, is one verification that the approach speed was correct.

    c.   Use the proper crosswind technique to ensure your airplane's longitudinal axis is aligned with and over the runway centerline and that you touch down with no side drift.

8. **Maintain crosswind correction and directional control throughout the approach and landing sequence.**

    a.   Use the crosswind and directional control techniques described in Task IV.B., Normal and Crosswind Approach and Landing, beginning on page 140.

9. **Apply brakes, as necessary, to stop in the shortest distance consistent with safety.**

    a.   Braking can begin aerodynamically by maintaining the landing attitude after touchdown. Once you are sure that the main gear wheels are solidly in ground contact, begin braking while holding back elevator pressure.

    1)   Increase back elevator pressure to hold the nosewheel off the runway until you have full back elevator pressure.

    2)   As the nosewheel begins to come down toward the runway, begin smoothly applying brakes by slowly increasing pressure evenly on the brakes.

    3)   Maintain and hold full back elevator pressure. This pressure is needed since the airplane tends to "lean" forward with heavy braking and you do not want to put too much stress on the nosewheel.

    a)   If you do not hold full back elevator pressure and you brake heavily, the stress on the nosewheel may cause it to collapse.

    b.   Airplanes with larger flap surfaces may benefit more from leaving the flaps down for drag braking, whereas smaller flaps may be retracted through the rollout to increase wheel contact with the ground and main wheel braking effectiveness.

    1)   Your author suggests that it is safer to wait on flap retraction until you are clear of the runway.

    a)   During the landing rollout, you are busy flying the airplane. Trying to retract the flaps is an unnecessary distraction, especially in retractable gear airplanes in which a misidentified control could lead to a gear-up landing.

    c.   Follow the procedures in your airplane's *POH*.

10. **Complete the appropriate checklist.**

    a.   The before-landing checklist should be completed on the downwind leg.

        1)   Avoid surprises by pumping the brakes while on the downwind leg to ensure that you have brake pressure.

        2)   Complete the last GUMPS check on short final.

    b.   After your airplane is clear of the runway, you should stop and complete the after-landing checklist.

C. Common Errors during a Short-Field Approach and Landing

    1.   **Improper use of landing performance data and limitations.**

        a.   Use your *POH* to determine the appropriate approach airspeed for a short-field approach.

        b.   In gusty and/or strong crosswinds, use the crosswind component chart to determine that you are not exceeding your airplane's crosswind limitations, if applicable.

        c.   Use your *POH* to determine minimum landing distances, and do not attempt to do better than the data.

        d.   The most common error, as well as the easiest to avoid, is to attempt a landing that is beyond the capabilities of your airplane and/or your flying skills. You need to remember that the distance needed for a safe landing is normally less than is needed for a safe takeoff. Plan ahead!

    2.   **Failure to establish approach and landing configuration at appropriate time or in proper sequence.**

        a.   Use the before-landing checklist in your *POH* to ensure that you follow the proper sequence in establishing the correct approach and landing configuration for your airplane.

        b.   You should initially start the checklist at midpoint on the downwind leg with the power reduction beginning once you are abeam your intended point of landing.

        1)   By the time you turn on final and align your airplane with the center of the runway, you should be in the final landing configuration. Confirm this by completing your checklist once again.

    3.   **Failure to establish and maintain a stabilized approach.**

        a.   Once you are on final and aligned with the center of the runway, you should make small adjustments to pitch and power to establish the correct descent angle (i.e., glide path) and airspeed.

        1)   Remember, you must make simultaneous adjustments to both pitch and power.
        2)   Large adjustments will result in a roller coaster ride.

    4.   **Improper technique in use of power, wing flaps, and trim.**

        a.   Use power and pitch adjustments simultaneously to maintain the proper descent angle and airspeed.

        b.   Wing flaps should be used in accordance with your airplane's *POH*.

        c.   Trim to relieve control pressures to help in stabilizing the final approach.

5.   **Inappropriate removal of hand from throttle.**

   a.   One hand should remain on the control yoke at all times.

   b.   The other hand should remain on the throttle unless you are operating the microphone or making an adjustment, such as trim or flaps.

      1)   Once you are on short final, your hand should remain on the throttle, even if ATC gives you instruction (e.g., cleared to land).

         a)   Your first priority is to fly your airplane and avoid doing tasks which may distract you from maintaining control.

         b)   Fly first; talk later.

   c.   You must be in the habit of keeping one hand on the throttle in case a sudden and unexpected hazardous situation should require an immediate application of power.

6.   **Improper technique during roundout and touchdown.**

   a.   Do not attempt to hold the airplane off the ground.

      1)   Remember that you should have minimal floating in a short-field landing. If floating is occurring, you should go around.

   b.   See Task IV.B, Normal and Crosswind Approach and Landing, beginning on page 140, for a detailed discussion of general landing errors.

   c.   Remember, you have limited runway, so when in doubt, go around.

7.   **Poor directional control after touchdown.**

   a.   Use rudder to steer your airplane on the runway, and increase aileron deflection into the wind as airspeed decreases.

   b.   See Common Errors of Task IV.B., Normal and Crosswind Approach and Landing, beginning on page 149, for a discussion on ground loops and other directional control problems after touchdown.

8.   **Improper use of brakes.**

   a.   Never attempt to apply the brakes until your airplane is firmly on the runway under complete control.

   b.   Use equal pressure on both brakes to prevent swerving and/or loss of directional control.

   c.   Follow the braking procedures described in your airplane's *POH*.

END OF TASK

POWER-OFF 180° ACCURACY APPROACH AND LANDING

IV.K. TASK: POWER-OFF 180° ACCURACY APPROACH AND LANDING

REFERENCE: FAA-H-8083-3.

Objective. To determine that the applicant:

1. Exhibits knowledge of the elements related to a power-off 180° accuracy approach and landing.	**4.** Abeam the specified touchdown point, closes throttle and establishes appropriate glide speed.
2. Considers the wind conditions, landing surface, obstructions, and selects an appropriate touchdown point.	**5.** Completes final airplane configuration.
3. Positions airplane on downwind leg, parallel to landing runway, and not more than 1000 feet AGL.	**6.** Touches down in a normal landing attitude, at or within 200 feet (60 meters) beyond the specified touchdown point.
	7. Completes the appropriate checklist.

A. General Information

   1. The objective of this task is for you to demonstrate your ability to judge a power-off glide and plan your approach to a specified touchdown point in the performance of a power-off 180° accuracy approach and landing.

B. Task Objectives

   1. Exhibit your knowledge of the elements related to a power-off 180° accuracy approach and landing.

      a. A power-off 180° accuracy approach and landing is an approach and landing made by gliding with the engine idling through a 180° pattern, begun abeam a specified touchdown point on the runway, to a touchdown at or within 200 feet beyond that point.

         1) The objective of this maneuver is to instill the judgement and procedures necessary for accurately flying the airplane to a safe landing without power.

         2) A practical application of this skill would be in the execution of a simulated or actual forced landing.

   2. Consider the wind conditions, landing surface, and obstructions, and select an appropriate touchdown point.

      a. Wind conditions have a major impact on the performance of a 180° accuracy approach and landing. As with any other approach and landing, you should plan this maneuver to land into the wind, but you must also take into account the effects of the wind on your glide path because power is considered to be fixed (i.e., the throttle is closed) and therefore is not available to help control the approach.

         1) You should begin the maneuver on the downwind leg at your airport's traffic pattern altitude. Abeam the intended point of touchdown, you will close the throttle and establish the manufacturer's recommended best glide speed.

            a) The point abeam the intended touchdown area on the downwind leg is called the "downwind key position."

            b) At this point, you should already have some idea as to the speed and direction of the wind based on any wind correction you have been holding during the downwind leg.

               i) Based on your knowledge of the wind at the downwind key position, you can begin planning the rest of your approach.

2) Plan your base turn according to the existing wind conditions.

    a) If the wind is strong, you will need to turn the base leg early in order to avoid landing short of the intended touchdown point.

        i) While heading into a strong wind on final approach, your ground speed will be lower than it would be with a light or calm wind, meaning that you cannot cover as much ground in a power-off glide from a given altitude.

            • Accordingly, you must turn your base leg sooner in order to create a shorter final approach leg so that you are able to reach your intended touchdown point from the altitude available.

    b) If the wind is light or calm, or if there is a tailwind, you will need to extend the downwind leg and turn the base leg later in order to avoid overshooting the intended touchdown point.

        i) While heading into a light or calm wind on final, or with a tailwind, your ground speed will be higher than it would be with a strong headwind, meaning that you can cover more ground in a power-off glide from a given altitude

            • Accordingly, you must turn your base leg later in order to create a longer final approach leg along which to dissipate altitude.

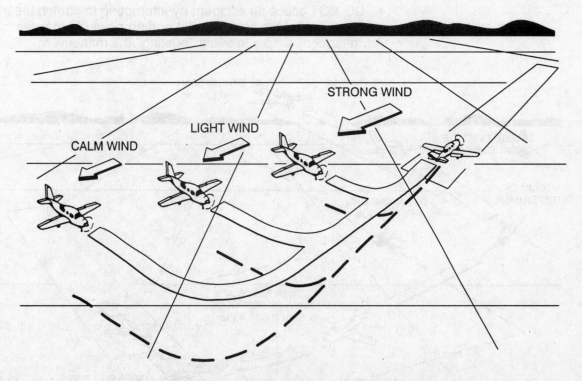

Figure 7-9 -- Plan the base leg for wind conditions.

    c) If it is necessary to land with a crosswind, you should select the runway that provides the greatest headwind component (comply with any ATC instructions, however). You must also take into account the effects of the crosswind on your approach.

i)   If you have a tailwind component on the base leg, the tendency is to be too high on the approach because you will not lose as much altitude during the base leg due to your higher ground speed.

- You must turn base later or fly a wider pattern (i.e., make the downwind leg farther from the runway) in order to lengthen the base leg.

ii)   If you have a headwind component on the base leg, you will tend to end up too low on the approach because you will lose more altitude during the base leg due to your lower ground speed.

- You must turn base earlier or fly a smaller pattern (i.e., make the downwind leg closer to the runway) in order to shorten the base leg.

d) Note that it is better to be slightly high and add some drag (e.g., lower flaps and/or perform a forward slip) or distance (e.g., S-turns) to your approach in order to make the touchdown point than to be slightly low and be forced to add power in order to avoid landing short of the point.

i)   Remember that this maneuver is intended to be performed with the throttle at idle, so any maneuver requiring the addition of power will be regarded as unsuccessful.

ii)   However, when performing this maneuver during practice or for your examiner, you should not hesitate to add power if necessary.

- DO NOT cause an accident by attempting to stretch the glide (i.e., raising the nose without adding power to maintain airspeed) simply to avoid "busting" the maneuver.

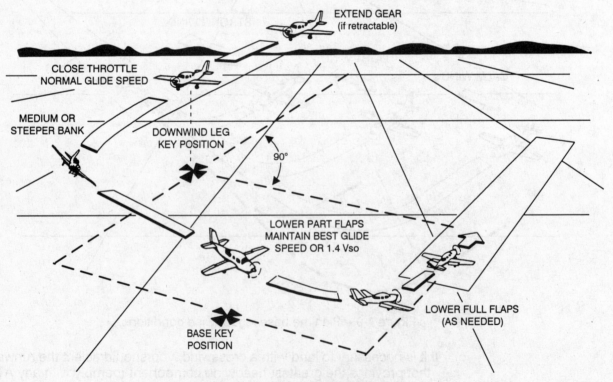

Figure 7-11 -- 180° power-off approach

3) Immediately after completing the turn to base, you will be in the "base key position," from which you can evaluate your approach.

a) At this position early in the base leg, you can evaluate how successful your planning has been up to that point and make any necessary corrections early, while you still have time to affect the outcome of the approach.

i) Observe the intended point of touchdown through the side window of your airplane and look for upward or downward relative motion in the window.

- Because of your orientation to the touchdown point while on the base leg, there will appear to be sideways relative movement of the touchdown point. This motion can be ignored because it will always be present and provides no useful information.

ii) If the point has no upward or downward relative motion, you are presently on an acceptable glide path.

- You should continue with a normal approach and square-off the turn from base to final.

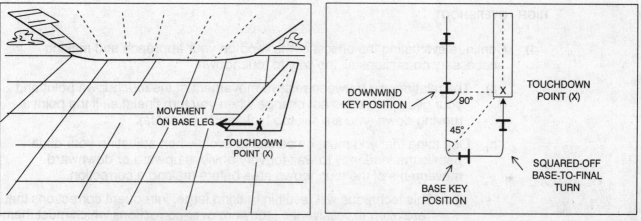

ON GLIDE PATH

iii) If the point appears to be moving upward, your present glide path will be too low if a normal approach is made and you will land short of your intended touchdown point.

- You should head directly for your intended touchdown point (i.e., "dogleg" the base).

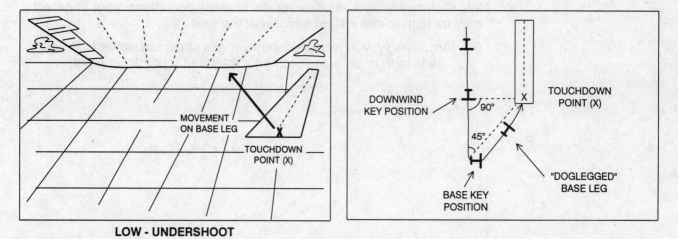

LOW - UNDERSHOOT

iv)   If the point appears to be moving downward, your present glide path will be too high if a normal approach is made and you will overshoot your intended touchdown point.

• You should increase drag by lowering flaps or performing a forward slip, or increase the length of your approach by performing S-turns.

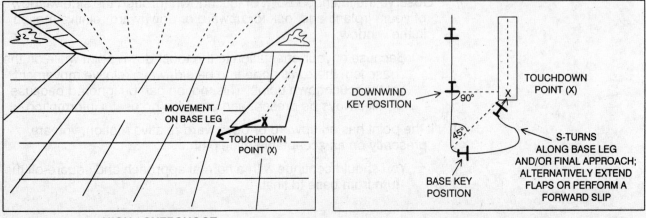

HIGH - OVERSHOOT

4)   Continue evaluating the effects of the wind on your approach and making necessary corrections all the way to touchdown.

a)   The relationship between relative movement of the touchdown point and your glide path does not change when you turn final (i.e., if the point is moving down, you are still too high, and vice-versa).

b)   One thing that you must be careful to avoid when adjusting your glide path is the tendency to wait for very obvious upward or downward movements of the touchdown area before making a correction.

i)   This technique will result in making large, infrequent corrections that are often excessive (i.e., they are over-corrections which must themselves be corrected for) or made too late to salvage the approach.

ii)   You must be alert to subtle movements of the touchdown area.

• In order to accurately interpret your glide path, you must "filter out" apparent movements of the touchdown area that are caused by turbulence and look for the general trend–up or down–of the touchdown point.

c)   Note that, due to updrafts/downdrafts or gusty conditions, your approach may be high at one instant and low at the next.

i)   Accordingly, you must constantly make small adjustments to your glide path in order to reach your intended touchdown point.

   b.   Because a power-off 180° accuracy approach is intended to be performed completely
        with the throttle at idle, you should not attempt this maneuver on a soft field because
        a soft-field touchdown requires the addition of power.

        1)   Accordingly, you should restrict this maneuver to paved runways or grass fields
             that are in good condition.

   c.   Before beginning the maneuver, you must take into account any obstacles that will
        affect your approach and select your touchdown point appropriately.

        1)   Do not choose a touchdown point that is too close to an obstacle or you may
             be tempted to get dangerously close to the obstacle in order to reach your
             intended touchdown point.

             a)   If you maintain a safe obstacle clearance, you may not be able to land on
                  or within 200 ft. beyond your intended touchdown point.

   d.   You should select a touchdown point within the first third of the runway.

        1)   Do not select a touchdown point at the edge of the usable landing area (e.g., on
             the numbers) because your aiming point will need to be short of the runway if
             you are to touch down "on the numbers."

             a)   Remember that you will always touch down beyond your aiming point
                  because the airplane floats down the runway during the roundout.

                  i)   Your aiming point should never be short of the runway because of
                       the increased risk of landing short of the runway threshold.

             b)   If obstacle clearance allows, choose a touchdown point that will allow you
                  to use the runway threshold line as an aiming point.

                  i)   For most light airplanes, aiming for the threshold line will result in a
                       touchdown 300 to 400 feet down the runway.

                  ii) You will become familiar with how far your airplane floats during
                       practice of power-off 180° accuracy approaches and landings.

        2)   Clearly identify the intended touchdown point to your examiner (e.g., the third
             centerline stripe).

3. ***Position your airplane on the downwind leg, parallel to the landing runway, at not
    more than 1,000 feet AGL.***

   a.   The maneuver should begin on the downwind leg at the traffic pattern altitude for the
        airport you are using.

        1)   If the traffic pattern altitude is above 1,000 ft. AGL, discuss with your examiner
             what altitude (s)he would like you to use.

4. **Abeam the specified touchdown point, close the throttle and establish the appropriate
    glide speed.**

   a.   When your airplane is abeam the touchdown point on the downwind leg, smoothly
        reduce power to idle and establish the airplane's best glide speed using pitch.

        1)   If your airspeed at the abeam point is more than the airplane's best glide speed
             (as it most likely will be), maintain altitude as the airplane decelerates to the
             best glide speed; then lower the nose to the appropriate pitch attitude to
             maintain the best glide speed and begin your descent.

             a)   If there is no manufacturer's recommended best glide speed, use 1.4 V_{so}.
             b)   Remember to use trim to relieve any control pressures.

5.   Complete the final airplane configuration.

a.   You should plan to touch down with the airplane in a normal landing configuration; i.e., gear and flaps down.

    1)   You should extend the landing gear abeam the touchdown point, just as with any other approach and landing.

        a)   DO NOT retract the gear during the approach in order to extend the glide–you may suffer a gear-up landing.

        b)   If the approach is not working out, go around. Explain to your examiner why the approach did not work and how you would correct your technique.

    2)   Use flaps as necessary to control the glide path during your approach.

        a)   Remember to re-trim the airplane to relieve control pressures after extending flaps.

        b)   Do not allow the airplane to touch down with less than the manufacturer's minimum recommended flap setting for landing.

           i)   If it is necessary to delay flap extension in order to make your touchdown point, extend the remaining flaps as you cross the runway threshold

6.   *Touch down in a normal landing attitude, at or within 200 ft. beyond the specified touchdown point.*

a.   You should make a normal landing in the proper touchdown attitude at or within 200 ft. beyond the touchdown point you have identified to your examiner.

    1)   It must be emphasized that, while accurate spot touchdowns are important, a safe and properly-executed approach and landing is essential.

    2)   You must never sacrifice a good approach or landing simply to make a touchdown on the desired spot.

        a)   Forcing the airplane onto the runway before it is ready to touch down will result in contacting the runway in a flat or nose-low attitude.

           i)   Wheelbarrowing or porpoising so severe as to cause structural damage may be the result.

        b)   Attempting to stretch the glide by increasing the pitch attitude without adding power may result in a stall at low altitude with insufficient room for recovery.

           i)   Alternatively, you may experience a hard landing or a bounce so severe as to cause structural damage.

7.   Complete the appropriate checklist.

a.   The before-landing checklist should be completed on the downwind leg before reaching the abeam point.

    1)   The GUMPS should be completed on both base leg and final

b.   Use the checklist in your *POH*.

C. Common Errors during a Power-Off 180°Accuracy Approach and Landing.

1. **Failure to establish the approach and landing configuration at the proper time or in the proper sequence.**

   a. Use the before-landing checklist in your *POH* to ensure that you follow the proper sequence in establishing the correct approach and landing configuration for your airplane.

   b. You should initially start the checklist at midpoint on the downwind leg with the throttle being closed once you are abeam your intended point of landing.

      1) By the time you turn on final and align your airplane with the runway centerline, you should be in the final landing configuration. Confirm this by completing your checklist once again.

2. **Failure to identify the key points in the pattern.**

   a. The two "key" points in a power-off 180° accuracy approach and landing are the downwind and base key positions.

      1) The downwind key position is on the downwind leg abeam the intended touchdown point.

      2) The base key position is on the base leg immediately after completion of the turn from downwind to base.

   b. Note that the PTS does not specify that you are required to point out these key positions to your examiner.

      1) Your failure to identify these points will be indicated by improper performance of the maneuver, e.g., not closing the throttle at the downwind key position or not recognizing and correcting for an improper glide path at the base key position.

3. **Failure to establish and maintain a stabilized approach.**

   a. Once you are on final and aligned with the runway centerline, you should make small adjustments to your pitch, configuration (e.g., flaps), and approach path in order to establish the correct descent angle (i.e., glide path) and airspeed.

      1) You must make corrections that are small and frequent as you continually evaluate your glide path.

      2) Large adjustments will result in a roller coaster ride.

   b. Lock in your airspeed and glide path as soon as possible.

      1) Never let your airspeed go below the appropriate glide speed.

      2) Make necessary corrections in order to stop any upward or downward movement of the touchdown point in the airplane's windscreen.

4. **Failure to consider the effects of the wind and landing surface.**

   a. Proper planning will ensure knowledge of the landing surface condition, e.g., wet, dry, grass, or paved.

      1) Because power is theoretically not available to perform a soft-field touchdown, do not attempt a power-off 180° accuracy approach and landing on a surface that is very soft or rough.

   b. Understand how the wind affects your approach path and plan accordingly.

5. Improper use of power, wing flaps, or trim.

    a.   By definition, a power-off 180° accuracy approach and landing is a power-off maneuver.

        1)   Accordingly, you must correct for deviations from the desired glide path and airspeed without the use of power.

        2)   Remember, however, that you must always demonstrate good judgment to your examiner.

            a)   Do whatever you feel is necessary if the approach does not look like it can be completed safely without the addition of power (i.e., add power or go around)

    b.   Wing flaps should be used in accordance with your *POH* to adjust the glide path.

    c.   Trim to relieve control pressures to help in stabilizing the final approach.

6. Improper procedure during roundout and touchdown.

    a.   See Task IV.B., Normal and Crosswind Approach and Landing, beginning on page 140, for a detailed discussion of general landing errors.

    b.   Remember, if you have any doubts about the outcome of the approach, go around.

7. Poor directional control after touchdown.

    a.   Use rudder to steer your airplane on the landing surface, and increase aileron deflection into the wind as airspeed increases.

    b.   See Common Errors of Task IV.B., Normal and Crosswind Approach and Landing, beginning on page 149, for a discussion on ground loops and other directional control problems after touchdown.

8. Improper use of brakes.

    a.   Use the minimum amount of braking required, and let your airplane slow by the friction and drag of the wheels on the ground, if runway length permits.

    b.   Never attempt to apply brakes until your airplane is firmly on the runway under complete control.

    c.   Use equal pressure on both brakes to help prevent swerving and/or loss of directional control.

END OF TASK

GO-AROUND/REJECTED LANDING

IV.L. TASK: GO-AROUND/REJECTED LANDING

REFERENCES: FAA-H-8083-3; Pilot's Operating Handbook, FAA-Approved Airplane Flight Manual.

Objective. To determine that the applicant:

1. Exhibits knowledge of the elements related to a go-around/rejected landing.

2. Makes a timely decision to discontinue the approach to landing.

3. Applies takeoff power immediately and transitions to climb pitch attitude for V_Y, and maintains V_Y, ±5 kt.

4. Retracts flaps as appropriate.

5. Retracts the landing gear, if appropriate, after a positive rate of climb is established.

6. Maneuvers to the side of the runway/landing area to clear and avoid conflicting traffic.

7. Maintains takeoff power and V_Y, ±5 kt. to a safe maneuvering altitude.

8. Maintains directional control and proper wind-drift correction throughout the climb.

9. Completes the appropriate checklist.

A. General Information

1. The objective of this task is for you to demonstrate your ability to make a proper decision to go around and then execute the go-around procedure.

2. For safety reasons, it may be necessary for you to discontinue your approach and attempt another approach under more favorable conditions.

a. This is called a go-around from a rejected (balked) landing.

B. Task Objectives

1. **Exhibit your knowledge of the elements related to a go-around/rejected landing.**

a. Occasionally it will be advisable, for safety reasons, to discontinue your approach and make another approach under more favorable conditions. Unfavorable conditions may include

1) Extremely low base-to-final turn

2) Too high or too low final approach

3) The unexpected appearance of hazards on the runway, e.g., another airplane failing to clear the runway on time

4) Wake turbulence from a preceding aircraft

5) Wind-shear encounter

6) Overtaking another aircraft on final approach

7) ATC instructions to "go around"

b. When takeoff power is applied in the go-around, you must cope with undesirable pitch and yaw.

1) Since you have trimmed your airplane for the approach (i.e., nose-up trim), the nose may rise sharply and veer to the left.

a) Proper elevator pressure must be applied to maintain a safe climbing pitch attitude.

b) Right rudder pressure must be increased to counteract torque, or P-factor, and to keep the nose straight.

2.   Make a timely decision to discontinue the approach to landing.

    a.   The need to discontinue a landing may arise at any point in the landing process, but the most critical go-around is one started when very close to the ground. A timely decision must be made.

        1)   The earlier you recognize a dangerous situation, the sooner you can decide to reject the landing and start the go-around, and the safer this maneuver will be.

        2)   Never wait until the last possible moment to make a decision.

    b.   Official reports concerning go-around accidents frequently cite "pilot indecision" as a cause. This happens when a pilot fixates on trying to make a bad landing good, resulting in a late decision to go around.

        1)   The pilot's reaction is natural, since the purpose of an approach is a landing.

        2)   Delays in deciding what to do cost valuable runway stopping distance. They also cause loss of valuable altitude as the approach continues.

        3)   If there is any question about making a safe touchdown and rollout, execute a go-around immediately.

    c.   Once you decide to go around, stick to it! Too many airplanes have been lost because a pilot has changed his/her mind and tried to land after all.

3.   *Apply takeoff power immediately, transition to the pitch attitude for V_Y, and maintain V_Y, ± 5 kt.*

    a.   Once you decide to go around, takeoff power should be applied immediately and your airplane's pitch attitude changed so as to stop the descent.

        1)   Power is the single most essential ingredient. Every precaution must be taken (i.e., completion of the before-landing checklist) to assure that power is available when you need it.

            a)   Adjust carburetor heat to OFF (cold) position, if appropriate.

            b)   Check that the propeller control is set at maximum (high) RPM and the mixture is full rich or appropriately leaned for high-density altitude airport operations. These steps should have been accomplished during the before-landing (GUMPS) checklist.

        2)   You should establish the pitch attitude for V_Y or V_X.

            a)   You may need to establish a pitch attitude for V_X initially, if you need to clear any obstacles.

            b)   After clearing any obstacles, accelerate to and maintain V_Y ± 5 kt.

    b.   As discussed earlier, you may have to cope with undesirable pitch and yaw due to the addition of maximum allowable (full) power in a nose-up trim configuration.

        1)   You must use whatever control pressure is required to maintain the proper pitch attitude and to keep your airplane straight. Considerable pressure may be required.

        2)   While holding your airplane straight and in a safe climbing attitude, you should retrim your airplane to relieve any heavy control pressures.

            a)   Since the airspeed will build up rapidly with the application of maximum allowable power and the controls will become more effective, this initial trim is to relieve the heavy pressures until a more precise trim can be made for the lighter pressures.

3) If the pitch attitude is increased excessively in an effort to prevent your airplane from mushing onto the runway, the airplane may stall.

    a) A stall is especially likely if no trim correction is made and the flaps remain fully extended.

c. During the initial part of an extremely low go-around (i.e., during the roundout), your airplane may "mush" onto the runway and bounce. This situation is not particularly dangerous if the airplane is kept straight and a constant, safe pitch attitude is maintained.

    1) Your airplane will be approaching safe flying speed rapidly, and the advanced power will cushion any secondary touchdown.

d. Establish a climb pitch attitude by use of outside visual references. You should have a knowledge of the visual clues to attain the attitude from your training.

e. Use the power setting and airspeed provided in your airplane's *POH*.

4. Retract the flaps as appropriate.

a. Immediately after applying power and raising the nose, you should partially retract or place the wing flaps in the takeoff position, as stated in your *POH*. Use caution in retracting the flaps.

    1) It will probably be wise to retract the flaps intermittently in small increments to allow time for the airplane to accelerate progressively as the flaps are being raised.

    2) A sudden and complete retraction of the flaps at a very low airspeed could cause a loss of lift, resulting in your airplane's settling onto the ground.

b. Your *POH* will specify the initial flap setting to be used during a go-around.

5. Retract the landing gear, if appropriate, after a positive rate of climb is established.

a. Unless otherwise noted in your *POH*, the flaps are normally retracted (at least partially) before retracting the landing gear.

    1) On most airplanes, full flaps create more drag than the landing gear.

    2) In case your airplane should inadvertently touch down as the go-around is initiated, it is desirable to have the landing gear in the down-and-locked position.

b. Never attempt to retract the landing gear until after a rough trim is accomplished and a positive rate of climb is established.

c. Follow the procedures in your airplane's *POH*.

6. Maneuver to the side of the runway/landing area to clear and avoid conflicting traffic.

a. Maintain a ground track parallel to the runway centerline and in a position where you can see the runway.

    1) This is important if the go-around was made due to another airplane on the runway because you need to maintain visual contact to avoid another dangerous situation, especially if that airplane is taking off.

b. When doing this, also consider the effect you may have on other traffic, especially if multiple runways are in use.

7. ***Maintain takeoff power and V$_Y$, ± 5 kt., to a safe maneuvering altitude.***

    a. After establishing V$_Y$ and completing gear and flap retraction, maintain takeoff power to a safe maneuvering altitude, normally 500 to 1,000 ft. AGL.

        1) Then the power (MP, RPM, and mixture) should be set to the climb power setting recommended in your airplane's *POH*.

            a) Adjust pitch as necessary to maintain airspeed.

    b. Maintain V$_Y$, ± 5 kt., until reaching traffic pattern altitude (normally 1,000 ft. AGL).

    c. If you are remaining in the traffic pattern, remember to fly the upwind leg at least ½ mile beyond the departure end of the runway before turning crosswind.

        1) Level off at traffic pattern altitude and set the power for the downwind leg.

    d. Follow the procedures in your *POH*.

8. **Maintain directional control and proper wind-drift correction throughout the climb.**

    a. Use wind drift correction to climb parallel to the extended runway centerline until you reach a safe maneuvering altitude that will allow you to reenter the traffic pattern.

    b. Now that you have your airplane under control, you can communicate with the tower or the appropriate ground station to advise that you are going around.

9. **Complete the appropriate checklist.**

    a. Consult your *POH* for the proper procedure to follow for your airplane.

        1) A go-around checklist is an excellent example of a checklist that you will "do and then review." When you execute a go-around, you will do it from memory and then review your checklist after you have initiated and stabilized your go-around.

    b. Complete the checklist for the climb to ensure that your airplane is in the proper configuration for climb to traffic pattern altitude.

C. Common Errors during a Go-Around

    1. **Failure to recognize a situation in which a go-around is necessary.**

        a. When there is any doubt of the safe outcome of a landing, the go-around should be initiated immediately.

        b. Do not attempt to salvage a possible bad landing.

    2. **Hazards of delaying a decision to go around.**

        a. Delay could lead to an accident because the remaining runway may be insufficient for landing or because delay could prevent you from clearing obstacles on the departure end of the runway.

    3. **Improper power application.**

        a. Power should be added smoothly and continuously.

        b. Assure that you have maximum power available at all times during the final approach by completing your before-landing checklist.

4. **Failure to control pitch attitude.**

   a. You must be able to divide your attention to adjust pitch attitude during the go-around and maintain control of your airplane.

   b. Learn the visual clues as to climb (V_Y and V_X) pitch attitudes, and then cross-check with the airspeed indicator.

5. **Failure to compensate for torque effect.**

   a. In a high-power, low-airspeed configuration, right rudder pressure must be increased to counteract torque and to keep the airplane's nose straight.

      1) Center the ball in the inclinometer.

6. **Improper trim technique.**

   a. Initial trim is important to relieve the heavy control pressures.

   b. Since your airplane may be in a nose-up trim configuration, the application of full power may cause the nose to rise sharply.

      1) In this configuration, a considerable amount of forward elevator pressure is required to maintain the proper pitch attitude and to prevent a stall/spin situation. The use of trim will decrease the pressure you will have to hold.

7. **Failure to maintain recommended airspeeds.**

   a. This error will reduce the climb performance of your airplane and may create unsafe conditions due to obstructions or, if too slow, a stall/spin situation.

8. **Improper wing flap or landing gear retraction procedure.**

   a. Follow the procedures in your *POH*.

   b. On most airplanes, the flaps create more drag than the landing gear; thus you should raise (at least partially) the flaps before the landing gear.

   c. Retract the landing gear only after a positive rate of climb is established, as indicated on the vertical speed indicator.

9. **Failure to maintain proper ground track during climbout.**

   a. Not maintaining the proper ground track may cause possible conflicts with other traffic and/or obstructions.

   b. You are expected by other traffic and/or ATC to maintain a ground track parallel to the runway centerline until at the proper position to turn crosswind.

10. **Failure to remain well clear of obstructions and other traffic.**

    a. Climb at V_X if necessary to clear any obstructions.

    b. Maintain visual contact with other traffic, especially if the go-around was due to departing traffic.

END OF TASK -- END OF CHAPTER

CHAPTER V
PERFORMANCE MANEUVERS

This chapter explains the four tasks (A-D) of Performance Maneuvers. These tasks include both knowledge and skill. Your examiner is not required to test you on all four tasks. The examiner must select at least either task A or B, and either task C or D.

STEEP TURNS

V.A. TASK: STEEP TURNS

REFERENCES: FAA-H-8083-3; Pilot's Operating Handbook, FAA-Approved Airplane Flight Manual.

Objective. To determine that the applicant:

1. Exhibits knowledge of the elements related to steep turns.

2. Establishes the manufacturer's recommended airspeed or if one is not stated, a safe airspeed not to exceed V_A.

3. Rolls into a coordinated 360° steep turn with at least a 50° bank, followed by a 360° steep turn in the opposite direction.

4. Divides attention between airplane control and orientation.

5. Maintains the entry altitude, ±100 ft. (30 meters); airspeed, ±10 knots; bank, ± 5°; and rolls out on the entry heading, ± 10°.

A. General Information

1. The objective of this task is for you to demonstrate your smoothness, coordination, orientation, division of attention, and control techniques in the performance of steep turns.

2. Additional reading: In Chapter 1, Airplanes and Aerodynamics, of *Pilot Handbook*, see the following:

a. Module 1.10, Airplane Stability, for a discussion on lateral stability or instability in turns

b. Module 1.11, Loads and Load Factors, for a discussion on the effect of turns on load factors, the effect of load factor on the stalling speed, and design maneuvering speed (V_A)

B. Task Objectives

1. **Exhibit your knowledge of the elements related to steep turns.**

a. Your airplane's turning performance is limited by the amount of power the engine is developing, its limit load factor (structural strength), and its aerodynamic characteristics.

b. The so-called **overbanking tendency** is the result of the airplane being banked steeply enough to reach a condition of negative static stability about the longitudinal axis.

1) Static stability can be positive, neutral, or negative. It is the tendency of the airplane, once displaced, to try to return to a stable condition as it was before being disturbed.

   a) In a shallow turn, the airplane displays positive static stability and tries to return to a wings-level attitude.

   b) In a medium bank turn, the airplane shows neutral static stability and will tend to remain in the medium bank, assuming calm air.

   c) In a steep turn, the airplane demonstrates negative static stability and tries to steepen the bank rather than remain stable. This is the overbanking tendency.

2) Why overbanking occurs: As the radius of the turn becomes smaller, a significant difference develops between the speed of the inside wing and the speed of the outside wing.

   a) The wing on the outside of the turn travels a longer circuit than the inside wing, yet both complete their respective circuits in the same length of time.

   b) Therefore, the outside wing must travel faster than the inside wing; as a result, it develops more lift. This creates a slight differential between the lift of the inside and outside wings and tends to further increase the bank.

   c) When changing from a shallow bank to a medium bank, the airspeed of the wing on the outside of the turn increases in relation to the inside wing as the radius of turn decreases, but the force created exactly balances the force of the inherent lateral stability of the airplane so that, at a given speed, no aileron pressure is required to maintain that bank.

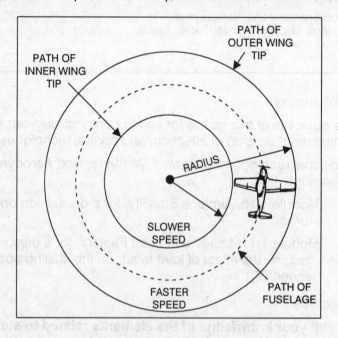

   d) As the radius decreases further when the bank progresses from a medium bank to a steep bank, the lift differential overbalances the lateral stability, and counteractive pressure on the ailerons is necessary to keep the bank from steepening.

    c.   The effects of torque (i.e., left-turning tendencies) should be anticipated.

        1)   In a left turn, there is a tendency to develop a slight skid. You may need to add more right rudder (or less left rudder) to maintain coordinated flight (i.e., ball centered).

        2)   In a right turn, there is a tendency to develop a slight slip. You may need to add more right rudder to maintain coordinated flight.

    d.   In this maneuver, a constant airspeed is required, so power must be added as necessary.

        1)   When back pressure is applied to increase lift in a steep bank, induced drag also increases. Thus, power will be required to maintain the entry altitude and airspeed.

2. *Establish and maintain the manufacturer's recommended entry airspeed, or if one is not stated, a safe airspeed not to exceed V_A.*

    a.   Before starting the steep turn, you should perform **clearing turns** to ensure that the area is clear of other air traffic since the rate of turn will be relatively rapid.

    b.   Establish and use the recommended entry speed found in your *POH*. If none is listed, then use a safe airspeed, not to exceed V_A (design maneuvering speed).

    c. V_A is the maximum speed at which the airplane will normally stall before the load limits are exceeded, avoiding structural damage.

        1) V_A is a function of the gross weight of your airplane.

        2)   See your *POH*.

           a)   In your airplane, V_A _____ at _____ lb.

    c.   Due to the increase in load factors during steep turns, you must not exceed V_A.

3. *Roll into a coordinated 360° steep turn with at least a 50° bank, followed by a 360° steep turn in the opposite direction.*

    a.   Note your heading toward your reference point and smoothly roll into a coordinated turn with at least a 50° angle of bank.

        1)   As the turn is being established, back pressure on the elevator control should be smoothly increased to increase the angle of attack.

    b.   As the bank steepens beyond 30°, you may find it necessary to hold a considerable amount of back elevator control pressure to maintain a constant altitude.

        1)   Additional back elevator pressure increases the angle of attack, which increases drag.

           a)   Additional power will be required to maintain entry altitude and airspeed.

        2)   Retrim your airplane of excess control pressures, as appropriate.

           a)   This will help you to maintain a constant altitude.

    c.   The rollout from the turn should be timed so that the wings reach level flight when your airplane is on the entry heading (i.e., toward your reference point).

        1)   Normally, you lead your desired heading by one-half of the number of degrees of bank, e.g., a 25° lead in a 50° bank.

        2)   During your training, you will develop your technique and knowledge of the lead required.

    d.   Your examiner will have you roll out of a steep turn and then roll into a steep turn in the opposite direction.

        1)   Remember to look and say "clear" (left or right) while rolling into a 50° bank in the opposite direction.

4.   Divide your attention between airplane control and orientation.

    a.   Do not stare at any one object during this maneuver.

    b.   To maintain orientation as well as altitude requires an awareness of the relative position of the nose, the horizon, the wings, and the amount of turn.

        1)   If you watch only the nose of your airplane, you will have trouble holding altitude constant and remaining oriented in the turn.

        2)   By watching all available visual and instrument references, you will be able to hold a constant altitude and remain oriented throughout the maneuver.

           a)   Keep attitude indicator at 50°.
           b)   Keep VSI at or near 0 fpm.
           c)   Check heading and altitude.
           d)   Scan outside for traffic.

    c.   Maintain control of your airplane throughout the turn.

        1)   To recover from an excessive nose-low attitude, you should first slightly reduce the angle of bank with coordinated aileron and rudder pressure.

           a)   Then back elevator pressure should be used to raise your airplane's nose to the desired pitch attitude.

           b)   After completing this, reestablish the desired angle of bank.

           c)   Attempting to raise the nose first will usually cause a tight descending spiral and could lead to overstressing the airplane.

        2)   If your altitude increases, the bank should be increased by coordinated use of aileron and rudder.

5.   *Maintain your entry altitude, ±100 ft.; airspeed, ±10 kt.; bank, ±5°; and rollout on the entry heading, ±10°.*

    a.   You must maintain your entry altitude and airspeed throughout the entire maneuver.

    b.   While the rollout is being made, back elevator pressure must be gradually released and power reduced as necessary to maintain the entry altitude and airspeed.

        1)   If trim was used during the steep turn, you will need to adjust the trim to relieve the control pressure.

    c.   Use whatever control pressure is necessary to keep the nose of the airplane on the horizon.

    d.   You must maintain your bank angle, ± 5°.

        1)   Note, however, that you must maintain at least a 50° bank.

        2)   Therefore, if you enter the maneuver with a 50° bank, your tolerance will be +5°/-0°.

    e.   The roll out from the turn should be timed so that the wings reach level flight when your airplane is on the entry heading (i.e., toward your reference point).

        1)   Normally, you lead your desired heading by one-half of the number of degrees of bank, e.g., a 25° lead in a 50° bank.

        2)   During your training, you should have developed your technique and knowledge of the lead required.

C. Common Errors during Steep Turns

1. **Improper pitch, bank, and power coordination during entry and rollout.**

    a. Do not overanticipate the amount of pitch change needed during entry and rollout.

        1) During entry, if the pitch is increased (nose up) before the bank is established, altitude will be gained.

        2) During recovery, if back pressure is not released, altitude will be gained.

    b. Power should be added as required during entry and then reduced during rollout.

        1) Do not adjust power during transition to turn in the opposite direction.

2. **Uncoordinated use of flight controls.**

    a. This error is normally indicated by a slip, especially in right-hand turns.

        1) Check inclinometer.

    b. If the airplane's nose starts to move before the bank starts, rudder is being applied too soon.

    c. If the bank starts before the nose starts turning, or the nose moves in the opposite direction, the rudder is being used too late.

    d. If the nose moves up or down when entering a bank, excessive or insufficient back elevator pressure is being applied.

3. **Inappropriate control applications.**

    a. This error may be due to a lack of planning.

    b. Failure to plan may require you to make a large control movement to attain the desired result.

4. **Improper technique in correcting altitude deviations.**

    a. When altitude is lost, you may attempt to raise the nose first by increasing back elevator pressure without shallowing the bank. This usually causes a tight descending spiral.

5. **Loss of orientation.**

    a. This error can be caused by forgetting the heading or reference point from which this maneuver was started.

    b. Select a prominent checkpoint to be used in this maneuver.

6. **Excessive deviation from desired heading during rollout.**

    a. This error is due to a lack of planning.
    b. The lead on the rollout should be one-half of the bank being used.

        1) With a 50° bank, 25° is needed for the rollout lead.

END OF TASK

STEEP SPIRAL

V.B. TASK: STEEP SPIRAL

REFERENCE: FAA-H-8083-3.

Objective. To determine that the applicant:

1. Exhibits knowledge of the elements related to a steep spiral.

2. Selects an altitude sufficient to continue through a series of at least three 360° turns.

3. Selects a suitable ground reference point.

4. Applies wind-drift correction to track a constant radius circle around selected reference point with bank not to exceed 60° at steepest point in turn.

5. Divides attention between airplane control and ground track, while maintaining coordinated flight.

6. Maintains the specified airspeed, ±10 knots, rolls out toward object or specified heading, ±10°.

A. General Information

   1.   The objective of this task is for you to demonstrate your smoothness, coordination, orientation, division of attention, and control techniques in the performance of steep spirals.

B. Task Objectives

   1.   **Exhibit your knowledge of the elements related to a steep spiral.**

      a.   A steep spiral is a continuous power-off gliding turn during which a constant radius around a point on the ground is maintained.

         1)   The maneuver is similar to a turn about a point, except that it is performed in a descent rather than at a constant altitude.

         2)   Steep spirals help you develop and maintain proficiency in power-off turns and control of wind drift, as well as planning, orientation, and division of attention.

      b.   Operating the engine at idle speed for a prolonged period during the glide may result in excessive engine cooling or spark plug fouling.

         1)   CAUTION: A steep spiral demonstration can become an actual emergency if you reach the completion of the maneuver with a cold engine. The engine may run roughly or stop altogether when you advance the throttle.

         2)   To avoid this situation, the manufacturer's recommendations regarding reduced-power operations (as outlined in the airplane's *POH*) should be followed. For example, leaning the mixture to maintain cylinder head temperatures when using reduced power settings may be recommended.

            a)   Also, the engine should be cleared periodically by briefly advancing the throttle to normal cruise power, while adjusting the pitch attitude to maintain a constant airspeed.

               i)   Preferably, this should be done while headed into the wind in order to minimize variations in groundspeed.

2. ***Select an altitude sufficient to continue through a series of at least three 360° turns.***

    a.   Steep spirals should be begun at an altitude that will allow for at least three 360° turns to be completed. The maneuver should not be continued below 1,000 ft. above the surface unless you are performing the steep spiral in conjunction with an emergency approach and landing exercise.

        1)   As you practice the maneuver, note how much altitude is normally lost during a 360° turn in your airplane.

        2)   Multiply the altitude lost by 3 and add 1,000 ft. to determine the minimum AGL entry altitude.

            a)   Add the terrain elevation to this figure to determine the minimum indicated altitude at which the maneuver should be begun.

3. **Select a suitable ground reference point.**

    a.   You should select a point that

        1)   Can be easily identified at a glance.

            a)   Do not select a vaguely-defined or non-unique point, such as one of several bales of hay scattered in a field, or you may lose track of exactly which point you are using.

        2)   Is located on or near a suitable emergency landing site.

            a)   Because the maneuver is normally completed at a low altitude, you must have emergency landing options available in case of an engine failure.

        3)   Is NOT in a congested area, near an open-air assembly of persons, on a federal airway, or near an area that might induce an undue hazard if a problem is experienced during the demonstration.

4. ***Apply wind-drift correction to track a constant radius circle around the selected reference point with the bank angle not to exceed 60° at the steepest point in the turn.***

    a.   The radius of the circle should be selected such that the steepest bank will not exceed 60°.

        1)   While not required as part of the PTS, you should enter the maneuver downwind so that your steepest bank will be required immediately.

            a)   Establishing the steepest bank immediately will aid you in determining the appropriate radius for the turn.

        2)   Because there is no minimum requirement for the steepest bank angle, we suggest that you plan for a 45° bank angle, as that bank angle will leave some room for error if you misjudge the wind speed or direction.

    b.   Begin the maneuver by performing clearing turns to carefully scan for traffic, especially below you. Flaps and landing gear (if retractable) should be up unless otherwise specified by your examiner.

        1)   When you are established on the desired entry heading (downwind) and almost abeam the reference point, smoothly reduce engine power to idle (or the manufacturer's recommended minimum power setting) and maintain altitude using back pressure.

            a)   Allow your airspeed to bleed off to the selected glide airspeed (e.g., best glide speed).

        2)   When you are abeam the reference point, roll into approximately a 45° bank and relax the back pressure to maintain the desired airspeed.

            a)   Re-trim the airplane as needed.

c.   During the descent, you must maintain a constant radius from the selected point by making bank adjustments to account for the effects of the wind, just as you must do when performing a turn about a point.

1)   On the downwind side of the maneuver, during which you will have a higher groundspeed, you must use a steeper bank angle in order to avoid being blown too far from the point (i.e., outside of the desired ground track).

a)   You must use a lower pitch attitude to maintain the desired airspeed while in a steeper bank.

2)   On the upwind side of the maneuver, during which you will have a slower groundspeed, you must use a shallower bank angle in order to avoid being blown on top of the point.

a)   You must use a higher pitch attitude to maintain the desired airspeed while in a shallower bank.

3)   Note that the speed and direction of the wind may vary as you descend.

5.   **Divide your attention between airplane control and ground track, while maintaining coordinated flight.**

a.   As with other ground reference maneuvers, you will be required to divide your attention between following the proper ground track and maintaining control of your airplane.

1)   Your attention must be divided among watching the ground reference point, maintaining the proper ground track, watching your flight instruments, and watching for other aircraft in your area.

b.   Since you will be changing bank constantly throughout this maneuver, you must actively maintain coordinated flight (i.e., keep the ball centered) and airspeed (i.e., vary the pitch attitude as the bank angle changes).

1)   Do not use rudder pressure alone to correct for wind drift.

a)   Use coordinated aileron and rudder to increase or decrease the bank.

c.   You must learn to divide your attention and not fixate on one item, such as your reference point.

6.   *Maintain the specified airspeed, ±10 knots, and roll out facing a specified ground object or on a specified heading, ±10°.*

a.   The steep spiral should be performed at a safe selected airspeed, presumably your airplane's best glide speed.

1)   The use of your airplane's best glide speed is consistent with the practical application of this maneuver, which is the dissipation of altitude over a selected landing site during the approach to a forced landing.

a)   By spiraling down over your intended touchdown point, you can avoid accidentally gliding too far from the field and leaving insufficient altitude to successfully complete the approach.

b)   See the discussion of Task IX. A., "Emergency Approach and Landing," beginning on page 255, for more information.

2)   A slight increase above best glide speed (e.g., 10 kt.) may be appropriate to avoid a stall during steep banks.

a)   Note that the airplane's stall speed is not increased to the same degree in a steep spiral as it is in a steep turn because the airplane does not maintain a constant altitude.

        b)   The descent helps to dissipate some of the "G" forces created by the steep bank.

    b.   During the roll-out at the completion of the maneuver, you should demonstrate good control, coordination, and smoothness so that the desired airspeed is maintained.

        1)   You must use back pressure to increase the pitch attitude as you roll the wings level to avoid increasing airspeed.

    c.   In order to roll out on the desired heading, lead the heading by one half the number of degrees of your bank angle; e.g., if you are in a 40° bank, begin leveling the wings 20° prior to the desired heading.

        1)   During training, you should have developed your own technique and knowledge of the lead required.

    d.   Complete the maneuver by increasing power and configuring the airplane as needed to maintain level flight or establish a climb, as directed by your examiner.

C.   Common Errors during Steep Spirals

    1.   **Improper pitch, bank, and power coordination during entry or completion.**

        a.   This error is indicated by

            1)   Allowing the nose to drop excessively or maintaining an excessively nose-high attitude upon starting the descent.

                a)   If the nose is allowed to drop too low, your airspeed may exceed the allowable tolerances. If an excessively nose-high attitude is maintained, a stall may occur.

                b)   You should determine the approximate correct pitch attitudes to establish for a straight glide and for beginning the descent during your training.

                      i)   Establish these attitudes during the entry and exit phases of the maneuver to avoid large airspeed changes; cross-check the airspeed indicator to fine-tune your attitude.

            2)   Allowing the bank angle to exceed 60°. The bank angle may become excessive if

                a)   The turn radius is too small.

                 b)   You do not correct for the effects of overbanking tendency by applying aileron opposite the direction of the bank while in a steep turn.

            3)   Forgetting to retard the throttle completely to idle (or to the manufacturer's recommended minimum power setting) before beginning the maneuver.

                a)   At completion of the maneuver, remember to increase power to maintain level flight or begin a climb, as directed by the examiner.

                b)   Do not allow a stall to occur.

    2.   **Uncoordinated use of flight controls.**

        a.   This error is normally indicated by the development of a slip or a skid as the bank angle changes, or by variations in airspeed.

            1)   Avoid this problem by frequently scanning the inclinometer (i.e., the ball) and cross-checking the airspeed indicator against the airplane's pitch attitude.

            2)   Do not correct for wind drift using rudder pressure alone.

3.   **Improper planning and failure to maintain constant airspeed and radius.**

    a.   This error is indicated by

        1)   The inability to complete three 360° turns before running out of altitude.

            a)   Be sure that you have sufficient altitude above the terrain before beginning the maneuver.

        2)   Losing track of the reference point during the maneuver.

            a)   This may be caused by beginning the maneuver with the reference point on the right side of an airplane with side-by-side seating, or by choosing a vaguely-defined reference point.

                i)   Unless the examiner specifies otherwise, you should perform the maneuver to the left because you will have a better view of the point and its surroundings.

        3)   The inability to maintain a constant distance from the reference point during the descent, or allowing the circle to drift downwind.

            a)   Be sure to vary the bank angle using coordinated rudder and aileron inputs in order to maintain the desired ground track as the airplane's orientation to the wind changes.

                i)   While upwind, use a shallow bank; while downwind, use a steeper bank.

            b)   As with a turn about a point, while directly crosswind on the downwind side, the airplane's nose will be pointed inside the circle, and while directly crosswind on the upwind side, the airplane's nose will be pointed outside the circle.

                i)   Do not attempt to keep the wing on the reference point throughout the maneuver.

4.   **Failure to stay oriented to the number of turns and the rollout heading.**

    a.   This error is indicated by completing fewer than three 360° turns or by rolling out on the incorrect heading or reference.

        1)   Avoid this error by starting the maneuver on a cardinal heading (i.e., north, south, east, or west) if possible.

            a)   If you cannot enter the maneuver downwind on a cardinal heading, try to use an entry heading that is shown on the heading indicator with digits, rather than tick marks (e.g., 150 instead of 165).

                i)   Use a heading bug, if available, or set the entry heading under the index of an unused VOR or ADF instrument to remind you.

            b)   Alternatively, pick a prominent landmark to use as an entry/roll-out reference.

        2)   Count the number of turns out loud each time the airplane passes through the entry heading or the reference landmark.

        3)   At completion of the maneuver, remember to lead the roll-out by an amount equal to one-half the bank angle to avoid overshooting the desired heading.

END OF TASK

CHANDELLES

V.C. TASK: CHANDELLES

       REFERENCE: FAA-H-8083-3.

Objective. To determine that the applicant:

1. Exhibits knowledge of the elements related to chandelles.

2. Selects an altitude that will allow the maneuver to be performed no lower than 1,500 ft. AGL (460 meters).

3. Establishes the recommended entry configuration, power, and airspeed.

4. Establishes the angle of bank at approximately 30°.

5. Simultaneously applies power and pitch to maintain a smooth, coordinated climbing turn to the 90° point with a constant bank.

6. Begins a coordinated constant rate rollout from the 90° point to the 180° point maintaining power and a constant pitch attitude.

7. Completes rollout at the 180° point, ±10° just above a stall airspeed, and maintaining that airspeed momentarily avoiding a stall.

8. Resumes straight and level flight with minimum loss of altitude.

A. General Information

    1. The objective of this task is for you to demonstrate your coordination, planning, and control techniques at varying airspeeds and attitudes in the performance of chandelles.

B. Task Objectives

    1. Exhibit your knowledge of the elements related to chandelles.

        a. A chandelle demands that the maximum flight performance of the airplane be obtained; that is, the airplane should gain the most altitude possible for a degree of bank and power setting without stalling.

           1) However, since numerous atmospheric variables beyond your control will affect the specific amount of altitude gained, the altitude gain is not a criterion of the quality of the chandelle.

        b. A chandelle is illustrated below.

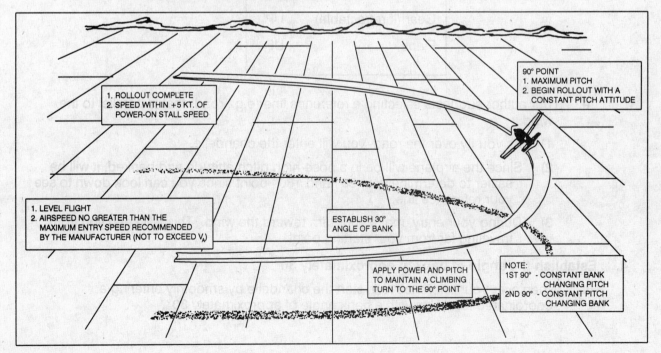

90° POINT
1. MAXIMUM PITCH
2. BEGIN ROLLOUT WITH A CONSTANT PITCH ATTITUDE

1. ROLLOUT COMPLETE
2. SPEED WITHIN +5 KT. OF POWER-ON STALL SPEED

1. LEVEL FLIGHT
2. AIRSPEED NO GREATER THAN THE MAXIMUM ENTRY SPEED RECOMMENDED BY THE MANUFACTURER (NOT TO EXCEED V$_A$)

ESTABLISH 30° ANGLE OF BANK

APPLY POWER AND PITCH TO MAINTAIN A CLIMBING TURN TO THE 90° POINT

NOTE:
1ST 90° - CONSTANT BANK
          CHANGING PITCH
2ND 90° - CONSTANT PITCH
          CHANGING BANK

2. **Select an altitude that will allow the maneuver to be performed no lower than 1,500 ft. AGL.**

    a.   Your author recommends that you use an altitude that is easy to read from your altimeter.

        1)   If the terrain elevation is 300 ft. MSL, the FAA requires the maneuver to be performed no lower than 1,800 ft. MSL (1,500 ft. AGL). Round this to the nearest 500-ft. increment (i.e., 2,000 ft. MSL) to make it easier to identify on your altimeter.

3. **Establish the recommended entry configuration, power, and airspeed.**

    a.   Prior to starting a chandelle, you should perform **clearing turns**, paying particular attention to possible traffic above and behind you.

        1)   Even though a chandelle is a 180° turn, you must perform **clearing turns** and check for traffic carefully.

    b.   The flaps and gear (if retractable) should be in the UP position.

    c.   Power should be adjusted to enter the maneuver at an airspeed no greater than the manufacturer's recommended entry speed, not to exceed V_A.

        1)   Remember that V_A is based on the airplane's weight, and the manufacturer's recommended airspeed is normally based on maximum gross weight. Calculate V_A so you do not exceed V_A.

    d.   Complete the following:

	Entry
Altitude	_____
Airspeed	_____
MP	_____
RPM	_____
Gear (if retractable)	UP
Flaps	UP

    e.   Your author suggests selecting a reference line (e.g., road) that is parallel to the wind.

        1)   As you fly over the road, you will enter the chandelle.

        2)   Since the airplane will be in a nose-high pitch attitude and banked, it will be easier to determine your 90° and 180° point since you can look down to see your reference line.

        3)   During your entry, make your turn toward the wind. This will keep you from traveling far from your starting point.

4. **Establish the angle of bank at approximately 30°.**

    a.   When over your reference line, start the chandelle by smoothly entering a coordinated level turn with a bank angle of approximately 30°.

5. **Simultaneously apply power and pitch to maintain a smooth, coordinated climbing turn to the 90° point with a constant bank.**

    a.   After you have established a level 30° banked turn, start a climbing turn by smoothly applying back elevator pressure to increase the pitch attitude at a constant rate and to attain the highest pitch attitude at the 90° point.

    b.   As the climb is initiated in an airplane with a fixed-pitch propeller, apply full power gradually.

        1)   In an airplane with constant-speed propeller, power may be left at the cruise power setting, or you may increase RPM to climb or takeoff setting prior to starting the chandelle. Then the MP is increased to climb or takeoff setting as the climb is started.

    c.   The angle of bank should remain constant to the 90° point.

        1)   Watch your bank angle because it may begin to increase without corrective control pressure.

            a)   As the airspeed decreases, the rate of turn will increase. This may cause an overbanking tendency, as discussed in Task V.A., Steep Turns, beginning on page 195.

    d.   Some pilots use the airspeed indicator as a reference for the proper pitch attitude at the 90° point.

        1)   The airspeed should be approximately at the midpoint between entry airspeed and the power-on stall speed.

            a)   The power-on stall speed varies with weight.

            b)   During your training, determine what the power-on stall speed is, given the normal loading of the airplane and the way the airplane will be loaded during your practical test.

        2)   You should try this while practicing chandelles.

    e.   Complete the following:

At 90°	
Airspeed	_____
Pitch attitude	_____
Bank angle	30°

6.   ***Begin a coordinated constant rate rollout from the 90° point to the 180° point maintaining power and a constant pitch attitude.***

   a.   When your airplane is headed parallel to your reference line (i.e., the 90° point), you should begin rolling out of the bank at a constant rate while maintaining a constant pitch attitude.

      1)   For planning purposes, the rate of rollout should be approximately 10° of bank for each 30° of heading change.

      2)   During the rollout, vertical lift increases, which tends to increase airspeed given a constant pitch attitude.

      3)   This tendency to increase airspeed should only reduce the rate at which you decrease your bank. As you plan and execute chandelles, your 90°-point pitch attitude has to be sufficient to accommodate the effect of the increased vertical component of lift.

      4)   Since the angle of bank will be decreasing and the vertical component of lift increasing, it **may** be necessary to release a small amount of back elevator pressure to prevent an increase in pitch attitude. Conversely, at the end of your rollout, your decreasing airspeed may require increased back pressure to offset the decreasing effectiveness of the elevator.

         a)   Use your outside visual reference and attitude indicator to maintain your pitch attitude.

   b.   Torque has a significant effect on rudder use during this maneuver. Since the chandelle calls for a gradual decrease of airspeed during the climbing turn, the right rudder pressure must be adjusted for the amount of torque effect being experienced.

      1)   Depending on the direction of the turn, aileron drag from the down aileron may act either in concert with torque, thus adding to it, or against torque.

         a)   To roll out of a left chandelle, the left wing must be raised. Thus, the left aileron is lowered and creates more drag than the aileron on the right wing, resulting in a tendency for the airplane to yaw to the left, in concert with the left torque effect. Therefore, significant right rudder correction is needed.

         b)   To roll out of a right chandelle, the right wing must be raised. Thus, the right aileron is lowered and creates more drag on that wing and tends to make the airplane yaw to the right, acting in the opposite direction from torque. Therefore, less right rudder correction is needed and may result in a cross-control situation during the rollout from a right chandelle.

      2)   When the wings are leveled, the aileron drag is neutralized, and torque is acting alone again.

7. **Complete the rollout at the 180° point, ± 10°, just above stall airspeed, and maintain that airspeed while momentarily avoiding a stall.**

   a. At the 180° point, your wings should be level within ± 10° of the reciprocal of your entry heading, and your airspeed should be within approximately +5 kt. of the power-on stall speed (your stall warning indicator should be on).

      1) Complete the following:

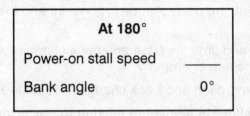

8. **Resume straight-and-level flight with a minimum loss of altitude.**

   a. After the wings are level, you must continue to correct for torque, which is prominent due to the low airspeed and high power.

   b. Gradually lower the nose to level flight while maintaining altitude.

      1) Right rudder pressure during the pitch decrease must be increased to counteract the additional torque caused by gyroscopic precession of the propeller.

   c. As airspeed increases, adjust pitch, power, and trim for cruise flight.

C. Common Errors during a Chandelle

   1. **Improper pitch, bank, and power coordination during entry or completion.**

      a. If the pitch attitude is increased quickly, a stall will occur before the airplane reaches the 180° point.

         1) If the pitch attitude is increased too slowly or if pitch is allowed to decrease, you will complete the 180° more than 5 kt. above the power-on stall speed.

      b. Rolling out too quickly will have the airplane at the 180° point at too high an airspeed.

         1) Rolling out too slowly will cause the airplane to stall before the 180° point.

      c. Power is used prior to entry to establish the proper airspeed and is increased only after the bank is established and pitch attitude has started to increase above the horizon.

         1) No other power adjustments are made during this maneuver.

   2. **Uncoordinated use of flight controls.**

      a. Maintain coordinated flight and use of controls throughout the maneuver.

      b. Ensure that you compensate for the torque and aileron drag effect throughout the maneuver.

      c. Check the ball in the inclinometer during all phases of the maneuver.

3. **Improper planning and timing of pitch and bank attitude changes.**

   a. During the first 90° of the turn, the bank is constant (approximately 30°) and pitch gradually increases.

   b. At the 90° point, you should have maximum pitch attitude and begin rollout.

   c. During the second 90°, pitch attitude remains constant and the bank is slowly rolled out.

   d. At the 180° point, the pitch attitude is constant and the rollout to wings-level flight is completed.

   e. You must plan and time the pitch and bank changes while dividing your attention to perform the maneuver properly.

      1) Subdividing pitch and bank changes will aid in this.

4. **Factors related to failure in achieving maximum performance.**

   a. Improper pitch throughout the maneuver
   b. Improper bank throughout the maneuver
   c. Lack of coordination, orientation, and planning

5. **A stall during the maneuver.**

   a. At no time during this maneuver should a stall develop.
   b. At the 180° point, your airspeed should be within +5 kt. of the power-on stall speed.

6. **Excessive deviation from desired heading during completion.**

   a. This error normally occurs because you did not maintain the corrections for the effects of torque at the completion of the maneuver.

END OF TASK

LAZY EIGHTS

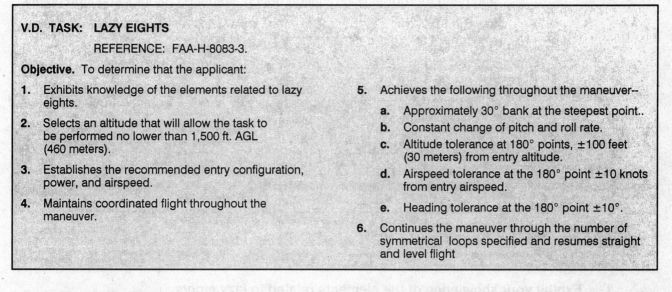

V.D. TASK: LAZY EIGHTS

REFERENCE: FAA-H-8083-3.

Objective. To determine that the applicant:

1. Exhibits knowledge of the elements related to lazy eights.

2. Selects an altitude that will allow the task to be performed no lower than 1,500 ft. AGL (460 meters).

3. Establishes the recommended entry configuration, power, and airspeed.

4. Maintains coordinated flight throughout the maneuver.

5. Achieves the following throughout the maneuver--

   a. Approximately 30° bank at the steepest point..

   b. Constant change of pitch and roll rate.

   c. Altitude tolerance at 180° points, ±100 feet (30 meters) from entry altitude.

   d. Airspeed tolerance at the 180° point ±10 knots from entry airspeed.

   e. Heading tolerance at the 180° point ±10°.

6. Continues the maneuver through the number of symmetrical loops specified and resumes straight and level flight

A.   General Information

1. The objective of this task is for you to demonstrate your ability to plan and remain oriented while maneuvering your airplane with positive, accurate control.

   a. This maneuver is used to develop a fine feel for constant, gradually changing control forces.

2. You may wish to experiment with the following tutorial maneuver with your CFI:

   a. After performing clearing turns to locate all nearby traffic, fly straight-and-level at a low cruise power setting.

   b. Visualize a square in front of the airplane equally divided above and below by the horizon.

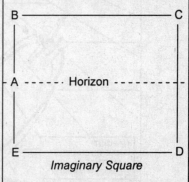

Imaginary Square

   1) Initially, you are at "A." Raise the nose to point "B" with back pressure, and hold the nose at "B" momentarily.

   2) Move the nose to "C" with coordinated aileron and rudder while maintaining back pressure. When at "C," level the wings and hold the nose at "C" momentarily.

   3) Move the nose to "D" with forward elevator pressure. Hold the nose at "D" momentarily.

   4) Move the nose to "E" with coordinated aileron and rudder pressure while maintaining forward pressure. When at "E," level the wings and hold the nose at "E" momentarily.

   c. Move the nose around the square once or twice more, stopping at each corner.

   1) Pay attention to the feel, movement, and need for rudder coordination during the speed changes and momentary stop points.

   d. Next, move the nose around the square without stopping at each corner.

   e. Next, convert the square to a circle equidistant above and below the horizon.

1)   Reverse the direction around the circle. Pay attention to the feel and movement and need for rudder coordination during airspeed changes and stop points.

2)   Slow the movement of the track of the forward extension of the nose so the movement about the circle is "lazy."

f.   Finally, convert the circles to a horizontally lying "8" equidistant above and below the horizon.

   1)   Again, this is where the lazy eight derives its name -- from the track of a forward extension of the longitudinal axis.

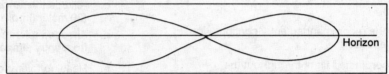

Airplane's nose projected to the horizon

B.   Task Objectives

1.   Exhibit your knowledge of the elements related to lazy eights.

a.   The lazy eight consists of two symmetrical 180° turns flown in opposite directions while climbing and descending during the turns.

   1)   The lazy eight gets its name from the flight pattern traced by the airplane. The maneuver is to be flown smoothly and appears very slow, i.e., lazy.

      a)   An extension of the longitudinal axis from the nose of the airplane to the horizon looks like a figure "8" lying on its side, one-half above the horizon and one-half below the horizon.

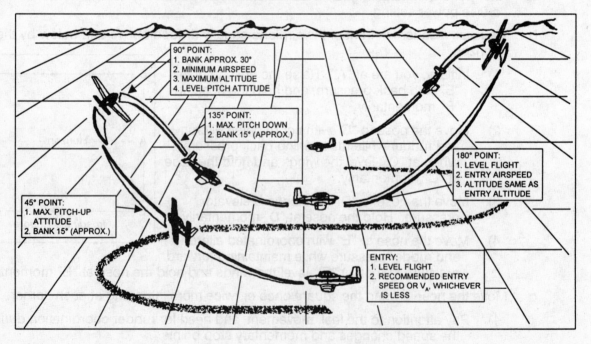

90° POINT:
1. BANK APPROX. 30°
2. MINIMUM AIRSPEED
3. MAXIMUM ALTITUDE
4. LEVEL PITCH ATTITUDE

135° POINT:
1. MAX. PITCH DOWN
2. BANK 15° (APPROX.)

180° POINT:
1. LEVEL FLIGHT
2. ENTRY AIRSPEED
3. ALTITUDE SAME AS ENTRY ALTITUDE

45° POINT:
1. MAX. PITCH-UP ATTITUDE
2. BANK 15° (APPROX.)

ENTRY:
1. LEVEL FLIGHT
2. RECOMMENDED ENTRY SPEED OR V$_A$, WHICHEVER IS LESS

b. Lazy eights require smooth, coordinated use of the flight controls.

1) At no time is the maneuver flown straight and level. The one point in the maneuver where a straight-and-level attitude is obtained is in the brief instant at the conclusion of each 180° turn just before the next turn is begun.

2) This maneuver requires constantly changing control pressures.

a) The control pressures need to change in accordance with changing combinations of climbing and descending turns at varying airspeeds.

c. The correct power setting for the lazy eight is that which will maintain the altitude for the maximum and minimum airspeeds used during the climbs and descents of the eight.

1) If excess power is used, your airplane will have gained altitude when the maneuver is completed.

2) If insufficient power is used, altitude will have been lost.

2. Select an altitude that will allow the task to be performed no lower than 1,500 ft. AGL.

a. Your author recommends that you use an altitude that is easy to read from your altimeter.

1) EXAMPLE: If the terrain elevation is 300 ft., the FAA requires the maneuver to be performed no lower than 1,800 ft. MSL (1,500 ft. AGL). Round this up to the nearest 500-ft. increment (2,000 ft. MSL) to make it easier to identify on your altimeter.

3. Establish the recommended entry configuration, power, and airspeed.

a. Perform **clearing turns** before starting this maneuver, especially to view the airspace behind and above you.

b. The flaps and gear (if retractable) should be in the UP position.

c. You will normally use the power setting required to obtain the airspeed recommended in your *POH*, or V_A if no airspeed is specified.

1) Remember that V_A is based on the airplane's weight, and the manufacturer's recommended airspeed is normally based on maximum gross weight. Calculate V_A for your airplane's weight and do not exceed V_A.

d. Complete the following:

Entry	
Altitude	____
Airspeed	____
MP	____
RPM	____
Gear (if retractable)	UP
Flaps	UP

4.   **Maintains coordinated flight throughout the maneuver.**

    a.   You should maintain coordinated (i.e., ball-centered) flight throughout the maneuver.

    b.   The maneuver is started from straight-and-level flight with a gradual climbing turn to the 45° point. Pitch must be increased at a faster rate than bank.

        1)   The rate of rolling into the bank must be slow enough to prevent the rate of turn from becoming too rapid.

            a)   As you raise the nose of your airplane, the airspeed decreases, causing the rate of turn to increase. Since the bank is also increasing, it too causes the rate of turn to increase.

        2)   Unless the maneuver is begun with a slow rate of roll, the combination of increasing pitch and increasing bank will cause the rate of turn to be so rapid that the 45° point is reached before the highest pitch attitude is attained.

    c.   At the 45° point, pitch is at its maximum, and the angle of bank should be at approximately 15°.

        1)   Complete the following:

At 45°	
Altitude	Increasing
Airspeed	Decreasing
Pitch attitude (max)	_____
Bank angle	approx. 15°

    d.   During the second 45° portion of the maneuver, the pitch attitude should decrease slowly, the airspeed should continue to decrease, and the bank should continue to increase.

        1)   Due to the decreasing airspeed, considerable right rudder pressure must be gradually applied to counteract torque.

            a)   More right rudder pressure will be needed during the climbing turn to the right because torque will be acting in the opposite direction of the turn.

            b)   In the left turn, torque correction is reduced because torque is acting in the same direction as the turn.

        2)   The controls may be slightly crossed in the right climbing turn because you may use left aileron to prevent overbanking and right rudder to correct for torque.

    e.   At the 90° point, your airplane should be at 30° angle of bank, maximum altitude, and minimum airspeed (5 to 10 kt. above stall speed).

        1)   It is at this time that an imaginary line, extending from your eyes and parallel to the longitudinal axis of your airplane, passes through your reference point at the 90° point.

2)   Complete the following:

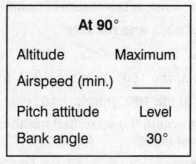

At 90°	
Altitude	Maximum
Airspeed (min.)	_____
Pitch attitude	Level
Bank angle	30°

f.   During the third 45° segment of the maneuver, the bank should be decreased gradually while the nose of the airplane is allowed to continue to lower.

1)   Remember to guide, not dive, the airplane during this segment.

g.   At the 135° point, your airplane should be at the lowest pitch attitude, and the bank angle should be approximately 15°.

1)   Complete the following:

At 135°	
Altitude	Decreasing
Airspeed	Increasing
Pitch attitude (min.)	_____
Bank angle	approx. 15°

h.   During the last 45° of the turn, you need to plan your rate of rollout and pitch change so that the wings become level and the entry airspeed and altitude are attained in level flight just as you reach the 180° point.

1)   During the descending turn, the airspeed will be increasing. Thus, it will be necessary gradually to relax rudder pressure (which was needed to correct for torque) as your airplane approaches your entry airspeed.

2)   Complete the following:

At 180°	
Altitude (entry)	_____
Airspeed (entry)	_____
Pitch attitude	Level
Bank angle	0°

    5. *Achieve the following throughout the maneuver:*

        a. *Approximately a 30° bank at the steepest point.*

        b. *Constant change of pitch and roll rate*

        c. *Altitude tolerance at the 180° points, ±100 ft. from the entry altitude*

        d. *Airspeed tolerance at the 180° points ± 10 kt. from entry airspeed*

        e. *Heading tolerance at the 180° points ±10°*

    6. **Continue the maneuver through the specified number of symmetrical loops and resume straight-and-level flight.**

C. Common Errors during a Lazy Eight

    1. **Poor selection of reference point(s).**

        a. Select reference points that are easily identified.

        b. If using a point, ensure that it is toward (or on) the horizon and not too close.

    2. **Uncoordinated use of flight controls.**

        a. Maintain coordinated flight and use of controls throughout this maneuver.

        b. Ensure that you properly compensate for the torque effect.

        c. Check inclinometer.

    3. **Unsymmetrical loops resulting from poorly planned pitch and bank attitude changes.**

        a. Excessive pitch-up attitude in the climbing turn may cause the airplane to stall before reaching the 90° point.

        b. Excessive pitch down during the second part of the turn results in an excessive dive, which causes the airplane to exceed the entry airspeed at the 180° point.

        c. Improper bank will cause you to hurry through the maneuver.

           1) A lazy eight should be a slow, lazy maneuver.

    4. **Inconsistent airspeed and altitude at key points.**

        a. If you tend to climb and/or your airspeed is becoming higher, reduce power slightly.

        b. If you tend to lose altitude and/or your airspeed is becoming slower, increase power slightly.

    5. **Loss of orientation.**

        a. This error may be due to not properly dividing your attention among the elements of the lazy eight. You may be concentrating on pitch and bank attitude without watching outside for your reference point.

        b. You may also forget your reference point, especially if you have selected poor reference points.

    6. **Excessive deviation from reference points.**

        a. You must plan for the proper bank and pitch attitude and airplane heading.

        b. Preplan the events in each 45° segment to help understand and anticipate the maneuver.

        c. Get in the habit of talking through the maneuver; what are the targets for altitude, airspeed, pitch, and bank at the next 45° checkpoint?

END OF TASK -- END OF CHAPTER

CHAPTER VI
GROUND REFERENCE MANEUVER

This chapter explains the one task of a ground reference maneuver. This task includes both knowledge and skill. Your examiner is required to test you on this task.

EIGHTS-ON-PYLONS

VI.A. TASK: EIGHTS-ON-PYLONS

   REFERENCE: FAA-H-8083-3

Objective.   To determine that the applicant:

1. Exhibits knowledge of the elements related to eights-on-pylons.

2. Determines the approximate pivotal altitude.

3. Selects suitable pylons that will permit straight-and-level flight, between the pylons.

4. Enters the maneuver at the appropriate altitude and airspeed and at a bank angle of approximately 30° to 40° at the steepest point.

5. Applies the necessary corrections so that the line-of-sight reference line remains on the pylon.

6. Divides attention between accurate coordinated airplane control and outside visual references.

7. Holds pylon using appropriate pivotal altitude avoiding slips and skids.

A. General Information

   1. The objective of eights-on-pylons is for you to demonstrate your ability to maneuver your airplane accurately while dividing your attention between your airplane's flight path and the selected points on the ground.

B. Task Objectives

   1. **Exhibit your knowledge of the elements related to eights-on-pylons.**

      a. Eights-on-pylons involves flying the airplane in circular paths, alternating left and right, in the form of a figure "8" around two selected points or pylons on the ground.

      b. The airplane is flown at an altitude and airspeed such that a line parallel to the airplane's lateral axis and extending from your eye appears to pivot on each of the pylons, as shown on page 218.

         1) No attempt is made to maintain a uniform distance from the pylon.

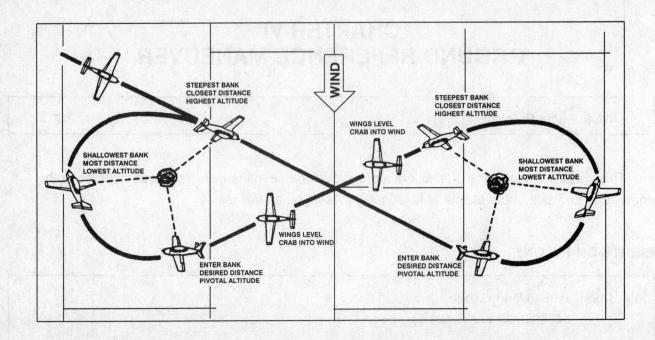

c.   In the correct performance of eights-on-pylons, you should use a sighting reference line which, from eye level, parallels the lateral axis of your airplane.

1)   High-wing, low-wing, swept-wing, and taper-wing airplanes, as well as those with tandem (fore and aft) or side-by-side seating, will all present different angles from your eyes to the wingtip.

a)   Your line-of-sight reference, while not necessarily on the wingtip itself, may be positioned in relation to the wingtip (ahead, behind, above, or below), as shown below.

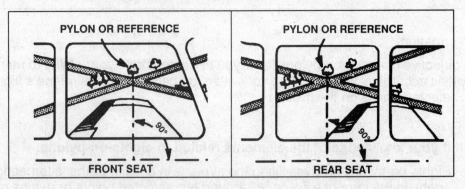

2)   The effects of using a correct and an incorrect line-of-sight reference to the pylon are shown on page 219.

d.   Relationship of groundspeed change to the performance of eights-on-pylons

1)   There is a specific altitude at which, when your airplane turns at a given groundspeed, a projection of your line-of-sight reference line to the selected point on the ground will appear to pivot on that point, i.e., **pivotal altitude**.

a)   The higher the groundspeed, the higher the pivotal altitude.
b)   The lower the groundspeed, the lower the pivotal altitude.

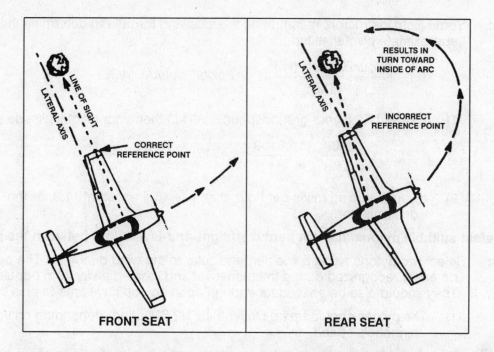

FRONT SEAT | REAR SEAT

2) Note carefully that the pivotal altitude is NOT a function of the angle of bank.

   a) In calm air, with the groundspeed constant around the pylon, the pivotal altitude would be constant throughout the maneuver.

   b) You could start the maneuver closer to the pylon with a resulting higher bank angle, and the pivotal altitude would NOT be different.

3) The strength (or speed) of the wind will affect the altitude changes to maintain the pivotal altitude.

   a) In a strong wind, the altitude changes will be greater (e.g., 100 to 200 ft.).
   b) In a light wind, the altitude changes will be smaller (e.g., 50 to 100 ft.).

2. Determine the approximate pivotal altitude.

a. At any altitude above the pivotal altitude, your reference line will appear to move rearward in relation to the pylon.

   1) When your airplane is below the pivotal altitude, your reference line will appear to move forward in relation to the pylon.

b. You can determine the approximate pivotal altitude by flying at an altitude well above the pivotal altitude.

   1) Reduce power and begin a descent at cruise speed in a continuous medium bank turn around the pylon.

      a) The apparent backward travel of your reference line with respect to the pylon will slow down as altitude is lost, stop for an instant, and then move forward if the descent is continued.

   2) The altitude at which your reference line apparently ceases to move but actually pivots on the pylon is the pivotal altitude.

   3) If your airplane descends below pivotal altitude, power should be added to maintain airspeed while altitude is regained to the pivotal altitude.

c.   Some flight instructors recommend the following formula to determine the approximate pivotal altitude.

$$\frac{Groundspeed \ (kt.)^2}{11.3} = Pivotal \ altitude \ (AGL)$$

1)   EXAMPLE: If your groundspeed is 90 kt., then your pivotal altitude is

$$\frac{(90)^2}{11.3} = \frac{8100}{11.3} = 717 \ ft. \ (AGL)$$

2)   If you are using miles per hour, then use 15, instead of 11.3, as the denominator.

3.   **Select suitable pylons that will permit straight-and-level flight between the pylons.**

a.   Select two pylons along a line perpendicular to the wind direction. The pylons should be easily recognized during the maneuver and located away from populated areas. They should also be spaced far enough apart so you have time to plan the turns.

1)   The pylons should be no closer than 1/2 SM apart, depending on your airplane's speed.

2)   You should have enough space between the pylons to allow for a brief period of straight-and-level flight while transitioning from one pylon to the other. This brief period of straight-and-level flight allows you to look for traffic and plan your next turn.

b.   When selecting suitable pylons, consider possible emergency landing areas within gliding distance, such as open fields or other nonwooded areas.

1)   Little time will be available to search for a suitable field for landing in the event the need arises, e.g., an engine failure.

c.   Perform **clearing turns** and carefully scan for other traffic.

1)   Look for obstacles, i.e., towers, since your altitude may be below 1,000 ft. AGL.

4.   **Enter the maneuver at the appropriate altitude and airspeed, and at a bank angle of approximately 30° to 40° at the steepest point.**

a.   You should be in the specified configuration and at the airspeed listed in your *POH*.

1)   If none is listed, use your normal cruise configuration and airspeed.

b.   Complete the following table with your CFI for eights-on-pylons planning:

Power MP: _____ RPM: _____	Airspeed: _____	Initial Altitude: _____

c.   Enter at the approximate pivotal altitude, as calculated in your planning.

d.   Enter the maneuver by flying diagonally crosswind between the pylons to a point downwind from the first pylon and then make the first turn into the wind.

1)   As your airplane approaches a position where the pylon appears to be just ahead of your line-of-sight reference, the turn should be started to keep the line-of-sight reference on the pylon.

2)   You should choose your entry point so that the steepest bank used in the maneuver (required when you are upwind of the pylon) will be approximately 30° to 40°.

5. **Apply the necessary corrections so that your line-of-sight reference line remains on the pylon.**

   a. Since your headings throughout the turns continually vary from directly downwind to directly upwind, your groundspeed will constantly change.

      1) Because of constantly changing groundspeed, the proper pivotal altitude will vary throughout the eight.

   b. As your airplane heads into the wind, the groundspeed decreases; consequently, the pivotal altitude decreases.

      1) Thus, you must descend to hold your reference line on the pylon.

   c. As the turn progresses on the upwind side of the pylon, the wind becomes more of a crosswind and drifts your airplane closer to the pylon.

      1) Since a constant distance from the pylon is not required, no correction to counteract drifting should be applied.

      2) Thus, with the airplane drifting closer to the pylon, the angle of bank must be increased to hold your reference line on the pylon.

   d. If the reference line appears to move ahead of the pylon, you should increase altitude.

      1) If the reference line appears to move behind the pylon, you should decrease altitude.

6. **Divide your attention between accurate, coordinated airplane control and outside visual references.**

   a. You must divide your attention between coordinated airplane control and outside visual references.

      1) Constantly be aware of the location of your line-of-sight reference in relation to the pylon.

   b. While performing this maneuver, you are still responsible for collision avoidance.

   c. You must also maintain orientation of the location of your pylons and the direction of the wind relative to your heading.

   d. As in any maneuver, you should always be planning ahead.

7. **Hold the pylon by using the appropriate pivotal altitude while avoiding slips or skids.**

   a. Hold the pylon by either climbing or descending to the pivotal altitude.

      1) Use rudder only for coordination, not as an adjustment to move the pylon forward or backward relative to your visual reference line.

      2) Do not attempt to cheat by using the rudder.

         a) Your CFI and your examiner will know if you do.

   b. Varying rudder pressure to yaw the airplane and force the reference line forward or backward to the pylon is a dangerous technique and must not be done.

C. Common Errors during Eights-on-Pylons

   1. **Faulty entry technique.**

      a. This error is normally due to poor planning.

         1) Not being at the approximate pivotal altitude

         2) Rolling into the bank too early, which requires you to shallow the bank, then roll back in

2. **Poor planning, orientation, and division of attention.**

   a. Poor planning is recognized by faulty entry technique and/or lack of anticipation of the changes in groundspeed.

   b. Poor orientation is recognized when you forget the wind direction or lose a pylon.

      1) Poor pylon selection will normally result in losing a pylon.

   c. Poor division of attention is recognized by uncoordinated flight control applications and failure to watch for traffic.

3. **Uncoordinated flight control application.**

   a. This error is normally due to poor division of attention.

4. **Use of improper "line-of-sight" reference.**

   a. The proper line-of-sight reference is parallel to the lateral axis of the airplane to the pylon -- your eye level.

   b. This visual reference line will be different for pilots seated in different positions.

5. **Application of rudder alone to maintain "line-of-sight" on the pylon.**

   a. This is the most common error in attempting to hold a pylon.

   b. You should not press the inside rudder to yaw the wing backward if the pylon is behind the reference line.

      1) When the pylon is ahead of the reference line, you should not press the outside rudder to yaw the wing forward.

   c. Use rudder for coordination only.

6. **Improper timing of turn entries and rollouts.**

   a. This error is due primarily to poor planning.

   b. When the pylon is just ahead of the reference line, the entry is started.

   c. Rollout should be timed to allow the airplane to proceed diagonally to a point on the downwind side of the second pylon.

7. **Improper correction for wind drift between pylons.**

   a. You must track a line to the next pylon by imagining a reference line.

   b. An improper correction is seen when arriving at the next pylon at a different distance than at the first pylon.

8. **Selection of pylons where there is no suitable emergency landing area within gliding distance.**

   a. This error is a part of poor planning; you should always to be prepared for any type of emergency.

9. **Large pitch and airspeed changes.**

   a. Such changes will result in errors in estimating groundspeed and pivotal altitude.

END OF TASK -- END OF CHAPTER

CHAPTER VII
NAVIGATION

This chapter explains the four tasks (A-D) of navigation. These tasks include both knowledge and skill. Your examiner is required to test you on all four tasks. Most pilots take pride in their ability to navigate with precision. To execute a flight which follows a predetermined plan directly to the destination and arrive safely with no loss of time because of poor navigation is a source of real satisfaction. Lack of navigational skill could lead to unpleasant and sometimes dangerous situations in which adverse weather, approaching darkness, or fuel shortage may force a pilot to attempt a landing under hazardous conditions.

PILOTAGE AND DEAD RECKONING

VII.A. TASK: PILOTAGE AND DEAD RECKONING
REFERENCES: AC 61-23/FAA-H-8083-25.

Objective. To determine that the applicant:

1. Exhibits knowledge of the elements related to pilotage and dead reckoning.

2. Follows the preplanned course by reference to landmarks.

3. Identifies landmarks by relating surface features to chart symbols.

4. Navigates by means of precomputed headings, groundspeed, and elapsed time.

5. Corrects for and records differences between preflight groundspeed and heading calculations and those determined en route.

6. Verifies the airplane's position within two (2) nautical miles of flight planned route.

7. Arrives at the en route checkpoints within three (3) minutes of the initial or revised ETA and provides a destination estimate.

8. Maintains the appropriate altitude, ±100 ft. (30 meters), and headings, ±10°.

A. General Information

1. The objective of this task is for you to demonstrate your ability to navigate by use of pilotage and dead reckoning techniques and procedures.

2. Additional reading: See *Pilot Handbook* for the following:

    a. Chapter 9, Navigation: Charts, Publications, Flight Computers, for a twenty-seven-page discussion on how to use a manual flight computer

    b. Chapter 11, Cross-Country Flight Planning, for an example of a standard navigation log and an abbreviated navigation log used and filled out during cross-country flight

3. You will not be required to fly an entire cross-country flight. Instead, your examiner will have you depart on the cross-country flight that you planned and discussed during the oral portion and will evaluate your ability to navigate by having you fly towards the first planned checkpoint.

B.   Task Objectives

   1.   Exhibit your knowledge of the elements related to pilotage and dead reckoning.

   a.   **Pilotage** is the action of flying cross-country using only a sectional chart to fly from one visible landmark to another.

   1)   Pilotage is accomplished by selecting two landmarks on your desired course and then maneuvering your airplane so that the two landmarks are kept aligned over the nose of your airplane.

   a)   Before the first of the two landmarks is reached, another more distant landmark should be selected and a second course steered.

   b)   When you notice wind drift away from your course, you must apply an adequate crab heading to maintain the desired ground track.

   2)   Pilotage can also be used by flying over, left or right of, or between two checkpoints to fly a straight line.

   3)   Pilotage becomes difficult in areas lacking prominent landmarks or under conditions of low visibility.

   4)   During your flight, you will use pilotage in conjunction with dead reckoning to verify your calculations and keep track of your position.

   b.   **Dead reckoning** is the navigation of your airplane solely by means of computations based on true airspeed, course, heading, wind direction and speed, groundspeed, and elapsed time.

   1)   Simply, dead reckoning is a system of determining where the airplane should be on the basis of where it has been. Literally, it is deduced reckoning, which is where the term originated, i.e., ded. or "dead" reckoning.

   2)   A good knowledge of the principles of dead reckoning will assist you in determining your position after having become disoriented or confused.

   a)   By using information from the part of the flight already completed, it is possible to restrict your search for identifiable landmarks to a limited area to verify calculations and to locate yourself.

   2.   Follow the preplanned course by reference to landmarks.

   a.   Departure

   1)   Just before taxiing onto the runway, write down the takeoff time on your navigation log.

   2)   Taxi onto the runway, align the airplane with the centerline, and come to a stop. Check the magnetic compass for a correct heading indication and reset the heading indicator to the compass.

   3)   After takeoff, there are two methods for establishing yourself on course.

   a)   After departing the traffic pattern, you can continue the climb to your planned cruising altitude and return to overfly the airport at least 500 ft. above the traffic pattern altitude.

   i)   Once over the airport, turn to your desired heading, look for your first checkpoint (landmark), and head toward it.

   ii)   This method is acceptable at an airport without an operating control tower.

   iii)   At an airport with an operating control tower, ATC would need to authorize this procedure.

      b)   Another method is to select a prominent landmark within 5 NM of the airport.

           i)   After takeoff, depart the traffic pattern and fly directly to the selected landmark. Once over the landmark, turn to your desired heading, locate your next checkpoint, and continue on course.

b.   En route

    1)   When using your sectional chart, arrange the chart so that your drawn course line runs up the page.

        a)   With this arrangement, what you see out the left/right side of the airplane should correspond with the left/right side of the course line.

    2)   Once at your cruising altitude, allow your airplane to accelerate, and then set the power and lean the mixture for cruise.

    3)   When appropriate, contact the FSS to open your flight plan.

        a)   On your practical test, inform your examiner that you would be opening your VFR flight plan.

    4)   By using your sectional chart and looking outside the airplane, you can locate the landmarks (checkpoints) used on your navigation log.

    5)   Locate a distant landmark that you will fly over and use that to assist you in your heading. Use closer landmarks to ensure that you remain on course.

c.   Arrival

    1)   Plan ahead by listening to the ATIS or an automated weather observation station broadcast, or by obtaining airport advisories, as appropriate.

    2)   If you are arriving at an unfamiliar airport, continuing to navigate by the selected landmarks to keep you on course will make it easier to locate the airport.

3.   Identify landmarks by relating surface features to chart symbols.

a.   The topographical information presented on sectional charts portrays surface elevation levels (contours and elevation tinting) and a great number of visual landmarks used for VFR flight.

    1)   These include airports, cities or towns, rivers and lakes, roads, railroads, and other distinctive landmarks.

    2)   Throughout your training, and especially on your cross-country flights, you should have been using your chart to identify landmarks and cross-checking with other landmarks nearby.

4.   Navigate by means of precomputed headings, groundspeed, and elapsed time.

a.   This objective refers to navigation by dead reckoning.

b.   During your cross-country preflight planning, you would have used all of the available information (e.g., winds aloft forecast, performance charts) to determine a heading, groundspeed, and elapsed time from your departure point to your destination.

c.   While en route, you will maintain your heading and keep track of your time between checkpoints.

    1)   During this time, you will be able to compute your actual elapsed time, groundspeed, and fuel consumption.

    2)   From this information, you should recompute your estimated time en route (ETE) to your next checkpoint/destination and deduce when you will be there.

    3)   These calculations are made by using your flight computer.

d.   Remember to determine where your airplane should be based on where it has been.

5. **Correct for and record differences between preflight groundspeed and heading calculations and those determined en route.**

    a. You must use and complete a navigation log when conducting the cross-country flight during your practical test.

    b. It is recommended that you use a navigation log for all of your cross-country flights.

6. ***Verify your airplane's position within 2 NM of the flight planned route.***

    a. By constantly dividing your attention among looking for other traffic, performing cockpit procedures, and navigating, you should have no problem in maintaining your route within 2 NM.

        1) Always be aware of where you have been and where you are going. Use landmarks all around you to help maintain your planned route.

7. ***Arrive at your en route checkpoints within 3 minutes of the initial or revised ETA and provide a destination estimate.***

    a. Once en route, you must mark down the time over each checkpoint.

    b. Since you already know the distance between the checkpoints, you can now use your flight computer to determine your actual groundspeed.

    c. Using the new groundspeed, you now need to revise your ETA to your next checkpoint and destination. Keep your examiner informed of these revised times.

8. ***Maintain the appropriate altitude, ±100 ft., and heading, ±10°.***

    a. While conducting your cross-country flight, you are required to maintain your selected cruising altitude, ±100 ft.

        1) Remember to divide your attention among all of your duties, but your primary duty is to maintain control of your airplane.

        2) Some pilots become so involved in looking at their charts, navigation log, and flight computer that they forget to look up, and when they do, they discover that the airplane is in an unusual flight attitude.

            a) Aviate first; then navigate.

    b. Make the needed adjustments to the heading to maintain your selected route, and maintain that heading. Tell your examiner when you are adjusting your heading.

C. Common Errors Using Pilotage and Dead Reckoning

1. **Poorly selected landmarks for planned checkpoints.**

    a. A road diagonally crossing the flight path is a poor choice.

2. **Poor division of attention.**

    a. You must divide your attention among flying your airplane, looking for traffic, identifying checkpoints, and working the flight computer.

        1) Dividing your attention is especially difficult when you are asked to alter your route.

    b. FLY YOUR AIRPLANE FIRST.

END OF TASK

NAVIGATION SYSTEMS AND RADAR SERVICES

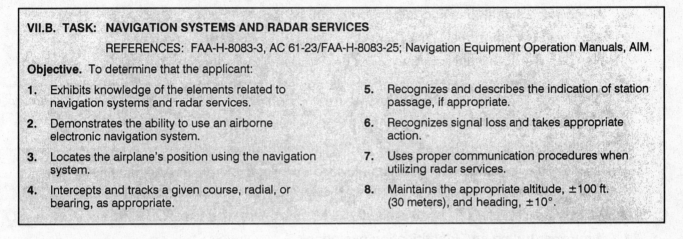

VII.B. TASK: NAVIGATION SYSTEMS AND RADAR SERVICES

REFERENCES: FAA-H-8083-3, AC 61-23/FAA-H-8083-25; Navigation Equipment Operation Manuals, AIM.

Objective. To determine that the applicant:

1. Exhibits knowledge of the elements related to navigation systems and radar services.

2. Demonstrates the ability to use an airborne electronic navigation system.

3. Locates the airplane's position using the navigation system.

4. Intercepts and tracks a given course, radial, or bearing, as appropriate.

5. Recognizes and describes the indication of station passage, if appropriate.

6. Recognizes signal loss and takes appropriate action.

7. Uses proper communication procedures when utilizing radar services.

8. Maintains the appropriate altitude, ±100 ft. (30 meters), and heading, ±10°.

A. General Information

1. The objective of this task is for you to demonstrate your ability to use properly the navigation systems installed in your airplane and to use ATC radar services.

2. Additional reading: See *Pilot Handbook* for the following:

   a. Chapter 3, Airports, Air Traffic Control, and Airspace, for a six-page discussion on ATC radar, transponder operation, and radar services available to VFR aircraft

   b. Chapter 10, Navigation Systems, for a 26-page discussion on various navigation systems, such as VOR, ADF, LORAN, and GPS

B. Task Objectives

1. **Exhibit your knowledge of the elements related to navigation systems and radar services.**

   a. The navigation systems that you will have in your airplane (VOR, ADF, LORAN, and GPS) operate by using the properties of radio waves.

      1) These navigation systems use a combination of ground or satellite transmitters and receivers in your airplane.

         a) You then determine and control ground track on the basis of the navigation instrument indications.

   b. ATC radar facilities provide a variety of services to participating VFR aircraft on a workload-permitting basis.

      1) To participate, you must be able to communicate with ATC, be within radar coverage, and be radar identified by the controller.

      2) Among the services provided are

         a) VFR radar traffic advisory service (commonly known as flight following)
         b) Terminal radar programs
         c) Radar assistance to lost aircraft

NOTE: For elements 2 through 6, listed beginning below, see the appropriate discussion in Chapter 10, Navigation Systems, in *Pilot Handbook*.

2. **Demonstrate the ability to use an airborne navigation system.**

3. **Locate your airplane's position using the navigation system.**

4. **Intercept and track a given course, radial, or bearing, as appropriate.**

5. **Recognize and describe the indication of station passage, if appropriate.**

6. **Recognize signal loss and take appropriate action.**

7. **Use proper communication procedures when utilizing radar services.**

    a. Use proper radio communication procedures when working with ATC.

    b. When working with a radar controller, you should repeat any altitude and/or heading clearances back to the controller.

        1) This is known as a **read back** of your clearance.

8. *Maintain the appropriate altitude, ±100 ft., and heading, ±10°.*

    a. You must divide your attention between using and interpreting the radio navigation instruments and/or ATC radar services and flying your airplane.

C. Common Errors Using Navigation Systems

1. **Improper tuning and identification of station.**

    a. The only positive way to know you are receiving signals from the proper VOR or NDB station is to verify its Morse code identifier.

    b. LORAN and GPS systems rely on the proper selection of the fix (airport, VOR, NDB, or intersection) identifier.

        1) Once you have selected and entered the identifier, check to see if the distance and bearing to your destination matches your planned course and distance.

2. **Poor orientation.**

    a. Follow the proper orientation procedures and understand the operating principles of the selected navigation system.

3. **Overshooting and undershooting radials/bearings during interception.**

    a. When you are using a VOR, this error is due to your not learning how to lead your turn to the desired heading.

    b. When you are using an ADF, this error is often due to your forgetting the course interception angle used.

4. **Failure to recognize station passage.**

    a. Know where you are at all times and anticipate station passage.

    b. You must also understand how station passage is displayed, especially on GPS and LORAN systems for which each manufacturer may be different.

5. **Failure to recognize signal loss.**

    a. The VOR TO/FROM indicator will show a neutral or off position. An alarm flag may appear on some VORs.

        1) All of these readings indicate that your equipment is receiving unreliable signals.

    b. With the ADF, you must monitor the NDB's Morse code identification at all times.

        1) If you cannot hear the identifier, you must not use that NDB station for navigation.

    c. The LORAN and GPS receiver will normally have some type of alarm indication if the signals are not reliable.

END OF TASK

DIVERSION

VII.C. TASK: DIVERSION

        REFERENCES: FAA-H-8083-25; AIM

Objective. To determine that the applicant:

1. Exhibits knowledge of the elements related to diversion.	3. Makes an accurate estimate of heading, groundspeed, arrival time, and fuel consumption to the alternate airport.
2. Selects an appropriate alternate airport and route.	4. Maintains the appropriate altitude, ±100 ft. (30 meters), and heading, ±10°.

A. General Information

    1.   The objective of the maneuver is for you to demonstrate your knowledge of the procedures for diverting to an alternate airport.

    2.   Among the aeronautical skills that you must have is the ability to plot courses in flight to alternate destinations when continuation of the flight to the original destination is impracticable.

        a.   Reasons include

            1)   Low fuel

            2)   Bad weather

            3)   Your own or passenger fatigue, illness, etc.

            4)   Airplane system or equipment malfunction

            5)   Any other reason that you decide to divert to an alternate airport

B. Task Objectives

    1.   Exhibit your knowledge of the elements related to diversion.

        a.   Procedures for diverting

            1)   Confirm your present position on your sectional chart.

            2)   Select your alternate airport and estimate a heading to put you on course.

            3)   Write down the time and turn to your new heading.

            4)   Use a straightedge to draw a new course line on your chart.

            5)   Refine your heading by pilotage and maximum use of available navigation systems.

            6)   Compute new estimated groundspeed, arrival time, and fuel consumption to your alternate airport.

b.   Adverse weather conditions are those conditions that decrease visibility and/or cloud ceiling height.

   1)   Understanding your preflight weather forecasts will enable you to look for signs of adverse weather (e.g., clouds, wind changes, precipitation).

      a)   Contact the nearest FSS or en route flight advisory service (EFAS) for updated weather information.

   2)   At the first sign of deteriorating weather, you should divert to an alternate. Attempting to remain VFR while the ceiling and visibility are getting below VFR minimums is a dangerous practice.

   3)   In order to remain VFR, you may be forced to lower altitudes and possibly marginal visibility. It is here that visibility relates to time as much as distance.

      a)   At 100 kt., your airplane travels approximately 170 ft./sec.; thus, related to 3 SM visibility, you can see approximately 90 sec. ahead.

         i)   The time decreases as speed increases and/or visibility decreases.

2.   Select an appropriate alternate airport and route.

a.   You should continuously monitor your position on your sectional chart and the proximity of useful alternative airports.

b.   Check the maximum elevation figure (MEF) on your sectional chart in each latitude-longitude quadrant of your route to determine the minimum safe altitude.

   1)   MEF is expressed in feet above MSL, which will enable you to make a quick determination by checking your altimeter.

c.   Determine that your alternate airport will meet the needs of the situation.

   1)   If the diversion is due to weather, ensure your alternate is in an area of good weather; otherwise, you may be forced into the same situation again.

   2)   If the diversion is due to mechanical reasons, ensure that repairs can be made at the selected alternate airport.

   3)   Ensure that the alternate airport has a runway long enough for your arrival and future departure.

d.   Determine that the intended route does not penetrate adverse weather or special-use airspace.

e.   Once you have decided on the best alternate airport, you should immediately estimate the magnetic course and turn to that heading.

   1)   The longer you wait, fewer are the advantages or benefits of making the diversion.

   2)   In the event the diversion results from an emergency, it is vital to divert to the new course as soon as possible.

3. **Make an accurate estimate of heading, groundspeed, arrival time, and fuel consumption to the alternate airport.**

   a. Courses to alternates can be estimated with reasonable accuracy using a straightedge and the compass roses shown at VOR stations on the sectional chart.

      1) The VOR radials and airway courses (already oriented to magnetic direction) printed on the chart can be used satisfactorily for approximation of magnetic bearings during VFR flights.

      2) Distances can be determined by using the measurements on a plotter, or by estimating point to point with a pencil and then measuring the approximate distance on the mileage scale at the bottom of the chart.

   b. If navigation systems are used to divert to an alternate, you should

      1) Select the appropriate identifier or coordinates (GPS, LORAN).
      2) Tune to the proper frequency and identify (VOR, ADF).
      3) Determine the course or radial to intercept or follow.

   c. Once established on your new course, use the known (or forecasted) wind conditions to determine estimated groundspeed, ETA, and fuel consumption to your alternate airport.

      1) Update as you pass over your newly selected checkpoints.

4. *Maintain the appropriate altitude, ±100 ft., and heading, ±10°.*

   a. Adjust your cruising altitude to your new magnetic course, if appropriate.

C. Common Errors during a Diversion

   1. **Not recognizing adverse weather conditions.**

      a. Any weather that is below the forecast has a potential to become an adverse weather condition.

      b. If there are any doubts about the weather, get an update from the nearest FSS or EFAS (Flight Watch).

   2. **Delaying the decision to divert to an alternate.**

      a. As soon as you suspect, or become uneasy about, a situation in which you may have to divert, you should decide on an alternate airport and proceed there directly.

      b. A delay will decrease your alternatives.

END OF TASK

LOST PROCEDURES

VII.D. TASK: LOST PROCEDURES

REFERENCES: FAA-H-8083-25; AIM

Objective. To determine that the applicant:

1. Exhibits knowledge of the elements related to lost procedures.

2. Selects an appropriate course of action.

3. Maintains an appropriate heading and climbs, if necessary.

4. Identifies prominent landmarks.

5. Uses navigation systems/facilities and/or contacts an ATC facility for assistance, as appropriate.

A. General Information

   1. The objective of this maneuver is to ensure that you know the steps to follow in the event you become lost.

   2. Steps to avoid becoming lost

      a. Always know where you are.

      b. Plan ahead and know what your next landmark will be and look for it.

         1) Similarly, anticipate the indication of your navigation systems.

      c. If your navigation systems or your visual observations of landmarks do not confirm your expectations, become concerned and take action.

B. Task Objectives

   1. Exhibit your knowledge of the elements related to lost procedures.

      a. The greatest hazard to a pilot failing to arrive at a given checkpoint at a particular time is panic.

         1) The natural reaction is for the pilot to fly to the assumed location of the checkpoint.

         2) On arriving at that point and not finding the checkpoint, the pilot usually assumes a second position and then, panicked, flies in another direction for some time.

         3) As a result of this wandering, the pilot may have no idea where the airplane is located.

      b. Generally, if planning was correct and the pilot used basic dead reckoning until the ETA, the airplane is going to be within a reasonable distance of the planned checkpoint.

      c. When you become lost you should

         1) Maintain your original heading and watch for landmarks.

         2) Identify the nearest concentration of prominent landmarks.

         3) Use all available navigation systems or facilities and/or ask for help from any ATC or FSS facility.

         4) Plan a precautionary landing if weather conditions get worse and/or your airplane is about to run out of fuel.

2. **Select an appropriate course of action.**

   a. As soon as you begin to wonder where you are, remember the point at which you last were confident of your location.

      1) Watch your heading. Know what it is and keep it constant.

      2) Do not panic. You are not "lost" yet.

      3) Recompute your expected navigation system(s) indications and visual landmarks.

         a) Reconfirm your heading (compass and heading indicator).
         b) Confirm correct radio frequencies and settings.
         c) Review your sectional chart, noting last confirmed landmark.

      4) Attempt to reconfirm present position.

   b. You should use all available means to determine your present location. This includes asking for assistance.

   c. You may want to climb to a higher altitude to ensure reception of navigation system signals, radar facilities, and communications.

   d. If available fuel is becoming a concern, you may want to adjust the power and mixture for maximum endurance until you can confirm your present location.

   e. The best course of action will depend on factors such as ceiling, visibility, hours of daylight remaining, fuel remaining, etc.

      1) Given the current circumstances, you will be the only one to decide the best course of action.

      2) Understand and respect your own and your airplane's limitations.

3. **Maintain an appropriate heading and climb, if necessary.**

   a. When unsure of your position, you should continue to fly your original heading and watch for recognizable landmarks while rechecking the calculated position.

      1) A climb to a higher altitude may assist you in locating more landmarks.

   b. By plotting the estimated distance and compass direction flown from your last noted checkpoint as though there were no wind, you will determine a point that will be the center of a circle within which your airplane's position may be located.

      1) If you are certain the wind is no more than 30 kt., and it has been less than 30 min. since the last known checkpoint was crossed, the radius of the circle should be approximately 15 NM.

   c. Continue straight ahead and check the landmarks within this circle.

      1) The most likely position will be downwind from your desired course.

4. **Identify prominent landmarks.**

   a. If the above procedure fails to identify your position, you should change course toward the nearest prominent landmark or concentration of prominent landmarks shown on your chart.

   b. If you have a very long known landmark, e.g., coastline, interstate highway, etc., you should proceed toward it.

   c. When a landmark is recognized, or a probable fix obtained, you should at first use the information both cautiously and profitably.

      1) No abrupt change in course should be made until a second or third landmark is positively identified to corroborate the first.

5. **Use navigation systems/facilities and/or contact an ATC facility for assistance, as appropriate.**

   a. Use all available navigation systems (VOR, ADF, LORAN, GPS) to locate your position.

      1) Use at least two VOR/NDB facilities to find the radial/bearing from the station that you are on. Draw these lines on your chart; where they intersect is your position.

      2) Most LORAN and GPS units have a function that will display the nearest airport and give its bearing and distance.

   b. If you encounter a distress or urgent condition, you can obtain assistance by contacting an ATC or FSS facility, or use the emergency frequency of 121.5 MHz.

      1) An urgent condition is one in which you are concerned about safety and you require timely but not immediate assistance. This is a potential distress condition.

         a) Begin your transmission by announcing PAN-PAN three times.

      2) A distress condition is one in which you feel threatened by serious and/or imminent danger and require immediate assistance.

         a) Begin your transmission by announcing MAYDAY three times.

      3) After establishing contact, work with the person to whom you are talking. Remain calm, cooperate, and remain in VFR conditions.

      4) ATC and FSS personnel are ready and willing to help, and there is no penalty for using them. Delay in asking for help has often caused accidents.

   c. If these conditions and others (e.g., darkness approaching) threaten, it is recommended that you make a precautionary landing while adequate visibility, fuel, and daylight are still available.

   d. It is most desirable to land at an airport, but if one cannot be found, a suitable field may be used.

      1) Prior to an off-airport landing, you should first survey the area for obstructions or other hazards.

      2) Identify your emergency landing area to your examiner, if appropriate.

C. Common Errors during Lost Procedures

   1. **Attempting to fly to where you assume your checkpoint is located.**

      a. Maintain your current heading and use available navigation systems and pilotage procedures to determine your position.

      b. Blindly searching tends to compound itself and leads to a panic situation.

   2. **Proceeding into marginal VFR weather conditions.**

      a. Use a 180° turn to avoid marginal weather conditions.

   3. **Failure to ask for help.**

      a. At any time that you are unsure of your position, ask for help.

      b. Do not let pride get in the way of safety.

      c. Recognizing the need for and seeking assistance is a sign of a mature, competent, and safe pilot.

END OF TASK -- END OF CHAPTER

CHAPTER VIII
SLOW FLIGHT AND STALLS

This chapter explains the four tasks (A-D) of Slow Flight and Stalls. Tasks A through C include both knowledge and skill, while Task D is knowledge only. Your examiner is required to test you on all four tasks.

MANEUVERING DURING SLOW FLIGHT

VIII.A. TASK: MANEUVERING DURING SLOW FLIGHT

REFERENCES: FAA-H-8083-3; Pilot's Operating Handbook, FAA-Approved Airplane Flight Manual.

Objective. To determine that the applicant:

1. Exhibits knowledge of the elements related to maneuvering during slow flight.

2. Selects an entry altitude that will allow the task to be completed no lower than 1,500 ft. (460 meters) AGL.

3. Establishes and maintains an airspeed at which any further increase in angle of attack, increase in load factor, or reduction in power, would result in an immediate stall.

4. Accomplishes coordinated straight-and-level flight, turns, climbs and descents with landing gear and flap configurations specified by the examiner.

5. Divides attention between airplane control and orientation.

6. Maintains the specified altitude, ±50 feet (15 meters); specified heading, ±10°; airspeed +5/-0 knots and specified angle of bank, ±5°.

A. General Information

1. The objective of this task is for you to demonstrate your ability to maneuver your airplane during slow flight in various configurations.

2. Additional reading: In Chapter 1, Airplanes and Aerodynamics, of *Pilot Handbook*, see Module 1.6, Dynamics of the Airplane in Flight, for a three-page discussion on the following:

    a. Lift, angle of attack, and airspeed
    b. Drag, angle of attack, and airspeed
    c. Pitch, power, and performance
    d. Slow flight

3. This maneuver demonstrates the flight characteristics and degree of controllability of your airplane in slow flight.

    a. It is of great importance that you know the characteristic control responses of your airplane during slow flight.

    b. You must develop this awareness in order to avoid stalls in your airplane (or any airplane that you may fly) at the slower airspeeds that are characteristic of takeoffs, climbs, and landing approaches.

B.   Task Objectives

   1.   Exhibit your knowledge of the elements related to maneuvering during slow flight.

      a.   It is important to know the relationship among parasite drag, induced drag, and the power needed to maintain a given altitude (or climb angle or glide slope) at a selected airspeed.

      b.   While straight-and-level flight is maintained at a constant airspeed, thrust is equal in magnitude to drag, and lift is equal in magnitude to weight, but some of these forces are separated into components.

         1)   In slow flight, thrust no longer acts parallel to and opposite to the flight path and drag, as shown below. Note that thrust has two components:

            a)   One acting perpendicular to the flight path in the direction of lift

            b)   One acting along the flight path

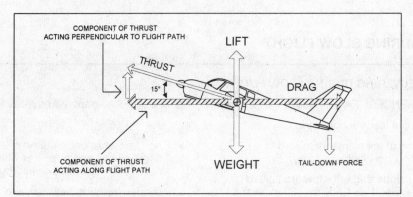

         2)   Because the actual thrust is inclined, its magnitude must be greater than drag if its component acting along the flight path is equal to drag.

            a)   Note that the forces acting upward (wing lift and the component of thrust) equal the forces acting downward (weight and tail-down force).

         3)   Wing loading (wing lift) is actually less during slow flight because the vertical component of thrust helps support the airplane.

      c.   The flight controls in slow flight are less effective than at normal cruise due to the reduced airflow over them (i.e., airplane controllability).

         1)   Anticipate the need of right rudder to counteract the torque effect in a low-airspeed, high-power-setting condition.

         2)   Large control movements may be required, but this does not mean rough or jerky movements.

   2.   Select an entry altitude that will allow the task to be completed no lower than 1,500 ft. AGL.

      a.   Your author recommends that you use an altitude that is easy to read from your altimeter.

         1)   If the terrain elevation is 300 ft. above sea level, the FAA requires the maneuver to be performed no lower than 1,800 ft. MSL (1,500 ft. AGL). Round this to the nearest 500-ft. increment (2,000 ft. MSL) to make it easier to identify on your altimeter.

      b.   Before you begin this task, your examiner should specify the airplane configuration to use (i.e., full flaps, partial flaps, gear up, gear down). If not, then ask your examiner for the desired configuration.

           1)   During this task, your examiner may have you change the airplane configuration to evaluate your knowledge of the elements related to slow flight.

      c.   Maintain your scan for other air traffic in your area, and perform **clearing turns**.

3.   *Establish and maintain an airspeed at which any further increase in angle of attack, increase in load factor, or reduction in power would result in an immediate stall.*

      a.   Begin slowing the airplane by gradually reducing power from the cruise power setting.

           1)   While the airspeed is decreasing, the position of the nose in relation to the horizon should be noted and should be raised as necessary to maintain altitude.

      b.   When the airspeed reaches the maximum allowable for landing gear operation (V_{LO}), the landing gear (if retractable) should be extended, as directed by your examiner.

           1)   Perform all gear-down checks, e.g., three in green.
           2)   In your airplane, V_{LO} _____.

      c.   As the airspeed reaches the maximum allowable speed for flap operation (V_{FE}), full flaps should be incrementally lowered to a setting specified by your examiner.

           1)   This will allow you to maintain pitch control of your airplane as flaps are extended.

           2)   In your airplane, V_{FE} _____.

      d.   Additional power will be required as airspeed decreases below L/D_{MAX} to maintain altitude.

           1)   Here, induced drag increases faster than parasite drag decreases.

           2)   This is known as "the backside of the power curve" or the "region of reverse command."

               a)   The region of reverse command means that you need more power (not less) to fly at a slower airspeed at a constant altitude.

      e.   As the flight conditions change, it is important to retrim your airplane as often as necessary to compensate for changes in control pressures.

      f.   When the desired airspeed and pitch attitude have been established, it is important to continually cross-check the attitude indicator, altimeter, and airspeed indicator, as well as outside references, to ensure that accurate control is being maintained.

           1)   In your airplane, the appropriate indicated airspeed for slow flight is _____.

      g.   Since you will be flying near the critical angle of attack, you cannot increase pitch to gain altitude.

           1)   To gain altitude, you need to increase power and adjust the pitch attitude.

4. **Accomplish coordinated straight-and-level flight, turns, climbs, and descents with landing gear and flap configurations specified by your examiner.**

   a. Once you have stabilized at the desired airspeed, you should maintain coordinated straight-and-level flight and level turns at a constant altitude.

   b. During the turns, the power will need to be increased to maintain airspeed and altitude and avoid a stall.

      1) Your examiner will specify the angle of bank to use.

   c. To climb, you will need to add power and adjust the pitch attitude to maintain airspeed.

   d. To descend, you will need to lower the nose and reduce power to maintain airspeed.

   e. Your examiner will specify the configuration to use (i.e., full flaps, no flaps, partial flaps, gear up, gear down).

5. **Divide your attention between airplane control and orientation.**

   a. When you are performing this maneuver, it is important to continually cross-check the attitude indicator, the altimeter, the airspeed indicator, and the ball of the turn coordinator, as well as outside references, to ensure that accurate control is being maintained.

      1) Do not become focused on one item, e.g., the altimeter.

   b. You must also divide your attention to watch for other aircraft in your area, i.e., practice collision avoidance.

6. *Maintain the specified altitude, ±50 ft.; the specified heading, ±10° ; airspeed, +5/-0 kt.; and the specified angle of bank, ±5°.*

C. Common Errors While Maneuvering during Slow Flight

1. **Failure to establish specified configuration.**

   a. This maneuver can be performed in various configurations of landing gear (if retractable) and flaps.

   b. You should form a habit of repeating instructions given to you for all maneuvers to ensure that you understand your examiner's instructions.

2. **Improper entry technique.**

   a. Perform clearing turns before beginning slow flight.

   b. To begin this maneuver, reduce power and gradually raise the nose. Use carburetor heat, if applicable.

   c. When the desired airspeed is attained, increase power and adjust both power and pitch to maintain airspeed and altitude.

      1) Anticipate the need of right rudder to counteract the effect of torque as power is applied.

   d. Retrim the airplane as often as necessary.

3. **Failure to establish and maintain the specified airspeed.**

   a. This error is caused by the improper use of power and pitch adjustments.

4. **Excessive variations of altitude, heading, and bank when a constant altitude, heading, and bank are specified.**

    a.   It is important to continually cross-check the attitude indicator, the altimeter, and the airspeed indicator, as well as outside references, to ensure that accurate control is being maintained.

5. **Rough or uncoordinated control technique.**

    a.   A stall may occur as a result of abrupt or rough control movements.
    b.   Uncoordinated control technique could risk the possibility of a crossed-control stall.

6. **Improper correction for torque effect.**

    a.   Because you will be at a high power setting, high angle of attack, and low airspeed, the airplane will exhibit pronounced tendencies to roll and yaw to the left.

        1)   Keep the ball centered using rudder and counteract any tendency to roll using aileron.

        2)   Right rudder will be required in level flight, and may even be required in a left turn.

7. **Faulty trim technique.**

    a.   Trim should be used to relieve control pressures.

    b.   Faulty trim technique may be evidenced by poor altitude control and by the pilot tiring quickly.

8. **Unintentional stall.**

    a.   A stall may be caused by uneven or sudden control inputs.
    b.   You must maintain your smooth control technique.
    c.   Check airspeed frequently.

9. **Inappropriate removal of hand from throttle.**

    a.   You should keep your hand on the throttle control at all times unless making an adjustment, such as trim.

END OF TASK

POWER-OFF STALLS

VIII.B. TASK: POWER-OFF STALLS

 REFERENCES: FAA-H-8083-3, AL 61-67; Pilot's Operating Handbook, FAA-Approved Airplane Flight Manual.

Objective. To determine that the applicant:

1. Exhibits knowledge of the elements related to power-off stalls.

2. Selects an entry altitude that allows the task to be completed no lower than 1,500 ft. (460 meters) AGL.

3. Establishes a stabilized descent in the approach or landing configuration, as specified by the examiner.

4. Transitions smoothly from the approach or landing attitude to a pitch attitude that will induce a stall.

5. Maintains a specified heading, ±10° in straight flight; maintains a specified angle of bank, not to exceed 20°, ±5°, in turning flight while inducing the stall.

6. Recognizes and recovers promptly as the stall occurs by simultaneously reducing the angle of attack, increasing power to maximum allowable, and leveling the wings to return to a straight-and-level flight attitude with a minimum loss of altitude appropriate for the airplane.

7. Retracts the flaps to the recommended setting, retracts the landing gear if retractable after a positive rate of climb is established.

8. Accelerates to V_x or V_y speed before the final flap retraction; returns to the altitude, heading, and airspeed specified by the examiner.

A. General Information

 1. The objective of this task is for you to demonstrate your ability to recognize and recover properly from a power-off stall.

 2. In Chapter 1, Airplanes and Aerodynamics, of *Pilot Handbook*, see Module 1.12, Stalls and Spins, for a four-page discussion on the aerodynamics of a stall and how to recognize an impending stall.

 3. Author's notes: This task does not differentiate between imminent and full stalls. You are required to announce to your examiner the onset of a stall (i.e., imminent) and promptly recover as the stall occurs (i.e., full).

  a. When the stall occurs, you must promptly recover so your airplane does not remain in a stalled condition.

B. Task Objectives

 1. **Exhibit your knowledge of the elements related to power-off stalls.**

  a. Power-off stalls are practiced to simulate approach and landing conditions and are usually performed with landing gear and flaps fully extended, i.e., landing configuration.

   1) Many stall/spin accidents have occurred in these power-off situations, including

    a) Crossed-control turns (aileron pressure in one direction, rudder pressure in the opposite direction) from base leg to final approach which result in skidding or slipping (uncoordinated) turns

    b) An attempt to recover from a high sink rate on final approach by only increasing pitch attitude

    c) Improper airspeed control on final approach or in other segments of the traffic pattern

    d) An attempt to "stretch" a glide in a power-off approach

    b.   The hazard of stalling during uncoordinated flight is that you may enter a spin.

        1)   Often a wing will drop at the beginning of a stall, and the nose of your airplane will attempt to move (yaw) in the direction of the low wing.

            a)   The correct amount of opposite rudder must be applied to keep the nose from yawing toward the low wing.

        2)   If you maintain directional control (coordinated flight), the wing will not drop further before the stall is broken, thus preventing a spin.

2.   Select an entry altitude that will allow the task to be completed no lower than 1,500 ft. AGL.

    a.   Your author recommends using an altitude that is easy to read from your altimeter.

        1)   If the terrain elevation is 300 ft. above sea level, the FAA requires a recovery no lower than 1,800 ft. MSL (1,500 ft. AGL). Round this to the nearest 500-ft. increment (2,000 ft. MSL) to make it easier to identify on your altimeter.

    b.   Do not let yourself be rushed into performing this maneuver. If you do not feel that you can recover before 1,500 ft. AGL (or a higher manufacturer's recommended altitude), explain this to your examiner and proceed to climb to a higher altitude.

        1)   During your training, you will learn how much altitude you need to perform this maneuver.

    c.   Perform **clearing turns** to ensure that the area is clear of other traffic.

3.   Establish a stabilized descent in the approach or landing configuration, as specified by your examiner.

    a.   Your examiner will specify the airplane configuration to use for this task. You should repeat these instructions back to your examiner to ensure that you heard the instructions correctly.

        1)   At this time, you should also confirm with your examiner the altitude, heading, and airspeed that you should return to after recovering from the stall.

    b.   Use the same procedure that you use to go into slow flight in the landing configuration.

    c.   Maintain a constant altitude and heading while you are slowing your airplane to the normal approach speed.

        1)   In your airplane, normal approach speed _____.

    d.   Perform your before-landing checklist (GUMPS).

    e.   As your airplane approaches the normal approach speed, adjust pitch and power to establish a stabilized approach (i.e., descent).

4.   Transition smoothly from the approach or landing attitude to a pitch attitude that will induce a stall.

    a.   Once established in a stabilized approach in the approach or landing configuration, you should smoothly raise the airplane's nose to an attitude that will induce a stall, while simultaneously reducing the power to idle.

        1)   In straight flight, maintain directional control with the rudder, level wings with the ailerons, and a constant pitch attitude with the elevator.

2) In turning flight, maintain coordinated flight with the rudder, bank angle with the ailerons, and a constant pitch attitude with the elevator.

    a) No attempt should be made to stall your airplane on a predetermined heading.

3) In most training airplanes, the elevator should be brought back smoothly and fully.

5. ***Maintain a specified heading, ±10°, if in straight flight; maintain a specified angle of bank not to exceed 20°, ±5°, if in turning flight, while inducing the stall.***

6. **Recognize the onset of the stall and recover promptly as the stall occurs by simultaneously reducing the angle of attack, increasing power to the maximum allowable setting, and leveling the wings to return to a straight-and-level flight attitude with a minimum loss of altitude that is appropriate for the airplane.**

    a. You should announce to your examiner when you recognize the first aerodynamic indications of the oncoming stall.

        1) The aerodynamic indications include the first signs of buffeting or decay of control effectiveness (i.e., a mushy feeling in the flight controls).

    b. Other signs of stall recognition include vision, hearing, kinesthesia, and stall warning indicators in the airplane.

    c. Though the recovery actions must be taken in a coordinated manner, they are broken down into three steps here for explanatory purposes.

    d. First, the key factor in recovering from a stall is regaining positive control of your airplane by reducing the angle of attack.

        1) Since the basic cause of a stall is always an excessive angle of attack, the cause must be eliminated by releasing the back elevator pressure that was necessary to attain that angle of attack or by moving the elevator control forward.

           a) Each airplane may require a different amount of forward pressure.

           b) Too much forward pressure can hinder the recovery by imposing a negative load on the wing.

        2) The object is to reduce the angle of attack but only enough to allow the wing to regain lift. Remember that you want to minimize your altitude loss.

           a) Your author suggests that the nose of the airplane should not go below the horizon.

    e. Second, promptly and smoothly apply maximum allowable power to increase airspeed and to minimize the loss of altitude. In most airplanes, the maximum allowable power will be full power, but do not exceed the RPM red line speed.

        1) If carburetor heat is on, you need to turn it off.

        2) Right rudder pressure will be necessary to overcome the torque effect as power is advanced and the nose is being lowered.

    f. Third, straight flight should be established with coordinated use of the controls.

        1) At this time, the wings should be leveled if they were previously banked.

        2) Do not attempt to deflect the ailerons until the angle of attack has been reduced.

           a) The adverse yaw caused by the downward aileron may place the airplane in uncoordinated flight, and if the airplane is still in a stalled condition, a spin could be induced.

g.   To minimize the loss of altitude, as power is applied and the wings are leveled, you should adjust the airplane's pitch to that required for V_x.

   1)   This pitch adjustment will place your airplane in a high angle of attack to stop the loss of altitude and to achieve the maximum climb performance.

h.   Maintain coordinated flight throughout the recovery.

7.   **Retract the flaps to the recommended setting, and retract the landing gear, if retractable, after a positive rate of climb is established.**

a.   Flaps should be partially retracted to reduce drag during recovery from the stall.

   1)   Flaps are partially raised before the gear because the flaps produce more drag.

   2)   Set the flaps as recommended for the go-around procedure in your airplane's *POH*.

b.   Landing gear, if retractable, should be retracted only after a positive rate of climb has been established on the vertical speed indicator and the altimeter.

   1)   Additionally, ensure that you have the airplane under control and clear of obstacles before reaching for the gear control.

8.   **Accelerate to V_x or V_y before the final flap retraction and return to the altitude, heading, and airspeed specified by the examiner.**

a.   Follow the procedures in your airplane's *POH*.

   1)   If your airplane recommends 0° flaps for V_x, then make the final flap retraction at V_x.

   2)   Otherwise, make the final flap retraction at V_y.

b.   Your examiner will normally provide you with the desired altitude, heading, and airspeed before you begin the maneuver.

   1)   If not, you must remember to ask for this information before you begin the maneuver.

C.   Common Errors during a Power-Off Stall

1.   **Failure to establish the specified flap and gear (if retractable) configuration prior to entry.**

a.   While maintaining altitude, reduce airspeed to slow flight with wing flaps and landing gear (if retractable) extended to the landing configuration.

   1)   Use your normal landing configuration.

b.   Remember to perform the required **clearing turns**.

2.   **Improper pitch, heading, and bank control during straight ahead stalls.**

a.   Use your visual and instrument references as in straight descents but with an increasing pitch attitude to induce a stall.

b.   Maintain directional control with the rudder and wings level with the ailerons.

3.   **Improper pitch and bank controls during turning stalls.**

a.   Use your visual and instrument references as in turning descents but with an increasing pitch attitude to induce a stall.

b.   Use whatever control pressure is necessary to maintain the specified angle of bank (not to exceed 30°) and coordinated flight.

4. **Rough or uncoordinated control technique.**

    a. As your airplane approaches the stall, the controls become increasingly sluggish, and you may assume that the controls need to be moved in a rough or jerky manner.

        1) Maintain smooth control applications at all times.

    b. Keep your airplane in coordinated flight, even if the controls feel crossed.

        1) If a power-off stall is not properly coordinated, one wing will often drop before the other, and the nose will yaw in the direction of the low wing during the stall.

5. **Failure to recognize the first indications of a stall.**

    a. The first indication of a stall is signaled by the first buffeting or decay of control effectiveness.

6. **Failure to achieve a stall.**

    a. You must maintain sufficient elevator back pressure to induce a stall.

        1) In many airplanes, this means the elevator control is full back to the stop.

    b. A full stall is evidenced by one or more of the following:

        1) Full back elevator pressure
        2) High sink rate
        3) Nose-down pitching
        4) Possible buffeting

7. **Improper torque correction.**

    a. During recovery, right rudder pressure is necessary to overcome the torque effects as power is advanced and the nose is raised.

    b. You must cross-check outside references with the turn coordinator to ensure that the ball remains centered.

8. **Poor stall recognition and delayed recovery.**

    a. Some pilots may attempt to hold a stall attitude because they are waiting for a particular event to occur, e.g., an abrupt pitch-down attitude.

        1) While the pilot is waiting for this event, the airplane is losing altitude from the high sink rate of a stalled condition.

    b. Delayed recovery aggravates the stall situation and, if you do not remain in coordinated flight, the airplane is likely to enter a spin.

    c. Recognition and recovery must be immediate and prompt.

9. **Excessive altitude loss or excessive airspeed during recovery.**

    a. Do not maintain a pitch-down attitude during recovery.

        1) Move the control yoke forward to reduce the angle of attack; then smoothly adjust the pitch to the desired attitude.

10. **Secondary stall during recovery.**

    a. A secondary stall occurs when you hasten to complete your stall recovery (to straight-and-level flight or climb) before the airplane has realigned itself with the flight path (relative wind).

END OF TASK

POWER-ON STALLS

VIII.C. TASK: POWER-ON STALLS

> REFERENCES: FAA-H-8083-3; AC 61-67; Pilot's Operating Handbook, FAA-Approved Airplane Flight Manual.
>
> NOTE: In some high performance airplanes, the power setting may have to be reduced below the practical test standards guideline power setting to prevent excessively high pitch attitudes (greater than 30° nose up).

Objective. To determine that the applicant:

1. Exhibits knowledge of the elements related to power-on stalls.

2. Selects an entry altitude that allows the task to be completed no lower than 1,500 ft. (460 meters) AGL.

3. Establishes the takeoff or departure configuration. Sets power to no less than 65% of available power.

4. Transitions smoothly from the takeoff or departure attitude to a pitch attitude that will induce a stall.

5. Maintains a specified heading ±5°, in straight flight; maintains a specified angle of bank, not to exceed 20°, ±10°, in turning flight, while inducing the stall.

6. Recognizes and recovers promptly as the stall occurs by simultaneously reducing the angle of attack, increasing power to maximum allowable, and leveling the wings to return to a straight-and-level flight attitude, with a minimum loss of altitude appropriate for the airplane.

7. Retracts flaps to the recommended setting, retracts the landing gear if retractable, after a positive rate of climb is established.

8. Accelerates to V_X or V_Y speed before the final flap retraction; returns to the altitude, heading, and airspeed specified by the examiner.

A. General Information

1. The objective of this task is for you to demonstrate your ability to recognize and recover properly from a power-on stall.

2. In Chapter 1, Airplanes and Aerodynamics, of *Pilot Handbook*, see Module 1.12, Stalls and Spins, for a four-page discussion on the aerodynamics of a stall and how to recognize an impending stall.

3. Author's note: This task does not differentiate between imminent and full stalls. You are required to announce to your examiner the onset of a stall (i.e., imminent) and promptly recover as the stall occurs (i.e., full).

   a. When the stall occurs, you must promptly recover so your airplane does not remain in a stalled condition.

B. Task Objectives

1. Exhibit your knowledge of the elements related to power-on stalls.

   a. Power-on stalls are practiced to simulate takeoff and climbout conditions and configurations.

      1) Many stall/spin accidents have occurred during these phases of flight, particularly during go-arounds.

         a) A causal factor in go-arounds has been the pilot's failure to maintain positive control due to a nose-high trim setting or premature flap retraction.

      2) Failure to maintain positive control during short-field takeoffs has also been an accident factor.

  b.   The likelihood of stalling in uncoordinated flight is increased during a power-on stall due to the greater torque from high pitch attitude, high power setting, and low airspeed.

    1)   A power-on stall will often result in one wing dropping.
    2)   Maintaining directional control with rudder is vital to avoiding a spin.

2.   **Select an entry altitude that will allow the task to be completed no lower than 1,500 ft. AGL.**

  a.   Your author recommends that you use an altitude that is easy to read from your altimeter.

    1)   If the terrain elevation is 300 ft. above sea level, the FAA requires a recovery no lower than 1,800 ft. MSL (1,500 ft. AGL). Round this to the nearest 500-ft. increment (2,000 ft. MSL) to make it easier to identify on your altimeter.

  b.   Do not let yourself be rushed into performing this maneuver. If you do not feel that you can recover before 1,500 ft. AGL (or a higher manufacturer's recommended altitude), explain this to your examiner and proceed to climb to a higher altitude.

    1)   During your training, you will learn how much altitude you need to perform this maneuver.

  c.   Before beginning the maneuver, confirm with your examiner the altitude, heading, and airspeed that you should return to after recovering from the stall.

  d.   Perform **clearing turns** to ensure that the area is clear of other traffic.

3.   **Establish the takeoff or departure configuration and set power to no less than 65% of available power.**

  a.   After the clearing turns are completed, reduce the power to slow the airplane to the normal liftoff speed, which is approximately V_R + 5 kt, or V_R.

    1)   Some CFIs will have you begin the airspeed reduction during your clearing turns to reduce the amount of time in performing this maneuver.

  b.   As the airplane slows below V_{FE}, lower the flaps to the takeoff setting, if appropriate.

    1)   If the examiner specifies that the maneuver is to be performed in the takeoff configuration, extend the landing gear below V_{LO}/V_{LE}, if retractable.

  c.   Maintain a constant heading and altitude as the airplane is properly configured and slowed.

  d.   The purpose of reducing the speed before the throttle is advanced to the recommended setting is to avoid an excessively steep nose-up attitude before your airplane stalls.

  e.   In your airplane, V_R _____.

  f.   When your airplane has slowed to V_R, you should set the power to the manufacturer's recommended climb power setting, while establishing a climb attitude.

    1)   In the absence of a manufacturer's recommended power setting, use no less than 65% of full power.

4.   **Transition smoothly from a takeoff or departure attitude to a pitch attitude that will induce a stall.**

  a.   After the climb attitude has been established, the nose is then brought smoothly upward to an attitude obviously impossible for the airplane to maintain (greater than V_X pitch attitude) and is held in that attitude until the stall occurs.

        1) Increased back elevator pressure will be necessary to maintain this attitude as the airspeed decreases.

        2) Do not use an extreme pitch attitude, which could result in loss of control.

    b. In straight flight, maintain directional control with the rudder, level wings with the ailerons, and a constant pitch attitude with the elevator.

        1) In turning flight, maintain coordinated flight while using a bank angle specified by your examiner, but not greater than 20°.

        2) Increasing right rudder pressure will be required during this maneuver as the airspeed decreases to counteract torque.

5. *Maintain a specified heading, ±10°, if in straight flight; maintain a specified angle of bank, not to exceed 20°, ±10°, if in turning flight.*

6. Recognize the onset of the stall and recover promptly as the stall occurs by simultaneously reducing the angle of attack, increasing power to the maximum allowable setting, and leveling the wings to return to a straight-and-level flight attitude, with minimum loss of altitude appropriate for the airplane.

    a. You should announce to your examiner when you recognize the first aerodynamic indications of the oncoming stall.

        1) The aerodynamic indications include the first signs of buffeting or decay of control effectiveness (i.e., a mushy feeling in the flight controls).

    b. Other signs of stall recognition include vision, hearing, kinesthesia, and stall warning indicators in the airplane

    c. Though the recovery actions must be taken in a coordinated manner, they are broken down into three steps here for explanatory purposes.

    d. First, the key factor in recovering from a stall is regaining positive control of your airplane by reducing the angle of attack.

        1) Since the basic cause of a stall is always an excessive angle of attack, the cause must be eliminated by releasing the back elevator pressure that was necessary to attain that angle of attack or by moving the elevator control forward.

            a) Each airplane may require a different amount of forward pressure.

            b) Too much forward pressure can hinder the recovery by imposing a negative load on the wing.

        2) The object is to reduce the angle of attack but only enough to allow the wing to regain lift. Remember that you want to minimize your altitude loss.

            a) Your author suggests that the nose of the airplane should not go below the horizon.

    e. Second, promptly and smoothly apply maximum allowable power to increase airspeed and to minimize the loss of altitude. In most airplanes, this will be full power, but do not exceed the RPM red line speed.

        1) Since the throttle is already at the takeoff or climb power setting, the addition of power will be relatively slight, if any.

            a) Use this step to confirm that you have maximum allowable power.

    f. Third, straight flight should be established with coordinated use of the controls.

        1) At this time, the wings should be leveled if they were previously banked.

        2)   Do not attempt to deflect the ailerons until the angle of attack has been reduced.

           a)   The adverse yaw caused by the downward aileron may place the airplane in uncoordinated flight, and if the airplane is still in a stalled condition, a spin could be induced.

   g.   To minimize the loss of altitude, you should establish the pitch attitude required for V_x.

   h.   Maintain coordinated flight throughout the recovery.

7.   Retract the flaps to the recommended setting and retract the landing gear, if retractable, after a positive rate of climb is established.

   a.   Once the airplane is under control and a positive rate of climb is established (as indicated by the vertical speed indicator and the altimeter), retract the flaps (if extended) and landing gear (if retractable).

   b.   The flaps should be retracted before the landing gear since the flaps create more drag.

   c.   Follow the procedures in your airplane's *POH*.

8.   Accelerate to V_x or V_y before final flap retraction and return to the altitude, heading, and airspeed specified by the examiner.

   a.   Follow the procedures in your airplane's *POH*.

        1)   If your airplane recommends 0° flaps for V_x, then make the final flap retraction at V_x.

        2)   Otherwise, make the final flap retraction at V_y.

   b.   Your examiner will normally provide you with the desired altitude, heading and airspeed before you begin the maneuver.

        1)   If not, you must remember to ask for this information before you begin the maneuver.

C.   Common Errors during a Power-On Stall

1.   Failure to establish the specified landing gear (if retractable) and flap configuration prior to entry.

   a.   Repeat the instructions that your examiner gave to you regarding the airplane configuration for the stall.

        1)   Your airplane will be configured for a takeoff or a normal departure climb.

   b.   Remember to perform the required **clearing turns**.

2.   Improper pitch, heading, and bank control during straight ahead stalls.

   a.   Use your visual and instrument references as in straight climbs but with a pitch attitude that will induce a stall.

   b.   Maintain heading and wings level during the straight ahead stall.

   c.   Use rudder pressure to counteract the increasing torque effects.

3.   Improper pitch and bank control during turning stalls.

   a.   Use your visual and instrument references as in a turning climb but with a pitch attitude that will induce a stall.

   b.   Use whatever control pressure is necessary to maintain a specified bank angle of not more than 20°, in coordinated flight.

4. **Rough or uncoordinated control technique.**

   a. As your airplane approaches the stall, the controls will become increasingly sluggish, and you may assume that the controls need to be moved in a rough or jerky manner.

      1) Maintain smooth control applications at all times.
      2) Do not try to muscle your way through this maneuver.

   b. Keep your airplane in coordinated flight even if the controls feel crossed.

      1) If a power-on stall is not properly coordinated, one wing will often drop before the other wing, and the nose will yaw in the direction of the low wing during the stall.

5. **Failure to recognize the first indications of a stall.**

   a. The first indication of a stall is signaled by the first buffeting or decay of control effectiveness.

6. **Failure to achieve a stall.**

   a. You must maintain sufficient elevator back pressure to induce a stall.

      1) In many airplanes, this means the elevator control is full back to the stop.

   b. A full stall is evident by one or more of the following:

      1) Full back elevator pressure
      2) High sink rate
      3) Nose-down pitching
      4) Possible buffeting

7. **Improper torque correction.**

   a. Since the airspeed is decreasing with a high power setting and a high angle of attack, the effect of torque becomes more prominent. Right rudder pressure must be used to counteract torque.

8. **Poor stall recognition and delayed recovery.**

   a. Some pilots may attempt to hold a stall attitude because they are waiting for a particular event to occur, e.g., an abrupt pitch-down attitude.

      1) While the pilot is waiting for this event, the airplane is losing altitude from the high sink rate of a stalled condition.

   b. Delayed recovery aggravates the stall situation and, if you do not remain in coordinated flight, the airplane is likely to enter a spin.

   c. Recognition and recovery must be immediate and prompt.

9. **Excessive altitude loss or excessive airspeed during recovery.**

   a. Do not maintain a pitch-down attitude during recovery.

      1) Move the control yoke forward to reduce the angle of attack; then smoothly adjust the pitch to the desired pitch attitude.

10. **Secondary stall during recovery.**

    a. A secondary stall happens when you rush your stall recovery to straight-and-level flight or climb before the airplane has realigned itself with the flight path (relative wind).

11. **Elevator trim stall.**

    a. Using excessive up elevator trim to hold a climb attitude during entry could make recovery difficult.

END OF TASK

SPIN AWARENESS

VIII.D. TASK: SPIN AWARENESS

> REFERENCES: FAA-H-8083-3, AC 61-67; Pilot's Operating Handbook, FAA-Approved Airplane Flight Manual.

Objective. To determine that the applicant exhibits knowledge of the elements related to spin awareness by explaining:

1. Aerodynamic factors related to spins.

3. Procedures for recovery from unintentional spins.

2. Flight situations where unintentional spins may occur.

A. General Information

    1. The objective of this task is for you to demonstrate your knowledge of spin awareness.

        a. You are not required to perform spins either during your training or on your practical test.

B. Task Objectives

    1. Explain the aerodynamic factors related to spins.

        a. A spin is an aggravated stall that results in what is termed autorotation, in which the airplane follows a corkscrew path in a downward direction.

        b. For a spin to occur, two conditions must exist.

            1) The airplane must be in a stall.
            2) The airplane must be in uncoordinated flight; i.e., the ball is not centered.

        c. If the nose of the airplane is allowed to yaw at the beginning of a stall, the wing will drop in the direction of the yaw.

            1) Unless rudder is applied to keep the nose from yawing, the airplane begins to slip toward the lowered wing.

            2) This slip causes the airplane to weathervane into the relative wind, i.e., toward the lowered wing, thus continuing the yaw.

        d. At the same time, the airplane continues to roll toward the lowered wing.

            1) The lowered wing has an increasingly greater angle of attack, due to the upward motion of the relative wind against its surfaces.

                a) It is then well beyond the critical angle of attack and suffers an extreme loss of lift and an increase in drag.

            2) The rising wing, since the relative wind is striking it at a smaller angle, has a smaller angle of attack than the opposite wing.

                a) The rising wing, in effect, becomes less stalled and thus develops some lift so that the airplane continues to roll.

            3) This autorotation, combined with the effects of centrifugal force and the different amounts of drag on the two wings, becomes a spin, and the airplane descends, rolling and yawing, until recovery is effected.

e.   Remember that, in order to spin, both of the airplane's wings must first be stalled; then one wing becomes less stalled than the other.

f.   A spin may be broken down into three phases.

1)   The incipient phase is the transient period between a stall and a fully developed spin, when a final balancing of aerodynamic and inertial forces has not yet occurred.

2)   The steady-state phase is that portion of the spin in which it is fully developed and the aerodynamic forces are in balance.

3)   The recovery phase begins when controls are applied to stop the spin and ends when level flight is attained.

g.   Use of the rudder is important during a stall. The correct amount of rudder must be applied to keep the nose from yawing. By maintaining directional control and not allowing the nose to yaw, the wing will not drop any more before the stall is broken. Thus, a spin will be averted.

2.   Explain the flight situations in which unintentional spins may occur.

a.   The primary cause of an inadvertent spin is stalling the airplane while executing a turn with excessive or insufficient rudder.

b.   The critical phases of flight for stall/spin accidents are

1)   Takeoff and departure
2)   Approach and landing and go-around
3)   Engine failure

c.   Spins can occur when practicing stalls with

1)   Uncoordinated flight control input
2)   Aileron deflection at critical angles of attack

3.   Explain the procedures for recovery from unintentional spins.

a.   Continued practice in stalls will help you to develop a more instinctive and prompt reaction in recognizing an approaching spin.

1)   It is essential to learn to apply immediate corrective action anytime it is apparent that your airplane is near a spin condition.

2)   If an unintentional spin can be prevented, it should be.

a)   Avoiding a spin shows sound pilot judgment and is a positive indication of alertness.

3)   If it is impossible to avoid a spin, you should execute an immediate recovery.

b.   In the absence of specific recovery techniques in your airplane's *POH*, the following technique is suggested for spin recovery:

1)   The first corrective action taken during any power-on spin is to close the throttle completely to eliminate power and minimize loss of altitude.

a)   Power aggravates the spin characteristics and causes an abnormal loss of altitude in the recovery.

2)   To recover from the spin, you should neutralize the ailerons, determine the direction of the turn, and apply full opposite rudder.

a)   Opposite rudder should be maintained until the rotation stops. Then the rudder should be neutralized. Continue to use the rudder for directional control.

b)   If the rudder is not neutralized at the proper time, the ensuing increased airspeed acting upon the fully deflected rudder will cause an excessive and unfavorable yawing effect. This places great strain on the airplane and may cause a secondary spin in the opposite direction.

3)   When the rotation slows, apply brisk, positive, straightforward movement of the elevator control (forward of the neutral position). The control should be held firmly in this position.

a)   The forceful movement of the elevator will decrease the excessive angle of attack and will break the stall.

4)   Once the stall is broken, the spinning will stop. When the rudder is neutralized, gradually apply enough back elevator pressure to return to level flight.

a)   Too much or abrupt back elevator pressure and/or application of rudder and ailerons during the recovery can result in a secondary stall and possibly another spin.

END OF TASK -- END OF CHAPTER

CHAPTER IX
EMERGENCY OPERATIONS

This chapter explains the three tasks (A-C) of Emergency Operations. These tasks include both knowledge and skill. Your examiner is required to test you on all three tasks.

There are several factors that may interfere with your ability to act promptly and properly when faced with an emergency.

1.   Reluctance to accept the emergency situation: Allowing your mind to become paralyzed by the emergency may lead to failure to maintain flying speed, delay in choosing a suitable landing area, and indecision in general.

2.   Desire to save the airplane: If you have been conditioned to expect to find a suitable landing area whenever your instructor simulated a failed engine, you may be apt to ignore good procedures to avoid rough terrain where the airplane may be damaged. There may be times that the airplane will have to be sacrificed so that you and your passengers can walk away.

3.   Undue concern about getting hurt: Fear is a vital part of self-preservation, but it must not lead to panic. You must maintain your composure and apply the proper concepts and procedures.

Emergency operations require that you maintain situational awareness of what is happening. You must develop an organized process for decision making that can be used in all situations. One method is to use **DECIDE**:

D etect a change -- Recognize immediately when indications, whether visual, aural, or intuitive, are different from those expected.

E stimate need to react -- Determine whether these different indications constitute an adverse situation and, if so, what sort of action, if any, will be required to deal with it.

C hoose desired outcome -- Decide how, specifically, you would like the current situation altered.

I dentify actions to control change -- Formulate a definitive plan of action to remedy the situation.

D o something positive -- Even if no ideal plan of action presents itself, something can always be done to improve things at least somewhat.

E valuate the effects -- Have you solved the predicament, or is further action required?

The following are ideas about good judgment and sound operating practice as you prepare to meet emergencies:

1. All pilots hope to be able to act properly and efficiently when the unexpected occurs. As a safe pilot, you should cultivate coolness in an emergency.

2. You must know your airplane well enough to interpret the indications correctly before you take the corrective action. This requires regular study of your airplane's *POH*.

3. While difficult, you must make a special effort to remain proficient in procedures you will seldom, if ever, have to use.

4. Do not be reluctant to accept the fact that you have an emergency. Take appropriate action immediately without overreacting. Explain your problem to ATC so they can help you plan alternatives and be in a position to grant you priority.

5. You should assume that an emergency will occur every time you take off, i.e., expect the unexpected. If it does not happen, you have a pleasant surprise. If it does, you will be in the correct mind-set to recognize the problem and handle it in a safe and efficient manner.

6. Avoid putting yourself into a situation where you have no alternatives. Be continuously alert for suitable emergency landing spots.

EMERGENCY APPROACH AND LANDING (SIMULATED)

IX.A. TASK: EMERGENCY APPROACH AND LANDING (SIMULATED)

   REFERENCES: FAA-H-8083-3; Pilot's Operating Handbook, FAA-Approved Airplane Flight Manual.

Objective. To determine that the applicant:

1. Exhibits knowledge of the elements related to emergency approach and landing procedures.

2. Analyzes the situation and selects an appropriate course of action.

3. Establishes and maintains the recommended best glide airspeed, ±10 kt.

4. Selects a suitable landing area.

5. Plans and follows a flight pattern to the selected landing area considering altitude, wind, terrain, and obstructions.

6. Prepares for landing, or go-around, as specified by the examiner.

7. Follows the appropriate checklist.

A. General Information

 1. The objective of this task is for you to demonstrate your ability to perform an emergency approach and landing.

 2. You will need to know and understand the procedures discussed in Section 3, Emergency Procedures, of your airplane's *POH*.

B. Task Objectives

 1. Exhibit your knowledge of the elements related to emergency approach and landing procedures.

  a. Emergency approaches and landings can be the result of a complete engine failure, a partial power loss, or a system and/or equipment malfunction that requires an emergency landing during which you may have engine power.

  b. During actual emergency landings, it is recommended that you maneuver your airplane to conform to a normal traffic pattern as closely as possible.

  c. If engine power is lost during the takeoff roll, pull the throttle to idle, apply the brakes, and slow the airplane to a stop.

   1) If you are just lifting off the runway and you lose your engine power, land the airplane straight ahead.

  d. If an actual engine failure occurs immediately after takeoff and before a safe maneuvering altitude (at least 500 ft. AGL) is attained, you should NOT attempt to turn back to the runway from which the takeoff was made.

   1) Instead, it is generally safer to establish immediately the proper glide attitude, and select a field directly ahead or slightly to either side of the takeoff path.

   2) The decision to continue straight ahead is often a difficult one to make unless you consider the problems involved in turning back.

    a) First, the takeoff was in all probability made into the wind. To get back to the runway, a downwind turn must be made which will increase your groundspeed and rush you even more in the performance of emergency procedures and in planning the approach.

        b)   Next, your airplane will lose considerable altitude during the turn and might still be in a bank when the ground is contacted, thus resulting in the airplane cartwheeling.

        c)   Last, but not least, after you turn downwind, the apparent increase in groundspeed could mislead you into attempting to slow down your airplane prematurely, thus causing it to stall.

    3)   Continuing straight ahead or making only a slight turn allows you more time to establish a safe landing attitude, and the landing can be made as slowly as possible.

        a)   Importantly, the airplane can be landed while under control.

  e.   The main objective when an emergency landing is imminent is to complete a safe landing in the largest and best field available.

    1)   Completing a safe landing involves getting the airplane on the ground in as near a normal landing attitude as possible without hitting obstructions.

    2)   Your airplane may suffer damage, but as long as you keep the airplane under control, you and your passengers should survive.

2.   Analyze the situation and select an appropriate course of action.

  a.   Several factors will affect your actions when you are faced with an engine failure:

    1)   Your altitude above the terrain will determine how much time (if any) can be spent troubleshooting the problem as well as how far you can glide to an emergency landing site.

    2)   The type of terrain and time of day will influence your choice of emergency landing sites (e.g., a road may be the best option in rough terrain or at night, but a road would be a poor choice if open fields were within gliding range).

    3)   The landing surface will influence whether to make a landing with the gear up or down.

3.   Establish and maintain the recommended best glide airspeed, ±10 kt.

  a.   Your examiner can and will normally simulate a complete power loss with the airplane in any configuration and/or altitude. This simulation is accomplished by the reduction of power to idle and the statement by your examiner that you have just experienced an engine failure.

  b.   Your first reaction should be to establish the best-glide attitude immediately and ensure that the landing gear and flaps are retracted.

    1)   Use the best-glide airspeed indicated in your *POH* for the appropriate weight. Best-glide airspeed decreases with a decrease in weight.

        a)   In your airplane, best-glide airspeed is _____ at _____ lb.

    2)   If the airspeed is above the proper glide speed, altitude should be maintained, and the airspeed allowed to dissipate to the best-glide speed.

        a)   When the proper glide speed is attained, the nose of your airplane should be lowered to maintain that speed and the airplane trimmed for the glide.

  c.   A constant gliding speed and pitch attitude should be maintained because variations of gliding speed will disrupt your attempts at accuracy in judging gliding distance and the landing spot.

  d.   In a complex airplane, set the propeller control as indicated in your airplane's *POH*.

    1)   Some manufacturers recommend that the propeller be set to low RPM, while others may state high RPM.

4. **Select a suitable landing area.**

   a. Many pilots select from locations in front or to the left of them when there may be a perfect site just behind or to the right. You may want to perform a 180° turn to the right to look for a suitable field if altitude permits and you do not have a suitable field in sight.

   b. Be aware of wind direction and velocity both for the desired landing direction and for their effect on glide distance.

   c. You should always be aware of suitable fields for an emergency landing. The perfect field would be an established airport or a hard-packed, long, smooth field with no high obstacles on the approach end. You need to select the best field available.

      1) An emergency landing is a soft-field touchdown without power.

      2) Attempt to land into the wind, although other factors may dictate a crosswind or downwind landing.

         a) Insufficient altitude may make it inadvisable or impossible to attempt to maneuver into the wind.

         b) Ground obstacles may make landing into the wind impractical or inadvisable because they shorten the effective length of the available field.

         c) The distance from a suitable field upwind from the present position may make it impossible to reach the field from the altitude at which the engine failure occurs.

         d) The best available field may be on a hill and at such an angle to the wind that a downwind landing uphill would be preferable and safer.

         e) See the top figure on the opposite page.

      3) Choose a smooth, grassy field if possible. If you land in a cultivated field, land parallel to the furrows. See the bottom figure on the opposite page.

   d. Roads should be used only as a last resort. They almost always have power lines crossing them which cannot be seen until you are committed to the road.

      1) Wires often are not seen at all, and the airplane just goes out of control, to the surprise of the pilot.

      2) The presence of wires can be assumed if you see telephone or power poles.

      3) Also, roads must be wide (e.g., four lanes) because of fences, adjacent trees, and road signs.

      4) Use roads only if clear of BOTH traffic and electric/telephone wires.

   e. Your altitude at the time of engine failure will determine

      1) The number of alternative landing sites available
      2) The type of approach pattern
      3) The amount of time available to determine and correct the engine problem

   f. Check for traffic and ask your examiner to check for traffic.

      1) Inform your examiner that you would ask your passengers, especially one sitting in the right front seat, to assist you in looking for other traffic and pointing it out to you.

      2) (S)he may instruct you to simulate that you are the only person in the airplane.

g.   Identify a suitable landing site and point it out to your examiner.

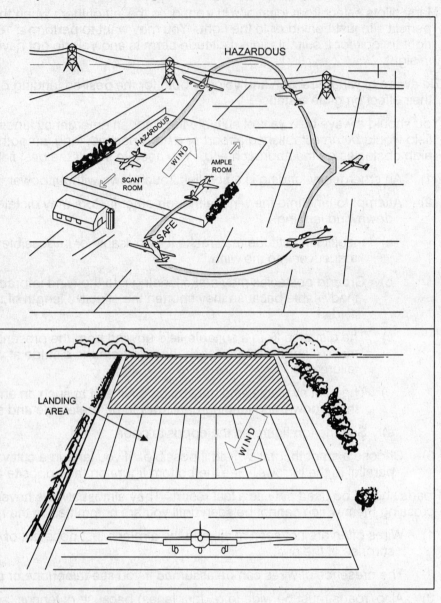

5.   ***Plan and follow a flight pattern to the selected landing area considering altitude, wind, terrain, and obstructions.***

a.   During your selection of a suitable landing area, you should have taken into account your altitude, the wind speed and direction, the terrain, obstructions, and other factors.

1)   Now you must finalize your plan and follow your flight pattern to the landing area.

2)   You are now executing what you planned.

b.   You can utilize any combination of normal gliding maneuvers, from wings level to spirals.

   1)   You should eventually arrive at a normal "key" position at a normal traffic pattern altitude for your selected field, i.e., abeam the touchdown point on downwind.

   a)   If you arrive at the key position significantly higher than pattern altitude, it is recommended that you circle your intended landing point until near pattern altitude.

   i)   Avoid extending your downwind leg too far from your landing site.

   2)   From this point on, your approach should be similar to a soft-field approach, except with no power.

   a)   Plan your turn onto final approach, as shown below.

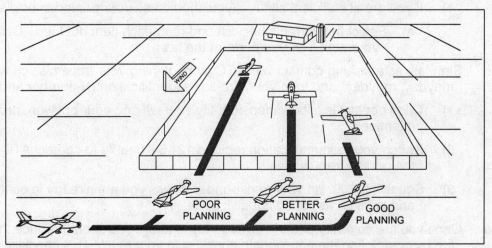

c.   You need to make a decision as to whether to land with the gear up or down (if retractable).

   1)   When the field is smooth and firm, and long enough to bring your airplane to a stop, a gear-down landing is appropriate.

   a)   If the field has stumps, rocks, or other large obstacles, having the gear down will better protect you and your passengers.

   b)   If you suspect the field to be excessively soft, wet, short, or snow-covered, a gear-up landing will normally be safer, to eliminate the possibility of your airplane nosing over as a result of the wheels digging in.

   2)   Allow time for the gear to extend or for you to lower the gear manually.

   3)   Lower the gear and any flaps only after a landing at your selected field is assured.

d.   The altitude is, in many ways, the controlling factor in the successful accomplishment of an emergency approach and landing.

   1)   If you realize you have selected a poor landing area (one that would obviously result in a disaster) AND there is a more advantageous field within gliding distance, a change should be made and explained to your examiner.

   a)   You must understand that this is an exception, and the hazards involved in last-minute decisions (i.e., excessive maneuvering at very low altitudes) must be thoroughly understood.

   2)   Slipping the airplane, using flaps, varying the position of the base leg, and varying the turn onto final approach are ways of correcting for misjudgment of altitude and glide angle.

6.   Prepare for a landing or go-around, as specified by your examiner.

a.   If your selected landing area is an airport, you can probably expect to make a landing on the runway.

b.   For all other fields, you can expect a low approach followed by a go-around.

c.   Ensure that you and your examiner effectively communicate as to how your approach will terminate.

   1)   If you have any doubts, ask your examiner.

7.   Follow the appropriate checklist.

a.   Use the appropriate checklist in your airplane's *POH*.

b.   You should be in the habit of performing from memory the first few critical steps necessary to get the engine operating again.

   1)   If you are at sufficient altitude, you should use your printed checklist.

      a)   Select the correct checklist and read each item out loud. Comment on your action as you perform the task.

c.   Simulate establishing contact with ATC by beginning your transmission with "Mayday, mayday, mayday" and then your airplane's identification (N-number and type).

   1)   Once contact is established, identify yourself and your position, problem, and intentions.

   2)   Switch your communication radio to 121.5 if unable to contact ATC or FSS on the normal frequencies.

   3)   Squawk "7700" on your transponder unless you are already in contact with ATC and have an assigned squawk code.

d.   Once you are committed to the emergency landing, you should reduce the chance of fire by completing the appropriate checklist in your *POH*. This checklist would normally include

   1)   Turn the fuel valve, the fuel pump (if electric), and the ignition switch to "OFF," and move the mixture to the idle cutoff position.

      a)   Turn off the master switch after electrically driven flaps and/or landing gear have been extended.

   2)   Wedge the door open to prevent it from being jammed shut upon impact.

      a)   Protect passengers from head injury with pillows, coats, or other padded items.

e.   For training or demonstrating emergencies, only simulate the procedures discussed in items c. and d. above.

C. Common Errors during an Emergency Approach and Landing (Simulated)

1. **Improper airspeed control.**

   a. Eagerness to get down to the ground is one of the most common errors.

      1) In your rush to get down, you will forget about maintaining your airspeed and arrive at the edge of the landing area with too much speed to permit a safe landing.

   b. Once you establish the best-glide airspeed, you should trim off the control pressures for hands-off flying.

      1) The proper trim will assist you in airspeed control as you perform the various tasks of the checklist(s) and plan your approach.

   c. Monitor your airspeed indicator and pitch attitude.

2. **Poor judgment in the selection of an emergency landing area.**

   a. Always be aware of suitable fields.

   b. Make timely decisions and stay with your decision. Even at higher altitudes this should be done in a timely manner.

3. **Failure to estimate the approximate wind speed and direction.**

   a. Use all available means to determine wind speed and direction.

      1) Smoke, trees, windsocks, and/or wind lines on water are good indicators of surface winds.

      2) Be aware of the crab angle you are maintaining for wind-drift correction.

   b. Failure to know the wind speed and direction will lead to problems during the approach to your selected field.

4. **Failure to fly the most suitable pattern for the existing situation.**

   a. Constantly evaluate your airplane's position relative to the intended spot for landing.

   b. Attempt to fly as much of a normal traffic pattern as possible since that is known to you and the key points will prompt you to make decisions.

   c. Do not rush to the landing spot and do not attempt to extend a glide to get to that spot.

5. **Failure to accomplish the emergency checklist.**

   a. The checklist is important from the standpoint that it takes you through all the needed procedures to regain power.

   b. If power is not restored, the checklist will prepare you and your airplane for the landing.

6. **Undershooting or overshooting selected emergency landing area.**

   a. This error is due to poor planning and failure to evaluate and make the needed corrections constantly during the approach.

   b. Familiarity with your airplane's glide characteristics and the effects of forward slips (if permitted), flaps, and gear (if retractable) is essential.

END OF TASK

SYSTEMS AND EQUIPMENT MALFUNCTIONS

IX.B. TASK: SYSTEMS AND EQUIPMENT MALFUNCTIONS

   REFERENCES: FAA-H-8083-3; Pilot's Operating Handbook, FAA-Approved Airplane Flight Manual.

Objective. To determine that the applicant:

1. Exhibits knowledge of the elements related to systems and equipment malfunctions appropriate to the airplane provided for the practical test.

2. Analyzes the situation and takes appropriate action for simulated emergencies appropriate to the airplane provided for the practical test for at least five (5) of the following:

   a. Partial or complete power loss.
   b. Engine roughness or overheat.
   c. Carburetor or induction icing.
   d. Loss of oil pressure.
   e. Fuel starvation.
   f. Electrical malfunction.

   g. Vacuum/pressure and associated flight instruments malfunction.
   h. Pitot/static.
   i. Landing gear or flap malfunction.
   j. Inoperative trim.
   k. Inadvertent door or window opening.
   l. Structural icing.
   m. Smoke/fire/engine compartment fire.
   n. Any other emergency appropriate to the airplane.

3. Follows the appropriate checklist or procedure.

A.   General Information

   1.   The objective of this task is to determine your knowledge and handling of various systems and equipment malfunctions appropriate to the most complex airplane you are using for your practical test.

B.   Task Objectives

   1.   Exhibit your knowledge of the elements related to system and equipment malfunctions appropriate to the airplane provided for the practical test.

      a.   To best prepare for this element, you must have a good working knowledge of all the systems and equipment in your airplane.

      b.   Since this task will be airplane specific, you will need to know Section 3, Emergency Procedures, of your airplane's *POH*.

         1)   This section will include both the checklists and the amplified procedures.
         2)   Have these checklists within easy access to you in the cockpit at all times.

2. **Analyze the situation and take appropriate action for at least five of the following:**

    NOTE: The following items are airplane make and model specific. You will need to research each item in your *POH* and, if you are uncertain about any, ask your CFI.

    a. **Partial or complete power loss**
    b. **Engine roughness or overheat**
    c. **Carburetor or induction icing**
    d. **Loss of oil pressure**
    e. **Fuel starvation**
    f. **Electrical malfunction**
    g. **Vacuum/pressure system and associated flight instruments malfunction**
    h. **Pitot/static system**
    i. **Landing gear or flap malfunction**
    j. **Inoperative trim**
    k. **Inadvertent door or window opening**
    l. **Structural icing**
    m. **Smoke/fire/engine compartment fire**
    n. **Any other emergency appropriate to the airplane**

3. **Follow the appropriate checklist or procedure.**

    a. Use the appropriate checklists for system and equipment malfunctions, which are in Section 3, Emergency Procedures, of your *POH*.

    b. Your emergency checklists must be readily available to you while you are in your airplane.

    c. While you may know the first few steps of the emergency checklists for some of the system and equipment malfunctions, you must use the appropriate checklist to ensure that you have followed the manufacturer's recommended procedures to correct the situation.

C. Common Errors during System and Equipment Malfunctions

1. **Failure to understand the systems and equipment in your airplane.**

    a. You must know how the various systems and equipment operate in your airplane.

        1) Then you will be able to analyze the malfunction correctly and take the appropriate steps to correct the situation.

        2) You will also understand the effect(s) the malfunction will have on the operation of your airplane.

2. **Failure to accomplish the emergency checklist or procedure.**

    a. Have your checklists readily available to you in the cockpit.

    b. Follow the checklist or procedure in order to take the appropriate steps to correct the malfunction and/or emergency.

END OF TASK

EMERGENCY EQUIPMENT AND SURVIVAL GEAR

IX.C. TASK: EMERGENCY EQUIPMENT AND SURVIVAL GEAR

　　　　REFERENCES: FAA-H-8083-3; Pilot's Operating Handbook, FAA-Approved Airplane Flight Manual.

Objective. To determine that the applicant:

1.　Exhibits knowledge of the elements related to
　　　emergency equipment and survival gear
　　　appropriate to the airplane and environment
　　　encountered during flight. Identifies appropriate
　　　equipment that should be aboard the airplane.

A.　General Information

　　1.　The objective of this task is to determine your knowledge of the emergency equipment and
　　　　survival gear appropriate to your airplane used for this practical test.

B.　Task Objectives

　　**1.　Exhibit your knowledge of the elements related to emergency equipment and survival
　　　　gear appropriate to the airplane and environment encountered during flight. Identify
　　　　appropriate equipment that should be aboard the airplane.**

　　　　a.　Emergency equipment

　　　　　　1)　Location in the airplane

　　　　　　　　a)　Most general aviation airplanes are equipped with an emergency locator
　　　　　　　　　　transmitter (ELT).

　　　　　　　　　　i)　Normally, the ELT is located in the aft fuselage section.

　　　　　　　　b)　Some airplanes are equipped with a fire extinguisher.

　　　　　　　　　　i)　The fire extinguisher is located near the pilot's seat to provide easy
　　　　　　　　　　　　access.

　　　　　　2)　Method of operation or use

　　　　　　　　a)　ELTs are normally automatically activated upon an impact of sufficient
　　　　　　　　　　force (approximately 5 Gs).

　　　　　　　　　　i)　There may be a switch in the cockpit with which you can manually
　　　　　　　　　　　　activate the ELT.

　　　　　　　　　　　　•　If not, you can access the ELT and manually activate it.
　　　　　　　　　　　　•　Ask your CFI to show you how to do this.

　　　　　　　　　　ii)　If you must make an emergency landing, you will want to use the
　　　　　　　　　　　　manual switch to activate the ELT since your landing may not
　　　　　　　　　　　　cause the ELT to activate automatically.

　　　　　　　　b)　Follow the instructions for operation and use of the fire extinguisher and
　　　　　　　　　　any other emergency equipment.

　　　　　　3)　Servicing requirements

　　　　　　　　a)　The batteries used in the ELT must be replaced (or recharged, if the
　　　　　　　　　　batteries are rechargeable) when the ELT has been in use for more than
　　　　　　　　　　1 cumulative hour or when 50% of their useful life (as established by the
　　　　　　　　　　manufacturer) has expired (FAR 91.207).

           i)   The new expiration date for replacing (or recharging) the battery must be marked on the outside of the transmitter and entered in the airplane's maintenance record.

           ii)   The ELT must be inspected annually and that date must be entered in the airplane's maintenance record.

    b)   A fire extinguisher will normally have a gauge by the handle to indicate if it is properly charged and a card attached to tell when the next inspection is required.

           i)   These should be checked during your visual inspection.

           ii)   Most fire extinguishers should be checked and serviced by an authorized person.

4) Method of safe storage

    a)   Ensure that the ELT and the fire extinguisher are stored and appropriately secured in the airplane.

b. Survival gear

1) Survival gear appropriate for operation in various climatological and topographical environments

    a)   Survival kits should have appropriate equipment and gear for the climate and the terrain over which your flight will be conducted.

    b)   Different items are needed for cold vs. hot weather and mountainous vs. flat terrain.

           i)   Survival manuals that are published commercially and by the government suggest items to be included.

    c)   While no FAR requires any type of survival gear for over-water operations under Part 91 (other than large and turbine-powered multiengine airplanes), it is a good operating practice to provide life preservers and a life raft(s) to accommodate everyone on the airplane.

    d)   It is best to be prepared for an emergency.

2) Location in the airplane

    a)   Survival gear should be located in an easily accessible location in the cabin, such as the baggage compartment.

3) Method of operation

    a)   Follow the instructions provided with your survival gear.

4) Servicing requirements

    a)   Periodically remove the items in your survival kit and check them for serviceability.

5) Method of safe storage

    a)   While in the airplane, your survival gear should be easily accessible and secured by tie-down or safety belts.

           i)   When you are not flying, your survival gear should be stored in a cool, dry place.

END OF TASK -- END OF CHAPTER

267

CHAPTER X
HIGH-ALTITUDE OPERATIONS

X.A. Supplemental Oxygen 268
X.B. Pressurization 270

This chapter explains the two tasks (A-B) of High-Altitude Operations. These tasks include both knowledge and skill. Your examiner is required to test you on Task A, Supplemental Oxygen. Task B, Pressurization, will be tested only if your airplane used on your practical test is pressurized.

FAR 61.31, Type Rating Requirements, Additional Training, and Authorization Requirements, states that no person may act as pilot in command of a pressurized airplane that has a service ceiling or maximum operating altitude, whichever is lower, above 25,000 ft. MSL, unless that person

1. Has completed the ground and flight training specified in FAR 61.31(g)(1) and (2)

2. Has a logbook endorsement from an authorized instructor certifying that the person is proficient in the operation of pressurized aircraft

For the purposes of FAR 61.31(g), flight operations conducted above 25,000 ft. MSL are considered to be high altitude. However, the high-altitude environment itself begins below 25,000 ft. MSL. For example, flight levels (FL) are used at and above 18,000 ft. to indicate levels of constant atmospheric pressure in relation to a reference datum of 29.92 in. Hg.

SUPPLEMENTAL OXYGEN

X.A. TASK: SUPPLEMENTAL OXYGEN

REFERENCES: 14 CFR Part 91; FAA-H-8083-3, AC 61-107; Pilot's Operating Handbook, FAA-Approved Flight Manual; AIM.

Objective.   To determine that the applicant exhibits knowledge of the elements related to supplemental oxygen by explaining:

1.   Supplemental oxygen requirements for flight crew and passengers when operating non-pressurized airplanes.

3.   Operational characteristics of continuous flow, demand, and pressure-demand oxygen systems.

2.   Identification and differences between "aviators' breathing oxygen" and other types.

A.   General Information

1.   The objective of this task is to determine your knowledge of the requirements and use of supplemental oxygen.

2.   The primary physiological reason to use supplemental oxygen is to prevent hypoxia.

a.   For optimal protection, you are encouraged to use supplemental oxygen above 10,000 ft. MSL during the day, and above 5,000 ft. MSL at night.

3.   You must use supplemental oxygen when required by the FARs.

B.   Task Objectives

1.   Explain the supplemental oxygen requirements for flight crew and passengers when operating nonpressurized airplanes.

a.   You may not operate a civil U.S.-registered airplane

1)   At cabin pressure altitudes above 12,500 ft. MSL up to and including 14,000 ft. MSL unless the required minimum flight crew uses supplemental oxygen for that part of the flight at those altitudes that is longer than 30 min.

2)   At cabin pressure altitudes above 14,000 ft. MSL unless the required minimum flight crew uses supplemental oxygen during the entire time at those altitudes

3)   At cabin pressure altitudes above 15,000 ft. MSL unless each occupant is provided with supplemental oxygen

b.   Supplemental oxygen use is more stringent under FAR Parts 121 and 135.

2.   Explain the identification and differences between "aviators' breathing oxygen" and other types.

a.   "Aviators' breathing oxygen" is specified at 99.5% pure oxygen and not more than .005 mg of water per liter.

1)   Oxygen bottles containing "aviators' breathing oxygen" should be clearly labeled.

b.   Medical oxygen contains too much water, which can collect in various parts of the supplemental oxygen system and freeze.

1)   Freezing may reduce, or stop, the flow of oxygen.

c.   Industrial oxygen is not intended for breathing.

3. **Explain the operational characteristics of continuous flow, demand, and pressure-demand oxygen systems.**

    a. The continuous flow oxygen system is the most common system found in general aviation airplanes. There are currently two types.

        1) The mask system is designed so the oxygen can be diluted with ambient air by allowing the user to exhale around the face piece, and comes with a rebreather bag which allows the individual to reuse part of the exhaled oxygen.

            a) Although certificated up to 41,000 ft., careful attention to system capabilities is required when using this type of system above 25,000 ft.

        2) A cannula has hollow flexible tubes positioned just under the user's nose. The tube has oxygen outlets under the nose and provides a very comfortable oxygen delivery method that does not interfere with headsets, microphones, drinking, or eating, and is certified for use up to 18,000 feet.

    b. The diluter-demand system increases efficiency compared to the continuous flow system by conserving oxygen at lower altitudes and increasing the oxygen flow at higher altitudes.

        1) This system is needed above 25,000 ft. and can be used safely up to 40,000 ft.

        2) This system allows the pilot to select either normal (cabin air and oxygen mixed) or 100% oxygen.

            a) 100% oxygen is normally automatically provided at approximately 30,000 ft.

    c. The pressure-demand system is normally installed in high-performance turboprop and jet airplanes.

        1) This system is needed for operations above 40,000 ft., and it delivers pressurized oxygen to your lungs.

        2) This differs from the two other systems because oxygen is delivered under positive pressure.

            a) You must exhale against the pressure of the incoming oxygen.

END OF TASK

PRESSURIZATION

> **X.B. TASK: PRESSURIZATION**
>
>   REFERENCES: FAA-H-8083-3, AC 61-107; AIM; Pilot's Operating Handbook, FAA-Approved Flight Manual.
>
> **Objective.** To determine that the applicant:
>
> 1. Exhibits knowledge of the elements related to pressurization by explaining --
>
>   **a.** Fundamental concept of cabin pressurization.
>   **b.** Supplemental oxygen requirements when operating airplanes with pressurized cabins.
>   **c.** Physiological hazards associated with high altitude flight and decompression.
>
> NOTE: Element 2 applies only if the airplane provided for the practical test is equipped for pressurized flight operations.
>
> 2. Operates the pressurization system properly, and reacts appropriately to simulated pressurization malfunctions.

A. General Information

   1. The objective of this task is to determine your knowledge of airplane pressurization systems.

       a. This task will be tested only if your airplane used on the practical test is a pressurized airplane.

B. Task Objectives

   1. **Exhibit your knowledge of the elements related to pressurization by explaining the following:**

       a. **Fundamental concept of cabin pressurization**

           1) Cabin pressurization is the compression of air in the airplane's cabin to maintain a cabin altitude lower than the actual flight altitude.

               a) Thus, the need for the full-time use of supplemental oxygen above certain altitudes is eliminated.

           2) Pressurization in most light airplanes is sent to the cabin from the turbocharger's compressor or from an engine-driven pneumatic pump.

               a) Since the compression of the air in the turbocharger causes the air to become hot, it is routed through a type of heat exchanger unit before it enters the cabin.

               b) The flow of compressed air into the cabin is regulated by an outflow valve which keeps the pressure constant by releasing excess pressure into the atmosphere.

                   i) This outflow valve also allows the exchange of air from inside to outside of the cabin to eliminate odors and to remove stale air.

3)   Pressurized airplanes have special structural specifications, such as windows of double thickness and doors with special seals and locking devices, to withstand differential pressures.

   a)   **Differential pressure** is the difference between cabin pressure and atmospheric pressure, and is normally expressed in pounds per square inch (psi).

   b)   Maximum differential pressure varies among makes and models of airplanes.

4)   A pressurized airplane has a cabin pressure control system which provides cabin pressure regulation, pressure relief, vacuum relief, and the means for selecting the desired cabin altitude in the isobaric differential pressure range.

   a)   A cabin pressure regulator, an outflow valve, and a safety valve are used to accomplish these functions.

   b)   Also, dumping the cabin pressure is a function of a pressure control system.

5)   The cabin pressure regulator controls cabin pressure to a selected value in the isobaric range and limits cabin pressure to a preset differential value in the differential range.

   a)   When the airplane reaches the altitude at which the maximum differential pressure is reached, a further increase in airplane altitude will result in an increase in the cabin pressure altitude.

   b)   Differential control is used to prevent the maximum differential pressure, for which the fuselage was designed, from being exceeded.

      i)   This differential pressure is determined by the structural strength of the cabin and often by the relationship of the cabin size to the probable areas of rupture, such as window areas and doors.

6)   The cabin air pressure safety valve is a combination pressure relief, vacuum relief, and dump valve.

   a)   The pressure relief valve prevents cabin pressure from exceeding the maximum differential pressure.

   b)   The vacuum relief valve prevents ambient pressure from exceeding cabin pressure by allowing external air to enter the cabin when ambient pressure exceeds cabin pressure.

   c)   The dump valve is actuated by the cockpit control switch.

      i)   When this switch is positioned to "dump" or "ram," a solenoid valve opens, causing the valve to dump the cabin air to the atmosphere.

7) Several instruments are used in conjunction with the pressurization controller.

   a) The cabin differential pressure gauge indicates the difference between inside and outside pressure.

      i) This gauge should be monitored to assure that the cabin does not exceed the maximum allowable differential pressure.

   b) A cabin altimeter is provided as a check on the performance of the system. In some cases, the differential pressure gauge and the cabin altimeter are combined into one instrument.

   c) A third instrument indicates the cabin rate of climb or descent.

   d) A cabin rate-of-climb instrument and a combination cabin altimeter/differential pressure gauge are shown below.

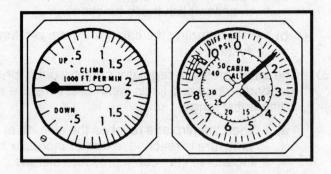

b. **Supplemental oxygen requirements when operating airplanes with pressurized cabins**

   1) Because of the ever-present possibility of decompression in a pressurized airplane, supplemental oxygen is still required.

      a) Pressurized airplanes meeting specific requirements of FAR Part 23 (Airworthiness Standards: Normal, Utility, Acrobatic, and Commuter Category Airplanes) and Part 25 (Airworthiness Standards: Transport Category Airplanes) have cabin altitude warning systems that are activated when cabin pressure altitudes exceed 10,000 ft.

         i) Pressurized airplanes meeting additional, more stringent requirements have automatic passenger oxygen-mask-dispensing devices that activate before cabin pressure altitude exceeds 15,000 ft.

   2) You may not operate a civil U.S.-registered airplane with a pressurized cabin

      a) At flight altitudes above FL 250 unless at least a 10-min. supply of supplemental oxygen is available for each occupant for use in the event that a descent is necessary due to a loss of cabin pressurization

         i) This oxygen supply is in addition to any supplemental oxygen required to satisfy the requirements for nonpressurized airplanes, as discussed in Task X.A., Supplemental Oxygen, on page 268.

   b) Above FL 350 unless one pilot at the controls of the airplane wears and uses an oxygen mask that is secured and sealed

      i) The mask must supply oxygen at all times or must automatically supply oxygen when the cabin pressure exceeds 14,000 ft. MSL.

      ii) An exception to this is for flights at or below FL 410. One pilot does not need to wear and use an oxygen mask if both pilots are at the controls and each has a quick-donning type mask that can be placed on the face with one hand from the ready position and secured, sealed, and operating within 5 sec.

         • If one pilot is away from the controls, the pilot at the controls must wear and use an oxygen mask that is secured and sealed.

   3) Supplemental oxygen use is more stringent under FAR Parts 121 and 135.

c. Physiological hazards associated with high-altitude flight and decompression

   1) The human body functions normally in the atmospheric area extending from sea level to 12,000 ft. MSL. In this range, brain oxygen saturation is at a level that allows for normal functioning. (Optimal functioning is 96% saturation.)

      a) At 12,000 ft., brain oxygen saturation is approximately 87%, which begins to approach a level that could affect performance.

   2) Hypoxia is a lack of sufficient oxygen in the body cells or tissues caused by an inadequate supply of oxygen, inadequate transportation of oxygen, or inability of the body tissues to use oxygen. A description of the four major hypoxia groups follows:

      a) **Hypoxic (altitude) hypoxia.** Altitude hypoxia poses the greatest potential physiological hazard to a pilot while flying in the high-altitude environment. This type of hypoxia is caused by an insufficient partial pressure of oxygen in the inhaled air resulting from reduced oxygen pressure in the atmosphere at altitude.

      b) **Histotoxic hypoxia.** This type of hypoxia is the inability of the body cells to use oxygen because of impaired cellular respiration. Histotoxic hypoxia, caused by alcohol or drug use, cannot be corrected by using supplemental oxygen because the uptake of oxygen is impaired at the tissue level.

         i) The only method of avoiding this type of hypoxia is to abstain, before flight, from alcohol or drugs that are not approved by a flight surgeon or an aviation medical examiner.

      c) **Hypemic (anemic) hypoxia.** This type of hypoxia is defined as a reduction in the oxygen-carrying capacity of the blood. Hypemic hypoxia is caused by a reduction in circulating red blood cells (hemoglobin) or contamination of blood with gases other than oxygen as a result of anemia, carbon monoxide poisoning, or excessive smoking.

d) **Stagnant hypoxia**. This type of hypoxia is an oxygen deficiency in the body resulting from poor circulation of the blood because of a failure of the circulatory system to pump blood (and oxygen) to the tissues.

   i)   In flight, this type of hypoxia can sometimes be caused by positive pressure breathing for long periods of time or by excessive G-forces.

NOTE: For additional information about hypoxia and its symptoms, refer to Task I.J., Aeromedical Factors, beginning on page 80.

3)   Prolonged oxygen use can also be harmful to human health. One hundred percent aviation oxygen can produce toxic symptoms if used for extended periods of time.

   a)   The symptoms can consist of bronchial cough, fever, vomiting, nervousness, irregular heart beat, and lowered energy.

   b)   The sudden supply of pure oxygen following a decompression can often aggravate the symptoms of hypoxia.

   c)   Therefore, oxygen should be taken gradually, particularly when the body is already suffering from lack of oxygen, to build up the supply in small doses.

4)   When nitrogen is inhaled, it dilutes the air we breathe. While most nitrogen is exhaled from the lungs along with carbon dioxide, some nitrogen is absorbed by the body.

   a)   The nitrogen absorbed into the body tissues does not normally present any problem because it is carried in a liquid state.

   b)   If the ambient surrounding atmospheric pressure lowers drastically, this nitrogen could change from a liquid and return to its gaseous state in the form of bubbles.

   c)   These evolving and expanding gases in the body are known as decompression sickness and are divided into two groups.

      i)   Trapped gas. Expanding or contracting gas in certain body cavities during altitude changes can result in abdominal pain, toothache, or pain in ears and sinuses if the person is unable to equalize the pressure changes.

         •   Above 25,000 ft., distention can produce particularly severe gastrointestinal pain.

      ii)   Evolved gas. When the pressure on the body drops sufficiently, nitrogen comes out of solution and forms bubbles which can have adverse effects on some body tissues. Fatty tissue contains more nitrogen than other tissue, thus making overweight people more susceptible to evolved gas decompression sicknesses.

         •   SCUBA diving will compound this problem because of the compressed air used in the breathing tanks.

5) Vision has a tendency to deteriorate with altitude. A reversal of light distribution at high altitudes (bright clouds below the airplane and darker, blue sky above) can cause a glare inside the cockpit.

   a) Glare effects and deteriorated vision are enhanced at night when the body becomes more susceptible to hypoxia.

   b) The empty visual field caused by cloudless, blue skies during the day can cause inaccuracies when judging the speed, size, and distance of other aircraft.

   c) Sunglasses are recommended to minimize the intensity of the sun's ultraviolet rays at high altitudes.

6) **Decompression** is defined as the inability of the airplane's pressurization system to maintain its designed pressure differential. Decompression can be caused by a malfunction in the pressurization system, by malfunction of door or window seals, or by structural damage to the airplane.

   a) During rapid decompression, there may be noise and, for a split second, one may feel dazed. The cabin air will fill with fog, dust, or flying debris. Fog occurs due to the rapid drop in temperature and the change of relative humidity. Normally, the ears clear automatically. Belching or passing of intestinal gas may occur. Air will rush from the mouth and nose due to the escape of air from the lungs.

   b) The primary danger of decompression is hypoxia. Unless proper utilization of oxygen equipment is accomplished quickly, unconsciousness may occur in a very short time. The period of useful consciousness is considerably shortened when a person is subjected to a rapid decompression. Oxygen in the lungs is exhaled rapidly. This, in effect, reduces the partial pressure of oxygen in the lungs and thus reduces the pilot's effective performance time by one-third to one-fourth of his/her normal time.

      i) Exposure to windblast and extremely cold temperatures are other hazards faced with a decompression.

   c) An explosive decompression is a change in cabin pressure faster than the lungs can decompress.

      i) Any decompression which occurs in less than 0.5 sec. is considered explosive and potentially dangerous.

      ii) To avoid potentially dangerous flying debris in the event of an explosive decompression, all loose items such as baggage and oxygen cylinders should be properly secured.

   d) Recovery from all types of decompression is similar. Oxygen masks should be donned, and an emergency descent initiated as soon as possible to avoid the onset of hypoxia.

      i) Although top priority in such a situation is reaching a safe altitude, pilots should be aware that cold-shock in piston engines can result from a high-altitude emergency descent, causing cracked cylinders or other engine damage.

      ii) The time allowed to make a recovery to a safe altitude before loss of useful consciousness is, of course, much less with an explosive than with a gradual decompression.

e)   Types of evolved gas decompression sickness

    i)   The **bends**, also known as caisson disease, is characterized by pain in and around the joints. The term "bends" is used because the resultant pain is eased by bending the joints.

- The pain gradually becomes more severe, can eventually become temporarily incapacitating, and can result in collapse.

    ii)   The **chokes** refers to a decompression sickness that manifests itself through chest pains and burning sensations, a desire to cough, possible cyanosis, a sensation of suffocation, progressively shallower breathing, and, if a descent is not made immediately, collapse and unconsciousness.

    iii)   **Paresthesia** is a third type of decompression sickness, characterized by tingling, itching, a red rash, and cold and warm sensations, probably resulting from bubbles in the central nervous system (CNS).

- CNS disturbances can result in visual deficiencies such as illusionary lines or spots, or a blurred field of vision.

- Some other effects of CNS disturbances are temporary partial paralysis, sensory disorders, slurred speech, and seizures.

f)   Shock can often result from decompression sicknesses as a form of body protest to disrupted circulation.

    i)   Shock can cause nausea, fainting, dizziness, sweating, and/or loss of consciousness.

    ii)   The best treatment for decompression sickness is descent to a lower altitude and landing.

2.   **Operate your airplane's pressurization system properly, and react appropriately to pressurization malfunctions.**

a.   If your airplane is equipped with a pressurization system, you must know the normal and emergency operating procedures.

1)   Follow the procedures explained in your airplane's *POH*.

END OF TASK -- END OF CHAPTER

CHAPTER XI
POSTFLIGHT PROCEDURES

This chapter explains the one task (A) of Postflight Procedures. This task includes both knowledge and skill. Your examiner is required to test you on this task.

AFTER LANDING, PARKING, AND SECURING

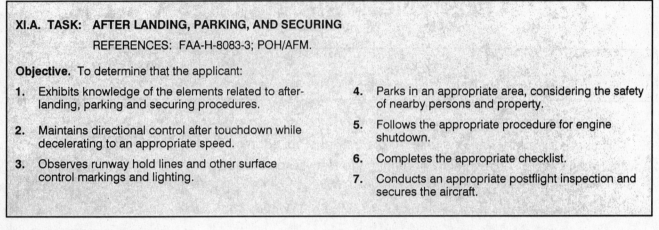

A.   General Information

   1.   The objective of this task is for you to demonstrate your ability to perform after-landing procedures and to park and secure your airplane.

   2.   A flight is never complete until the airplane is parked, the engine shut down, and the airplane secured.

B.   Task Objectives

   1.   **Exhibit your knowledge of the elements related to after-landing, parking, and securing procedures.**

      a.   After you have landed and reached a safe taxi speed, you should exit the runway without delay at the first available taxiway or on a taxiway as instructed by ATC.

         1)   At an airport with an operating control tower, ATC will instruct you to contact ground control for a clearance to taxi.

            a)   You should cross the runway holding position markings before contacting ground control.

            b)   Ask for "progressive taxi" if unfamiliar or unsure of airport procedures.

      b.   Before taxiing, you should normally complete the after-landing checklist for your airplane.

      c.   While operating your airplane on the ramp, you should be constantly aware of what is happening around you. Be careful of people walking to and from vehicles and aircraft.

      d.   Hand signals are used by all ground crews and are similar at all airports; i.e., this is an international language.

         1)   When taxiing on a ramp, a lineman may give you hand signals to tell you where to taxi and/or where to park your airplane.

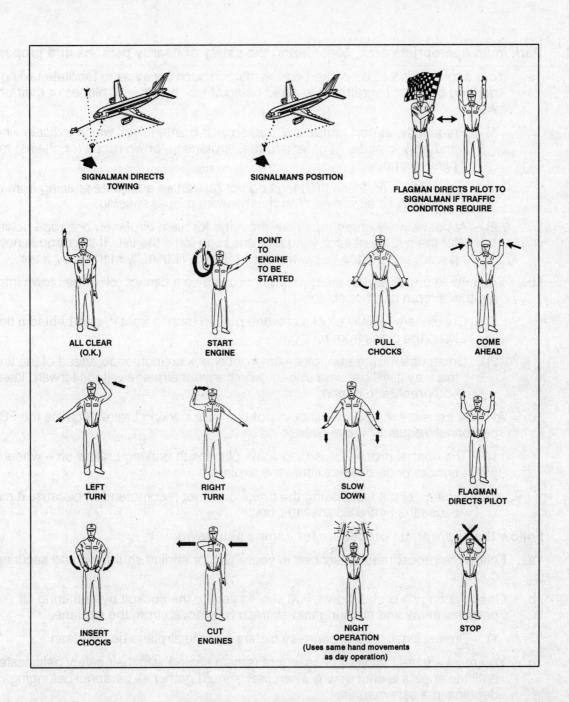

2. **Maintain directional control after touchdown while decelerating to an appropriate speed.**

3. **Observe runway hold lines and other surface control markings and lightings.**

    a. Remember to read back any runway hold short instructions given to you by ATC.

    b. If you are unsure if you are cleared to cross a runway, simply ask.

        1) ASKING FOR HELP IS BETTER THAN HAVING A RUNWAY INCURSION.

4. **Park in an appropriate area, considering the safety of nearby persons and property.**

    a.   Your airplane should be parked on the ramp in such a way as to facilitate taxiing and parking by other aircraft and to avoid being struck by other airplanes or their prop/jet wash.

        1)   Frequently, airport ramps are marked with painted lines which indicate where and how to park. At other airports, airplane tie-down ropes (or chains) mark parking spots.

           a)   However, these markings do not guarantee adequate spacing from other parked airplanes. You must ensure proper spacing.

        2)   Almost always, three ropes are provided for each airplane: one rope positioned for the middle of each wing and one rope to tie the tail. If the ramp is not paved, each of the tie-down ropes (chains) is usually marked by a tire.

    b.   You should chock and/or tie down your airplane so it cannot roll or be blown into another aircraft or other object.

        1)   Chocks are usually blocks of wood placed both in front of and behind a tire to keep the plane from rolling.

        2)   On an unfamiliar ramp, place the front chock an inch or so ahead of the tire. In this way it will become evident whether your airplane will roll forward later as you prepare to depart.

    c.   At most transient ramps, you should **not** use your parking brake because the FBO personnel frequently move aircraft.

        1)   The normal procedure is to lock the plane with parking brakes off -- wheel chocks or tie-downs secure the airplane.

        2)   In many airplanes, leaving the brake on is not recommended because it may cause the hydraulic lines to burst.

5. **Follow the appropriate procedure for engine shutdown.**

    a.   Follow the procedures prescribed in your *POH* for engine shutdown and securing the cockpit.

    b.   Once the engine is shut down, you should secure the cockpit by gathering all personal items and ensuring that all trash is removed from the airplane.

        1)   Professionalism and courtesy dictate that the airplane be left clean.

    c.   You must ensure that your passengers remain seated with their safety belts fastened until the engine is shut down. Then they should gather all personal belongings and deplane in a safe manner.

        1)   You should inform them of the safe exit from the ramp area to the terminal or have them remain next to your airplane while you finish conducting the postflight procedures.

           a)   At that time, you can safely escort them off the ramp area.

6. **Complete the appropriate checklists.**

    a.   Complete the appropriate checklists in your *POH* for parking and securing your airplane.

7. **Conduct an appropriate postflight inspection and secure the aircraft.**

    a. Obviously, hangar storage is the best means of protecting aircraft from the elements, flying debris, vehicles, vandals, etc. Even in hangars, airplanes should be chocked to avoid scrapes and bumps from rolling.

    b. Airplanes stored outside are normally tied down.

        1) Chains or ropes are used to secure the airplane to the ground from three locations on the airplane: usually, the midpoint of each wing and the tail.

        2) Tie-down hooks or eyelets are provided at these locations on most airplanes.

    c. When leaving the airplane tied down for an extended period of time or when expecting windy weather, you should install the control or gust locks which hold the control yoke stationary so the control surfaces cannot bang back and forth in the wind.

        1) On older planes, this is sometimes accomplished by clamping the aileron, elevator, and rudder to adjacent stationary surfaces so they cannot move.

        2) Alternatively, the control yoke (or stick) can be secured tightly with a safety belt.

    d. You should inspect the outside of your airplane for any damage that may have occurred during the flight.

    e. You should also inspect the underside of the fuselage to note any excessive oil being blown out of the engine.

    f. Finally, note any malfunctions (discrepancies) in the proper logbooks, and signal to other pilots when an unairworthy condition exists. Always take the airplane out of service if there is an airworthiness problem.

C. Common Errors After Landing and While Parking and Securing

    1. **Hazards resulting from failure to follow recommended procedures.**

        a. The after-landing checklist is as important as those for any other situation. You must follow recommended procedures to prevent creating unsafe situations.

        b. See Common Errors during Taxiing in Task II.D., Taxiing, on page 105.

    2. **Poor planning, improper technique, or faulty judgment in performance of postflight procedures.**

        a. Just because this is the end of a flight, do not let yourself get rushed or develop bad habits in conducting postflight procedures.

        b. This task must be approached in the same professional manner as the preflight and flying procedures.

END OF TASK - END OF CHAPTER

APPENDIX A
FAA COMMERCIAL PILOT
PRACTICAL TEST STANDARDS REPRINTED
(FAA-S-8081-12A with Change 3)
SINGLE ENGINE LAND ONLY

The purpose of this appendix is to reproduce verbatim what you would get in PTS reprint books that are normally sold for $5.00 at FBOs.

All of these PTSs are reproduced (and explained, discussed, and illustrated!!) elsewhere throughout this book.

INTRODUCTION

General Information

The Flight Standards Service of the Federal Aviation Administration (FAA) has developed this practical test book as the standard that shall be used by FAA inspectors and designated pilot examiners when conducting commercial pilot—airplane practical tests. Flight instructors are expected to use this book when preparing applicants for practical tests. Applicants should be familiar with this book and refer to these standards during their training.

Information considered directive in nature is described in this practical test book in terms, such as "shall" and "must" indicating the actions are mandatory. Guidance information is described in terms, such as "should" and "may" indicating the actions are desirable or permissive, but not mandatory.

The FAA gratefully acknowledges the valuable assistance provided by many individuals and organizations throughout the aviation community who contributed their time and talent in assisting with the revision of these practical test standards.

This practical test standard may be downloaded from the Regulatory Support Division's, AFS-600, web site at http://afs600.faa.gov. Subsequent changes to this standard, in accordance with AC 60-27, Announcement of Availability: Changes to Practical Test Standards, will also be available on AFS-600's web site and then later incorporated into a printed revision.

This publication can be purchased from the Superintendent of Documents, U.S. Government Printing Office, Washington, DC 20402.

Comments regarding this publication should be sent to:

U.S. Department of Transportation
Federal Aviation Administration
Flight Standards Service
Airman Testing Standards Branch, AFS-630
P.O. Box 25082
Oklahoma City, OK 73125

Practical Test Standard Concept

Title 14 of the Code of Federal Regulations (14 CFR) part 61 specifies the AREAS OF OPERATION in which knowledge and skill must be demonstrated by the applicant before the issuance of a commercial pilot certificate or rating. The CFRs provide the flexibility to permit the FAA to publish practical test standards containing the AREAS OF OPERATION and specific TASKs in which pilot competency shall be demonstrated. The FAA shall revise this book whenever it is determined that changes are needed in the interest of safety. *Adherence to the provisions of the regulations and the practical test standards is mandatory for the evaluation of commercial pilot applicants.*

Practical Test Book Description

This test book contains the following Commercial Pilot—Airplane Practical Test Standards:

Section 1 Airplane—Single-Engine Land and Sea
Section 2 Airplane—Multiengine Land and Sea

The Commercial Pilot Practical Test Standards—Airplane includes the AREAS OF OPERATION and TASKs for the issuance of an initial commercial pilot certificate and for the addition of category ratings and/or class ratings to that certificate.

Practical Test Standards Description

AREAS OF OPERATION are phases of the practical test arranged in a logical sequence within each standard. They begin with Preflight Preparation and end with Postflight Procedures. The examiner, however, may conduct the practical test in any sequence that will result in a complete and efficient test; *however, the ground portion of the practical test shall be accomplished before the flight portion.*

TASKs are titles of knowledge areas, flight procedures, or maneuvers appropriate to an AREA OF OPERATION. The abbreviation(s) within parentheses immediately following a TASK refer to the category and/or class aircraft appropriate to that TASK. The meaning of each abbreviation is as follows.

ASEL Airplane—Single-Engine Land
AMEL Airplane—Multiengine Land
ASES Airplane—Single-Engine Sea
AMES Airplane—Multiengine Sea

NOTE: When administering a test based on sections 1 and 2 of this PTS, the TASKs appropriate to the class airplane (ASEL, ASES, AMEL, or AMES) used for the test shall be included in the plan of action. The absence of a class indicates the TASK is for all classes. NOTE is used to emphasize special considerations required in the AREA OF OPERATION or TASK.

REFERENCE identifies the publication(s) that describe(s) the TASK. Descriptions of TASKs are not included in these standards because this information can be found in the current issue of the listed reference. Publications other than those listed may be used for references if their content conveys substantially the same meaning as the referenced publications.

These practical test standards are based on the following references.

14 CFR part 43	Maintenance, Preventive Maintenance, Rebuilding, and Alteration
14 CFR part 61	Certification: Pilots, Flight Instructors, and Ground Instructors
14 CFR part 91	General Operating and Flight Rules
AC 00-6	Aviation Weather
AC 00-45	Aviation Weather Services
AC 61-23/ FAA-H-8083-25	Pilot's Handbook of Aeronautical Knowledge
AC 61-65	Certification: Pilots and Flight Instructors
AC 61-67	Stall and Spin Awareness Training.
AC 61-84	Role of Preflight Preparation
AC 90-48	Pilots' Role in Collision Avoidance
AC 90-66	Recommended Standard Traffic Patterns and Practices for Aeronautical Operations At Airports Without Operating Control Towers.
AC 91-69	Seaplane Safety for FAR Part 91 Operations
AC 120-51	Crew Resource Management Training
FAA-H-8083-1	Aircraft Weight and Balance Handbook
FAA-H-8083-3	Airplane Flying Handbook
FAA-H-8083-15	Instrument Flying Handbook
AIM	Aeronautical Information Manual
AFD	Airport Facility Directory
NOTAMs	Notices to Airmen
Other	Pilot Operating Handbook FAA-Approved Flight Manual Navigation Charts Seaplane Supplement

The Objective lists the elements that must be satisfactorily performed to demonstrate competency in a TASK. The Objective includes:

1. Specifically what the applicant should be able to do;
2. Conditions under which the TASK is to be performed; and
3. Acceptable performance standards

Use of the Practical Test Standards Book

The FAA requires that all commercial pilot practical tests be conducted in accordance with the appropriate commercial practical test standards and the policies set forth in the INTRODUCTION. Applicants shall be evaluated in **ALL** TASKs included in each AREA OF OPERATION of the appropriate practical test standard, unless otherwise noted.

An applicant, who holds at least a commercial pilot certificate seeking an additional airplane category rating and/or class rating at the commercial pilot level, shall be evaluated in the AREAS OF OPERATION and TASKs listed in the Additional Rating Task Table. At the discretion of the examiner, an evaluation of the applicant's competence in the remaining AREAS OF OPERATION and TASKs may be conducted.

If the applicant holds two or more category or class ratings at least at the commercial level, and the ratings table indicates differing required TASKs, the "least restrictive" entry applies. For example, if "ALL" and "NONE" are indicated for one AREA OF OPERATION, the "NONE" entry applies. If "B" and "B, C" are indicated, the "B" entry applies.

In preparation for each practical test, the examiner shall develop a written "plan of action." The "plan of action" shall include all TASKs in each AREA OF OPERATION, unless noted otherwise. If the elements in one TASK have already been evaluated in another TASK, they need not be repeated. For example, the "plan of action" need not include evaluating the applicant on complying with markings, signals, and clearances at the end of the flight, if that element was sufficiently observed at the beginning of the flight. *Any TASK selected for evaluation during a practical test shall be evaluated in its entirety.*

The examiner is not required to follow the precise order in which the AREAS OF OPERATION and TASKs appear in this book. The examiner may change the sequence or combine TASKs with similar Objectives to have an orderly and efficient flow of the practical test. For example, Radio Communications and ATC Light Signals may be combined with Traffic Patterns. The examiner's "plan of action" shall include the order and combination of TASKs to be demonstrated by the applicant in a manner that will result in an efficient and valid test.

The examiner is expected to use good judgment in the performance of simulated emergency procedures. The use of the safest means for simulation is expected. Consideration must be given to local conditions, both meteorological and topographical, at the time of the test, as well as the applicant's workload, and the condition of the aircraft used. If the procedure being evaluated would jeopardize safety, it is expected that the applicant will simulate that portion of the maneuver.

Special Emphasis Areas

Examiners shall place special emphasis upon areas of aircraft operations considered critical to flight safety. Among these are:

1. Positive aircraft control;
2. Positive exchange of the flight controls procedure (who is flying the airplane);
3. Stall/spin awareness;
4. Collision avoidance;
5. Wake turbulence avoidance;
6. Land and Hold Short Operations (LAHSO);
7. Runway incursion avoidance;
8. Controlled flight into terrain (CFIT);
9. Aeronautical decision making (ADM);
10. Checklist usage; and
11. Other areas deemed appropriate to any phase of the practical test.

Although these areas may not be specifically addressed under each **TASK, they are essential to flight safety and will be evaluated during the** practical test. In all instances, the applicant's actions will relate to the complete situation.

Commercial Pilot—Airplane Practical Test Prerequisites

An applicant for the Commercial Pilot—Airplane Practical Test is required by 14 CFR part 61 to:

1. Be at least 18 years of age;
2. Be able to read, speak, write, and understand the English language. If there is a doubt, use AC 60-28, English Language Skill Standards;
3. Possess a private pilot certificate with an airplane rating, if a commercial pilot certificate with an airplane rating is sought, or meet the flight experience required for a private pilot certificate (airplane rating) and pass the private airplane knowledge and practical test;
4. Possess an instrument rating (airplane) or the following limitation shall be placed on the commercial pilot certificate: "Carrying passengers in airplanes for hire is prohibited at night or on cross-country flights of more than 50 nautical miles;"
5. Have passed the appropriate commercial pilot knowledge test since the beginning of the 24th month before the month in which he or she takes the practical test;
6. Have satisfactorily accomplished the required training and obtained the aeronautical experience prescribed;
7. Possess at least a current third class medical certificate;
8. Have an endorsement from an authorized instructor certifying that the applicant has received and logged training time within 60 days preceding the date of application in preparation for the practical test, and is prepared for the practical test; and
9. Also have an endorsement certifying that the applicant has demonstrated satisfactory knowledge of the subject areas in which the applicant was deficient on the airman knowledge test.

Aircraft and Equipment Required for the Practical Test

The commercial pilot—airplane applicant is required by 14 CFR section 61.45, to provide an airworthy, certificated airplane for use during the practical test. This section further requires that the aircraft must:

1. Be of U.S., foreign or military registry of the same category, class, and type, if applicable, for the certificate and/or rating for which the applicant is applying;
2. Have fully functioning dual controls, except as provided for in 14 CFR section 61.45(c) and (e);
3. Be capable of performing all AREAS OF OPERATION appropriate to the rating sought and have no operating limitations which prohibit its use in any of the AREAS OF OPERATION required for the practical test; and
4. Be a complex airplane furnished by the applicant, unless the applicant currently holds a commercial pilot certificate with a single-engine or multiengine class rating as appropriate, for the performance of takeoffs, landings, and appropriate emergency procedures. A complex landplane is one having retractable landing gear, flaps, and controllable propeller or turbinepowered. A complex seaplane is one having flaps and controllable propeller.

Use of FAA-Approved Flight Simulator or Flight Training Device

An airman applicant for commercial pilot—airplane certification may be authorized to use an FAA-qualified and approved flight simulator or flight training device, to complete certain flight TASK requirements listed in this practical test standard.

An airman applicant seeking an added rating to a commercial certificate may also use a qualified and approved flight simulator or flight training device to complete the flight task requirements in accordance with Appendix 1 and 2 of these practical test standards. These appendices should be consulted to identify which flight TASKs may be accomplished in an approved flight simulator or flight training device. The level of flight simulator or flight training device required for each maneuver or procedure will also be found in the appropriate appendix. An appropriate class airplane is required to complete the remaining flight TASKs for certification.

When flight TASKs are accomplished in an aircraft, certain TASK elements may be accomplished through "simulated" actions in the interest of safety and practicality, but when accomplished in a flight simulator or flight training device, these same actions would not be "simulated." For example, when in an aircraft, a simulated engine fire may be addressed by retarding the throttle to idle, simulating the shutdown of the engine, simulating the discharge of the fire suppression agent, if applicable, simulating the disconnect of associated electrical, hydraulic, and pneumatics systems, etc. However, when the same emergency condition is addressed in a flight simulator or flight training device, all TASK elements must be accomplished as would be expected under actual circumstances.

Similarly, safety of flight precautions taken in the aircraft for the accomplishment of a specific maneuver or procedure (such as limiting altitude in an approach to stall or setting maximum airspeed for an engine failure expected to result in a rejected takeoff) need not be taken when a flight simulator or flight training device is used.

It is important to understand that whether accomplished in an aircraft, flight simulator or flight training device, all TASKs and elements for each maneuver or procedure shall have the same performance standards applied equally for determination of overall satisfactory performance.

Flight Instructor Responsibility

An appropriately rated flight instructor is responsible for training the commercial pilot applicant to acceptable standards in **all** subject matter areas, procedures, and maneuvers included in the TASKs within each AREA OF OPERATION in the appropriate commercial pilot practical test standard.

Because of the impact of their teaching activities in developing safe, proficient pilots, flight instructors should exhibit a high level of knowledge, skill, and the ability to impart that knowledge and skill to students.

Throughout the applicant's training, the flight instructor is responsible for emphasizing the performance of effective visual scanning and collision avoidance procedures.

Examiner[1] Responsibility

The examiner conducting the practical test is responsible for determining that the applicant meets the acceptable standards of knowledge and skill of each TASK within the appropriate practical test standard. Since there is no formal division between the "oral" and "skill" portions of the practical test, this becomes an ongoing process throughout the test. Oral questioning, to determine the applicant's knowledge of TASKs and related safety factors, should be used judiciously at all times, especially during the flight portion of the practical test. Examiner' shall test to the greatest extent practicable the applicant's correlative abilities rather than mere rote enumeration of facts throughout the practical test.

If the examiner determines that a TASK is incomplete, or the outcome uncertain, the examiner may require the applicant to repeat that TASK, or portions of that TASK. This provision has been made in the interest of fairness and does not mean that instruction, practice, or the repeating of an unsatisfactory task is permitted during the certification process. When practical, the remaining TASKs of the practical test phase should be completed before repeating the questionable TASK.

Throughout the flight portion of the practical test, the examiner shall evaluate the applicant's use of visual scanning and collision avoidance procedures.

Satisfactory Performance

Satisfactory performance to meet the requirements for certification is based on the applicant's ability to safely:

1. Perform the TASKs specified in the AREAS OF OPERATION for the certificate or rating sought within the approved standards;
2. Demonstrate mastery of the aircraft with the successful outcome of each TASK performed never seriously in doubt;
3. Demonstrate satisfactory proficiency and competency within the approved standards;
4. Demonstrate sound judgment; and
5. Demonstrate single-pilot competence if the aircraft is type certificated for single-pilot operations.

Unsatisfactory Performance

The tolerances represent the performance expected in good flying conditions. If, in the judgment of the examiner, the applicant does not meet the standards of performance of any TASK performed, the associated AREA OF OPERATION is failed and therefore, the practical test is failed.

The examiner or applicant may discontinue the test at any time when the failure of an AREA OF OPERATION makes the applicant ineligible for the certificate or rating sought. *The test may be continued ONLY with the consent of the applicant.* If the test is discontinued, the applicant is entitled credit for only those AREAS OF OPERATION and their associated TASKs satisfactorily performed. However, during the retest, and at the discretion of the examiner, any TASK may be reevaluated, including those previously passed.

---

[1] The word "examiner" is used throughout the standards to denote either the FAA inspector or FAA designated pilot examiner who conducts an official practical test.

Typical areas of unsatisfactory performance and grounds for disqualification are:

1. Any action or lack of action by the applicant that requires corrective intervention by the examiner to maintain safe flight.
2. Failure to use proper and effective visual scanning techniques to clear the area before and while performing maneuvers.
3. Consistently exceeding tolerances stated in the Objectives.
4. Failure to take prompt corrective action when tolerances are exceeded.

When a notice of disapproval is issued, the examiner shall record the applicant's unsatisfactory performance in terms of the AREA OF OPERATION and specific TASK(s) not meeting the standard appropriate to practical test conducted. The AREA(s) OF OPERATION/TASK(s) not tested and the number of practical test failures shall also be recorded. If the applicant fails the practical test because of a special emphasis area, the Notice of Disapproval shall indicate the associated task. i. e.: AREA OF OPERATION VIII, Maneuvering During Slow Flight, failure to use proper collision avoidance procedures.

Crew Resource Management (CRM)

CRM refers to the effective use of all available resources: human resources, hardware, and information. Human resources include all groups routinely working with the cockpit crew or pilot who are involved with decisions that are required to operate a flight safely. These groups include, but are not limited to dispatchers, cabin crewmembers, maintenance personnel, air traffic controllers, and weather services. CRM is not a single TASK, but a set of competencies that must be evident in all TASKs in this practical test standard as applied to either single pilot operations or crew.

Applicant's Use of Checklists

Throughout the practical test, the applicant is evaluated on the use of an appropriate checklist. Proper use is dependent on the specific TASK being evaluated. The situation may be such that the use of the checklist, while accomplishing elements of an Objective, would be either unsafe or impractical, especially in a single-pilot operation. In this case, a review of the checklist after the elements have been accomplished, would be appropriate. Division of attention and proper visual scanning should be considered when using a checklist.

Use of Distractions During Practical Tests

Numerous studies indicate that many accidents have occurred when the pilot has been distracted during critical phases of flight. To evaluate the applicant's ability to utilize proper control technique while dividing attention both inside and/or outside the cockpit, the examiner shall cause realistic distractions during the flight portion of the practical test to evaluate the applicant's ability to divide attention while maintaining safe flight.

Positive Exchange of Flight Controls

During flight training, there must always be a clear understanding between students and flight instructors of who has control of the aircraft. Prior to flight, a briefing should be conducted that includes the procedure for the exchange of flight controls. A positive three-step process in the exchange of flight controls between pilots is a proven procedure and one that is strongly recommended.

When the instructor wishes the student to take control of the aircraft, he or she will say, "You have the flight controls." The student acknowledges immediately by saying, "I have the flight controls." The flight instructor again says, "You have the flight controls." When control is returned to the instructor, follow the same procedure. A visual check is recommended to verify that the exchange has occurred. There should never by any doubt as to who is flying the aircraft.

Metric Conversion Initiative

To assist pilots in understanding and using the metric measurement system, the practical test standards refer to the metric equivalent of various altitudes throughout. The inclusion of meters is intended to familiarize pilots with its use. The metric altimeter is arranged in 10 meter increments; therefore, when converting from feet to meters, the exact conversion, being too exact for practical purposes, is rounded to the nearest 10 meter increment or even altitude as necessary.

SECTION 1

COMMERCIAL PILOT--AIRPLANE SINGLE-ENGINE LAND

CONTENTS

Airplane Single-Engine Land

ADDITIONAL RATING TASK TABLE

CHECKLISTS:

AREAS OF OPERATION:

ADDITIONAL RATING TASK TABLE
Airplane Single-Engine Land

Addition of an Airplane Single-Engine Land Rating to an existing Commercial Pilot Certificate

Required TASKS are indicated by either the TASK letter(s) that apply(s) or an indication that all or none of the TASKS must be tested based on the notes in each AREA OF OPERATION.

Areas of Operation	ASES	AMEL	AMES	RH	RG	Glider	Balloon	Airship
			COMMERCIAL PILOT RATING(S) HELD					
I	F,G	F,G	F,G	F,G	F,G	F,G	F,G	F,G
II	D	NONE	D	A,C,D,F	A,D,F	A,B,C,D,F	A,B,C,D,F	A,B,C,D,F
III	C	NONE	C	B,C	NONE	B,C	B,C	B,C
IV	A,B,C,D,E,F,K	A,B,C,D,E,F,K	A,B,C,D,E,F,K	A,B,C,D,E,F,K,L	A,B,C,D,E,F,K,L	A,B,C,D,E,F,K,L	A,B,C,D,E,F,K,L	A,B,C,D,E,F,K,L
V	NONE	B,C,D	B,C,D	ALL	ALL	ALL	ALL	ALL
VI	NONE	ALL	ALL	ALL	ALL	ALL	ALL	ALL
VII	NONE	NONE	NONE	NONE	NONE	ALL	ALL	NONE
VIII	NONE	NONE	NONE	ALL	ALL	ALL	ALL	ALL
IX	A,B	A,B	A,B	ALL	ALL	ALL	ALL	ALL
X	NONE	NONE	NONE	ALL	ALL	ALL	ALL	ALL
XI	A	NONE	A	A	A	A	A	A

APPLICANT'S PRACTICAL TEST CHECKLIST

APPOINTMENT WITH EXAMINER:

EXAMINER'S NAME _____

LOCATION _____

DATE/TIME _____

ACCEPTABLE AIRCRAFT

- ☐ Aircraft Documents:
  Airworthiness Certificate
  Registration Certificate
  Operating Limitations
- ☐ Aircraft Maintenance Records:
  Logbook Record of Airworthiness Inspections and AD Compliance
- ☐ Pilot's Operating Handbook, FAA-Approved Airplane Flight Manual

PERSONAL EQUIPMENT

- ☐ View-Limiting Device
- ☐ Current Aeronautical Charts
- ☐ Computer and Plotter
- ☐ Flight Plan Form
- ☐ Flight Logs
- ☐ Current AIM, Airport Facility Directory, and Appropriate Publications

PERSONAL RECORDS

- ☐ Identification - Photo/Signature ID
- ☐ Pilot Certificate
- ☐ Current and Appropriate Medical Certificate
- ☐ Completed FAA Form 8710-1, Airman Certificate and/or Rating Application with Instructor's Signature (if applicable)
- ☐ Computer Test Report
- ☐ Pilot Logbook with appropriate Instructor Endorsements
- ☐ FAA Form 8060-5, Notice of Disapproval (if applicable)
- ☐ Approved School Graduation Certificate (if applicable)
- ☐ Examiner's Fee (if applicable)

EXAMINER'S PRACTICAL TEST CHECKLIST

Airplane Single-Engine Land

APPLICANT'S NAME _____

LOCATION _____

DATE/TIME _____

I. PREFLIGHT PREPARATION

- ☐ A. CERTIFICATES AND DOCUMENTS
- ☐ B. AIRWORTHINESS REQUIREMENTS
- ☐ C. WEATHER INFORMATION
- ☐ D. CROSS-COUNTRY FLIGHT PLANNING
- ☐ E. NATIONAL AIRSPACE SYSTEM
- ☐ F. PERFORMANCE AND LIMITATIONS
- ☐ G. OPERATION OF SYSTEMS
- ☐ H. AEROMEDICAL FACTORS

II. PREFLIGHT PROCEDURES

- ☐ A. PREFLIGHT INSPECTION
- ☐ B. COCKPIT MANAGEMENT
- ☐ C. ENGINE STARTING
- ☐ D. TAXIING
- ☐ E. BEFORE TAKEOFF CHECK

III. AIRPORT OPERATIONS

- ☐ A. RADIO COMMUNICATIONS AND ATC LIGHT SIGNALS
- ☐ B. TRAFFIC PATTERNS
- ☐ C. AIRPORT, RUNWAY, AND TAXIWAY SIGNS, MARKINGS, AND LIGHTING

IV. TAKEOFFS, LANDINGS, AND GO-AROUNDS

- ☐ A. NORMAL AND CROSSWIND TAKEOFF AND CLIMB
- ☐ B. NORMAL AND CROSSWIND APPROACH AND LANDING
- ☐ C. SOFT-FIELD TAKEOFF AND CLIMB
- ☐ D. SOFT-FIELD APPROACH AND LANDING
- ☐ E. SHORT-FIELD TAKEOFF AND MAXIMUM PERFORMANCE CLIMB
- ☐ F. SHORT-FIELD APPROACH AND LANDING
- ☐ G. POWER-OFF 180° ACCURACY AND LANDING
- ☐ H. GO-AROUND/REJECTED LANDING

V. PERFORMANCE MANEUVERS

- ☐ A. STEEP TURNS
- ☐ B. STEEP SPIRAL
- ☐ C. CHANDELLES
- ☐ D. LAZY EIGHTS

VI. GROUND REFERENCE MANEUVER

- ☐ EIGHTS ON PYLONS

VII. NAVIGATION

- ☐ A. PILOTAGE AND DEAD RECKONING
- ☐ B. NAVIGATION SYSTEMS AND ATC RADAR SERVICES
- ☐ C. DIVERSION
- ☐ D. LOST PROCEDURE

VIII. SLOW FLIGHT AND STALLS

- ☐ A. MANEUVERING DURING SLOW FLIGHT
- ☐ B. POWER-OFF STALLS
- ☐ C. POWER-ON STALLS
- ☐ D. SPIN AWARENESS

IX. EMERGENCY OPERATIONS

- ☐ A. EMERGENCY APPROACH AND LANDING (SIMULATED)
- ☐ B. SYSTEMS AND EQUIPMENT MALFUNCTIONS
- ☐ C. EMERGENCY EQUIPMENT AND SURVIVAL GEAR

X. HIGH ALTITUDE OPERATIONS

- ☐ A. SUPPLEMENTAL OXYGEN
- ☐ B. PRESSURIZATION

XI. POSTFLIGHT PROCEDURES

- ☐ A. AFTER LANDING, PARKING, AND SECURING

I.   AREA OF OPERATION: PREFLIGHT PREPARATION

NOTE: The examiner shall develop a scenario based on real time weather to evaluate TASKs C and D.

A. TASK: CERTIFICATES AND DOCUMENTS

REFERENCES: 14 CFR parts 43, 61, 91; FAA-H-8083-3; AC 61-23/FAA-H-8083-25; POH/AFM.

Objective. To determine that the applicant exhibits knowledge of the elements related to certificates and documents by:

1.   Explaining—

   a.   commercial pilot certificate privileges limitations and recent flight experience requirements.
   b.   medical certificate class and duration.
   c.   pilot logbook or flight records.

2.   Locating and explaining—

   a.   airworthiness and registration certificates.
   b.   operating limitations, placards, instrument markings, and POH/AFM.
   c.   weight and balance data and equipment list.

B. TASK: AIRWORTHINESS REQUIREMENTS

REFERENCES: 14 CFR part 91; AC 61-23/FAA-H-8083-25.

Objective. To determine that the applicant exhibits knowledge of the elements related to airworthiness requirements by:

1.   Explaining–

   a.   required instruments and equipment for day/night VFR.
   b.   procedures and limitations for determining airworthiness of the airplane with inoperative instruments and equipment with and without an MEL.
   c.   requirements and procedures for obtaining a special flight permit.

2.   Locating and explaining—

   a.   airworthiness directives.
   b.   compliance records.
   c.   maintenance/inspection requirements.
   d.   appropriate record keeping.

C. TASK: WEATHER INFORMATION

REFERENCES: 14 CFR part 91; AC 00-6, AC 00-45, AC 61-23/FAA-H-8083-25, AC 61-84; AIM.

Objective. To determine that the applicant:

1.   Exhibits knowledge of the elements related to weather information by analyzing weather reports, charts, and forecasts from various sources with emphasis on—

   a.   METAR, TAF, and FA.
   b.   surface analysis chart.
   c.   radar summary chart.
   d.   winds and temperature aloft chart.
   e.   significant weather prognostic charts.
   f.   convective outlook chart.
   g.   AWOS, ASOS, and ATIS reports.

2.   Makes a competent "go/no-go" decision based on available weather information.

D. TASK: CROSS-COUNTRY FLIGHT PLANNING

REFERENCES: 14 CFR part 91; AC 61-23/FAA-H-8083-25, AC 61-84; Navigation Charts; A/FD; AIM.

Objective. To determine that the applicant:

1.   Exhibits knowledge of the elements related to cross-country flight planning by presenting and explaining a pre-planned VFR crosscountry flight, as previously assigned by the examiner. On the day of the practical test, the final flight plan shall be to the first fuel stop, based on maximum allowable passengers, baggage, and/or cargo loads using real time weather.
2.   Uses appropriate and current aeronautical charts.
3.   Properly identifies airspace, obstructions, and terrain features.
4.   Selects easily identifiable en route checkpoints.
5.   Selects most favorable altitudes considering weather conditions and equipment capabilities.
6.   Computes headings, flight time, and fuel requirements.
7.   Selects appropriate navigation system/facilities and communication frequencies.
8.   Applies pertinent information from NOTAMs, A/FD, and other flight publications.
9.   Completes a navigation log and simulates filing a VFR flight plan.

E. TASK: NATIONAL AIRSPACE SYSTEM

REFERENCES: 14 CFR part 71, 91; Navigation Charts; AIM.

Objective. To determine that the applicant exhibits knowledge of the elements related to the National Airspace System by explaining:

1.   Basic VFR weather minimums—for all classes of airspace.
2.   Airspace classes—their operating rules, pilot certification, and airplane equipment requirements for the following—

   a. Class A.
   b. Class B.
   c. Class C.
   d. Class D.
   e. Class E.
   f. Class G.

3.   Special use and other airspace areas.

F. TASK: PERFORMANCE AND LIMITATIONS

REFERENCES: AC 61-23/FAA-H-8083-25; FAA-H-8083-1; AC 61-84, POH/AFM.

Objective. To determine that the applicant:

1.   Exhibits knowledge of the elements related to performance and limitations by explaining the use of charts, tables, and data to determine performance and the adverse effects of exceeding limitations.
2.   Computes weight and balance. Determines if the computed weight and center of gravity is within the airplane's operating limitations and if the weight and center of gravity will remain within limits during all phases of flight.
3.   Demonstrates use of the appropriate performance charts, tables, and data.
4.   Describes the effects of atmospheric conditions on the airplane's performance.

G. TASK: OPERATION OF SYSTEMS

REFERENCES: AC 61-23/FAA-H-8083-25; POH/AFM.

Objective. To determine that the applicant exhibits knowledge of the elements related to the operation of systems on the airplane provided for the practical test, by explaining at least five (5) of the following systems.

1. Primary flight controls and trim.
2. Flaps, leading edge devices, and spoilers.
3. Water rudders (ASES).
4. Powerplant and propeller.
5. Landing gear.
6. Fuel, oil, and hydraulic.
7. Electrical.
8. Avionics.
9. Pitot-static, vacuum/pressure and associated flight instruments.
10. Environmental.
11. Deicing and anti-icing.

H. TASK: AEROMEDICAL FACTORS

REFERENCES: AC 61-23/FAA-H-8083-25; AIM.

Objective. To determine that the applicant exhibits knowledge of the elements related to aeromedical factors by explaining:

1. The symptoms, causes, effects, and corrective actions of at least four (4) of the following—

   a. hypoxia.
   b. hyperventilation.
   c. middle ear and sinus problems.
   d. spatial disorientation.
   e. motion sickness.
   f. carbon monoxide poisoning.
   g. stress and fatigue.
   h. dehydration.

2. The effects of alcohol, drugs, and over-the-counter medications.
3. The effects of excess nitrogen during scuba dives upon a pilot or passenger in flight.

II. AREA OF OPERATION: PREFLIGHT PROCEDURES

A. TASK: PREFLIGHT INSPECTION

REFERENCES: FAA-H-8083-3; POH/AFM.

Objective. To determine that the applicant:

1. Exhibits knowledge of the elements related to preflight inspection. This shall include which items must be inspected, the reasons for checking each item, and how to detect possible defects.
2. Inspects the airplane with reference to an appropriate checklist.
3. Verifies that the airplane is in condition for safe flight.

B. TASK: COCKPIT MANAGEMENT

REFERENCES: FAA-H-8083-3; POH/AFM.

Objective. To determine that the applicant:

1. Exhibits knowledge of the elements related to cockpit management procedures.
2. Ensures all loose items in the cockpit and cabin are secured.
3. Organizes material and equipment in an efficient manner so they are readily available.
4. Briefs occupants on the use of safety belts, shoulder harnesses, doors, and emergency procedures.

C. TASK: ENGINE STARTING

REFERENCES: FAA-H-8083-3, AC 61-23/FAA-H-8083-25, AC 91-13, AC 91-55; POH/AFM.

Objective. To determine that the applicant:

1. Exhibits knowledge of the elements related to recommended engine starting procedures. This shall include the use of an external power source, hand propping safety, and starting under various atmospheric conditions.
2. Positions the airplane properly considering structures, surface conditions other aircraft, and the safety of nearby persons and property.
3. Utilizes the appropriate checklist for starting procedure.

D. TASK: TAXIING

REFERENCES: FAA-H-8083-3; POH/AFM.

Objective. To determine that the applicant:

1. Exhibits knowledge of the elements related to safe taxi procedures.
2. Performs a brake check immediately after the airplane begins moving.
3. Positions flight controls properly for the existing wind conditions.
4. Controls direction and speed without excessive use of brakes.
5. Complies with airport/taxiway markings, signals, ATC clearances and instructions.
6. Taxies so as to avoid other aircraft and hazards.

E. TASK: BEFORE TAKEOFF CHECK

REFERENCES: FAA-H-8083-3; POH/AFM.

Objective. To determine that the applicant:

1. Exhibits knowledge of the elements related to the before takeoff check. This shall include the reasons for checking each item and how to detect malfunctions.
2. Positions the airplane properly considering other aircraft/vessels, wind and surface conditions.
3. Divides attention inside and outside the cockpit.
4. Ensures the engine temperatures and pressure are suitable for run-up and takeoff.
5. Accomplishes the before takeoff checklist and ensures the airplane is in safe operating condition.
6. Reviews takeoff performance airspeeds, takeoff distances, departure and emergency procedures.
7. Avoids runway incursion and/or ensures no conflict with traffic prior to taxiing into takeoff position.

III. AREA OF OPERATION: AIRPORT OPERATIONS

A. TASK: RADIO COMMUNICATIONS AND ATC LIGHT SIGNALS

REFERENCES: 14 CFR part 91, AC 61-23/FAA-H-8083-25; AIM.

Objective. To determine that the applicant:

1. Exhibits knowledge of the elements related to radio communications and ATC light signals.
2. Selects appropriate frequencies
3. Transmits using recommended phraseology.
4. Acknowledges radio communications and complies with instructions.

B. TASK: TRAFFIC PATTERNS

REFERENCES: FAA-H-8083-3, AC 61-23/FAA-H-8083-25, AC90-66; AIM.

Objective. To determine that the applicant:

1. Exhibits knowledge of the elements related to traffic patterns. This shall include procedures at airports with and without operating control towers, prevention of runway incursions, collision avoidance, wake turbulence avoidance, and wind shear.
2. Complies with proper traffic pattern procedures.
3. Maintains proper spacing from other traffic.
4. Corrects for wind-drift to maintain proper ground track.
5. Maintains orientation with runway/landing area in use.
6. Maintains traffic pattern altitude ±100 feet (30 meters), and appropriate airspeed ±10 knots.

C. TASK: AIRPORT, RUNWAY, AND TAXIWAY SIGNS, MARKINGS, AND LIGHTING

REFERENCES: AC 61-23/FAA-H-8083-25; AIM.

Objective. To determine that the applicant:

1. Exhibits knowledge of the elements related to airport, runway, and taxiway operations with emphasis on runway incursion avoidance.
2. Properly identifies and interprets airport, runway, and taxiway signs, markings, and lighting.

IV. AREA OF OPERATION: TAKEOFFS, LANDINGS, AND GO-AROUNDS

A. TASK: NORMAL AND CROSSWIND TAKEOFF AND CLIMB

NOTE: If a crosswind condition does not exist, the applicant's knowledge of crosswind elements shall be evaluation through oral testing.

REFERENCES: FAA-H-8083-3; POH/AFM.

Objective. To determine that the applicant:

1. Exhibits knowledge of the elements related to normal and crosswind takeoff, climb operations and rejected takeoff procedures.
2. Positions the flight controls for the existing wind conditions.
3. Clears the area, taxies onto the takeoff surface, and aligns the airplane on the runway center/takeoff path.
4. Lifts off at the recommended airspeed, and accelerates to V_Y.
5. Establishes a pitch attitude that will maintain V_Y ±5 knots.
6. Retracts the landing gear if appropriate, and flaps after a positive rate of climb is established.
7. Maintains takeoff power and V_Y ±5 knots to a safe maneuvering altitude.
8. Maintains directional control and proper wind-drift correction throughout the takeoff and climb.
9. Complies with noise abatement procedures.
10. Completes appropriate checklists.

B. TASK: NORMAL AND CROSSWIND APPROACH AND LANDING

NOTE: If a crosswind condition does not exist, the applicant's knowledge of the crosswind elements shall be evaluated through oral testing.

REFERENCES: FAA-H-8083-3; POH/AFM

Objective. To determine that the applicant:

1. Exhibits knowledge of the elements related to normal and crosswind approach and landing.
2. Considers the wind conditions, landing surface, obstructions, and selects a suitable touchdown point.
3. Establishes the recommended approach and landing configuration and airspeed and adjusts pitch attitdue and power as required.
4. Maintains a stabilized approach and recommended airspeed, or in its absence not more than 1.3 V_{SO}, ±5 knots, with wind gust factor applied.
5. Makes smooth, timely, and correct control application during the roundout and touchdown.
6. Touches down at or within 200 feet (60 meters) beyond a specified point with no drift, and with the airplane's longitudinal axis aligned with and over the runway center/landing path.
7. Maintains crosswind correction and directional control throughout the approach and landing sequence.
8. Completes appropriate checklist.

C. TASK: SOFT-FIELD TAKEOFF AND CLIMB

REFERENCES: FAA-H-8083-3; POH/AFM

Objective. To determine that the applicant:

1. Exhibits knowledge of the elements related to a soft-field takeoff and climb.
2. Positions the flight controls for existing conditions and to maximize lift as quickly as possible.
3. Clears the area, taxies onto the takeoff surface at a speed consistent with safety without stopping while advancing the throttle smoothly to takeoff power.
4. Establishes and maintains a pitch attitude that will transfer the weight of the airplane from the wheels to the wings as rapidly as possible.
5. Lifts off at the lowest possible airspeed and remains in ground effect while accelerating to V_X or V_Y, as required.
6. Establishes a pitch attitude for V_X or V_Y, as appropriate, and maintains selected airspeed ±5 knots, during the climb.
7. Retracts the landing gear, if appropriate and flaps after clear of any obstacles or as recommended by the manufacturer.
8. Maintains takeoff power and V_X or V_Y ±5 knots to a safe maneuvering altitude.
9. Maintains directional control and proper wind-drift correction throughout the takeoff and climb.
10. Completes appropriate checklists.

D. TASK: SOFT-FIELD APPROACH AND LANDING

REFERENCES: FAA-H-8083-3; POH/AFM.

Objective. To determine that the applicant:

1. Exhibits knowledge of the elements related to a soft-field approach and landing.
2. Considers the wind conditions, landing surface, and obstructions, and selects the most suitable touchdown area.
3. Establishes the recommended approach and landing configuration and airspeed; adjusts pitch attitude and power as required.
4. Maintains a stabilized approach and recommended airspeed, or in its absence, not more than 1.3 V_{SO}, ±5 knots, with wind gust factor applied.
5. Makes smooth, timely, and correct control application during the roundout and touchdown.
6. Touches down softly, with no drift, and with the airplane's longitudinal axis aligned with the runway/landing path.
7. Maintains crosswind correction and directional control throughout the approach and landing.
8. Maintains crosswind correction and directional control throughout the approach and landing sequence.
9. Completes appropriate checklist.

E. TASK: SHORT-FIELD TAKEOFF AND MAXIMUM PERFORMANCE CLIMB

REFERENCES: FAA-H-8083-3; POH/AFM.

Objective. To determine that the applicant:

1. Exhibits knowledge of the elements related to a short-field (confined area) takeoff and maximum performance climb.
2. Positions the flight controls for the existing wind conditions, sets flaps as recommended.
3. Clears the area, taxies into takeoff position utilizing maximum available takeoff area and aligns the airplane on the runway center/takeoff path..
4. Applies brakes (if appropriate) while advancing the throttle smoothly to takeoff power.
5. Lifts off at the recommended airspeed, and accelerates to recommended obstacle clearance airspeed, or V_X.
6. Establishes a pitch attitude that will maintain the recommended obstacle clearance airspeed, or V_X, +5/-0 knots, until the obstacle is cleared, or until the airplane is 50 fee (20 meters) above the surface.
7. After clearing the obstacle, establishes the pitch attitude for V_Y, accelerates to V_Y, and maintains V_Y, ±5 knots during the climb.
8. Retracts the landing gear, if appropriate and flaps after clear of any obstacles or as recommended by manufacturer.
9. Maintains takeoff power and V_Y ±5 knots to a safe maneuvering altitude.
10. Maintains directional control and proper wind-drift correction throughout the takeoff and climb.
11. Completes appropriate checklists.

F. TASK: SHORT-FIELD APPROACH AND LANDING

REFERENCES: FAA-H-8083-3; POH/AFM.

Objective. To determine that the applicant:

1. Exhibits knowledge of the elements related to a short-field approach and landing.
2. Considers the wind conditions, landing surface, obstructions, and selects the most suitable touchdown point.
3. Establishes the recommended approach and landing configuration and airspeed and adjusts pitch attitude and power.
4. Maintains a stabilized approach and recommended approach airspeed, or in its absence, not more than 1.3 V_{SO}, ±5 knots, with wind gust factor applied.
5. Makes smooth, timely, and correct control application during the roundout and touchdown.
6. Touches down smoothly at minimum control airspeed.
7. Touches down at or within 100 feet (30 meters) beyond a specified point, with no side drift, minimum float and with the airplane's longitudinal axis aligned with and over the runway center/landing path.
8. Maintains crosswind correction and directional control throughout the approach and landing sequence.
9. Applies brakes or elevator control, as necessary, to stop in the shortest distance consistent with safety.
10. Completes appropriate checklist.

G. TASK: POWER-OFF 180° ACCURACY APPROACH
          AND LANDING

REFERENCE: FAA-H-8083-3.

Objective. To determine that the applicant:

1. Exhibits knowledge of the elements related to a
    power-off 180° accuracy approach and landing.
2. Considers the wind conditions, landing surface,
    obstructions, and selects an appropriate touchdown
    point.
3. Positions airplane on downwind leg, parallel to
    landing runway, and not more than 1000 feet AGL.
4. Abeam the specified touchdown point, closes throttle
    and establishes appropriate glide speed.
5. Completes final airplane configuration.
6. Touches down in a normal landing attitude, at or
    within 200 feet (60 meters) beyond the specified
    touchdown point.
7. Completes the appropriate checklist.

H. TASK: GO-AROUND/REJECTED LANDING

REFERENCES: FAA-H-8083-3; POH/AFM.

Objective. To determine that the applicant:

1. Exhibits knowledge of the elements related to a
    go-around/rejected landing.
2. Makes a timely decision to discontinue the approach to
    landing.
3. Applies takeoff power immediately and transitions to
    climb pitch attitude for V_Y, and maintains V_Y ±5 knots.
4. Retracts flaps as appropriate.
5. Retracts the landing gear if appropriate after a positive
    rate of climb is established.
6. Maneuvers to the side of runway/landing area to clear
    and avoid conflicting traffic.
7. Maintains takeoff power and V_Y ±5 knots to a safe
    maneuvering altitude.
8. Maintains directional control and proper wind-drift
    correction throughout the transition to climb.
9. Completes appropriate checklist.

V. AREA OF OPERATION:
  PERFORMANCE MANEUVERS

NOTE: The examiner shall at least select either TASK A or B, and
either C or D.

A. TASK: STEEP TURNS

REFERENCES: FAA-H-8083-3; POH/AFM.

Objective. To determine that the applicant:

1. Exhibits knowledge of the elements related to steep
    turns.
2. Establishes the manufacturer's recommended airspeed
    or if one is not stated, a safe airspeed not to exceed V_A.
3. Rolls into a coordinated 360° steep turn with at least a
    50° bank, followed by a 360° steep turn in the opposite
    direction.
4. Divides attention between airplane control and
    orientation.
5. Maintains the entry altitude, ± 100 feet (30 meters),
    airspeed, ±10 knots, bank, ±5°; and rolls out on the
    entry heading ±10°.

B. TASK: STEEP SPIRAL

REFERENCE: FAA-H-8083-3.

Objective. To determine that the applicant:

1. Exhibits knowledge of the elements related to a
    steep spiral.
2. Selects an altitude sufficient to continue through a
    series of at least three 360° turns.
3. Selects a suitable ground reference point.
4. Applies wind-drift correction to track a constant
    radius circle around selected reference point with
    bank not to exceed 60° at steepest point in turn.
5. Divides attention between airplane control and
    ground track, while maintaining coordinated flight.
6. Maintains the specified airspeed, ±10 knots, rolls out
    toward object or specified heading, ±10°.

C. TASK: CHANDELLES

REFERENCES: FAA-H-8083-3

Objective. To determine that the applicant:

1. Exhibits knowledge of the elements related to
    chandelles.
2. Selects an altitude that will allow the maneuver to be
    performed no lower than 1,500 feet AGL (460 meters).
3. Establishes the recommended entry configuration,
    power, and airspeed.
4. Establishes the angle of bank at approximately 30°.
5. Simultaneously applies power and pitch to maintain a
    smooth, coordinated climbing turn to the 90° point with
    a constant bank.
6. Begins a coordinated constant rate of rollout from the
    90° point to the 180° point maintaining power and a
    constant pitch attitude.
7. Completes rollout at the 180° point, ±10° just above a
    stall airspeed, and maintaining that airspeed
    momentarily avoiding a stall.
8. Resumes straight and level flight with minimum loss of
    altitude.

D. TASK: LAZY EIGHTS

REFERENCES: FAA-H-8083-3.

Objective. To determine that the applicant:

1. Exhibits knowledge of the elements related to lazy
    eights.
2. Selects an altitude that will allow the task to be
    performed no lower than 1,500 feet AGL (460 meters).
3. Establishes the recommended entry configuration,
    power, and airspeed.
4. Maintains coordinated flight throughout the maneuver
5. Achieves the following throughout the maneuver-

    a. approximately 30° bank at the steepest point.
    b. constant change of pitch and roll rate.
    c. altitude tolerance at 180° points, ±100 feet (30
        meters from entry altitude.
    d. airspeed tolerance at the 180° point plus ±10°
        knots from entry airspeed.
    e. heading tolerance at the 180° point plus ±10°.

6. Continues the maneuver through the number of
    symmetrical loops specified and resumes straight and
    level flight.

VI. AREA OF OPERATION: GROUND REFERENCE MANEUVER

TASK: EIGHTS ON PYLONS

REFERENCE: FAA-H-8083-3.

Objective. To determine that the applicant:

1. Exhibits knowledge of the elements related to eights on pylons.
2. Determines the approximate pivotal altitude.
3. Selects suitable pylons, that will permit approximately 3 to 5 seconds of straight and level flight between the pylons.
4. Enters the maneuver at the appropriate altitude and airspeed and at a bank angle or approximately 30° to 40° at the steepest point.
5. Applies the necessary corrections so that the line-of-sight reference line remains on the pylon.
6. Divides attention between accurate coordinated airplane control and outside visual references.
7. Holds pylon using appropriate pivotal altitude avoiding slips and skids.

VII. AREA OF OPERATION: NAVIGATION

A. TASK: PILOTAGE AND DEAD RECKONING

REFERENCES: AC 61-23/FAA-H-8083-25.

Objective. To determine that the applicant:

1. Exhibits knowledge of the elements related to pilotage and dead reckoning.
2. Follows the preplanned course by reference to landmarks.
3. Identifies landmarks by relating the surface features to chart symbols.
4. Navigates by means of precomputed headings, groundspeed, and elapsed time.
5. Corrects for and records differences between preflight groundspeed and heading calculations and those determined en route.
6. Verifies the airplane's position within 2 nautical miles of flight planned route.
7. Arrives at the en route checkpoints within 3 minutes of the initial or revised ETA and provides a destination estimate.
8. Maintains appropriate altitude, ±100 feet (30 meters), and headings, ±10°.

B. TASK: NAVIGATION SYSTEMS AND RADAR SERVICES

REFERENCES: FAA-H-8083-3, AC 61-23/FAA-H-8083-25; Navigation Equipment Operations Manuals, AIM.

Objective. To determine that the applicant:

1. Exhibits knowledge of the elements related to navigation systems and radar services.
2. Demonstrates the ability to use an airborne electronic navigation system.
3. Locates the airplane's position using the navigation system.
4. Intercepts and tracks a given course, radial, or bearing as appropriate.
5. Recognizes and describes the indication of station passage if appropriate.
6. Recognizes signal loss and takes appropriate action.
7. Uses proper communication procedures when utilizing radar services.
8. Maintains the appropriate altitude, ±100 feet (30 meters), heading, ±10°.

C. TASK: DIVERSION

REFERENCES: FAA-H-8083-25; AIM

Objective. To determine that the applicant:

1. Exhibits knowledge of the elements related to diversion.
2. Selects an appropriate alternate airport and route.
3. Makes an accurate estimate of heading, groundspeed, arrival time, and fuel consumption to the alternate airport.
4. Maintains the appropriate altitude, ±100 feet (30 meters), and heading, ±10°.

D. TASK: LOST PROCEDURE

REFERENCES: FAA-H-8083-25; AIM.

Objective. To determine that the applicant:

1. Exhibits knowledge of the elements related to lost procedures.
2. Selects the best course of action.
3. Maintains an appropriate heading and climbs, if necessary.
4. Identifies prominent landmark(s).
5. Uses navigation systems/facilities and/or contacts an ATC facility for assistance as appropriate.

VIII. AREA OF OPERATION: SLOW FLIGHT AND STALLS

A. TASK: MANEUVERING DURING SLOW FLIGHT

REFERENCES: FAA-H-8083-3; POH/AFM

Objective. To determine that the applicant:

1. Exhibits knowledge of the elements related to maneuvering during slow flight.
2. Selects an entry altitude that will allow the task to be completed no lower than 1,500 feet (460 meters) AGL.
3. Establishes and maintains an airspeed at which any further increase in angle of attack, increase in load factor, or reduction in power, would result in an immediate stall.
4. Accomplishes coordinated straight-and-level flight, turns, climbs, and descents with landing gear and flap configurations specified by the examiner.
5. Divides attention between airplane control and orientation.
6. Maintains the specified altitude, ±50 feet (15 meters); specified heading, ±10°; airspeed +5/-0 knots, and specified angle of bank, ±5°.

B. TASK: POWER-OFF STALLS

REFERENCES: FAA-H-8083-3; AC 61-67; POH/AFM.

Objective. To determine that the applicant:

1. Exhibits knowledge of the elements related to power-off stalls.
2. Selects an entry altitude that allows the task to be completed no lower than 1,500 feet (460 meters) AGL.
3. Establishes a stabilized descent, in the approach or landing configuration, as specified by the examiner.
4. Transitions smoothly from the approach or landing attitude to a pitch attitude that will induce a stall.
5. Maintains a specified heading, ±10°, in straight flight; maintains a specified angle of bank, not to exceed 20°, +0/−5°, in turning flight, while inducing a stall.
6. Recognizes and recovers promptly as the stall occurs by simultaneously reducing the angle of attack, increasing power to maximum allowable, and leveling the wings to return to a straight-and-level flight atttude with a minimum loss of altitude appropriate for the airplane.
7. Retracts the flaps to the recommended setting, retracts the landing gear if retractable after a positive rate of climb is established.
8. Accelerates to V_x or V_y speed before final flap retraction; returns to the altitude, heading, and airspeed specified by the examiner.

C. TASK: POWER-ON STALLS

REFERENCES: FAA-H-8083-3, AC 61-17; POH/AFM.

NOTE: In some high-performance airplanes, the power setting may have to be reduced below the practical test standards guideline power setting to prevent excessively high pitch attitudes (greater than 30° nose up).

Objective. To determine that the applicant:

1. Exhibits knowledge of the elements related to power-on stalls.
2. Selects an entry altitude that allows the task to be completed no lower than 1,500 feet (460 meters) AGL.
3. Establishes the takeoff or departure configuration. Sets power to no less than 65 percent available power.
4. Transitions smoothly from the takeoff or departure attitude to a pitch attitude that will induce a stall.
5. Maintains a specified heading, ±5°, in straight flight; maintains a specified angle of bank, not to exceed a 20°, ±10°, in turning flight, while inducing the stall.
6. Recognizes and recovers promptly as the stall occurs by simultaneously reducing the angle of attack, increasing power to maximum allowable, and leveling the wings to return to a straight-and-level flight attitude, with a minimum loss of altitude appropriate for the airplane.
7. Retracts flaps to the recommended setting, retracts the landing gear if retractable, after a positive rate of climb is established.
8. Accelerates to V_x or V_y speed before the final flap retraction; returns to the altitude, heading, and airspeed specified by the examiner.

D. TASK: SPIN AWARENESS

REFERENCES: FAA-H-8083-3, AC 61-67; POH/AFM.

Objective. To determine that the applicant exhibits knowledge of the elements related to spin awareness by explaining:

1. Aerodynamic factors related to spins.
2. Flight situations where unintentional spins may occur.
3. Procedures for recovery from unintentional spins.

IX. AREA OF OPERATION: EMERGENCY OPERATIONS

A. TASK: EMERGENCY APPROACH AND LANDING (SIMULATED)

REFERENCES: FAA-H-8083-3; POH/AFM.

Objective. To determine that the applicant:

1. Exhibits knowledge of the elements related to emergency approach and landing procedures.
2. Analyzes the situation and selects an appropriate course of action.
3. Establishes and maintains the recommended best glide airspeed, ±10 knots.
4. Selects a suitable landing area.
5. Plans and follows a flight pattern to the selected landing area considering altitude, wind, terrain, and obstructions.
6. Prepares for landing, or go-around, as specified by the examiner.
7. Follows the appropriate checklist.

B. TASK: SYSTEMS AND EQUIPMENT MALFUNCTIONS

REFERENCES: FAA-H-8083-3; POH/AFM.

Objective. To determine that the applicant:

1. Exhibits knowledge of the elements related to systems and equipment malfunctions appropriate to the airplane provided for the practical test.
2. Analyzes the situation and takes appropriate action for simulated emergencies appropriate to the airplane provided for the practical test for least five (5) of the following—

   a. partial or complete power loss.
   b. engine roughness or overheat.
   c. carburetor or induction icing.
   d. loss of oil pressure.
   e. fuel starvation.
   f. electrical malfunction.
   g. vacuum/pressure, and associated flight instruments malfunction.
   h. pitot/static.
   i. landing gear or flap malfunction.
   j. inoperative trim.
   k. inadvertent door or window opening.
   l. structural icing.
   m. smoke/fire/engine compartment fire.
   n. any other emergency appropriate to the airplane.

3. Follows the appropriate checklist or procedure.

C. TASK: EMERGENCY EQUIPMENT AND SURVIVAL GEAR

REFERENCES: FAA-H-8083-3; POH/AFM.

Objective. To determine that the applicant:

1. Exhibits knowledge of the elements related to emergency equipment and survival gear appropriate to the airplane and environment encountered during flight. Identifies appropriate equipment that should be above the airplane.

X. AREA OF OPERATION: HIGH ALTITUDE OPERATIONS

A. TASK: SUPPLEMENTAL OXYGEN

REFERENCES: 14 CFR part 91; FAA-H-8083-3, AC 61-107; AIM; POH/AFM.

Objective. To determine that the applicant exhibits knowledge of the elements related to supplemental oxygen by explaining:

1. Supplemental oxygen requirements for flight crew and passengers when operating non-pressurized airplanes.
2. Distinctions and differences between "aviators' breathing oxygen" and other types.
3. Operational characteristics of continuous flow, demand, and pressure-demand oxygen systems.

B. TASK: PRESSURIZATION

REFERENCES: FAA-H-8083-3, AC 61-107; AIM; POH/AFM.

Objective. To determine that the applicant:

1. Exhibits knowledge of the elements related to pressurization by explaining—

   a. fundamental concept of cabin pressurization.
   b. supplemental oxygen requirements when operating airplanes with pressurized cabins.
   c. physiological hazards associated with high altitude flight and decompression.

NOTE: Element 2 applies only if the airplane provided for the practical test is equipped for pressurized flight operations.

2. Operates the pressurization system properly, and reacts appropriately to simulated pressurization malfunctions.

XI. AREA OF OPERATION: POSTFLIGHT PROCEDURES

NOTE: The examiner shall select TASK A and for ASES applicants at least one other TASK.

A. TASK: AFTER LANDING, PARKING, AND SECURING

REFERENCES: FAA-H-8083-3; POH/AFM.

Objective. To determine that the applicant:

1. Exhibits knowledge of the elements related to after landing, parking, and securing procedures.
2. Maintains directional control after touchdown while decelerating to an appropriate speed.
3. Observes runway hold lines and other surface control markings and lighting.
4. Parks in an appropriate area, considering the safety of nearby persons and property.
5. Follows the appropriate procedure for engine shutdown.
6. Completes the appropriate checklist.
7. Conducts an appropriate postflight inspection and secures the aircraft.

APPENDIX B
COMPLEX AND HIGH-PERFORMANCE AIRPLANES

OPERATING LARGER ENGINES

A. Operating engines with higher horsepower requires more finesse in starting and shutdown procedures. Also, there may be additional considerations such as turbocharging and/or fuel injection.

1. Higher-horsepower engines are more affected by temperature and fuel/air mixture during starting than smaller engines. They are usually less difficult to start when cold but more difficult to start when hot.

   a. The range of favorable mixtures for starting decreases considerably as the size of the engine increases, especially when it is hot.

B. High-horsepower engines are susceptible to vapor lock, which can make starting almost impossible. **Vapor lock** is caused by the heat of the engine vaporizing the fuel in the fuel lines. As a result, adequate fuel and fuel pressure are not available to start the engine.

1. The engine must be allowed to cool adequately. Opening the engine cowling may help speed up the process.

2. An auxiliary fuel pump may also be beneficial in helping start the engine.

3. Review the hot engine start procedures in the airplane's *POH*.

C. In-flight operations require gentle throttle movements and careful control of the mixture. Some high-performance engines have throttle controls that permit adjustments by turning the knob (called a vernier control) rather than pushing and pulling.

1. Always make throttle adjustments smoothly.

   a. Even if you need full power immediately for a short-field takeoff, you should use your brakes to run up your engine slowly, and then release your brakes when at full power.

2. The objective is to prevent too-rapid cooling and heating of various engine parts and to promote smooth operation of the airplane.

3. Cowl flaps and proper fuel leaning techniques are used to regulate engine temperature.

D.   Most high-performance airplanes have additional instruments to aid the pilot in proper leaning of the engine.

    1.   **Exhaust gas temperature (EGT) gauges** indicate the temperature of the exhaust gas just as it exits the cylinder.

        a.   Usually an EGT gauge is calibrated in 25°F increments.

        b.   At full takeoff power, you use full rich mixture (except at high-altitude airports).

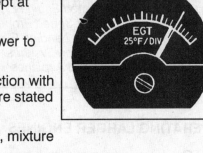

        c.   After takeoff, as you reduce power from takeoff power to climb settings, the EGT will decrease.

           1)   Usually the mixture can be leaned in conjunction with the power reduction based on the procedure stated in the *POH*.

           2)   The idea is to allow a rich, but not overly rich, mixture to help cool the engine during climb.

        d.   At altitude for your desired cruise, and at your desired power setting (RPM and MP),

           1)   Slowly lean the engine and watch the EGT rise.

           2)   Note the lag in EGT movement after mixture change. Change the mixture slowly enough so as to read the corresponding change in EGT.

           3)   At some point, the EGT will stop increasing and begin decreasing, i.e., reach the peak.

           4)   Note that, once it starts decreasing, the engine may begin running rough because it is excessively lean.

           5)   Some engines are designed to operate at peak EGT; others at 25°, 50°, 75°, etc., rich of peak; and some lean of peak.

           6)   Many pilots with single-probe EGTs run 25° to 50° richer than recommended to compensate for another cylinder being a little leaner than the cylinder with the EGT probe.

               a)   **Probe** refers to the sensor that measures temperature. More sophisticated EGT gauges have a probe for each cylinder.

    2.   **Cylinder head temperature (CHT) gauges** measure temperature of the metal at the top of the cylinder.

        a.   This gauge allows the pilot to avoid running the engine too hot, which is a by-product of a too-lean situation.

           1)   Inadequate cooling air flow may contribute to a high CHT.

        b.   The CHT is generally not used to lean the engine, as it is not immediately sensitive to slight changes in the fuel/air mixture.

           1)   Opening cowl flaps or increasing airspeed (in climb or descent) will decrease CHT.

        c.   Rather, the CHT, like the oil temperature gauge, indicates the overall engine temperature and well-being.

E.   With large engines, airplane responses are amplified with changes in power settings. A slight movement of the throttle can produce large horsepower changes. In addition, as engine size increases, the allowable duration for running the engine at maximum power decreases; i.e., damage can occur more easily.

    1.   Many engines have set power limitations, usually expressed in minutes of operation (e.g., takeoff power may be maintained for a maximum of only 5 min.). After takeoff, the maximum power available is called METO (maximum except for takeoff) power. Generally, it is better to operate at less than maximum power, especially for the climb. The enemy of high-performance engines is excess heat, so operating with cruise climb settings will keep engine wear to a minimum.

        a.   A reduced power setting will also reduce engine noise for noise abatement procedures.

    2.   During cruise, operating at 65% to 75% power, in general, reduces engine wear and fuel consumption and offers significant benefits.

F.   The operation of a small airplane engine can be compared to a lawnmower, and the operation of a large airplane engine can be compared to a high-performance race car. Additional care and warm-up periods must be utilized in the operation of a large engine.

    1.   Rapid descents must be carefully monitored because an excessive rate of descent and high airspeed at a low power setting may damage the larger engine as a result of its cooling too rapidly and unevenly (shock cooling).

    2.   Rapid, uneven cooling is potentially a very serious problem, especially in descents from higher altitudes where the temperature is low.

        a.   The problem is frequently compounded by turbulence, which requires even lower power settings to preclude airspeed buildup.

    3.   The solution frequently is to lower the landing gear, which acts as a speed brake.

        a.   Remember to first reduce your airspeed to the lower of V_{LE}/V_{LO} so as not to damage the landing gear or the landing gear doors.

        b. V_{LO} is the maximum airspeed for landing gear operation. V_{LE} is the maximum airspeed for flight with the landing gear extended. These airspeeds may differ; check your *POH*.

    4.   Some high-performance aircraft have speed brakes installed. Speed brakes are small plates that can be extended several inches up out of the top of the wing to create drag and reduce lift. They permit a good rate of descent and lower airspeeds at moderate power settings, just as landing gear extension does.

OPERATING TURBOCHARGED ENGINES

A.   Turbocharging in single-engine airplanes has become popular due to the availability of smaller and lighter turbochargers.

    1.   Turbochargers compress air going to the carburetor or cylinder intake.

        a.   Exhaust gases drive a turbine, which powers the compressor.

    2.   The increased air density provides greater power and improved performance.

B. Turbocharging is a method of overcoming reduced engine power, which usually occurs with increases in altitude or at high density altitudes. By forcing compressed air into the cylinder, outside air density is a less significant factor in the engine's performance.

1. Turbocharged engines usually maintain sea-level horsepower up to a certain altitude, called the critical altitude.

2. From the critical altitude up to the service ceiling, the engine will have a decrease in available power with increasing altitude.

3. There are two types of turbocharging systems:

    a. The **normalizer system**, which allows the engine to develop sea-level pressure of approximately 29 in. of MP up to a critical altitude (generally between 14,000 and 16,000 ft. MSL)

    b. The **supercharger system**, a more powerful system, which allows the engine to develop higher-than-sea-level pressure (up to 60 in. of MP) up to a critical altitude

C. For a better understanding of the typical turbocharging system, follow the induction air through the engine until it is expelled as exhaust gases, as shown below.

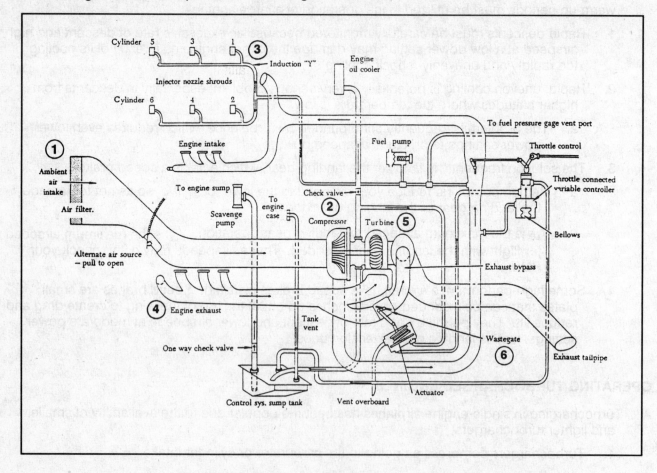

1. Induction air is taken in through the air intake.
2. The air is then compressed by the compressor.
3. This compressed air is then forced into the cylinders through the intake manifold.

4. The air and fuel are burned, and the exhaust gases are routed from the exhaust manifold toward the turbine.

5. The exhaust gases drive the turbine which, in turn, drives the compressor.

6. The **waste gate** is a damper-like device that controls the amount of exhaust gas that is routed through the turbine.

    a. As the waste gate closes with altitude, it allows more gas through the turbine, causing the compressor to spin faster and resulting in more compression.

        1) This compression allows the engine to maintain selected manifold pressure as altitude increases up to the critical altitude.

    b. There are three types of waste gates: manual, fixed, and automatic. The most common is the automatic waste gate.

        1) The automatic waste gate operates on internal pressure. When pressure builds toward an **overboost** (excessive manifold pressure), the waste gate automatically opens to relieve pressure, keeping the engine within normal operating limits regardless of air density.

D. The operation of turbocharged engines requires much care. When advancing and retarding the throttle, smooth motions should be used at slow rates. Harsh, abrupt movement of the throttle can be very damaging to the turbocharger and the engine.

    1. The trade-off for the increased performance and high-altitude capabilities is that, in general, turbocharging an engine will normally result in an engine that will burn more fuel in all phases of flight.

        a. This additional fuel consumption must be taken into consideration on cross-country flights.

        b. It can be offset, however, by the higher true airspeed possible at high altitudes and the potential to use beneficial tailwinds.

    2. Another in-flight consideration is cylinder head temperature. At higher altitudes where the air is thin (where turbocharged engines are frequently flown), cylinder head temperatures tend to be higher than normal because the engine is subjected to less cooling air.

        a. Thus, the engine has a greater tendency to exceed its temperature limits.

        b. Extra care and vigilance must be exercised, and the mixture may have to be richened, or a cowl flap opened.

    3. Shutting-down procedures also differ. Turbocharged engines must be allowed to idle for periods of up to 10 min. in order for cooling and lubricating liquids to cool the turbocharger and to avoid excessive wear on bearings and other metal-to-metal surfaces within the turbocharger. Also, due to the extremely high RPM of the turbine, this time allows the turbine to slow down.

    4. Before flying an airplane with a turbocharger, you must be thoroughly familiar with its operation, including the type of waste gates, MP limits, and critical altitude.

OPERATING FUEL-INJECTED ENGINES

A.   Fuel injectors are used in place of carburetors in some complex airplanes and almost all high-performance airplanes. As implied, fuel is injected either directly into the cylinders or just at the intake valve.

B.   There are several types of fuel injection systems in use today. Most designs include an engine-driven fuel pump, a fuel/air control unit, a fuel distributor, and discharge nozzles for each cylinder.

1.   The fuel pump provides pressurized fuel to the fuel injector unit.

2.   Based on the throttle setting, the mixture setting, and the air flow to the engine, a metered amount of fuel is sent to the fuel flow divider where it is divided and an equal amount is sent to each injector.

3.   Here, the fuel passes out the discharge nozzle and is atomized, then vaporized, in the cylinder's intake port.

4.   The pilot monitors the system through a fuel-flow gauge on the instrument panel.

a.   The fuel-flow gauge is usually marked in gallons or pounds of fuel flow per hour.

C.   Operation of fuel-injected engines is very similar to carburetor-equipped engines in terms of engine controls and pilot actions. The only major difference is that an electric fuel pump is needed to pressurize the system to start the engine. After the start, the engine-driven fuel pump maintains fuel pressure. The electric pump provides supplemental pressure to combat fuel vapors or provides backup in case of an engine-driven fuel pump failure.

D.   The fuel injection system is generally less susceptible to icing than the carburetor system.

1.   Impact icing of the air intake, however, is a possibility in either system. Impact icing occurs when ice forms on the exterior of the airplane and results in clogging openings such as the engine air intake.

2.   The air intake for the fuel injection system is somewhat similar to that used in the carburetor system. The fuel injection system, however, is equipped with an alternate air source located within the engine cowling. This source is used if the external air source is obstructed by ice or by other matter.

E.   Some of the advantages of fuel injection are

1.   Less susceptibility to icing
2.   Better fuel flow
3.   Faster throttle response
4.   Precise control of mixture
5.   Better fuel distribution
6.   Easier cold-weather starts

F.   Disadvantages of fuel injection are usually associated with

1.   Difficulty in starting a hot engine
2.   Vapor locks during ground operations on hot days

a.   Vapor lock is a term used when fuel vaporizes and forms a vapor pocket in the fuel lines between the fuel tank and the induction system. These vapor pockets can result in a partial or complete block of fuel flow.

3.   Problems associated with restarting an engine that quits because of fuel starvation

OPERATING A CONSTANT-SPEED PROPELLER

A. Another difference in complex high-performance airplanes is that they are equipped with a controllable-pitch propeller, of which the constant-speed propeller system is the most common.

B. An airplane equipped with a constant-speed propeller has two main power controls:

    1. The throttle controls the power output of the engine (registered on the manifold pressure gauge).

        a. The manifold pressure (MP) gauge is a simple barometer that measures the air pressure in the engine intake manifold in inches of mercury.

    2. The propeller control regulates the engine RPM and, in turn, the propeller RPM.

        a. The RPM is registered on the tachometer.

C. The propeller control is usually found between the mixture and the throttle controls, and in some airplanes it is operated by turning rather than pushing and pulling.

    1. Since all three controls are adjacent and operate similarly, i.e., turn or push-pull, you must be careful to adjust the correct control. Learn the relative position and the "feel" of each knob.

    2. Usually, each control has a differently shaped knob and/or a different color to assist in distinguishing it from the others.

    3. You must be in the habit of confirming which control you have before making any adjustment to ensure that you have the correct control. Standard colors are throttle (black), prop (blue), and mixture (red).

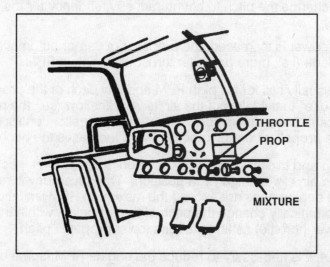

D. Power instruments include the RPM and MP gauges. The RPM gauge indicates the engine speed (and thus the propeller speed), and the MP gauge indicates the air pressure in the engine intake manifold in inches of mercury (i.e., the throttle setting).

E. Constant-speed propeller systems consist of a governor unit which controls the pitch angle of the blades so the engine's speed (RPM) remains constant. The governor regulates the flow of engine oil into and out of the propeller hub to control the blade angle.

    1. The propeller governor can be controlled by the pilot so that any desired propeller blade angle setting (within manifold pressure limits) and engine RPM can be obtained. By means of the propeller governor, the airplane's operational efficiency can be increased in various flight conditions.

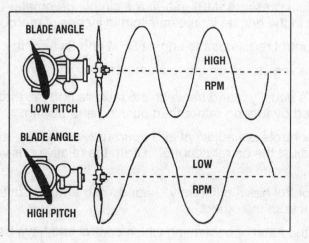

    2. Once the pilot has set the propeller to a given RPM, the propeller governor will automatically change the pitch to counteract any tendency for the engine to vary from this RPM.

        a. If engine power is increased, the propeller governor automatically increases the pitch of the blade (i.e., more propeller thrust) to maintain RPM.

F. Starting procedures usually call for full high RPM and low pitch of the propeller. At low pitch, the propeller angle, or "bite" that it takes of the air, is very shallow (i.e., the propeller blade is approximately vertical). Low pitch is obtained with the propeller control knob all the way forward. Moving the propeller control knob rearward increases the pitch, i.e., increases the bite.

G. During engine starting and taxiing, a low pitch position is used. On takeoff, power is advanced and the propeller remains in the high RPM position. The governor will regulate the RPM of the propeller so that the engine does not exceed the maximum RPM limitations. Adjusting the power (MP) will automatically change the pitch of the propeller, within the limits of the governor system. Higher power (throttle) settings require lower propeller pitch.

H. During initial climb-out, it is necessary to reduce the engine RPM (some engines are limited as to the time permitted for the engine to run at full high RPM and full throttle). This step is taken **after** reduction of MP, i.e., after the reduction of the throttle. Thus, **after** reduction of the MP to climb power, RPM should be reduced.

    1. The reduced RPM will also reduce the noise heard on the ground, which is important for noise abatement procedures.

I.   Most engine failures occur during the first power change and/or RPM reduction, i.e., just after the takeoff. Therefore, special care should be taken to be alert for an engine failure when making the initial propeller RPM change.

    1.   That change should be made at a safe altitude, e.g., 500 to 1,000 ft. AGL.

    2.   Takeoff and initial climb power settings vary by engine and manufacturer.

        a.   Thus, you should refer to your airplane's *POH* for these recommended settings.

J.   Once in cruise flight, additional power adjustments are usually necessary. The throttle should be retarded prior to increasing the pitch of the propeller (i.e., reducing RPM), and the propeller should be advanced prior to advancing the throttle. These adjustments will avoid overloading the engine, i.e., having too high a manifold pressure for too low an RPM (in which case the engine may be damaged). Consult your airplane's *POH* for the MP/RPM combination for the desired cruise performance.

K.   Before landing, i.e., as part of the final landing checklist, the propeller should be advanced to full high RPM position (low pitch) so that, if an increase in power becomes necessary (e.g., a go-around), full power can be used without causing excessive MP relative to RPM. After landing and throughout taxiing and engine shutdown, the propeller should be kept in the high RPM position.

L.   The propeller governor is designed with a fail-safe system in the event of an oil pressure failure. On some propeller models, the oil pressure is used to push the blade into a high-pitch, low-RPM setting. If an oil pressure failure occurred, the blade would be driven by centrifugal force into the low-pitch, high-RPM position that is desired for takeoffs and landings. Certain propeller models are aided by counterweights, springs, or air pressure in going to the high RPM setting after an oil pressure failure.

    1.   Not all single-engine planes are like this. Some go to high pitch, low-RPM to increase glide ratio in case of engine failure.

OPERATING RETRACTABLE LANDING GEAR

A.   All complex airplanes and most high-performance airplanes are equipped with retractable landing gear. They provide several benefits:

    1.   The primary benefit is the reduction in parasitic drag when the gear is retracted. Remember, as speed is doubled, drag is quadrupled.

    2.   The reduction in drag has a corresponding and related increase in airspeed. By having a clean airframe, more airspeed can be obtained with the same amount of horsepower.

Fixed Gear

Retractable Gear

B.   Gear systems can be operated in a number of different ways. Some are electric, some are hydraulic, and some are hybrids called electro-hydraulic.

   1.   The electric system uses a reversible electric motor to power the system. Through a gear assembly, the electric motor turns a bellcrank, operating the push-pull cables and tubes that extend and retract the landing gear. As a backup, most have a handcrank to manually lower the gear.

   2.   The hydraulic system uses an engine-driven hydraulic pump to force fluid under pressure through a series of valves, pipes, and actuators. The hydraulic pressure drives the gear up or down. For emergencies, a hand pump, compressed nitrogen, or a combination of both is used.

   3.   The electro-hydraulic system uses a reversible electric motor to drive the hydraulic pump. The gear selector switch is an electric switch which activates the electric motor and controls its direction. For emergency use, a hydraulic pressure dump switch is usually used. The dump switch releases the pressure, and the gear free-falls to the down and (sometimes) locked position.

C.   Prior to landing, the pilot should look for a positive indication (such as three green lights) that the gear is down and locked. Many airplanes are equipped with gear warning devices that provide a visual or audible warning in case the pilot forgets to lower the landing gear prior to landing. These warning devices are activated in various manners.

   1.   Some have switches on the throttle that sense the reduction in power.

   2.   Others have sensors that are activated by external devices with the ability to sense slow airspeed.

   3.   On more advanced airplanes, radar altimeters cause the warning.

      a.   Radar altimeters determine height above the ground with radar, rather than atmospheric pressure.

D.   When flying an airplane with retractable landing gear, you should incorporate a landing gear down check prior to landing; e.g., always say "Gear down and locked" as you make your turn to final, and remember to look at the landing gear indicator one last time on short final. This check should be in addition to your normal landing checklist during which you lower your landing gear.

   1.   One method that is frequently used is thinking of the gear lever as a descent switch.

      a.   When VFR in the traffic pattern, lower the gear just prior to descending from pattern altitude.

      b.   When on an instrument approach, lower the gear just prior to making your final descent for landing.

         1)   On a precision approach, the gear is lowered at glideslope intercept.

         2)   On a nonprecision approach, the gear is lowered at the final approach fix inbound.

   2.   Exceptions to this rule are necessary when conditions of flight warrant an early or delayed extension of the gear to maintain the safety of the flight.

      a.   Early extension is called for when extension is to be done manually.

      b.   A partial or complete engine failure indicates delaying the gear extension until the **field is made**.

3. If an off-airport landing becomes necessary, a decision must be made by the pilot, depending on the terrain, whether to make the landing with the gear up or down.

   a. An emergency landing on a rough surface or a plowed field, or a water ditching, requires gear up.

   b. When an emergency landing is to be made on a hard, smooth surface, the landing gear should be lowered once the landing is assured.

E. Finally, note that most retractable-gear airplanes require you to reduce your airspeed to a particular speed (V_{LO}) prior to lowering the landing gear (similar to slowing down before using flaps). Some airplanes also have a limited speed for retraction. These speeds must be understood, committed to memory, and used during flight operations.

   1. V_{LO} -- maximum speed at which the gear may be operated

      a. This may be two speeds: one for gear extension and one for gear retraction.

   2. V_{LE} -- maximum speed at which you may fly with the gear extended

      a. V_{LE} may be higher than V_{LO}.

      b. On some airplanes, gear doors close again after the gear is extended, resulting in a higher V_{LE}.

OPERATING PRESSURIZATION SYSTEMS

A. **Pressurization** is the process of increasing the airplane cabin pressure to sufficient levels to permit normal breathing while the airplane is flying at high altitudes. Pressurization is available on a limited number of single-engine airplanes. High-altitude flight is desirable to

   1. Get above bad weather
   2. Avoid congested airways
   3. Get a more direct routing
   4. Avoid low-altitude turbulence
   5. Decrease fuel consumption
   6. Increase true airspeed

   NOTE: The latter two occur due to the lower density of air at higher altitudes.

B. For more information on pressurization systems, see Task X.B., Pressurization, beginning on page 270.

FLYING HIGHER-AIRSPEED AIRPLANES

A. Higher performance means an increase in airspeed and climb and descent rates. It is important to plan ahead when operating high-performance airplanes as everything happens more quickly. High-performance airplanes also tend to be much cleaner in configuration; i.e., they may have much less drag. This reduced drag makes it more difficult to slow the airplane and much easier to accelerate.

B. Airspeed is most critical when landing and operating in a traffic pattern. It often becomes necessary to fly a wider traffic pattern, or extend the downwind leg, in order to give the airplane enough room to follow slower airplanes safely. S-turns on final approach, as well as using full flaps and flying the airplane more slowly, are sometimes used to increase spacing. High-performance airplanes require longer runway lengths and stopping distances. It is important to remember that higher gross weight and higher density altitude also affect takeoff and stopping distances. See your *POH* for flight planning purposes.

C. It is a good idea to experiment with your airplane in various configurations during your initial checkout with a CFI. Find out what power settings work for

   1. Traffic pattern entry speed
   2. Approach flap extension
   3. Landing gear extension
   4. Straight and level

      a. Slow cruise
      b. Approach flaps extended
      c. Gear and approach flaps extended

   5. Normal descent

      a. Approach flaps extended
      b. Gear and approach flaps extended
      c. Gear and full flaps extended

   6. Final approach speed

APPENDIX C
FLIGHT AND GROUND TRAINING SYLLABUS

This appendix contains 18 flight training lessons and 12 ground training lessons for the commercial pilot certificate, airplane single-engine land rating, under FAR Part 61.129. The requirements of Part 61.129 are summarized on pages 2 and 3.

The Gleim system focuses on helping you develop "PTS proficiency," with respect to the 43 PTS tasks required by the FAA on your practical test, as quickly and easily as possible.

In developing this syllabus, we had to make some assumptions. You and your CFI are encouraged to make adjustments to the syllabus to meet your requirements. We made the following assumptions:

1. You have an instrument rating; thus, you do NOT need 10 hr. of instrument flight training.

2. You have at least 5 hr. of solo night VFR and at least 10 takeoffs and landings at an airport with an operating control tower during your commercial flight training.

3. You do NOT have a complex airplane logbook endorsement.

    a. If you have a complex airplane logbook endorsement, one or more of the first four flight lessons will not be needed.

    b. Note that 10 hr. of flight training (dual) is required in a complex airplane.

4. You have NOT met the commercial flight training requirement that one day and one night dual VFR cross-country flights be performed.

    a. If you have met the flight training requirements for the day and night VFR cross-country flights, flight lessons 5 and 6 may not be needed.

5. Flight lessons 1 through 4 are designed to provide you with the minimum training for a complex airplane logbook endorsement to act as PIC.

    a. If you are instrument rated, we recommend that you seek the service of a CFII and obtain instrument flight transition training in that complex airplane.

6. Flight lessons 5 and 6 are provided to meet the commercial aeronautical experience for cross-country flight training and to accumulate the 10 hr. of complex airplane training.

    a. Cross-country flight training in a complex airplane is essential in your transition training program.

7. You must decide whether you will use a complex airplane for your entire practical test or use two airplanes: a complex airplane for tasks requiring such an airplane and a primary trainer airplane for the remaining tasks.

    a. Seek the advice of your CFI for the pros and cons of each choice.

Note: This syllabus is designed for pilots with over 200 hours and an instrument rating (see above). Gleim also has a commercial pilot syllabus for pilots who have just completed their instrument training.

The following is a list of the flight and ground lessons:

Flight Training		Ground Training	
Lesson	**Topic**	**Lesson**	**Topic**
1.	Intro to complex airplanes	1.	Airplanes and aerodynamics
2.	Slow flight and stalls	2.	Airplane instruments, engines, and systems
3.	Emergency operations		
4.	Complex airplane review	3.	Airports, ATC, and airspace
5.	Dual cross-country	4.	FARs
6.	Dual night cross-country	5.	Airplane performance and weight and balance
7.	Solo cross-country		
8.	Chandelles, lazy eights, steep turns	6.	Aeromedical factors and ADM
9.	Eights-on-pylons and steep spirals	7.	Aviation weather
10.	Solo practice	8.	Aviation weather services
11.	Review of slow flight and stalls	9.	Navigation
12.	Review of emergency operations	10.	Navigation systems
13.	Solo practice	11.	Flight operations
14.	Maneuvers review	12.	Practice knowledge test
15.	Solo practice		
16.	Maneuvers review		
17.	Solo practice		
18.	Practice practical test		

FLIGHT TRAINING SYLLABUS

The following is a brief description of the parts of each one-page Gleim lesson in this syllabus:

Objective: We open each lesson with an objective, usually a sentence or two, to help you gain perspective and understand the goal for that particular lesson.

Text References: This section tells you which reference books you will need to study or refer to while mastering the tasks within the lesson. Abbreviations are given to facilitate the cross-referencing process.

Content: Each lesson contains a list of the tasks required to be completed before moving to the next lesson. A task may be listed as a "review item" (a task covered in a previous lesson) or as a "new item" (a task introduced to you for the first time). Each task is preceded by three blank "checkoff" boxes which may be used by your CFI to keep track of your progress and to indicate that each task was completed.

There are three boxes because it may take more than one flight to complete the lesson. Your CFI may mark the box(es) next to each task in one of the following methods (or any other method desired):

✓ - task completed to lesson completion standards	D - demonstrated by CFI A - accomplished by you S - safe/satisfactory P - meets PTS standards	1 - above lesson standard 2 - meets lesson standard 3 - below lesson standard

Most tasks are followed by book and page references that tell you exactly where to find the information you need to accomplish the task successfully.

Completion Standards: Based on these standards, your CFI determines how well you have met the objective of the lesson in terms of knowledge and skill.

Notes: Space is provided for your CFI's critique of the lesson, which you can refer to later. You CFI may also write any specific assignment for the next lesson. Additionally, you can write any questions you may have for your CFI.

FLIGHT LESSON 1: Introduction to Complex Airplanes

Objective

To familiarize the student with the complex airplane, its operating characteristics, the cockpit controls, and the instruments and systems. The student will be introduced to preflight and postflight procedures, the use of checklists, and the safety precautions to be followed.

Text References

Commercial Pilot Flight Maneuvers and Practical Test Prep (FM)

Pilot Handbook (PH)

Pilot's Operating Handbook (POH)

Content

1. Preflight briefing
2. New items

    ☐☐☐ Use of checklists - CFI

    ☐☐☐ Preflight inspection - FM 87-92; POH-4

        ☐☐☐ Airplane servicing - CFI

    ☐☐☐ Location of emergency equipment and survival gear - CFI

    ☐☐☐ Airplane systems - POH-7; CFI

    ☐☐☐ Engine starting - FM 97-101; POH-4

    ☐☐☐ Taxiing - FM 102-105

    ☐☐☐ Before-takeoff check - FM 106-109; POH-4

    ☐☐☐ Normal and crosswind takeoff and climb - FM 132-139; POH-4

    ☐☐☐ Collision avoidance procedures - FM 107-108; PH 134-135

    ☐☐☐ Traffic patterns - FM 114-121; PH 126-127

    ☐☐☐ Normal and crosswind approach and landing - FM 140-155; POH-4

    ☐☐☐ After-landing procedures - FM 278-281; POH-4

    ☐☐☐ Parking and securing the airplane - FM 278-281; POH-4

3. Postflight critique and preview of next lesson

Completion Standards

The lesson will have been successfully completed when the student displays an understanding of the airplane's systems, the use of checklists, preflight procedures, and postflight procedures.

Notes:

FLIGHT LESSON 2: Slow Flight and Stalls

Objective

To improve the student's proficiency in the operation of a complex airplane and to introduce slow flight, stalls, short-field takeoffs and landings, and power-off 180° accuracy approach and landings.

Text References

Commercial Pilot Flight Maneuvers and Practical Test Prep (FM)

Pilot Handbook (PH)

Pilot's Operating Handbook (POH)

Content

1. Preflight briefing
2. Review items

    ☐☐☐ Use of checklists - CFI
    ☐☐☐ Airplane systems - FM 75-79; PH 55-104; POH-7
    ☐☐☐ Preflight inspection - FM 87-92
    ☐☐☐ Engine starting - FM 97-101; POH-4
    ☐☐☐ Taxiing - FM 102-105
    ☐☐☐ Traffic patterns - FM 114-121; PH 126-127
    ☐☐☐ Postflight procedures - FM 278-281

3. New items

    ☐☐☐ Short-field takeoff and climb - FM 167-173; POH-4
    ☐☐☐ Maneuvering during slow flight - FM 235-239; PH 29
    ☐☐☐ Power-off stalls (entered from straight flight and turns) - FM 240-244; PH 48-52
    ☐☐☐ Power-on stalls (entered from straight flight and turns) - FM 245-249; PH 48-52
    ☐☐☐ Spin awareness - FM 250-252; PH 52-54; POH-3
    ☐☐☐ Short-field approach and landing - FM 174-179; POH-4
    ☐☐☐ Power-off 180° accuracy approach and landing - FM 180-188

4. Postflight critique and preview of next lesson

Completion Standards

The lesson will have been successfully completed when the student displays an increased proficiency in the operation of a complex airplane by maintaining altitude, ±100 ft.; heading, ±15°; and airspeed, ±10 kt. During this and subsequent flights, the student will perform the preflight inspection, engine starting, taxiing, the before-takeoff check, and the postflight procedures without instructor assistance. Finally, the student will display an understanding of maneuvering during slow flight, the indications of an approaching stall, the proper recovery procedures, and the conditions necessary for a spin to occur.

Notes:

FLIGHT LESSON 3: Emergency Operations

Objective

To improve the student's proficiency in the operation of a complex airplane and to introduce emergency operations; go-around procedures; and soft-field takeoffs and landings.

Text References

Commercial Pilot Flight Maneuvers and Practical Test Prep (FM)

Pilot Handbook (PH)

Pilot's Operating Handbook (POH)

Content

1. Preflight briefing
2. Review items

   ☐☐☐ Airplane systems - FM 75-79; PH 55-104; POH-7
   ☐☐☐ Short-field takeoff and climb - FM 167-173 ; POH-4
   ☐☐☐ Short-field approach and landing - FM 174-179; POH-4
   ☐☐☐ Power-off 180° accuracy approach and landing - FM 180-188
   ☐☐☐ Maneuvering during slow flight - FM 235-239; PH 29
   ☐☐☐ Power-off stalls - FM 240-244; PH 48-52
   ☐☐☐ Power-on stalls - FM 245-249; PH 48-52

   ---

3. New items

   ☐☐☐ Soft-field takeoff and climb - FM 156-161; POH-4
   ☐☐☐ Soft-field approach and landing - FM 162-166; POH-4
   ☐☐☐ Go-around - FM 189-193; POH-4
   ☐☐☐ Emergency descent - CFI; POH-3
   ☐☐☐ Emergency approach and landing - FM 255-261; POH-3
   ☐☐☐ Systems and equipment malfunctions - FM 262-263; POH-3

       ☐☐☐ Emergency gear extension - POH-3
       ☐☐☐ Propeller overspeed - POH-3

   ☐☐☐ Emergencies during takeoff roll, initial climb, cruise, descent, and in the traffic pattern - FM 108; POH-3

4. Postflight critique and preview of next lesson

Completion Standards

The lesson will have been successfully completed when the student displays proficiency in short-field takeoffs and landings, power-off 180° accuracy approaches and landings, slow flight, and recovery from stalls. Additionally, the student will display an understanding of the emergency procedures, go-around procedures, and soft-field takeoffs and landings. The student will maintain altitude, ±100 ft.; airspeed, ±10 kt.; and heading, ±15°.

Notes:

FLIGHT LESSON 4: Complex Airplane Review

Objective

To review previous lessons so that the student can gain proficiency and demonstrate the necessary skills to act as pilot in command of a complex airplane.

Text References

Commercial Pilot Flight Maneuvers and Practical Test Prep (FM)

Pilot Handbook (PH)

Pilot's Operating Handbook (POH)

Content

1. Preflight briefing
2. Review items

- ☐☐☐ Airplane systems - FM 75-79 ; PH 55-104; POH-7
- ☐☐☐ Normal takeoff and landing - FM 132-139; POH-4
- ☐☐☐ Soft-field takeoff and landing - FM 156-166; POH-4
- ☐☐☐ Short-field takeoff and landing - FM 167-179; POH-4
- ☐☐☐ Go-around - FM 189-193; POH-4
- ☐☐☐ Maneuvering during slow flight - FM 235-239; PH 29
- ☐☐☐ Power-off stall - FM 240-244; PH 48-52
- ☐☐☐ Power-on stall - FM 245-249; PH 48-52
- ☐☐☐ Emergency descent - CFI; POH-3
- ☐☐☐ Emergency approach and landing - FM 255-261; POH-3
- ☐☐☐ Systems and equipment malfunctions - FM 262-263; POH-3

  - ☐☐☐ Emergency gear extension - POH-3
  - ☐☐☐ Propeller overspeed - POH-3

- ☐☐☐ Traffic patterns - FM 114-121; PH 126-127

3. Postflight critique and preview of next lesson

☐ Instructor will endorse student's logbook for complex airplanes and high-performance airplanes, if appropriate.

Completion Standards

The lesson will have been successfully completed when the student demonstrates proficiency in the operation of a complex airplane as a pilot in command. The student will maintain altitude, ±100 ft.; airspeed, ±10 kt.; and heading, ±10°. The instructor will endorse the student's logbook to certify the student is proficient to operate a complex airplane. If the complex airplane has an engine of more than 200 horsepower, then the instructor will make an additional endorsement that the student is proficient to operate a high-performance airplane.

Notes:

FLIGHT LESSON 5: Dual Cross-Country

Objective

To introduce the student to cross-country procedures in a complex airplane. This flight must be at least 2 hr. in day VFR conditions, consisting of a total straight-line distance of more than 100 NM from the original departure point.

Text References

Commercial Pilot Flight Maneuvers and Practical Test Prep (FM)

Pilot Handbook (PH)

Pilot's Operating Handbook (POH)

Sectional chart

Airport/Facility Directory (A/FD)

Content

1. Preflight briefing
2. Review items

☐☐☐ Aeronautical charts - PH 343-352
☐☐☐ *Airport/Facility Directory*, Notice to Airmen
   (NOTAM), and other publications -
   PH 352-359
☐☐☐ National airspace system - FM 65-70
☐☐☐ Route selection - FM 62-64; PH 413-414
☐☐☐ Navigation log - PH 428
☐☐☐ Obtaining weather information - FM 50-67;
   PH 303-342
☐☐☐ Determining performance and limitations -
   FM 71-74; PH 235-251; POH-2, 5
☐☐☐ Weight and balance computations -
   PH 252-263; POH-6
☐☐☐ Cockpit management - FM 93-96
☐☐☐ Aeromedical factors - FM 80-85; PH 265-277
☐☐☐ Filing a VFR flight plan - PH 418-420

☐☐☐ Soft-field takeoffs and landings - FM 156-166;
   POH-4
☐☐☐ Course interception - FM 223-226
☐☐☐ Open VFR flight plan - CFI
☐☐☐ Pilotage & dead reckoning - FM 223-226; PH 421
☐☐☐ Navigation system(s) - FM 227-228; PH 387-412
☐☐☐ ATC radar services - FM 227-228; PH 146-151
☐☐☐ Computing groundspeed, ETA, and fuel
   consumption - PH 363-369
☐☐☐ Lost procedures - FM 232-234; PH 424-426
☐☐☐ Diversion to alternate airport - FM 229-231;
   PH 422-423
☐☐☐ Closing a VFR flight plan - PH 420

3. New items

☐☐☐ Supplemental oxygen - FM 268-269
☐☐☐ Pressurization (if appropriate) - FM 270-276
☐☐☐ Setting power and fuel mixture - POH-4, 5
☐☐☐ Profile planning (departure, cruise, descent) - CFI

4. Postflight critique and preview of next lesson

Completion Standards

This lesson will have been successfully completed when the student is able to perform the cross-country flight, planning and flying the planned course and computing groundspeed, ETA, and fuel consumption. The student will display the ability to navigate by means of pilotage and dead reckoning and by any other navigation systems. Additionally, the student will perform lost procedures and a diversion to an alternate airport. The student will maintain the appropriate altitude, ±100 ft., and heading, ±10°; arrive at the en route checkpoints or destination, ±3 min. of ETA; and verify the airplane's position within 1 NM of the flight plan route at all times.

Notes:

FLIGHT LESSON 6: Dual Night Cross-Country

Objective

To increase the student's proficiency in planning and flying a night cross-country flight in a complex airplane. The flight must be at least 2 hr. in night VFR conditions, consisting of a total straight-line distance of more than 100 NM from the original point of departure.

Text References

Commercial Pilot Flight Maneuvers and Practical Test Prep (FM)

Pilot Handbook (PH)

Pilot's Operating Handbook (POH)

Sectional chart

Airport/Facility Directory (A/FD)

Content

1. Preflight briefing
2. Review items

    ☐☐☐ Aeromedical factors - FM 80-85; PH 273-277
    ☐☐☐ Personal equipment and preparation - CFI
    ☐☐☐ Obtaining weather information - FM 50-61; PH 303-342
    ☐☐☐ Determining performance and limitations - FM 71-74; PH 235-251; POH-2, 4, 5, 6
    ☐☐☐ Route selection - FM 62-64
    ☐☐☐ Night VFR fuel requirements (FAR 91.151) - PH 209
    ☐☐☐ Short-field takeoffs and landings - FM 167-179
    ☐☐☐ Go-around - FM 189-193
    ☐☐☐ Collision avoidance procedures - FM 114-115; PH 134-135
    ☐☐☐ Pilotage and dead reckoning - FM 223-226; PH 421
    ☐☐☐ Navigation systems - FM 227-228; PH 387-412
    ☐☐☐ ATC radar services - FM 227-228; PH 146-151
    ☐☐☐ Lost procedures - FM 232-234; PH 424-426
    ☐☐☐ Diversion to an alternate airport - FM 229-231; PH 422-423

3. Postflight critique and preview of next lesson

Completion Standards

The lesson will have been successfully completed when the student demonstrates commercial pilot proficiency in the planning and flying of a night cross-country flight. The student will maintain altitude, ±100 ft., and heading, ±10°. At the completion of this lesson, the student will have met the dual cross-country aeronautical experience requirements for a commercial pilot certificate.

Notes:

FLIGHT LESSON 7: Solo Cross-Country

Objective

To increase the student's proficiency in cross-country procedures. This cross-country flight must not be less than 300 NM total distance, with landings at a minimum of three points, one of which is a straight-line distance of at least 250 NM from the original departure point. In Hawaii, the longest segment must have a straight-line distance of at least 150 NM.

Text References

Commercial Pilot Flight Maneuvers and Practical Test Prep (FM)

Pilot Handbook (PH)

Pilot's Operating Handbook (POH)

Aeronautical charts and publications

Content

1. Preflight briefing

   ☐☐☐ Instructor ensures that the planned flight meets the requirements

2. Review items

   ☐☐☐ Obtaining weather information - FM 50-61; PH 303-342
   ☐☐☐ Cross-country flight planning - FM 62-64; PH 413-428
   ☐☐☐ Determining performance and limitations - FM 71-74; PH 235-251; POH-2, 4, 5, 6
   ☐☐☐ Pilotage and dead reckoning - FM 223-226; PH 421
   ☐☐☐ Navigation systems and ATC radar services - FM 227-228; PH 146-151, 387-412
   ☐☐☐ Computing groundspeed, ETAs, and fuel consumption - PH 363-369
   ☐☐☐ Short-field takeoffs and landings - FM 167-179
   ☐☐☐ Power-off 180° accuracy approach and landing - FM 180-188
   ☐☐☐ Soft-field takeoffs and landings - FM 156-166

3. Postflight critique and preview of next lesson

Completion Standards

The lesson will have been successfully completed when the student completes this cross-country flight as planned.

Notes:

FLIGHT LESSON 8: Chandelles, Lazy Eights, and Steep Turns

Objective

To introduce the student to chandelles, lazy eights, and steep turns.

Text References

Commercial Pilot Flight Maneuvers and Practical Test Prep (FM)

Pilot Handbook (PH)

Pilot's Operating Handbook (POH)

Content

1. Preflight briefing
2. Review items

    ☐☐☐ Soft-field takeoffs and landings - FM 156-166; POH-4
    ☐☐☐ Go-around - FM 189-193; POH-4
    ☐☐☐ Wake turbulence avoidance - FM 115-116; PH 127-133

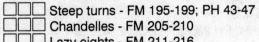

3. New items

    ☐☐☐ Steep turns - FM 195-199; PH 43-47
    ☐☐☐ Chandelles - FM 205-210
    ☐☐☐ Lazy eights - FM 211-216

4. Postflight critique and preview of next lesson

Completion Standards

The lesson will have been successfully completed when the student demonstrates the proper entry procedures and understands the control techniques required for steep turns, chandelles, and lazy eights. Additionally, the student will demonstrate increased proficiency in soft-field takeoffs and landings and go-around procedures.

Notes:

FLIGHT LESSON 9: Eights-on-Pylons and Steep Spirals

Objective

To review previous lessons to gain proficiency and to introduce the student to eights-on-pylons and steep spirals.

Text References

Commercial Pilot Flight Maneuvers and Practical Test Prep (FM)

Pilot Handbook (PH)

Pilot's Operating Handbook (POH)

Content

1. Preflight briefing
2. Review items

    ☐☐☐ Short-field takeoffs and landings - FM 167-179; POH-4
    ☐☐☐ Steep turns - FM 195-199; PH 43-45
    ☐☐☐ Chandelles - FM 205-210
    ☐☐☐ Lazy eights - FM 211-216
    ☐☐☐ Emergency descent - POH-3
    ☐☐☐ Emergency approach and landing - FM 255-261; POH-3

    _____

3. New items

    ☐☐☐ Steep spirals - FM 200-204
    ☐☐☐ Eights-on-pylons - FM 217-222

4. Postflight critique and preview of next lesson

Completion Standards

The lesson will have been successfully completed when the student understands the proper entry procedure of both eights-on-pylons and steep spirals, and understands how to keep the line-of-sight reference line correctly on the pylon during the performance of eights-on-pylons. The student will also demonstrate increased proficiency in steep turns, chandelles, lazy eights, and emergency procedures.

Notes:

FLIGHT LESSON 10: Solo Practice

Objective

To develop the student's confidence and proficiency through solo practice of the assigned maneuvers.

Text References

Commercial Pilot Flight Maneuvers and Practical Test Prep (FM)

Pilot Handbook (PH)

Pilot's Operating Handbook (POH)

Content

1. Preflight briefing
2. Review items

    □□□ Soft-field takeoffs and landings - FM 156-166; POH-4
    □□□ Short-field takeoffs and landings - FM 167-179; POH-4
    □□□ Power-off 180° accuracy approach and landing - FM 180-188
    □□□ Traffic patterns - FM 114-121; PH 126-127
    □□□ Collision avoidance procedures - PH 134-135
    □□□ Steep turns - FM 195-199; PH 43-47
    □□□ Chandelles - FM 205-210
    □□□ Lazy eights - FM 211-216
    □□□ Eights-on-pylons - FM 217-222
    □□□ Steep spirals - FM 200-204
    □□□ Postflight procedures - FM 278-281; POH-4

3. Postflight critique and preview of next lesson

Completion Standards

The lesson will have been successfully completed when the student completes the listed maneuvers assigned for the solo flight. The student will gain confidence and proficiency as a result of the solo practice.

Notes:

FLIGHT LESSON 11: Review of Slow Flight and Stalls

Objective

To increase the student's proficiency in the flight maneuvers with emphasis on slow flight and stalls.

Text References

Commercial Pilot Flight Maneuvers and Practical Test Prep (FM)

Pilot Handbook (PH)

Pilot's Operating Handbook (POH)

Content

1. Preflight briefing
2. Review items

   ☐☐☐ Soft-field takeoffs and landings - FM 156-166; POH-4
   ☐☐☐ Maneuvering during slow flight - FM 235-239; PH 29
   ☐☐☐ Power-off stalls - FM 240-244; PH 48-52
   ☐☐☐ Power-on stalls - FM 245-249; PH 48-52
   ☐☐☐ Spin awareness - FM 250-252; PH 52-54; POH-3
   ☐☐☐ Chandelles - FM 205-210
   ☐☐☐ Lazy eights - FM 211-216
   ☐☐☐ Traffic patterns - FM 114-121; PH 126-127
   ☐☐☐ Wake turbulence avoidance - FM 115-116; PH 127-133

3. Postflight critique and preview of next lesson

Completion Standards

The lesson will have been successfully completed when the student demonstrates increased proficiency while performing the maneuvers. The student will maintain the desired altitude, ±100 ft.; airspeed, ±10 kt. (except (s)he will maintain V_Y on takeoff, ±5 kt., and the approach airspeed, ±5 kt.); and heading, ±10°.

Notes:

FLIGHT LESSON 12: Review of Emergency Operations

Objective

To increase the student's proficiency in the flight maneuvers with emphasis on emergency operations.

Text References

Commercial Pilot Flight Maneuvers and Practical Test Prep (FM)

Pilot Handbook (PH)

Pilot's Operating Handbook (POH)

Content

1. Preflight briefing
2. Review items

    ☐☐☐ Short-field takeoffs and landings - FM 167-179; POH-4
    ☐☐☐ Power-off 180° accuracy approach and landing - FM 180-188
    ☐☐☐ Emergency descent - CFI; POH-3
    ☐☐☐ Emergency approach and landing - FM 255-261; POH-3
    ☐☐☐ Systems and equipment malfunctions - FM 262-263; POH-3
    ☐☐☐ Eights-on-pylons - FM 217-222
    ☐☐☐ Steep spirals - FM 200-204
    ☐☐☐ Chandelles - FM 205-210
    ☐☐☐ Lazy eights - FM 211-216
    ☐☐☐ Power-off stall - FM 240-244; PH 48-52
    ☐☐☐ Power-on stall - FM 245-249; PH 48-52
    ☐☐☐ Go-around - FM 189-193; POH-4

3. Postflight critique and preview of next lesson

Completion Standards

The lesson will have been successfully completed when the student demonstrates increased proficiency while performing the maneuvers. The student will maintain the desired altitude, ±100 ft.; heading, ±10°; and airspeed, ±10 kt. (except (s)he will maintain V_X, +5/-0 kt., and V_Y, ±5 kt.).

Notes:

FLIGHT LESSON 13: Solo Practice

Objective

To further develop the student's proficiency through solo practice of assigned maneuvers.

Text References

Commercial Pilot Flight Maneuvers and Practical Test Prep (FM)

Pilot Handbook (PH)

Pilot's Operating Handbook (POH)

Content

1. Preflight briefing
2. Review items

    ☐☐☐ Soft-field takeoffs and landings - FM 156-166; POH-4
    ☐☐☐ Short-field takeoffs and landings - FM 167-179; POH-4
    ☐☐☐ Power-off 180° accuracy approach and landing - FM 180-188
    ☐☐☐ Steep turns - FM 195-199; PH 43-47
    ☐☐☐ Chandelles - FM 205-210
    ☐☐☐ Lazy eights - FM 211-216
    ☐☐☐ Eights-on-pylons - FM 217-222
    ☐☐☐ Steep spirals - FM 200-204
    ☐☐☐ Maneuvering during slow flight - FM 235-239; PH 29
    ☐☐☐ Power-off stalls - FM 240-244; PH 48-52
    ☐☐☐ Power-on stalls - FM 245-249; PH 48-52

3. Postflight critique and preview of next lesson

Completion Standards

The lesson will have been successfully completed when the student completes the assigned maneuvers. The student will gain confidence and improve performance as a result of the solo practice period.

Notes:

FLIGHT LESSON 14: Maneuvers Review

Objective

To determine the student's proficiency level in the maneuvers and procedures covered previously.

Text References

Commercial Pilot Flight Maneuvers and Practical Test Prep (FM)

Pilot Handbook (PH)

Pilot's Operating Handbook (POH)

Content

1. Preflight briefing
2. Review items

 ☐☐☐ Certificates and documents - FM 41-49
 ☐☐☐ Operation of systems - FM 75-79; PH 14-21, 55-104; POH-7
 ☐☐☐ Preflight inspection - FM 87-92; POH-4
 ☐☐☐ Cockpit management - FM 93-96
 ☐☐☐ Engine starting - FM 97-107; POH-4
 ☐☐☐ Radio communications and ATC light signals - FM 111-113; PH 135-145
 ☐☐☐ Airport, runway, and taxiway signs, markings, and lighting - FM 122-130; PH 105-125
 ☐☐☐ Taxiing - FM 102-105
 ☐☐☐ Before-takeoff check - FM 106-109; POH-4
 ☐☐☐ Soft-field takeoff and climb - FM 156-161; POH-4
 ☐☐☐ Steep turns - FM 195-199; PH 43-47
 ☐☐☐ Chandelles - FM 205-210
 ☐☐☐ Lazy eights - FM 211-216
 ☐☐☐ Maneuvering during slow flight - FM 235-239; PH 29
 ☐☐☐ Power-off stalls - FM 240-244; PH 48-52
 ☐☐☐ Power-on stalls - FM 245-249; PH 48-52
 ☐☐☐ Spin awareness - FM 250-252; PH 52-54; POH-3
 ☐☐☐ Traffic patterns - FM 114-121; PH 126-127
 ☐☐☐ Soft-field approach and landing - FM 162-166; POH-4
 ☐☐☐ Go-around - FM 189-193; POH-4
 ☐☐☐ After-landing procedures - FM 278-281; POH-4
 ☐☐☐ Parking and securing the airplane - FM 278-281; POH-4

3. Postflight critique and preview of next lesson

Completion Standards

The lesson will have been successfully completed when the student demonstrates improved proficiency in the various tasks given. The student will maintain the altitude, airspeed, and heading standards specified for the appropriate task in the current FAA *Commercial Pilot Practical Test Standards*.

Notes:

FLIGHT LESSON 15: Solo Practice

Objective

To further develop the student's proficiency through solo practice of assigned maneuvers.

Text References

Commercial Pilot Flight Maneuvers and Practical Test Prep (FM)

Pilot Handbook (PH)

Pilot's Operating Handbook (POH)

Content

1. Preflight briefing
2. Review items

   ☐☐☐ Soft-field takeoffs and landings - FM 156-166; POH-4
   ☐☐☐ Traffic patterns - FM 114-121; PH 126-127
   ☐☐☐ Steep turns - FM 195-199; PH 43-47
   ☐☐☐ Chandelles - FM 205-210
   ☐☐☐ Lazy eights - FM 211-216
   ☐☐☐ Eights-on-pylons - FM 217-222
   ☐☐☐ Steep spirals - FM 200-204
   ☐☐☐ Maneuvering during slow flight - FM 235-239; PH 29
   ☐☐☐ Power-off stalls - FM 240-244; PH 48-52
   ☐☐☐ Power-on stalls - FM 245-249; PH 48-52

3. Postflight critique and preview of next lesson

Completion Standards

The lesson will have been successfully completed when the student completes the assigned maneuvers. The student will gain confidence and improve performance as a result of the solo practice period.

Notes:

FLIGHT LESSON 16: Maneuvers Review

Objective

To develop improved performance and proficiency in the procedures and maneuvers covered previously.

Text References

Commercial Pilot Flight Maneuvers and Practical Test Prep (FM)

Pilot Handbook (PH)

Pilot's Operating Handbook (POH)

Content

1. Preflight briefing
2. Review items

   ☐☐☐ Short-field takeoff and climb - FM 167-173; POH-4
   ☐☐☐ Cross-country procedures - FM 62-64, 199-210
   ☐☐☐ High-altitude operations - FM 267-276
   ☐☐☐ Emergency descent - CFI; POH-3
   ☐☐☐ Emergency approach and landing - FM 255-261; POH-3
   ☐☐☐ Systems and equipment malfunctions - FM 262-263; POH-3
   ☐☐☐ Steep turns - FM 195-199; PH 43-47
   ☐☐☐ Chandelles - FM 205-210
   ☐☐☐ Lazy eights - FM 211-216
   ☐☐☐ Eights-on-pylons - FM 217-222
   ☐☐☐ Steep spirals - FM 200-204
   ☐☐☐ Short-field approach and landing - FM 174-179; POH-4
   ☐☐☐ Power-off 180° accuracy approach and landing - FM 180-188
   ☐☐☐ Go-around - FM 189-193; POH-4
   ☐☐☐ Postflight procedures - FM 278-281; POH-4

3. Postflight critique and preview of next lesson

Completion Standards

The lesson will have been successfully completed when the student demonstrates improved proficiency in the maneuvers and procedures given. The student will complete each task to the standards specified in the current FAA *Commercial Pilot Practical Test Standards*.

Notes:

FLIGHT LESSON 17: Solo Practice

Objective

To further develop the student's proficiency of assigned maneuvers through solo practice.

Text References

Commercial Pilot Flight Maneuvers and Practical Test Prep (FM)

Pilot Handbook (PH)

Pilot's Operating Handbook (POH)

Content

1. Preflight briefing
2. Review items

   ☐☐☐ Soft-field takeoffs and landings - FM 156-166; POH-4
   ☐☐☐ Short-field takeoffs and landings - FM 167-179; POH-4
   ☐☐☐ Steep turns - FM 195-199; PH 43-47
   ☐☐☐ Chandelles - FM 205-210
   ☐☐☐ Lazy eights - FM 211-216
   ☐☐☐ Eights-on-pylons - FM 217-222
   ☐☐☐ Steep spirals - FM 200-204
   ☐☐☐ Maneuvering during slow flight - FM 235-239; PH 29
   ☐☐☐ Power-off stalls - FM 240-244; PH 48-52
   ☐☐☐ Power-on stalls - FM 245-249; PH 48-52
   ☐☐☐ Maneuvers as assigned by the instructor - CFI

3. Postflight critique and preview of next lesson

Completion Standards

The lesson will have been successfully completed when the student completes the assigned maneuvers. The student will gain confidence and proficiency as a result of this practice period.

Notes:

FLIGHT LESSON 18: Practice Practical Test

Objective

The student will be able to demonstrate the required proficiency of a commercial pilot by utilizing the current FAA *Commercial Pilot Practical Test Standards*. A complex airplane must be used for all takeoffs, landings, and appropriate emergency procedures.

Text References

Commercial Pilot Flight Maneuvers and Practical Test Prep (FM)

Pilot Handbook (PH)

Pilot's Operating Handbook (POH)

Content

1. Commercial Pilot Practical Test tasks

☐☐☐ Certificates and documents - FM 41-49
☐☐☐ Obtaining weather information - FM 50-61; PH 303-342
☐☐☐ Cross-country flight planning - FM 62-64
☐☐☐ National airspace system - FM 65-70
☐☐☐ Performance and limitations - FM 71-74
☐☐☐ Operation of systems - FM 75-79; PH 55-104; POH-7
☐☐☐ Aeromedical factors - FM 80-85
☐☐☐ Physiological aspects of night flying - CFI
☐☐☐ Lighting and equipment for night flying - CFI
☐☐☐ Preflight inspection - FM 87-92
☐☐☐ Cockpit management - FM 93-96
☐☐☐ Engine starting - FM 97-101
☐☐☐ Taxiing - FM 102-105
☐☐☐ Before-takeoff check - FM 106-109
☐☐☐ Radio communications and ATC light signals - FM 111-113
☐☐☐ Traffic patterns - FM 114-121
☐☐☐ Airport, runway, and taxiway signs, markings, and lighting - FM 122-130; PH 105-125
☐☐☐ Normal and crosswind takeoff and climb - FM 132-139
☐☐☐ Soft-field takeoff and climb - FM 156-161
☐☐☐ Short-field takeoff and climb - FM 167-173

☐☐☐ Pilotage and dead reckoning - FM 223-226
☐☐☐ Navigation systems and ATC radar services - FM 227-228
☐☐☐ Diversion - FM 229-231
☐☐☐ Lost procedure - FM 232-234
☐☐☐ Steep turns - FM 195-199
☐☐☐ Chandelles - FM 205-210
☐☐☐ Lazy eights - FM 211-216
☐☐☐ Eights-on-pylons - FM 217-222
☐☐☐ Steep spirals - FM 200-204
☐☐☐ Maneuvering during slow flight - FM 235-239
☐☐☐ Power-off stalls - FM 240-244
☐☐☐ Power-on stalls - FM 245-249
☐☐☐ Spin awareness - FM 250-252
☐☐☐ Emergency descent - CFI
☐☐☐ Emergency approach and landing - FM 255-261
☐☐☐ Systems and equipment malfunctions - FM 262-263
☐☐☐ Emergency equipment and survival gear - FM 264-265
☐☐☐ Supplemental oxygen - FM 268-269
☐☐☐ Pressurization (if appropriate) - FM 270-276
☐☐☐ Normal and crosswind approach and landing - FM 140-155
☐☐☐ Soft-field approach and landing - FM 162-166
☐☐☐ Short-field approach and landing - FM 174-179
☐☐☐ Power-off 180° accuracy approach and landing - FM 180-188
☐☐☐ Go-around - FM 189-193
☐☐☐ After-landing procedures - FM 278-281
☐☐☐ Parking and securing the airplane - FM 278-281

2. Postflight critique

Completion Standards

The lesson will have been successfully completed when the student demonstrates the required level of proficiency in all tasks of the current FAA *Commercial Pilot Practical Test Standards*. The instructor will assist the student in completing the Airman Certificate and/or Rating Application (FAA Form 8710-1), sign the back of FAA Form 8710-1, and make the necessary logbook endorsements in the student's logbook.

Notes:

GROUND TRAINING SYLLABUS

The following ground training lessons are based on the chapters of Gleim's *Commercial Pilot FAA Written Exam* book, with the modules of each chapter comprising the contents of a lesson. Use *Pilot Handbook* to supplement your study.

GROUND LESSON 1: Airplanes and Aerodynamics

Objective:

To further develop the student's knowledge of aerodynamics to ensure a complete understanding of the various factors affecting flight.

Text References:

Commercial Pilot FAA Written Exam, Chapter 1, Airplanes and Aerodynamics
Pilot Handbook, Chapter 1, Airplanes and Aerodynamics

Content:

Flaps	Ground Effect
Airplane Wings	Airplane Stability
Stalls	Turns
Spins	Load Factor
Lift and Drag	

Completion Standards:

The lesson will be complete when the student can answer the 61 FAA questions in Chapter 1, Airplanes and Aerodynamics, of *Commercial Pilot FAA Written Exam* and/or *FAA Test Prep* software with a minimum passing grade of 70%.

GROUND LESSON 2: Airplane Instruments, Engines, and Systems

Objective:

To further develop the student's understanding of airplane instruments, engines, and systems.

Text References:

Commercial Pilot FAA Written Exam, Chapter 2, Airplane Instruments, Engines, and Systems
Pilot Handbook, Chapter 2, Airplane Instruments, Engines, and Systems

Content:

Magnetic Compass	Detonation and Preignition
Airspeed Indicator	Airplane Ignition Systems
Turn Coordinator/Turn-and-Slip Indicator	Engine Cooling
Fuel/Air Mixture	Airplane Propellers
Carburetor Heat	

Completion Standards:

The lesson will be complete when the student can answer the 45 FAA questions in Chapter 2, Airplane Instruments, Engines, and Systems, of *Commercial Pilot FAA Written Exam* and/or *FAA Test Prep* software with a minimum passing grade of 70%.

GROUND LESSON 3: Airports, Air Traffic Control, and Airspace

Objective:

To ensure the student's understanding of airspace, air traffic control, and airports.

Text References:

Commercial Pilot FAA Written Exam, Chapter 3, Airports, Air Traffic Control, and Airspace
Pilot Handbook, Chapter 3, Airports, Air Traffic Control, and Airspace

Content:

Airspace
VHF/DF
Airport Signs
Collision Avoidance
Wake Turbulence
Land and Hold Short Operations (LAHSO)

Completion Standards:

The lesson will be complete when the student can answer the 39 FAA questions in Chapter 3, Airports, Air Traffic Control, and Airspace, of *Commercial Pilot FAA Written Exam* and/or *FAA Test Prep* software with a minimum passing grade of 70%.

GROUND LESSON 4: Federal Aviation Regulations

Objective:

To develop the student's understanding of FAR Parts 1, 23, 61, and 91 and the accident reporting requirements of NTSB Part 830.

Text References:

Commercial Pilot FAA Written Exam, Chapter 4, Federal Aviation Regulations
Pilot Handbook, Chapter 4, Federal Aviation Regulations

Content:

FAR Part 1
FAR Part 23
FAR Part 61

FAR Part 91
NTSB Part 830

Completion Standards:

The lesson will be complete when the student can answer the 126 FAA questions in Chapter 4, Federal Aviation Regulations, of *Commercial Pilot FAA Written Exam* and/or *FAA Test Prep* software with a minimum passing grade of 70%.

GROUND LESSON 5: Airplane Performance and Weight and Balance

Objective:

To ensure the student's understanding of calculating airplane performance, including weight and balance.

Text References:

Commercial Pilot FAA Written Exam, Chapter 5, Airplane Performance and Weight and Balance
Pilot Handbook, Chapter 5, Airplane Performance and Weight and Balance

Content:

Density Altitude
Density Altitude Computations
Takeoff Distance
Time, Fuel, and Distance to Climb
Maximum Rate of Climb
Cruise and Range Performance

Crosswind/Headwind Component
Landing Distance
Weight and Balance
Weight and Moment Computations
Weight Change and Weight Shift Computations

Completion Standards:

The lesson will be complete when the student can answer the 63 FAA questions in Chapter 5, Airplane Performance and Weight and Balance, of *Commercial Pilot FAA Written Exam* and/or *FAA Test Prep* software with a minimum passing grade of 70%.

GROUND LESSON 6: Aeromedical Factors and Aeronautical Decision Making

Objective:

To further develop the student's understanding of the aeromedical factors related to flight and to the aeronautical decision making (ADM) process.

Text References:

Commercial Pilot FAA Written Exam, Chapter 6, Aeromedical Factors and Aeronautical Decision Making (ADM)
Pilot Handbook, Chapter 6, Aeromedical Factors and Aeronautical Decision Making

Content:

Hypoxia and Alcohol
Hyperventilation
Spatial Disorientation
Pilot Vision
Aeronautical Decision Making (ADM)

Completion Standards:

The lesson will be complete when the student can answer the 32 FAA questions in Chapter 6, Aeromedical Factors and Aeronautical Decision Making (ADM), of *Commercial Pilot FAA Written Exam* and/or *FAA Test Prep* software with a minimum passing grade of 70%.

GROUND LESSON 7: Aviation Weather

Objective:

To further develop the student's understanding of the fundamentals of weather, as associated with the operation of an airplane.

Text References:

Commercial Pilot FAA Written Exam, Chapter 7, Aviation Weather
Pilot Handbook, Chapter 7, Aviation Weather

Content:

Causes of Weather	Fog
High/Low Pressure Areas	Stability
Jet Stream	Thunderstorms and Icing
Temperature	Turbulence
Clouds	Wind Shear

Completion Standards:

The lesson will be complete when the student can answer the 92 FAA questions in Chapter 7, Aviation Weather, of *Commercial Pilot FAA Written Exam* and/or *FAA Test Prep* software with a minimum passing grade of 70%.

GROUND LESSON 8: Aviation Weather Services

Objective:

To further develop the student's ability to interpret and use weather charts, reports, and forecasts. Additionally, the student will develop an understanding of high-altitude weather and associated charts and forecasts.

Text References:

Commercial Pilot FAA Written Exam, Chapter 8, Aviation Weather Services
Pilot Handbook, Chapter 8, Aviation Weather Services

Content:

Sources of Weather Information	Terminal Aerodrome Forecast (TAF)
Aviation Routine Weather Report (METAR)	Aviation Area Forecast (FA)
Radar Weather Report (SD)	In-Flight Weather Advisories
Surface Analysis Chart	Low-Level and High-Level Prognostic Charts
Constant Pressure Charts	Other Charts and Forecasts

Completion Standards:

The lesson will be complete when the student can answer the 46 FAA questions in Chapter 8, Aviation Weather Services, of *Commercial Pilot FAA Written Exam* and/or *FAA Test Prep* software with a minimum passing grade of 70%.

GROUND LESSON 9: Navigation: Charts, Publications, Flight Computers

Objective:

To further develop the student's understanding of, and the ability to use, navigation charts, publications, and a flight computer in planning a VFR cross-country flight.

Text References:

Commercial Pilot FAA Written Exam, Chapter 9, Navigation: Charts, Publications, Flight Computers
Pilot Handbook, Chapter 9, Navigation: Charts, Publications, Flight Computers

Content:

Sectional Charts
Fuel Consumption
Time, Distance, and Fuel to Station
Wind Direction and Speed
Time, Compass Heading, etc., on Climbs and En Route
Time, Compass Heading, etc., on Descents

Completion Standards:

The lesson will be complete when the student can answer the 58 FAA questions in Chapter 9, Navigation: Charts, Publications, Flight Computers, of *Commercial Pilot FAA Written Exam* and/or *FAA Test Prep* software with a minimum passing grade of 70%.

GROUND LESSON 10: Navigation Systems

Objective:

To further develop the student's knowledge and understanding of various navigation systems.

Text References:

Commercial Pilot FAA Written Exam, Chapter 10, Navigation Systems
Pilot Handbook, Chapter 10, Navigation Systems

Content:

Automatic Direction Finder (ADF)
VOR Use and Receiver Checks
Radio Magnetic Indicator (RMI)
Horizontal Situation Indicator (HSI)

Completion Standards:

The lesson will be complete when the student can answer the 32 FAA questions in Chapter 10, Navigation Systems, of *Commercial Pilot FAA Written Exam* and/or *FAA Test Prep* software with a minimum passing grade of 70%.

GROUND LESSON 11: Flight Operations

Objective:

To review the student's knowledge of normal and emergency flight operations and general safety precautions.

Text References:

Commercial Pilot FAA Written Exam, Chapter 11, Flight Operations
Pilot Handbook, Chapter 3, Airports, Air Traffic Control, and Airspace

Content:

Flight Fundamentals
Taxiing
Landings
Emergencies
Anti-Collision Light System
Cold Weather Operation
Turbulence
Night Flying Operations

Completion Standards:

The lesson will be complete when the student can answer the 22 FAA questions in Chapter 11, Flight Operations, of *Commercial Pilot FAA Written Exam* and/or *FAA Test Prep* software with a minimum passing grade of 70%.

GROUND LESSON 12: Practice Knowledge Test

Objective:

To evaluate the student's comprehension of the aeronautical knowledge necessary to successfully pass the FAA commercial pilot written test.

Text References:

Commercial Pilot FAA Written Exam, Appendix A, Commercial Pilot Practice Test, or *FAA Test Prep* software

Content:

Commercial Pilot Practice Test

Completion Standards:

The lesson will be complete when the student can complete the commercial pilot practice test using Appendix A, Commercial Pilot Practice Test, of *Commercial Pilot FAA Written Exam* and/or *FAA Test Prep* software with a minimum passing grade of 70%. The instructor will review each incorrect answer to ensure complete understanding before the instructor provides an endorsement to take the FAA written test.

END OF APPENDIX

APPENDIX D
ORAL EXAM GUIDE

Most flight schools and many CFIs recommend that pilots preparing for their practical test study an "Oral Exam Guide." We agree: this book is both an "oral exam guide" and a "flight exam guide." With the Gleim system you are well-prepared. This book has everything you need to know to pass your FAA practical test with confidence. Four other Gleim books that may be applicable to the commercial pilot oral exam and the entire FAA practical test are

Aviation Weather and Weather Services (AWWS),
Commercial Pilot FAA Written Exam (CPWE),
Pilot Handbook (PH), and
FAR/AIM

These books contain all the information you need to do well on your commercial pilot practical test. *Pilot Handbook* and *FAR/AIM* are part of our Private Pilot Kit, and *Aviation Weather and Weather Services* is part of our Instrument Pilot Kit. Thus, these books are not included in our Commercial Pilot Kit. *Pilot Handbook*, *FAR/AIM*, and *Aviation Weather and Weather Services*, however, are recommended.

Consider this appendix your **ORAL EXAM GUIDE**.

1. Review the requirements to obtain a commercial pilot certificate on page 2 of CPFM (this book).

2. Read "Oral Portion of the Practical Test" on page 35 (CPFM).

3. Relatedly, read the following on pages 28 through 34 (CPFM):

    Airplane and Equipment Requirements
    What to Take to Your Practical Test
    Practical Test Application Form
    Authorization to Take the Practical Test

4. In *Pilot Handbook*, Chapter 4 "Federal Aviation Regulations," read the outlines through 61.60, 61.121 to 61.133, all of Part 91, and NTSB 830.

    Note: FARs ARE NOW REFERRED TO AS CFRs: The FAA now abbreviates Federal Aviation Regulations as "14 CFR" rather than "FARs." CFR stands for Code of Federal Regulations, and the Federal Aviation Regulations are in Title 14. For example, FAR Part 1 and FAR 61.109 are now referred to as 14 CFR Part 1 and 14 CFR Sec. 61.109, respectively. CFIs and pilots continue to use the acronym FAR.

Airplane Specification Sheet:

Photocopy the back side of this page and make as many notes as possible about your airplane. This will help you organize the information you should know about your airplane, especially for your practical test.

Consult your POH and bring it to your practical test.

Examiner Questions:

You will be ready for your practical test. Follow the advice on page 35. The following pages contain questions previously asked by designated examiners on commercial pilot practical tests. In addition to our brief answers, there are cross references to Gleim books if you wish to study further.

AIRPLANE SPECIFICATION SHEET

GENERAL

N-number _____

Make & Model _____

Max. Ramp Wt. _____

Fuel Capacity _____

Min. Fuel for Flight _____

Oil Capacity _____

Min. Oil for Flight _____

AIRSPEEDS (MPH or KTS)

V_{SO} _____

V_{S1} _____

V_R _____

V_X _____

V_Y _____

V_{FE} _____

V_A _____

V_{NO} _____

V_{NE} _____

Best Glide _____

ELECTRICAL SYSTEM

Voltage _____

Amps _____

LANDING GEAR SYSTEM _____

_____

_____

FLIGHT CONTROL SYSTEM _____

_____

FUEL SYSTEM _____

_____

_____

EMERGENCY EXITS SYSTEM _____

_____

_____

OTHER NOTES:

Part I: Preflight Preparation

1. Certificates and Documents

1. What certificates and documents must be on board the aircraft during a Part 91 flight for it to be considered legal?

Remember **A.R.R.O.W. A**irworthiness certificate, **R**egistration, **R**adio station license (if you are flying outside the U.S.), **O**perating limitations, and **W**eight and balance. (PH Ch. 4)

2. What are the items required to be carried with you in order to act as pilot in command (PIC)?

To act as PIC of an aircraft, you are required to carry your pilot's certificate and medical certificate. (CPWE Ch. 4)

3. How long is a third-class medical certificate valid? A second-class? A first-class?

A third-class medical certificate is valid until the end of the 36th calendar month following the date of the examination if you were under 40 years of age on the day of the medical exam. If you were 40 years old or older on the day of the exam, then the certificate is valid until the end of the 24th calendar month following the date of the examination. A second-class medical certificate is valid for operations requiring a commercial pilot certificate for 12 months following the date of the examination, regardless of age. A first-class medical certificate is valid for operations requiring an airline transport pilot certificate for 6 months, or for operations requiring a commercial pilot certificate for 12 months, following the date of the examination, regardless of age. (CPWE Ch. 4)

4. What class medical certificate must you have to apply for a certificate or rating?

To apply for a certificate or rating, you are required to have a third-class medical certificate. (CPWE Intro)

5. What minimum class of medical certificate is required to act as PIC on a commercial flight conducted under Part 91 or Part 135? What about under Part 121?

To act as PIC on a commercial flight conducted under Parts 91 and 135, you are required to have a second-class medical certificate. To act as PIC under Part 121, you are required to have a first-class medical certificate. (CPWE Intro)

a. Pilot Logbooks

6. What is required to act as PIC of a complex, high performance, or tailwheel airplane?

To act as PIC of a complex, high performance, or tail-wheel airplane, you are required to receive and log ground and flight training and obtain a logbook endorsement from an appropriately rated CFI. (CPWE Ch. 4)

7. What is required to act as PIC of a turbojet-powered aircraft, or one with a gross weight over 12,500 lbs.?

To act as PIC of a turbojet-powered aircraft, or one with a gross weight of over 12,500 lbs., you are required to have a type rating. (CPWE Ch. 4)

8. What is a flight review? Within what time period must a flight review have been satisfactorily completed in order to act as PIC?

A flight review is a minimum of one hour of ground training and one hour of flight training that must have been completed within the preceding 24 calendar months for you to be able to act as PIC. Alternatively, you may have passed a pilot proficiency check conducted by an examiner/inspector, a company check airman, or a U.S. Armed Force, for a pilot certificate, rating, or operating privilege within the preceding 24 calendar months. (CPWE Ch. 4)

9. What must be done to remain current to act as PIC of an aircraft carrying passengers under Part 91?

To act as PIC of an aircraft carrying passengers, you must complete three takeoffs and landings (to a full stop in a tailwheel airplane) every 90 days, and complete a flight review every 24 calendar months. To carry passengers at night, you must complete three landings to a full stop at night every 90 days. (CPWE Ch. 4)

10. When can a pilot log second-in-command flight time?

You can only log second-in-command time when the aircraft you are flying requires a second-in-command, or the regulations under which the operation is conducted require a second-in-command, and you are appropriately rated in the aircraft. (CPWE Ch. 4)

11. What flight experience must be entered into a pilot logbook?

The only flight experience that is required to be entered into a pilot logbook is that experience which is required for obtaining a certificate or rating, completing a flight review, or meeting recency of experience requirements. (CPWE Ch. 4)

b. Maintenance Records and Aircraft Logbooks

12. What type of airframe inspections is an aircraft required to have undergone to be considered airworthy?

An aircraft must have undergone an annual inspection within the preceding 12 calendar months to be considered airworthy if it is used for non-commercial operations. If an aircraft is used for commercial operations, it is also required to have been through an inspection within the preceding 100 hours. (CPWE Ch. 4)

13. Is an airplane owner who is not an A&P mechanic allowed to perform any type of maintenance on his/her airplane?

Yes. An airplane owner who is not a certified mechanic is allowed to perform preventive maintenance, such as oil changes. (CPWE Ch. 4)

14. How often must a transponder be tested and inspected to be considered airworthy?

You may not operate a transponder unless it has been inspected and tested within the preceding 24 calendar months. (CPWE Ch. 4)

15. What is an STC? When is an STC required?

An STC is a Supplemental Type Certificate. An STC is required whenever there is a major change or modification made to the airplane that doesn't warrant a new type certificate. (CPFM Ch. 1)

16. Who is responsible for keeping the airplane in an airworthy condition?

The owner or operator is responsible for making sure the airplane is kept in an airworthy condition. (CPWE Ch. 4)

17. What is an Airworthiness Directive (AD)? Why are they issued?

An AD is issued by the FAA when there is a safety issue with a particular type of aircraft. ADs are mandatory and must be complied with within a certain time frame, unless the AD specifically indicates otherwise. (CPFM Ch. 1)

18. What type of maintenance records is the owner required to keep for an aircraft?

Maintenance records must be kept for the current status of life-limited parts (propeller, engine, etc.), the current status of all ADs, and any preventive maintenance done by the pilot. (CPWE Ch. 4)

Author Note: As of August 1, 2002, the FAA introduced a new task, Airworthiness Requirements, in the Commercial PTSs. See pages 45-49.

c. Commercial Pilot FARs

19. Must you notify the FAA of a change of address?

Yes. If your address changes, you must notify the FAA in writing within 30 days, or you may not exercise the privileges of your pilot certificate. (CPWE Ch. 4)

20. Define the responsibility and authority of the pilot in command.

The pilot in command is the final authority as to the operation of the aircraft. (S)he is responsible for the safety of the crew and all passengers on board the aircraft. (CPWE Ch. 4)

21. How long must one wait after consuming alcohol before acting as a required crewmember on a civil airplane?

You must wait eight hours after consuming alcohol before acting as a required crewmember on a civil airplane. (PH Ch. 4)

22. What is the maximum allowable blood alcohol content while acting as a required crewmember on a civil airplane?

You may not act as a required cremember on a civil aircraft while having .04% by weight or more blood alcohol content. (PH Ch.4)

23. Above what altitude must all passengers be provided with supplemental oxygen?

All passengers must be provided with supplemental oxygen when the cabin altitude is above 15,000 ft. MSL. The required flight crew must be provided with and use supplemental oxygen for all time in excess of 30 minutes spent above 12,500 ft. MSL, and for the entire time spent above 14,000 ft. MSL. (CPWE Ch. 4)

24. Within what time frame must an accident report be filed with the National Transportation Safety Board (NTSB)?

You are required to notify the NTSB immediately when an aircraft accident (an occurence that results in death or serious injury to any person, or substantial damage to the aircraft) occurs. A report must be filed within 10 days after an accident. (CPWE Ch. 4)

25. Is damage to the landing gear or tire considered substantial damage by the NTSB?

Damage to a tire or landing gear is not considered substantial damage, and a report to the NTSB is not required. A definition of exactly what is and is not considered substantial damage is found in NTSB Part 830. (PH Ch. 4)

26. Which occurrences require immediate notification to the NTSB?

You must immediately notify the NTSB when an aircraft accident or any of the following incidents occur: the inability of a required crewmember to perform his/her duties, an in-flight fire, a flight control system malfunction, a mid-air collision, failure of the structural components of a turbine engine (excluding compressor and turbine blades/vanes), damage to property (other than the aircraft) in excess of $25,000, or when an aircraft is overdue and is believed to have been involved in an accident. (PH Ch. 4)

27. How is a "serious injury" defined by the NTSB?

A serious injury is defined by NTSB Part 830 as an injury requiring hospitalization for more than 48 hours, most bone fractures, muscle or nerve damage, internal organ damage, second or third degree burns, or any burns, affecting over 5% of the body. (PH Ch. 4)

28. When are safety belts required to be worn by all occupants?

Safety belts and shoulder harnesses, if installed, are required to be worn by all occupants during taxi, takeoff, and landing. (CPWE Ch. 4)

29. As PIC, what is your responsibility to your passengers with regard to safety belts?

As PIC, you must brief your passengers on the operation of the safety belts, and notify your passengers when belts must be worn. (PH Ch. 4)

30. What is common carriage?

Common carriage is considered a willingness to fly anyone or anything for hire. With common carriage, customers usually come as a result of advertising or through an intermediary.

31. What is holding out?

Holding out is advertising or working with an intermediary to gain customers in order to fly for hire. A business that is holding out is usually practicing common carriage.

32. Are you authorized to hold out as a Part 91 commercial operator?

No. By definition, holding out requires an air carrier certificate. Part 119 regulates the certification of air carriers and commercial operators.

33. What is a NASA Aviation Safety Reporting Program (ASRP) report? When should one be filed?

The NASA ASRP is a voluntary program designed to gather information about deficiencies in the aviation system. When an FAR is violated inadvertently without involving a criminal offense, filing a NASA ASRP report within 10 days may prevent an enforcement action. (PH Ch. 4)

2. Weather Information

a. Weather Theory

34. What is a weather-based scenario?

The FAA is changing their focus on weather theory and weather services to a more scenario-based system. This means that questions on the oral portion of the practical test will be related to a hypothetical weather situation. For example, your examiner may ask you about the expected weather along your flight route for the pre-planned cross-country.

35. What is standard sea level temperature and pressure?

Standard sea level temperature is 15°C. Standard sea level pressure is 29.92" Hg. These numbers are important for completing important calculations, such as true airspeed, current lapse rate, and density altitude. (AWWS PI-Ch. 3)

36. What is the standard lapse rate?

The standard lapse rate is 2°C per 1,000 ft. of altitude gained. (AWWS PI-Ch. 6)

37. What is the Coriolis force?

The Coriolis force is a theory that explains how things deflect to the right in the Northern Hemisphere. It applies to wind, pressure, and general weather patterns. The Coriolis force is the reason wind and weather patterns generally move from West to East (left to right) in the United States. (AWWS PI-Ch. 4)

38. Why is wind shear dangerous?

Wind shear is dangerous because it is unpredictable, and it can cause significant changes in heading, airspeed, and altitude, especially close to the ground. (AWWS PI-Ch. 4)

39. What is the significance of a close temperature-dew point spread?

A close temperature-dew point spread indicates the probable formation of visible moisture in the form of dew, mist, fog, or clouds. The decrease in temperature (most frequently at night) can result in a close temperature-dew point spread and fast forming fog. (AWWS PI-Ch. 5)

40. What are the characteristics of stable air? What are the characteristics of unstable air?

Stable air is characterized by continuous precipitation, smooth air, and poor visibility. Unstable air is characterized by showery precipitation, rough air, and good visibility. (AWWS PI-Ch. 8)

41. What are the four types of fronts and what significance is this to aviation?

The four types of fronts are high, low, stationary, and occluded. Each front indicates a different type of weather. (AWWS PI-Ch. 8)

42. What type of weather is associated with a cold front?

Cold fronts usually contain the most volatile weather. Because cold air replaces warm air quickly, the difference in pressure is the greatest with the potential for violent weather. (AWWS PI-Ch. 8)

43. What type of weather is associated with a warm front?

The weather associated with warm fronts is usually relatively mild. Warm front weather is usually much more widespread and longer lasting then that of cold front weather. (AWWS PI-Ch. 8)

44. What type of weather is associated with a stationary front?

A stationary front is when warm and cold air masses meet, but do not mix. Wind always blows along the frontal boundary of a stationary front, and in some cases embedded storms occur. (AWWS PI-Ch. 8)

45. What is an occluded front?

An occluded front is a combination of cold, warm, and cool air. Thus, weather in occluded fronts are a combination of cold and warm front weather. (AWWS PI-Ch. 8)

46. What is clear air turbulence? Why is it dangerous?

Clear air turbulence is turbulence not associated with thunderstorms. It usually occurs along an upper level temperature inversion. It is dangerous because it is often unexpected, and it can be severe. (AWWS PI-Ch. 13)

47. What are three types of structural icing?

The three types of structural icing are clear, rime, and mixed ice. Clear ice forms when drops are large as in rain or in cumuliform clouds. It is hard, heavy, and unyielding. Rime ice forms as a result of small drops found in stratified clouds and drizzle. Air becomes trapped in between the drops and makes the ice appear white. Mixed ice is a combination of clear and rime ice. (AWWS PI-Ch. 10)

48. How much can ice or frost degrade performance?

It is important not to operate with frost on the wings because it can degrade performance by up to 40%. (AWWS PI-Ch. 10)

49. What are the types of fog and how are they formed?

The fog types include radiation, advection, precipitation-induced, upslope, and ice. Radiation fog forms when the air close to the ground is cooled faster than the air above it. It usually forms at night or near daybreak. Advection fog forms along coastal areas when the water is warmer than the air around it. Precipitation-induced fog forms when relatively warm rain or drizzle falls through cool air and evaporation from the precipitation saturates the cool air. Upslope fog forms as a result of moist, stable air being cooled adiabatically as it moves up sloping terrain. Ice fog occurs in cold weather when the temperature is well below freezing and water vapor sublimates directly as ice crystals. (AWWS PI-Ch. 12)

50. What conditions must be present for a thunderstorm to form?

Formation of a thunderstorm requires a lifting action, an unstable lapse rate, and sufficient water vapor. (AWWS PI-Ch. 11)

51. What is a microburst? Why is it hazardous to aircraft? How long does a microburst typically last?

A microburst is a heavy downdraft occurring within a thunderstorm. It is hazardous to aircraft because of the extreme down force. The downdrafts become stronger outflowing horizontal surface winds flowing outward from the base of the thunderstorm. A microburst usually lasts for a total of 10 minutes with the maximum intensity winds lasting for 2 to 4 minutes. (AWWS PI-Ch. 11)

b. Weather services

52. Where is weather information available on the ground?

Weather information is available on the ground from a Flight Service Station (FSS), Direct User Access Terminal System (DUATS), and Telephone Information Briefing Service (TIBS). You can speak to a pre-flight briefer at FSS and/or receive TIBS by calling 1-800-WX-BRIEF anywhere in the country. DUATS is a free service available to pilots on the Internet. Here you can receive weather information, and file a flight plan. TIBS is recorded weather information that can be obtained by calling 1-800-WX-BRIEF. (AWWS PIII-Ch. 1)

53. Where is weather information available in-flight?

Weather information is available in-flight with

EFAS   En-route Flight Advisory Service
HIWAS   Hazardous In-Flight Weather Advisory Service
FSS   Flight Service Station
TWEB   Transcribed Weather Broadcast
ATIS   Automatic Terminal Information Service
ASOS   Automated Surface Observation Service
AWOS   Automatic Weather Observation Service

EFAS is also known as "Flight Watch" and is available almost anywhere in the country on 122.0. You can file a PIREP and obtain numerous types of weather information with EFAS. HIWAS is a recorded briefing of hazardous weather over select VOR frequencies. FSS frequencies are shown on navigational charts and are usually available for ATC. TWEB is a recorded broadcast of current and adverse weather conditions over select VOR and NDB frequencies. ATIS is recorded weather information for a terminal area. AWOS and ASOS are automated weather reporting stations found at many airports. (AWWS PIII-Ch. 1)

54. What is a METAR?

A METAR is a current weather observation that is updated at a regular interval, and applies for a 5-mile radius around the observation point (usually at any airport). (AWWS PIII-Ch. 2)

55. What is a TAF? How often are TAFs updated?

A TAF is a forecast of conditions for the next 24 hours that applies to a 5-mile radius around the place of the report. TAFs are updated four times a day. (AWWS PIII-Ch. 7)

56. What is a PIREP? How is one submitted? How can a pilot receive one?

A PIREP is a Pilot Weather Report. They are important sources of observed weather aloft. PIREPs are submitted by pilots on EFAS, and can be received by EFAS or a FSS. (AWWS PIII-Ch. 3)

57. What type of information can be found in an area forecast (FA)? How often is an area forecast updated? What are the four sections of an area forecast?

An area forecast (FA) is a forecast of clouds and general weather conditions over an area of several states, and is updated three times a day. An FA contains four sections, the communication and product header, precautionary statement, synopsis, and VFR clouds/weather section. The communication and product header indicates the date and time of issuance, valid times, and area of coverage. The precautionary statement icing, low-level wind shear, and IFR conditions, and non-MSL heights are denoted by AGL or CIG. The synopsis is a brief summary of the location and movement of fronts, pressure systems, and circulation patterns. The VFR clouds/weather section contains a 12-hr. specific forecast and a 6-hr. outlook and covers possible weather hazards such as IFR conditions, icing, thunderstorms, and wind shear. (AWWS PIII-Ch. 8)

58. What is the difference between a Radar summary chart and a visible satellite report?

A Radar summary chart displays areas of precipi-tation, as well as information about the type, intensity, configuration, coverage, echo top, and cell movement of that precipitation. A visible satellite report is a type of imagery of clouds and their thickness. (AWWS PIII-Chs. 5, 18)

59. What is a SIGMET? What is a convective SIGMET? What is an AIRMET?

SIGMETs are issued for all aircraft and may include severe icing not associated with thunderstorms, clear air turbulence, dust storms, and volcanic eruptions. Convective SIGMETs are issued for severe thunderstorms, embedded thunderstorms, lines of thunderstorms, and tornados, all of which imply severe or greater turbulence, severe icing, and low-level wind shear. AIRMETS are issued for moderate icing, moderate turbulence, IFR conditions over 50% of an area, sustained surface winds of 30 kt. or greater, nonconvective low-level windshear, and mountain obscuration. (AWWS PIII-Ch. 10)

60. What do winds and temperatures aloft forecasts indicate? What can a pilot determine from these forecasts?

Winds and temperatures aloft forecasts indicate the wind speed and direction, as well as temperature at various altitudes. Pilots are interested in most favorable winds and temperature inversions. (AWWS PIII-Ch. 21)

61. What is a Center Weather Advisory?

A Center Weather Advisory is an advisory provided by ATC for potentially hazardous weather expected to happen within the next 2 hours. (AWWS PIII-Ch. 1)

3. Cross-country Flight Planning

a. National Airspace System

62. What are the minimum VFR cloud clearance and visibility requirements for Class E airspace below 10,000 ft. MSL? What are they above 10,000 ft. MSL?

The minimum VFR cloud clearance and visibility requirements in Class E airspace below 10,000 ft. MSL are 500 ft. below clouds, 1,000 ft. above clouds, 2,000 ft. horizontally from clouds, and 3 miles visibility. The minimum VFR cloud clearance and visibility requirements in Class E airspace above 10,000 ft. MSL are 1,000 ft. below clouds, 1,000 ft. above clouds, 1 SM horizontally from clouds, and 5 miles visibility. (PH Ch. 3)

63. What are the minimum VFR cloud clearance and visibility requirements for Class G airspace below 1,200 ft. AGL during the day? What are they at night?

The minimum VFR cloud clearance and visibility requirements in Class G airspace below 1,200 ft. AGL during the day are clear of clouds and 1 mile visibility. The minimum VFR cloud clearance and visibility requirements in Class G airspace below 1,200 ft. AGL at night are 500 ft. below clouds, 1,000 ft. above clouds, 2,000 ft. horizontally from clouds, and 3 miles visibility. (PH Ch. 3)

64. What are the minimum VFR cloud clearance and visibility requirements for Class G airspace above 1,200 ft. AGL but below 10,000 ft. MSL during the day? What are they at night?

The minimum VFR cloud clearance and visibility requirements in Class G airspace above 1,200 ft. AGL but below 10,000 ft. MSL during the day are 500 ft. below clouds, 1,000 ft. above clouds, 2,000 ft. horizontally from clouds, and 1 mile visibility. The minimum VFR cloud clearance and visibility requirements in Class G airspace above 1,200 ft. AGL but below 10,000 ft. MSL at night are 500 ft. below clouds, 1,000 ft. above clouds, 2,000 ft. horizontally from clouds, and 3 miles visibility. (PH Ch. 3)

65. What are the minimum VFR cloud clearance and visibility requirements for Class B airspace? What are they for Class C airspace? What are they for Class D airspace?

The minimum VFR cloud clearance and visibility requirements in Class B airspace are clear of clouds and 3 miles visibility. The minimum VFR cloud clearance and visibility requirements in Class C and Class D airspace are 500 ft. below clouds, 1,000 ft. above clouds, 2,000 ft. horizontally from clouds, and 3 miles visibility. (PH Ch. 3)

66. What is required for a student pilot to fly solo in Class B airspace?

To fly solo in Class B airspace, a student pilot must have received all of the standard pre-solo endorsements, as well as an endorsement stating that (s)he has received training for the specific Class B area in which the solo flight is to be conducted. (PH Ch. 3)

67. What class of airspace requires a clearance prior to entry? What classes of airspace require that 2-way radio communication be established prior to entry?

Class B airspace requires a clearance prior to entry, and Class C and Class D airspace require that 2-way radio communication be established prior to entry. (PH Ch. 3)

68. How do you determine when 2-way radio communication has been established?

Two-way radio communication has been established when ATC responds with your correct call sign. (PH Ch. 3)

69. When is a transponder with Mode C required for VFR flight?

A working transponder with Mode C is required any time you are above 10,000 ft. MSL, inside Class B or Class C airspace, and above Class B or Class C airspace up to 10,000 ft. MSL, or within 30 NM of a Class B primary airport. (PH Ch. 3)

70. What are the typical dimensions of Class D airspace?

Class D airspace typically extends upward from the surface to 2,500 ft. AGL and outward to a 5 SM radius from the primary airport. Airspace dimensions may vary according to local requirements, however. (PH Ch. 3)

71. What are the typical dimensions of Class C airspace?

Class C airspace is typically composed of two sections that are referred to as the surface area and the shelf area. The surface area typically extends upward from the surface to 4,000 ft. MSL and outward to a 5 NM radius upward from the primary airport. The shelf area typically extends upward from 1,200 ft. MSL to 4,000 ft. MSL and outward to a 10 NM radius from the primary airport. Airspace dimensions may vary according to local requirements, however. (PH Ch. 3)

72. What is a TRSA?

TRSA stands for Terminal Radar Service Area. TRSAs are established around Class D airports that have radar service capability, but do not meet all of the criteria to be designated as Class C airspace. Participation in TRSA service is voluntary (though it is recommended), but 2-way radio communication must still be established prior to entering Class D airspace. (PH Ch. 3)

73. What are the minimum cloud clearance and visibility requirements to obtain a special VFR clearance?

To obtain a special VFR clearance, you must be able to remain clear of clouds and have at least 1 mile visibility. (PH Ch. 3)

74. What is a Prohibited Area? What is a Restricted Area? What is a Military Operations Area? What is an Alert Area? What is a Warning Area?

Prohibited Areas are established for reasons of national security; flight is prohibited at all times within them. Restricted Areas are established to contain unusual, often invisible hazards to aircraft such as aerial gunnery or missile tests. Flight is restricted within a Restricted Area when that area is active. Military Operations Areas (MOAs) are established to separate IFR and military traffic. VFR flight is always permitted within MOAs. Alert Areas are established to notify pilots of unusual aerial activity such as a high volume of flight training but flight is always permitted within them. Warning areas are located offshore and are established to alert pilots. (PH Ch. 3)

75. When should you contact ATC after leaving from an uncontrolled satellite airport located in Class C or Class D airspace?

After departing an uncontrolled satellite airport in Class C or Class D airspace, contact ATC as soon as practicable. (PPWE pg. 62-63)

76. What is a Military Training Route?

Military Training Routes are depicted on sectional charts to alert pilots to establish flight paths used for military training, usually occurring at high speeds and low altitudes. (PH Ch. 3)

b. Available publications

77. What information do Airport/Facilities Directories provide?

Airport/Facilities Directories (A/FD) provide all the information needed for an airport or radio navigation aid (NAVAID). A/FDs also provide published NOTAMS and areas of parachute and aerobatic activity. (PPFM pg. 54)

78. What type of information do sectional charts provide?

Sectional charts provide topographical, physical (roads, railroad tracks, etc.), airport, NAVAID, and airspace information for a specific geographic location. (PH Ch. 9)

79. What information does the Airmen's Information Manual (AIM) provide?

The AIM provides information regarding airport operations, navigation aids, airspace, flight operations, and ATC procedures. (PH Ch. 9)

80. Where can pilot certification information be found?

Pilot certification information can be found in FAR part 61.

81. Where can information on oxygen requirements, fuel requirements, airspace, and all other regulatory flight rules be found?

All flight rules that apply to general aviation are in FAR part 91.

82. What is an Advisory Circular (AC)?

ACs are used by the FAA as a means of issuing nonregulatory information to pilots, mechanics, and manufacturers. (PH Ch. 9)

c. Performance Charts

83. How is density altitude calculated?

To calculate density altitude

a.   Obtain the field elevation

b.   Barometric pressure: Add (if below standard) or subtract (if above standard) to obtain pressure altitude. For example, if the field elevation is 2,000 ft. and the barometric pressure is 30.00, you will subtract 80 ft. (30.00 – 29.92 x 100) from 2,000.

c.   Line up the pressure altitude and temperature on your flight computer to find density altitude. If temperature is above standard, density altitude will be greater than pressure altitude; the opposite will occur if temperature is below standard.

84. What are the typical performance charts found in a POH?

Performance charts common to all POHs include takeoff, climb, cruise, landing, maximum glide chart, and the density altitude chart. You should be proficient with each of the performance charts in your POH. Be able to use each chart and explain it to your examiner. (PH Ch. 5)

85. How does density altitude affect airplane performance?

High density altitude has a noticeably negative effect on aircraft performance. First, because the air going into the engine is not as dense with high density altitude, the engine does not develop as much power. Second, the propeller is an airfoil and does not develop as much thrust in the thinner air at high density altitude. Third, at high density altitude, the wing is not as efficient, and therefore requires more airflow to produce the same amount of lift as would be produced at lower density altitudes. Thus, high density altitude has a negative effect on your takeoff roll, climb rate, and cruise performance.

86. What are some factors that affect takeoff performance?

The common factors that affect takeoff performance are density altitude, the weight of the aircraft, wind speed and direction, and the surface of the runway. With a higher density altitude, the aircraft will have a longer takeoff roll. Increased weight also increases the takeoff roll. If the wind speed is high and it is close to a headwind, the ground roll will be reduced because of the increased relative wind. Finally, a soft runway surface will make the takeoff roll longer.

87. What is maximum range? What is maximum endurance?

Maximum range is the maximum distance an aircraft can fly on full fuel. Maximum endurance is the maximum time an aircraft can fly on full fuel. (PH Ch. 5)

88. What is the definition of best glide speed?

Best glide speed is the point in the drag curve in which total drag is the lowest, or L/D $_{max}$. (PH Ch. 5 and your airplane's POH)

89. What are some factors that affect landing distance?

The most common factors that affect landing distance are wind speed and direction, the runway surface, and the weight of the airplane. The stronger the headwind, the slower the airplane's normal speed at landing and the shorter landing distance. A poor runway surface decreases braking efficiency. A heavier airplane has more inertia and requires more landing distance. (PH Ch. 5)

d. Weight and Balance

90. How is the center of gravity (CG) calculated?

The center of gravity is calculated by dividing the airplane's total weight by the total moment. Total moment is the sum of the product of the weight of each item in the airplane, e.g, occupant, baggage, fuel, etc., times the arm. Arm is the distance of the item from the datum. (PH Ch. 5)

91. What are some of the effects that being over gross weight can have on an airplane?

Being over gross weight is illegal and very dangerous and can increase the takeoff and landing distance, decrease climb performance, cause possible structural damage, and accelerate metal fatigue. (PH Ch. 5)

92. Where are the measurements taken for the computation of the CG?

The CG is computed from the reference datum, which is defined by the airplane manufacturer. It is frequently the firewall or the leading edge of the wing. (PH Ch. 5)

93. What are the handling characteristics of an airplane with an aft CG?

An airplane with an aft CG is generally unstable. It will fly at a higher airspeed, but it may be impossible to recover from a stall or spin. (PH Ch. 5)

94. What are the handling characteristics of an airplane with a forward CG?

An airplane with a forward CG is generally more stable than one with an aft CG. It will fly at a slower airspeed (more drag), and it will stall at a higher indicated stall speed. (PH Ch. 5)

95. Why should a weight and balance be calculated with both current conditions and with zero or low fuel under the given conditions before departing?

Before beginning any flight, you must compute a weight and balance with the current conditions. However, as fuel burns during a flight, the CG moves. To make sure the CG will stay within limits the entire flight, you should calculate a theoretical weight and balance with no or low fuel as well. (PH Ch. 5)

96. What is the difference between the moment and the arm?

The arm is the distance from the datum to the center of the item for which the moment is being calculated. The moment is the product of the weight of the object being measured and its distance from the datum (arm). (PH Ch. 5)

4. Operation of Systems

a. Avionics

97. Which flight instruments are part of the pitot-static system?

Typically, the airspeed indicator, vertical speed indicator, and altimeter are the flight instruments in the pitot-static system. (PH Ch. 2)

98. Which instruments are driven by a vacuum pump?

Typically, the gyros in the attitude indicator and heading indicator are driven by the vacuum system. (PH Ch. 2)

99. What are the definitions of four types of airspeeds?

Indicated airspeed is what is read on the airspeed indicator. Calibrated airspeed is determined by engineers and has no practical use for pilots. However, many performance charts are listed in calibrated airspeed and a chart that gives indicated versus calibrated must be used to determine the indicated airspeed. True airspeed is calibrated airspeed or indicated airspeed corrected for non-standard temperature and pressure. True airspeed at higher altitudes are higher than shown on the airspeed indicator due to the higher density altitude, which means less dense air. Ground speed is the actual speed in which you are moving over the ground.

100. Define the different types of altitude?

Altitude types include indicated, true, pressure, absolute, and density. Indicated altitude is read directly from the altimeter after it is set to the local altimeter setting. True altitude is the vertical distance of the aircraft above sea level. Pressure altitude is the altitude indicated on the altimeter when the altimeter setting is adjusted to standard pressure. It is also indicated altitude or actual altitude adjusted for nonstandard pressure. Density altitude is pressure altitude corrected for nonstandard temperature. (PH Ch. 2)

101. How does the vertical speed indicator (VSI) work?

The VSI is a sealed case with a calibrated leak and a diaphragm inside it. Slight difference in air pressure expands or contracts the diaphragm that is linked to the needles on the face of the instrument. (PH Ch. 2)

102. How do the gyroscopic instruments work?

Gyroscopic instruments work on the principle of rigidity in space. A vacuum pump or electrical power source spins a gyro in the instrument at a high rate of speed, thus keeping it rigid in space. If a force is applied, then precession happens 90° ahead of the force. (PH Ch. 2)

103. What errors are magnetic compasses subject to?

Magnetic compasses are subject to magnetic variation, northerly and southerly turning, acceleration, and compass card oscillation errors. (PH Ch. 2)

104. What is magnetic variation?

Magnetic variation is the difference in degrees between true and magnetic north. Although the magnetic field of the Earth lies roughly north and south, the Earth's magnetic poles do not coincide with its geographic poles, which are used in construction of aeronautical charts. (PH Ch. 2)

105. What is magnetic dip?

Magnetic dip is the tendency of the compass needles to point down as well as point to the magnetic pole. The resultant error is known as dip error, greatest at the poles and zero at the magnetic equator. It causes northerly and southerly turning errors and acceleration errors. (PH Ch. 2)

106. What is northerly and southerly turning error?

Northerly and southerly turning error is the most pronounced of the dip errors. If the airplane is on a northerly heading and turns east or west, the compass will lag if the airplane is on a southerly heading and turns east or west, the compass will lead the actual airplane heading. REMEMBER, North Lags, South Leads. (PH Ch. 2)

107. What is acceleration error?

Acceleration error is also due to the dip of the Earth's magnetic field. Because the compass is mounted like a pendulum, the aft end of the compass card is tilted upward when accelerating and downward when decelerating during changes of airspeed. When on east or west headings, acceleration causes compasses to indicate a turn to the north. Deceleration causes compasses to indicate a turn to the south. ANDS (Accelerate North, Decelerate South). (PH Ch. 2)

108. What is compass card oscillation?

Compass card oscillation error results from erratic movement of the compass card, which may be caused by turbulence or abrupt flight control movement. (PH Ch. 2)

b. Systems

109. What is the purpose of a magneto? Why are there usually two magnetos in airplane engines?

A magneto provides electrical current to the spark plugs. Most general aviation engines have two magnetos because there are two spark plugs per cylinder. Each magneto provides current to one set of spark plugs. The result is a redundant system and also better performance. (PH Ch. 2)

110. What is the function of the mixture control?

The mixture controls the amount of fuel going to the carburetor or cylinders. It makes for better fuel efficiency, less wear on the spark plugs, and a more efficient engine. (PH Ch. 2)

111. What is the purpose of a carburetor? What is one of its limitations?

The carburetor is where the fuel mixes with the air before it is sent to the cylinders. It is subject to induction icing. (PH Ch. 2)

112. How does the fuel system work on this airplane? How does the electrical system work? How do the brakes work?

Learn how all the systems work on your airplane. Consult your POH and complete the worksheet on page 338.

113. When making power adjustments with a constant-speed propeller, what should be changed first?

When making a power adjustment with a constant-speed propeller, it is important to keep the manifold pressure setting below the RPM setting. When decreasing power, always reduce manifold pressure before reducing RPM. When increasing power, always increase RPM before increasing manifold pressure. (CPWE pg. 43)

114. What does the throttle control on an engine with a constant-speed prop? What does the propeller control operate?

The throttle controls manifold pressure, and the propeller control operates RPM with a constant-speed propeller. (CPWE pg. 43)

c. Aerodynamics and Stability

115. How does lift develop?

Lift develops as a result of differential pressure between the upper and lower surfaces of the wing. The air that travels over the top of the wing must go farther and faster, and thus has a lower pressure than the air which travels under the bottom side of the wing. The pressure difference pulls the wing upward as a result. (CPWE pg. 20)

116. How is total drag affected by an increase in airspeed? How is parasite drag affected? How is induced drag affected?

As airspeed increases, total drag increases above L/D_{max}. Parasite drag is the resistance of air as the airplane passes through it. As airspeed increases, parasite drag increases as the square of the velocity. If the speed is doubled, four times as much parasite drag is produced. Induced drag is the by-product of lift and varies inversely as the square of the airspeed. For example, reducing airspeed by half (from 120 kt. to 60 kt.) increases the induced drag by four times. (PH Ch. 1)

117. What is static stability?

Static stability is the airplane's initial tendency to return to its original attitude after its equilibrium is disrupted. If an airplane flies through turbulence, and its immediate tendency is to return to its original attitude, it has positive static stability. (CPWE Ch. 1)

118. What is dynamic stability?

Dynamic stability is the airplane's tendency to enter increasing oscillations OR decreasing oscillations after its equilibrium is disrupted. For example, if an airplane flies through turbulence and the oscillations it experiences diverge from its original trimmed attitude, the airplane exhibits negative dynamic stability; or if the oscillations decrease in size, the airplane has positive dynamic stability. (CPWE pg. 22)

119. What is the purpose of wing dihedral?

Airplanes are designed with wing dihedral to increases lateral stability. If a momentary gust of wind forces one wing of the airplane to rise and the other to lower, the airplane will roll into a bank. When an airplane is banked without turning, it tends to sideslip, or slide downward, toward the lowered wing. Since the wings have dihedral, the air strikes the low wing at a much greater angle of attack than the high wing. Thus, the low wing produces more lift than the high wing, and level flight will be restored. (PH Ch. 1)

120. What is adverse yaw? How is it corrected?

Adverse yaw occurs in turns. As the airplane turns, the high, outside wing moves faster through the air than the inside wing. Becuase of this, the high wing creates more drag and pulls the nose of the airplane towards it. Adverse yaw can be corrected by using proper rudder control. (PH Ch. 1)

121. What is the purpose of flaps?

Wing flaps create both lift and drag. They can be used to shorten the takeoff roll and/or to increase the descent angle on approach without increasing airspeed. (CPWE Ch. 1)

122. Why is more back pressure required to maintain level flight while turning?

When an airplane is banked to change direction, some of its vertical component of lift transfers to a horizontal component. As a result, more back elevator pressure is required to keep the airplane at a constant altitude. (CPWE Ch. 1)

5. Aeromedical Factors

123. What is hypoxia? How can it be prevented?

Hypoxia is insufficient oxygen in the blood. It can be prevented by flying at a lower altitude or by using supplemental oxygen. (PH Ch. 6)

124. What is hyperventilation? How can it be treated?

Hyperventilation is insufficient carbon dioxide in the blood. It can be treated by taking slow, deep breaths, or by breathing into a bag. (PH Ch. 6)

125. How can stress affect your flying?

Stress degrades decision making ability and slows your reactions. (PH Ch. 6)

126. What is a good rule for flying if taking medication?

Do NOT fly if you are taking medication unless the medication is approved by the FAA or you are certain that the medicine will NOT impair your abilities. (PH Ch. 6)

127. What is carbon monoxide poisoning? What is the primary source of it in aircraft cockpits?

Carbon monoxide poisoning occurs when carbon monoxide enters the blood, thereby causing hypoxia. The most common source of carbon monoxide in aircraft cockpits is exhaust fumes from a defective heater or other source. (PH Ch. 6)

128. How long should pilots and passengers wait to fly after SCUBA diving?

If a controlled ascent was required during the dive, wait 24 hours before flying. If a controlled ascent was not required, wait 12 hours before flying up to 8,000 ft. and 24 hours for any altitude above 8,000 ft. (PH Ch. 6)

129. What is the graveyard spiral?

If descending during a coordinated constant-rate turn that has ceased stimulating, the motion-sensing system can create the illusion of being in a descent with the wings level. A disoriented pilot will pull back on the controls, tightening the spiral and increasing the loss of altitude. (PH Ch. 6)

130. How can you recover from spatial disorientation?

The best way to recover from spatial disorientation is to focus on the flight instruments and rely on their indications. (PH Ch. 6)

a. Physiology of Night Flight

131. How long does it take your eyes to fully adapt to darkness?

It takes your eyes 30 minutes to fully adapt to darkness. If you accidentally view a bright light, your night vision will be lost instantly. (PH Ch. 6)

132. What is the recommended altitude to begin using oxygen at night to reduce the risk of hypoxia and impaired vision?

It is recommended that supplemental oxygen be used above 5,000 ft. at night to avoid the risk of hypoxia and impaired vision. (PH Ch. 6)

133. How should one scan for traffic at night?

Scanning for traffic at night should be done with peripheral vision. This is because the rods are concentrated outside of the fovea. (PH Ch. 6)

Part II: Flight Operations

1. Night Flight Operations

134. What additional equipment is your airplane required to have for night flight?

In addition to the equipment required for day VFR flight, your airplane is also required to have an approved anti-collision light, position lights, an adequate electrical source, and a spare set of fuses if resettable fuses (e.g., circuit breakers) are not equipped. (PH Ch. 4)

135. What makes the preflight at night different from the preflight during the day?

The night preflight is difficult to perform because you cannot see as well at night. In addition to the normal checks and inspections, your night preflight should include a check of all lights and lighting systems. (CPFM pg. 75)

136. What additional equipment should you bring with you on a night flight?

It is a good idea to bring two flashlights and spare batteries with you on a night flight. (CPFM pg. 76)

137. How much fuel reserve is required for VFR night flight?

The FARs require a VFR fuel reserve of 45 minutes at night. More is better. (PH Ch. 4)

138. What color are runway lights?

Runway lights are primarily white, though some turn red to indicate a lessening amount of runway remaining. (PH Ch. 3)

2. Spin Awareness

139. What is a spin?

A spin is an aggravated stall that results in autorotation. (PH Ch. 1)

140. In what situations is a spin likely to occur?

Spins can occur in almost any situation. However, the most common places where spins happen are in the pattern on the turn from base to final and during a go-around. (CPFM Ch. 8)

141. What is the difference between a steep spiral and a spin?

By definition, an airplane must be stalled to be in a spin but not in a steep spiral. (CPFM Ch. 8)

142. What is the recommended spin recovery for your airplane?

Though every airplane has a slightly different spin recovery procedure, it is usually throttle to idle, neutralize the ailerons, full rudder deflection in the opposite direction of the turn, break the stall with forward elevator pressure, level the wings if necessary, and recover from the descent. (CPFM Ch. 8)

3. Emergency Procedures
The following questions are airplane specific. The answers given here are a general guide only. To fully understand the correct procedure for every situation in your airplane, refer to the POH.

143. What would happen if the vacuum pump failed in your airplane? Is it considered an emergency situation in VFR conditions?

A failed vacuum pump will result in the loss of the attitude indicator and the heading indicator. A vacuum pump failure often goes unnoticed by pilots because the gyros take a long time to wind down. This is not considered an emergency situation in VFR conditions because these instruments are not necessary for safe flight. (PH Ch. 2)

144. What would happen to the altimeter if the pitot-static system were obstructed? What would happen to the VSI? What would happen to the airspeed indicator?

If the pitot-static system was blocked, the altimeter would indicate the altitude where the system became blocked. The VSI would give no indication in a climb or descent. The airspeed indicator would read zero. (PH Ch. 2)

145. What error does the altimeter indicate if you are using an alternate static source?

Because alternate static sources are usually located inside the cockpit where the pressure is lower than it is outside the airplane, the altimeter indicates higher than normal. (PH Ch. 2)

146. What does a low voltage light indicate when it is illuminated? How would you address this situation?

A low voltage light indicates that the alternator or generator is not working and the electrical equipment is running from the battery. To effectively deal with the situation, turn off all non-essential electrical equipment and land as soon as practical. (PH Ch. 2)

147. What is the procedure if a circuit breaker pops?

If a circuit breaker pops and it is resettable, push it back in once. If it pops out again, leave it out and determine the next course of action. Pushing the breaker in more than once may lead to an electrical fire. (PH Ch. 2)

148. What are some common causes of a rough running engine in flight?

Though there are numerous factors that can cause an engine to run rough, the most common causes are carburetor ice, a problematic magneto, or fouled spark plugs. (PH Ch. 2)

149. What is the necessary action if you lose a magneto in flight?

If a magneto is lost in flight, determine the bad magneto by switching from both to either left or right. The bad magneto will be evident when the engine will not run on that particular magneto. After you identify the bad magneto, run on the good one and land as soon as practical. (PH Ch. 2)

150. Is using all the fuel from one tank before switching to another a good practice? Why?

Using all the fuel from one tank is not a good practice because it may cause vapor lock in the fuel line. The result may be an engine failure without the ability to restart it inflight. (PH Ch. 2)

151. What should you do if you notice that you are losing oil pressure?

A loss of oil pressure should be viewed as an emergency situation. The engine will not continue to run with low oil pressure. Be prepared for a forced landing. Attempt to fly to the nearest airport. (PH Ch. 2)

a. Emergency Equipment and Survival Gear

152. What are the required inspections for an ELT?

An ELT must have been inspected in the preceding 12 calendar months to be legal. Also, the ELT battery must be replaced after 1 hour of cumulative use or after 50% of its useful life. (PH Ch. 4)

153. Must your airplane be equipped with a working ELT before beginning a flight?

Yes. ELTs are always required unless exempt under FAR Part 91.207. An example of where an aircraft is not required to have an ELT is if that aircraft is used for flight instruction within 50 NM of the home airport. (PH Ch. 4)

154. How is an ELT activated?

An ELT can be activated either manually by flipping the switch on the physical unit, or automatically by an impact to the airplane.

155. What signal does an ELT emit?

ELTs emit a distress signal on 121.5.

156. What other survival gear is your airplane equipped with?

Some small airplanes are equipped with a fire extinguisher and/or life vests. Know what your airplane is equipped with and be able to describe its location and explain how to use it.

157. Are you required to have flotation devices for all occupants when flying over water?

Only flights that are operated for hire beyond power-off gliding distance from shore are required to have flotation devices for all occupants when flying over open water. (FAR Part 91)

4. High Altitude Flight and Cabin Pressurization

158. How is cabin pressurization normally accomplished in light airplanes?

Pressurization in most light airplanes is sent to the cabin from the turbo-charger's compression or from an engine-driven pneumatic pump. (CPFM Ch. 9)

159. What happens when a pressurized airplane reaches its maximum differential pressure?

If a pressurized airplane reaches its maximum differential cabin pressure, any increase in flight altitude will result in an increase in cabin altitude. (CPFM Ch. 9)

160. What is the purpose of a cabin differential pressure gauge?

The purpose of a cabin differential pressure gauge is to indicate the difference between outside and inside pressure. (CPFM Ch. 9)

161. What is the purpose of a cabin altimeter?

The purpose of a cabin altimeter is to provide a check of the pressurization system by indicating cabin altitude. (CPFM Ch. 9)

162. How can a sudden supply of pure oxygen affect hypoxia symptoms?

A sudden supply of oxygen can aggravate the symptoms of hypoxia. (CPFM Ch. 9)

163. What action should take place following any type of decompression?

Following any type of decompression, oxygen masks should be donned, immediately followed by an emergency descent. (CPFM Ch. 9)

164. What is the most dangerous and harmful type of decompression?

The most dangerous and harmful type of decompression is an explosive one. (CPFM Ch. 9)

165. Why is it a good idea for all passengers to wear their safety belts at all times during a flight?

It is a good idea for all passengers to wear their safety belts at all times because in the event of a rapid or explosive decompression, it is less likely that they will be ejected from the airplane. (CPFM Ch. 9)

Be confident; you will do fine. You can never be totally prepared. If you have studied this book, you will pass with confidence. This book contains the answer to virtually every question, issue, and requirement that is possible on the commercial pilot practical test. GOOD LUCK!

The night flight tasks in Preflight Preparation Area of Operation have been removed from the Commercial Practical Test Standards. There are six knowledge test questions in Chapter 11 of CPWE.

The questions contained in this oral exam guide cover primarily the oral tasks listed in the PTS. Some tasks that can be tested by either the oral exam or flight portion of the exam are also included. Tasks that are considered only testable in flight have not been included. The discussion of flight maneuvers in Chapters I to XI will prepare you well for the flight portion of your practical test.

ABBREVIATIONS AND ACRONYMS IN
COMMERCIAL PILOT PRACTICAL TEST PREP
AND FLIGHT MANEUVERS

AC	Advisory Circular		min.	minute
AD	Airworthiness Directive		MMEL	master MEL
ADF	automatic direction finder		MOA	military operations area
ADM	aeronautical decision making		MP	manifold pressure
A/FD	*Airport/Facility Directory*		MSL	mean sea level
AGL	above ground level		MTR	military training route
AIM	*Aeronautical Information Manual*		NAVID	navigational aid
ATC	air traffic control		NDB	nondirectional beacon
CFI	certificated flight instructor		NM	nautical mile
CG	center of gravity		NOTAM	Notice to Airmen
CNS	central nervous system		PAPI	precision approach path indicator
CRM	cockpit resource management		PIC	pilot in command
CTAF	common traffic advisory frequency		PIREP	pilot weather report
EFAS	En Route Flight Advisory Service		POH	*Pilot's Operating Handbook*
EGT	exhaust gas temperature		PSI	pound per square inch
ELT	emergency locator transmitter		PTS	Practical Test Standards
ETA	estimated time of arrival		sec.	second
ETE	estimated time en route		SM	statute mile
FAA	Federal Aviation Administration		STC	supplemental type certificate
FAR	Federal Aviation Regulation		SUA	special-use airspace
FBO	fixed-base operator		TRSA	terminal radar service area
FL	flight level		V_A	design maneuvering speed
FMAS	Flight Maneuver Analysis Sheets		VASI	visual approach slope indicator
FSDO	Flight Standards District Office		V_{FE}	maximum flap extended speed
FSS	Flight Service Station		VFR	visual flight rules
ft.	feet		VHF	very high frequency
GPS	global positioning system		VHF/DF	VHF direction finder
IFR	instrument flight rules		V_{LE}	maximum landing gear extended speed
IR	instrument reference		V_{LO}	maximum landing gear operating speed
kt.	knot		V_{NE}	never-exceed speed
km.	kilometer		VOR	VHF omnidirectional range
LAA	local airport advisory		VR	visual reference
L/D_{MAX}	maximum lift-to-drag ratio		V_R	rotation speed
LLWAS	low-level wind-shear alert system		V_{S1}	stalling speed in a specified configuration
LORAN	long-range navigation		V_{SO}	stalling speed in the landing configuration
MEF	maximum elevation figure		V_X	best-angle-of-climb speed
MEL	minimum equipment list		V_Y	best-rate-of-climb speed

LOGBOOK ENDORSEMENT FOR PRACTICAL TEST

The following endorsement must be in your logbook and presented to your examiner at your practical test.

1. Endorsement for flight proficiency/practical test: FAR 61.39(a)(6), 61.123(e), and 61.127

I certify that (First name, MI, Last name) has received the required training of Secs. 61.127 and 61.129. I have determined he/she is prepared for the commercial pilot (airplane, single-engine land) practical test. He/She has demonstrated satisfactory knowledge of the subject areas found deficient on his/her knowledge test.

_____ _____ _____ _____ _____

        Signed   *Date*   *Name*   *CFI Number*   *Expiration Date*

GLEIM
KNOWLEDGE
TRANSFER
SYSTEMS™

AUTHOR'S RECOMMENDATION

The Experimental Aircraft Association, Inc. is a very successful and effective nonprofit organization that represents and serves those of us interested in flying, in general, and in sport aviation, in particular. I personally invite you to enjoy becoming a member:

$40 for a 1-year membership
$23 per year for students under 19 years old
Family membership available for $50 per year

Membership includes the monthly magazine *Sport Aviation*.

Write to: Experimental Aircraft Association, Inc.   *Or call:*   (920) 426-4800
              P.O. Box 3086   (800) 843-3612
              Oshkosh, Wisconsin 54903-3086

The annual EAA Oshkosh AirVenture is an unbelievable aviation spectacular with over 12,000 airplanes at one airport! Virtually everything aviation-oriented you can imagine! Plan to spend at least 1 day (not everything can be seen in a day) in Oshkosh (100 miles northwest of Milwaukee).

Convention dates: 2002 -- July 23 through July 29
                          2003 -- July 29 through August 4
                          2004 -- July 27 through August 2

The annual Sun 'n Fun EAA Fly-In is also highly recommended. It is held at the Lakeland, FL (KLAL) airport (between Orlando and Tampa). Visit the Sun 'n Fun web site at http://www.sun-n-fun.org.

Convention dates: 2002 -- April 7 through 13
                          2003 -- April 2 through April 8
                          2004 -- April 14 through April 20
                          2005 -- April 13 through April 19

BE-A-PILOT: INTRODUCTORY FLIGHT

Be-A-Pilot is an industry-sponsored marketing program designed to inspire people to "Stop dreaming, start flying." Be-A-Pilot has sought flight schools to participate in the program and offers a $49 introductory flight certificate that can be redeemed at a participating flight school.

The goal of this program is to encourage people to experience their dreams of flying through an introductory flight and to begin taking flying lessons.

For more information, you can visit the Be-A-Pilot home page at http://www.beapilot.com or call 1-888-BE-A-PILOT.

CIVIL AIR PATROL: CADET ORIENTATION FLIGHT PROGRAM

The Civil Air Patrol (CAP) Cadet Orientation Flight Program is designed to introduce CAP cadets to general aviation operations. The program is voluntary and primarily motivational, and it is designed to stimulate the cadet's interest in and knowledge of aviation.

Each orientation flight includes at least 30 min. of actual flight time, usually in the local area of the airport. Except for takeoff, landing, and a few other portions of the flight, cadets are encouraged to handle the controls. The Cadet Orientation Flight Program is designed to allow five front-seat and four back-seat flights. But you may be able to fly more.

For more information about the CAP cadet program nearest you, visit the CAP home page at http://www.cap.gov or call 1-800-FLY-2338.

GLEIM'S FREE E-MAIL UPDATE SERVICE
update@gleim.com

All updates are available at www.gleim.com/Aviation/Updates

Your message to Gleim must include (in the subject or body) the acronym for your book or software, followed by the edition-printing for books and the version for software. The edition-printing is indicated on the book's spine and at the bottom right corner of the cover. The software version is indicated on the CD-ROM label.

GLEIM	Written Exam		Flight Maneuvers
	Book	Software	Book
Private Pilot	PPWE	FAATP PP	PPFM
Instrument Pilot	IPWE	FAATP IP	IPFM
Commercial Pilot	CPWE	FAATP CP	CPFM
Flight/Ground Instructor	FIGI	FAATP FIGI	FIFM
Fundamentals of Instructing	FOI	FAATP FOI	
Airline Transport Pilot	ATP	FAATP ATP	
Flight Engineer	FEWE	FAATP FEWE	

GLEIM	Reference Books
Pilot Handbook	PH
Aviation Weather and Weather Services	AWWS
Private Pilot Syllabus and Logbook	PPSYL
Instrument Pilot Syllabus	IPSYL
Commercial Pilot Syllabus	CPSYL
FAR/AIM	FARAIM

EXAMPLES

For *Commercial Pilot Flight Maneuvers*, fourth edition-first printing:

To: update@gleim.com
From: your e-mail address
Subject: CPFM 4-1

For *FAA Test Prep* software, Commercial Pilot, version 4.1:

To: update@gleim.com
From: your e-mail address
Subject: FAATP CP 4.1

IT ONLY TAKES A MINUTE

If you do not have e-mail, have a friend send e-mail to us and print our response for you.

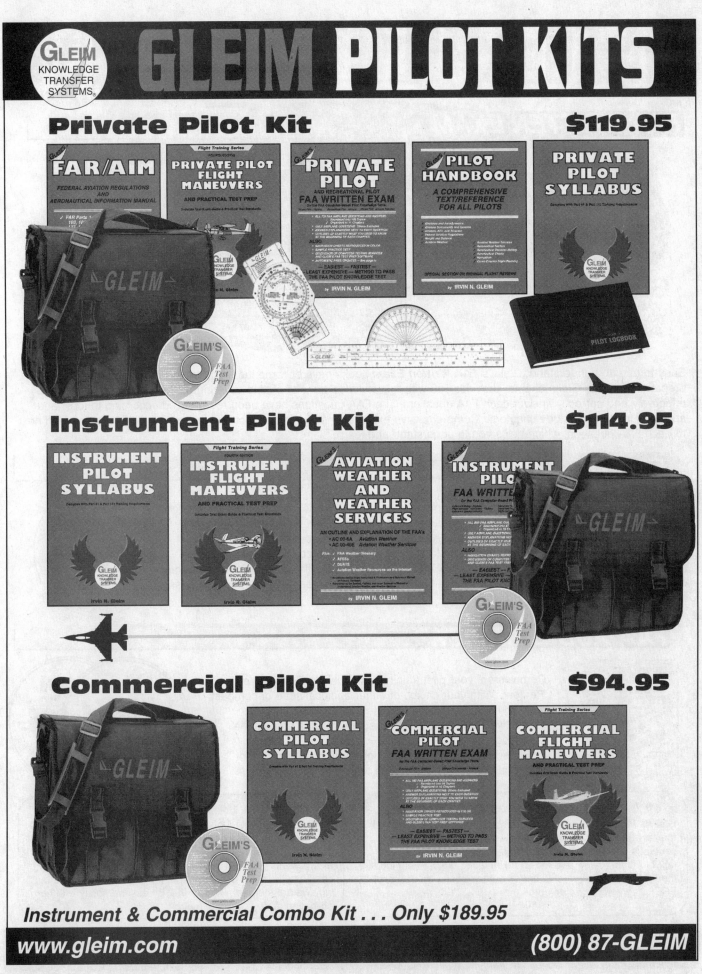

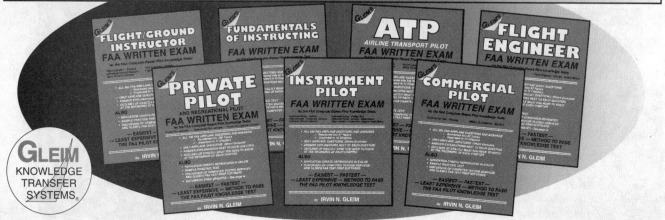

FLIGHT MANEUVERS

Gleim's Flight Training Series is designed to be used from your introductory flight through your checkride. All of the tasks and flight maneuvers you will be required to learn and master for your oral and practical test are thoroughly outlined and explained. Our outlines integrate all of the various FAA books, advisory circulars, FARs, Practical Test Standards, etc. into one easy-to-use book. We also explain the common errors for each flight maneuver so you can learn from the mistakes of pilots before you. Save time and money by knowing exactly what is required and how to complete each outlined task. Our **Flight Maneuvers** books will thoroughly prepare you for each flight lesson and the practical test. Included as an appendix in each book is a reprint of the FAA Practical Test Standards.

REFERENCE BOOKS / SYLLABI

Aviation Weather and Weather Services is a complete re-write of FAA AC 00-6A and AC 00-45E compiled into a single easy-to-understand text. This book contains all the maps, diagrams, charts, and color figures that appear in the FAA publications. Pilots who desire to learn and understand this subject matter can now do so much more efficiently and cost effectively.

Pilot Handbook is a complete ground school text in outline format and is loaded with diagrams to facilitate learning and understanding. It contains expanded weather coverage and special sections on the flight review and instrument proficiency checks. With a detailed index, *Pilot Handbook* will be your first choice for an all-round reference manual.

The purpose of Gleim's *FAR/AIM* is to consolidate the Federal Aviation Regulations (FAR) and the Aeronautical Information Manual (AIM) into one easy-to-use reference book. Similar books of this type create additional work for the user. In
contrast, our **FAR/AIM** SIMPLIFIES and FACILITATES your effort. The text format, larger type, indentations, two-column structure, and spacing are designed to make it easier to read, learn, and understand. The comprehensive FAR index in front of the book and the AIM index at the back of the book make finding pertinent information easier than when using the standard government indexes.

Gleim's *Syllabi* provide step-by-step lesson plans for your flight training. Each syllabus will simplify and facilitate your studies and training so you can achieve your goals efficiently and cost effectively. A complete flight training program for both Part 61 and Part 141 operations, each syllabus contains a thorough course overview with separate ground and flight training sections.

370

TYPICAL COMMENTS ABOUT GLEIM PRODUCTS

Dear Dr. Gleim:

This is a note of appreciation for your fine text, *Private Pilot FAA Written Exam*.

As a layman, I am not a scientifically trained person, my first look at the questions for the private pilot exam made it seem impossible. The [name of competitor] book left me stymied and discouraged.

Fortunately, Aeroflight at Westheimer Field in Norman carried your book. I bought it and the whole subject quickly came into focus. I passed the test the first time.

You have an outstanding sense of organization and a superior sense of instructional psychology. I am much in your debt. Thank you for sharing your knowledge, for your assistance, insight, and indirect encouragement.

Lloyd P. Williams
Washington, Oklahoma

Dear Irvin,

I just got back from taking my Private Pilot Test by computer in 20 minutes and getting a score of 97.

I want to thank you and congratulate you on a job well done with your software.

I am a software developer myself and I have to hand it to you, I couldn't have done better. The installation was easy, using the screens was easy, and, if I could change anything it would be that screen that always comes up at the end of a study session that says "you have answered all the questions," but I don't have a better way of doing it.

Well done.

Charles F. Armantrout
Denver, CO

Dear Dr. Gleim:

First I would like to thank you for *Instrument Pilot FAA Flight Maneuvers and Practical Test Prep*. I am currently using it as I prepare for my check ride later this month. I am finding it as useful as the *Private Pilot Flight Maneuvers and Practical Test Prep*. (The one about which I wrote the original letter to you.) I have a few suggestions and a correction that I will send when I pass my check ride.

I again would like to give you and your books more credit and thanks by letting you know I got a 97% on my Instrument Written Test. I got an 86% on my Private Written Test without the use of your books. I can honestly say that the difference, more than 10%, is attributed to your book with the red cover. Its format is a teaching tool in itself. As a secondary mathematics teacher I commend the use of an outline followed by the questions for that concept. It was nice not having to turn to the back of the book to find the answer and the explanation. What a time saver! I am not sure if I will go on to get any more ratings after I get my instrument ticket, but if I do I will be using a book with a red cover.

Thanks again and happy flying.

Brian E. Radcliffe
Kingsville, Maryland

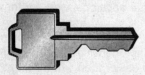 The KEY TO SUCCESS in your flight training, which also minimizes cost and frustration, is your study and preparation at home before flying with your flight instructor. The more you know about flying, flight training, and each flight lesson, the better you will do.

INDEX

Gleim Publications, Inc.
P.O. Box 12848
Gainesville, FL 32604

TOLL FREE: (800) 87-GLEIM/(800) 874-5346
LOCAL: (352) 375-0772
FAX: (888) 375-6940 (toll free)
INTERNET: http://www.gleim.com
E-MAIL: sales@gleim.com

Customer service is available:
8:00 a.m. - 7:00 p.m., Mon. - Fri. (Eastern Time)
9:00 a.m. - 2:00 p.m., Saturday (Eastern Time)
Please have your credit card ready or save
time by ordering online!

Gleim's PRIVATE PILOT KIT
Includes everything you need to pass the FAA pilot knowledge (written) test and FAA practical test.
Our price is far lower than similarly equipped kits found elsewhere .... $119.95 _____

Gleim's INSTRUMENT PILOT KIT
Everything you need, just like our Private Pilot Kit. With CD-ROM .... $114.95 _____

Gleim's COMMERCIAL PILOT KIT
Everything you need to prepare for your commercial certificate. With CD-ROM .... $94.95 _____

SPECIAL COMBO: INSTRUMENT/COMMERCIAL KIT .... $189.95 _____

KNOWLEDGE TEST

	Books	Software*	Book/Software	Audios**	Book/Software*/ Audios**	
Private/Recreational Pilot	☐ @ $15.95	☐ @ $49.95	☐ @ $58.95	☐ @ $60	☐ @ $106.95	_____
Instrument Pilot	☐ @ $18.95	☐ @ $59.95	☐ @ $70.95	☐ @ $60	☐ @ $117.95	_____
Commercial Pilot	☐ @ $14.95	☐ @ $59.95	☐ @ $66.95	**Please select audio format.		_____
Fundamentals of Instructing	☐ @ $12.95	☐ } both for		☐ CDs ☐ Cassettes		_____
Flight/Ground Instructor	☐ @ $14.95	☐ } $59.95	☐ @ $66.95			_____
Airline Transport Pilot	☐ @ $26.95	☐ @ $59.95	☐ @ $77.95			_____
Flight Engineer	☐ @ $26.95	☐ @ $59.95	☐ @ $77.95			_____

*CD-ROM (Windows) includes all questions, figures, charts, and outlines for each of the pilot knowledge tests.

REFERENCE AND FLIGHT MANEUVERS/PRACTICAL TEST PREP BOOKS
FAR/AIM ($10.00 with any other purchase) .... $15.95 _____
Aviation Weather and Weather Services .... 22.95 _____
Pilot Handbook .... 13.95 _____
Private Pilot Flight Maneuvers and Practical Test Prep .... 19.95 _____
Instrument Pilot Flight Maneuvers and Practical Test Prep .... 18.95 _____
Commercial Pilot Flight Maneuvers and Practical Test Prep .... 16.95 _____
Flight Instructor Flight Maneuvers and Practical Test Prep .... 17.95 _____

OTHER BOOKS AND ACCESSORIES
Private Pilot Syllabus and Logbook .... $ 9.95 _____
Instrument Pilot Syllabus .... 14.95 _____
Commercial Pilot Syllabus .... 14.95 _____
Pilot Logbook *NEW* .... 7.95 _____
Flight Computer .... 9.95 _____
Navigational Plotter .... 5.95 _____
Flight Bag .... 29.95 _____

Shipping (nonrefundable): **First item = $5; each additional item = $1** $_____
Add applicable sales tax for shipments within the State of Florida. _____
Please FAX, e-mail, or write for additional charges for outside the 48 contiguous United States. **TOTAL** $_____

Printed 07/02. Prices subject to change without notice.

1. We process and ship orders daily, within one business day over 98.8% of the time. Call by noon for same-day service!
2. Please PHOTOCOPY this order form for others.
3. No CODs. Orders from individuals must be prepaid. Library and company orders may be purchased on account.
4. Gleim Publications, Inc. guarantees the immediate refund of all resalable texts and unopened software and audios if returned within 30 days. Applies only to items purchased direct from Gleim Publications, Inc. Our shipping charge is nonrefundable.
5. Components of specially priced package deals are nonreturnable.

NAME (please print) _____

ADDRESS _____ Apt. _____
(street address required for UPS)

_____

CITY _____ STATE ____ ZIP _____

____ MC/VISA/DISC ____ Check/M.O. Daytime Telephone (____)_____

Credit Card No. ____ - ____ - ____ - ____

Exp. ___/___ Signature _____
Mo./Yr.

E-mail Address _____

020

PILOT KNOWLEDGE (WRITTEN EXAM) BOOKS AND SOFTWARE

Before pilots take their FAA airmen knowledge tests, they want to understand the answer to every FAA test question. Gleim's pilot knowledge test books and software are widely used because they help pilots learn and understand exactly what they need to know to pass. Each chapter opens with an outline of exactly what you need to know to answer the FAA test questions. Additional information can be found in our reference books and flight maneuver/practical test prep books.

PRIVATE PILOT FAA WRITTEN EXAM BOOK ($15.95) / **FAA TEST PREP SOFTWARE** ($49.95):

Prepares you for PAR, RPA, and PAT knowledge tests.

INSTRUMENT PILOT FAA WRITTEN EXAM BOOK ($18.95) / **FAA TEST PREP SOFTWARE** ($59.95):

Prepares you for IRA, CFII, and IGI knowledge tests.

COMMERCIAL PILOT FAA WRITTEN EXAM BOOK ($14.95) / **FAA TEST PREP SOFTWARE** ($59.95):

Prepares you for the CAX and MCA knowledge tests.

FUNDAMENTALS OF INSTRUCTING FAA WRITTEN EXAM BOOK ($12.95) / **FAA TEST PREP SOFTWARE COMBINED WITH FLIGHT/GROUND INSTRUCTOR** ($59.95):

Prepares you for the FOI knowledge test.

FLIGHT/GROUND INSTRUCTOR FAA WRITTEN EXAM BOOK ($14.95) / **FAA TEST PREP SOFTWARE** ($59.95):

Prepares you for the Flight Instructor--Airplane (FIA), Basic Ground Instructor (BGI), and the Advanced Ground Instructor (AGI) knowledge tests.

AIRLINE TRANSPORT PILOT FAA WRITTEN EXAM BOOK ($26.95) / **FAA TEST PREP SOFTWARE** ($59.95):

Prepares you for the ATP Part 121, ATP Part 135, and the flight dispatcher certificate.

FLIGHT ENGINEER FAA WRITTEN EXAM BOOK ($26.95) / **FAA TEST PREP SOFTWARE** ($59.95):

This book and/or software is to be used for the turbojet and basic (FEX) and the turbojet-added rating (FEJ) knowledge tests.

FLIGHT MANEUVERS/PRACTICAL TEST PREP BOOKS

Our Flight Maneuvers and Practical Test Prep books are designed to simplify and facilitate your flight training and will help prepare pilots for FAA practical tests as much as the Gleim written exam books help prepare pilots for FAA pilot knowledge tests. Each task, objective, concept, requirement, etc., in the FAA's practical test standards is explained, analyzed, illustrated, and interpreted so pilots will gain practical test proficiency as quickly as possible.

Private Pilot Flight Maneuvers and Practical Test Prep	368 pages	($19.95)
Instrument Pilot Flight Maneuvers and Practical Test Prep	432 pages	($18.95)
Commercial Pilot Flight Maneuvers and Practical Test Prep	384 pages	($16.95)
Flight Instructor Flight Maneuvers and Practical Test Prep	544 pages	($17.95)

REFERENCE

PILOT HANDBOOK ($13.95)

A complete pilot ground school text in outline format with many diagrams for ease in understanding. This book is used in preparation for private, commercial, and flight instructor certificates and the instrument rating. A complete, detailed index makes it more useful and saves time. It contains a special section on biennial flight reviews.

AVIATION WEATHER AND WEATHER SERVICES ($22.95)

A complete rewrite of the FAA's Aviation Weather 00-6A and Aviation Weather Services 00-45E into a single easy-to-understand book complete with maps, diagrams, charts, and pictures. Learn and understand the subject matter much more easily and effectively with this book.

FAR/AIM ($15.95)

The purpose of this book is to consolidate the common Federal Aviation Regulations (FAR) parts and the Aeronautical Information Manual into one easy-to-use reference book. The Gleim book is better because of bigger type, better presentation, improved indexes, and full-color figures. FAR Parts 1, 43, 61, 67, 71, 73, 91, 97, 103, 105, 119, Appendices I and J of 121, 135, 137, 141, and 142 are included.

NEW PILOT LOGBOOK ($7.95)

A professional high-quality logbook with improved entry categories.

GLEIM'S PILOT KITS

Gleim's pilot kits provide students with a complete training program to successfully pass the FAA knowledge and practical tests. At a price for less than similarly equipped kits, Gleim's kits represent the best training value in the aviation industry.

PRIVATE PILOT KIT ($119.95)

INSTRUMENT PILOT KIT ($114.95)

COMMERCIAL PILOT KIT ($94.95)

Please forward your suggestions, corrections, and comments to **Irvin N. Gleim • c/o Gleim Publications, Inc. • P.O. Box 12848 • University Station • Gainesville, Florida • 32604** for inclusion in the next edition of *Commercial Pilot Practical Test Prep and Flight Maneuvers*. Please include your name and address on the back of this page so we can properly thank you for your interest.

1. _____

2. _____

3. _____

4. _____

5. _____

6. _____

7. _____

8. _____

9. _____

10. _____

11. _____

12. _____

13. _____

14. _____

15. _____

16. _____

Remember for superior service: <u>Mail</u>, <u>e-mail</u>, or <u>fax</u> questions about our books or software.
<u>Telephone</u> questions about orders, prices, shipments, or payments.

Name: _____

Address: _____

City/State/Zip: _____

Telephone: Home: _____ Work: _____ Fax: _____

E-mail: _____